American Identity and the Politics of Multiculturalism

The civil rights movement and immigration reform transformed American politics in the mid-1960s. Demographic diversity and identity politics raised the challenge of *e pluribus unum* anew, and multiculturalism emerged as a new ideological response to this dilemma. This book uses public opinion data from both national and Los Angeles surveys to compare ethnic differences in patriotism and ethnic identity as well as in support for multicultural norms and group-conscious policies. The authors find evidence of strong patriotism among all groups and the classic pattern of assimilation among the new wave of immigrants. They argue that there is a consensus in rejecting harder forms of multiculturalism that insist on group rights but also a widespread acceptance of softer forms that are tolerant of cultural differences and do not challenge norms, such as by insisting on the primacy of English. There is little evidence of a link between strong group consciousness and a lack of patriotism, even in the most disadvantaged minority groups. The authors conclude that the United States is not breaking apart due to the new ethnic diversity.

Jack Citrin is Heller Professor of Political Science at the University of California, Berkeley. He currently serves as the Director of the Institute of Governmental Studies and has previously served as the Director of University of California Data and as the Acting Director of the Survey Research Center. His publications include *Tax Revolt: Something for Nothing in California* (with David O. Sears, 1982); *How Race, Immigration and Ethnicity Are Shaping the California Electorate* (2002); and *Ethnic Context, Race Relations, and California Politics* (with Bruce E. Cain and Cara Wong, 2000). His work has appeared in such journals as the *American Political Science Review*, the *American Journal of Political Science*, and the *Journal of Politics*. Two of his articles have won prizes from the American Political Science Association. He is a founding member of the International Society of Political Psychology.

David O. Sears is Distinguished Professor of Psychology and Political Science at the University of California, Los Angeles. He has twice been a Fellow at the Center for Advanced Study in the Behavioral Sciences. He has served as Dean of Social Sciences and as Director of the Institute for Social Science Research at UCLA. He is a member of the American Academy of Arts and Sciences and has been a Guggenheim Fellow and the president of the International Society of Political Psychology. Among his publications are *Social Psychology* (twelve editions); *Obama's Race: The 2008 Election and the Dream of a Post-Racial America* (with Michael Tesler, 2010); *The Politics of Violence: The New Urban Blacks and the Watts Riot* (with John B. McConahay, 1973); and more than 150 journal articles and book chapters on psychology and political science.

Cambridge Studies in Public Opinion and Political Psychology

Series Editors

DENNIS CHONG, University of Southern California and Northwestern University
JAMES H. KUKLINKSI, University of Illinois, Urbana-Champaign

Cambridge Studies in Public Opinion and Political Psychology publishes innovative research from a variety of theoretical and methodological perspectives on the mass public foundations of politics and society. Research in the series focuses on the origins and influence of mass opinion; the dynamics of information and deliberation; and the emotional, normative, and instrumental bases of political choice. In addition to examining psychological processes, the series explores the organization of groups, the association between individual and collective preferences, and the impact of institutions on beliefs and behavior.

Cambridge Studies in Public Opinion and Political Psychology is dedicated to furthering theoretical and empirical research on the relationship between the political system and the attitudes and actions of citizens.

Books in the series are listed following the Index.

American Identity and the Politics of Multiculturalism

JACK CITRIN
University of California, Berkeley

DAVID O. SEARS
University of California, Los Angeles

CAMBRIDGE
UNIVERSITY PRESS

CAMBRIDGE
UNIVERSITY PRESS

32 Avenue of the Americas, New York, NY 10013-2473, USA

Cambridge University Press is part of the University of Cambridge.

It furthers the University's mission by disseminating knowledge in the pursuit of education, learning, and research at the highest international levels of excellence.

www.cambridge.org
Information on this title: www.cambridge.org/9780521535786

© Jack Citrin and David O. Sears 2014

First published 2014

Printed in the United States of America

A catalog record for this publication is available from the British Library.

Library of Congress Cataloging in Publication Data
Citrin, Jack.
American identity and the politics of multiculturalism / Jack Citrin, University of California, Berkeley; David O. Sears, University of California, Los Angeles.
    pages   cm – (Cambridge studies in public opinion and political psychology)
ISBN 978-0-521-82883-3 (hardback)
    1. Multiculturalism – United States – Public opinion.   2. Cultural pluralism – United States – Public opinion.   3. Public opinion – United States.   4. Multiculturalism – Political aspects – United States.   5. Ethnicity – Political aspects – United States.   6. Group identity – United States.   I. Sears, David O.   II. Title.
JV6477.C59   2014
305.800973–dc23   2014001849

ISBN 978-0-521-82883-3 Hardback
ISBN 978-0-521-53578-6 Paperback

We dedicate this book to our wives, Bonnie McKellar and Carrie Sears.
Their care and support made its completion possible.

Contents

List of Figures   *page* x

List of Tables   xi

Preface   xiii

Prologue   xvii

1   The Challenge of *E Pluribus Unum*   1

2   The Political Psychology of Identity Choice   30

3   Contours of American National Identity   56

4   The Ethnic Cauldron and Group Consciousness   88

5   Public Opinion and Multiculturalism's Guiding Norms   120

6   When Do Ethnic and National Identities Collide?   145

7   Group-Conscious Policies: Ethnic Consensus and Cleavage   175

8   The Dynamics of Group-Conscious Policy Preferences   204

9   Multiculturalism and Party Politics   223

10 Conclusion   261

Appendices

2.1   Ethnic Composition in Los Angeles County Social Surveys,
      by Year and Level of Education   285

3.1   Question Wording for Survey Items   286

7.1   Precise Question Wordings in National Data   288

7.2   Precise Wordings of Pew Research Center Questions   290

9.1   Roll-Call Votes on Group-Conscious Policies and Factor
      Analysis of Issue Constraint   291

Bibliography   293

Index   311

Figures

1.1   Ethnic Change in the United States, California, and Los
Angeles County   *page* 14
3.1   Foci of National Pride in America, by Ethnicity   68
3.2   Normative Content of American Identity, by Ethnicity   83
4.1   Ethnic Groups in Conflict, by Ethnic Group and Year   93
6.1   Strength of Ethnic Identity by American vs. Ethnic
Self-Categorization, within Ethnicity   153
6.2   Patriotism by American vs. Ethnic Self-Categorization, within
Ethnicity   154

Tables

2.1   Demographic Composition of Ethnic Groups in Los Angeles
      County   *page* 51
2.2   Classification of Ethnic Groups by Immigration Status and
      Language Spoken at Home in Los Angeles County   53
2.3   Characteristics of Latinos in Los Angeles, by Immigration Status   54
3.1   Percent with Strong Affective Attachment to America, by Race
      and Ethnicity   61
3.2   Patriotism: Latinos by Immigration Status, and All Whites   72
3.3   Affective Attachment to America: The White Vanguard Hypothesis   77
3.4   The Vanguard Hypothesis: Predictors of Patriotism   79
4.1   Perceptions of Ethnic Group Distinctiveness and Conflict, by Ethnicity 91
4.2   What Group Is Your Ethnic Group Most in Conflict With?
      (Los Angeles Data)   95
4.3   Ethnic Differences in Group Consciousness (Los Angeles Data)   103
4.4   Ethnic Group Consciousness Typology (Los Angeles Data)   109
4.5   The Effects of Immigration Status on Strength of Latinos' Ethnic
      Group Consciousness (Los Angeles Data)   112
4.6   Explaining Strength of Ethnic Identity: Regression Equations
      (Los Angeles Data)   114
5.1   Support for Social Multiculturalism, by Ethnicity   123
5.2   Support for Political Multiculturalism, by Ethnicity   130
5.3   Support for Multiculturalism: The Ethnic Minority Group
      Consciousness Hypothesis   135
5.4   Support for Multiculturalism: The Latino Immigration Status
      Hypothesis   137
5.5   Are White Vanguards Supporting Multiculturalism?   139
6.1   American vs. Ethnic Self-Categorization, by Ethnicity   150
6.2   American vs. Ethnic Self-Categorization, by Ethnicity and Latino
      Immigration Status   157
6.3   Latinos' National and Ethnic Identifications, by Language Spoken
      at Home   159

6.4	Correlations of Ethnic and National Attachment	163
6.5	Correlations of Support for Multiculturalism Norms, by Attachment to Nation and Ethnicity	169
6.6	National Attachment and Ethnic Identity Effects on Support for Assimilation (National Data)	171
7.1	Support for Group-Conscious Policies: Trends in National Data over Time, by Ethnicity	179
7.2	Support for Group-Conscious Policies: Los Angeles Surveys	181
7.3	Support for Group-Conscious Policies: Episodic National Data	183
7.4	Issue Constraint: Whites in National Surveys	200
7.5	Issue Constraint by Ethnicity: Los Angeles Surveys	201
8.1	Ethnic Identification, National Identity, and Support for Group-Conscious Policies: Los Angeles Surveys and 2012 American National Election Studies (ANES)	207
8.2	Correlations of National Attachment and National Identity with Support for Group-Conscious Policies: National Surveys (Whites Only)	210
8.3	Origins of Support for Group-Conscious Positions on Race-Targeted Policies: Los Angeles Surveys	213
8.4	Origins of Support for Group-Conscious Positions on Immigration Policy: Los Angeles Surveys	215
8.5	Origins of Support for Group-Conscious Positions on Language Policy: Los Angeles Surveys	216
8.6	Predictors of Whites' Support for Group-Conscious Policies: National Surveys	218
8.7	Predictors of Minorities' Support for Group-Conscious Policies: 2012 ANES	219
9.1	Mean Affective Attachment to the Nation among Whites, by Party Identification and Ideology	232
9.2	Cross-Tabulations of Whites' Conception of a "True American," by Party Identification and Ideology	234
9.3	Cross-Tabulations of Ideology by National and Ethnic Identity, by Ethnicity	235
9.4A	Whites' Beliefs about Social Multiculturalism, by Party Identification and Ideology	241
9.4B	Whites' Beliefs about Political Multiculturalism, by Party Identification and Ideology	242
9.5	Attitudes toward Group-Conscious Policies, by Party Identification and Ideology: National Surveys	249
9.6	Cross-Tabulations of Support for Group-Conscious Policies by Party Identification and Ideology within Ethnic Groups: Los Angeles Surveys	251
9.7	Whites' Issue Constraint: National Data (ANES)	255

Preface

This book has both psychological and professional origins. On a personal level, what it means to have a national identity and how minority and majority groups coexist were daily questions for Jack Citrin as he grew up in a family of Russian Jewish refugees in China and Japan. Landing in the United States with a student visa in the mid-1960s, he moved from immigrant to citizen in 1978, feeling grateful to a country in which one could quite readily belong yet understanding that his skin color and unaccented English helped make this possible. The first Sears in what is now the United States shows up on the tax lists in Plymouth Colony in 1633, although little is known about him. In contrast, there are compelling family legends about David O. Sears's maternal great-grandmother Anna O'Keefe who fled the Irish Potato Famine as a teenager in the 1840s and found work in the Lowell cotton mills. Among other things she provided his middle name. Later generations of Sears's family progressed from farming to academia, yielding descendants with blessedly secure, classically "American" social identities. Perhaps a by-product of this security has been a deep concern about the treatment of minorities in a nation committed so early and so publicly to equality.

On a professional level, this book uses the important demographic changes in postwar American society to pursue our long-term research agendas. We regard ourselves as students of the psychology of politics, although one of us comes originally from the discipline of political science and the other from psychology. But throughout our careers and several earlier collaborations, our primary focus has always been on understanding the underpinnings and political consequences of public opinion. We also have shared an interest in symbolic politics theory as a conceptual starting point in analyzing public responses to societal changes and public events. Citrin has been a longtime student of American political culture, with a particular interest in political disaffection and system support and, more recently, in the future of national identity in a globalizing world. Sears has long done research on both sides of the American black–white racial divide, from black activism and political violence to white resistance to civil rights and racial equality.

The specific story developed here can be said to begin in an important way in the 1960s. That tumultuous and fascinating decade produced some momentous political successes as a result of direct attacks on the system of formal racial inequality that had marked American society almost from its inception. One residue of the 1960s was a civil rights ideology that interpreted those successes as resulting from the recognition and privileging of collective racial identities, something of a change from traditional American individualism. A second residue was a largely unnoticed set of reforms in immigration policy that later had equally momentous but unanticipated societal effects, most notably in a dramatic new wave of immigrants, both legal and illegal, especially from Latin America and Asia.

These two historic changes converged in the 1980s and 1990s with an evolved form of the civil rights ideology that has often been described as "identity politics." It extrapolated the lessons many felt they had learned in the 1960s about the necessity for the recognition of racial differences and for collective action on behalf of minorities beyond the singular case of African Americans to many other mobilizing groups in American society – most notably ethnic groups such as Latinos, Asian Americans, and Native Americans – but to other relatively less advantaged groups as well, such as women, the elderly, homosexuals, the disabled, and the mentally ill.

The lesson drawn by some from the civil rights era, if it may be called that, is that advancing equal treatment of disadvantaged groups requires the explicit identification of particular group cultures and official efforts to recognize and represent them in public life. The heightened group consciousness in many of these mobilized new minorities was accompanied by, we suggest, a common multiculturalist political ideology that centers on subgroup identities and privileges the promotion of those groups' interests. We conceive of multiculturalism as an alternative formula to the individualist conception of American identity and the emphasis on assimilation that undergirded earlier views of how to accommodate waves of immigration. Underlying our empirical analysis is the question of how deeply this multiculturalist ideology has penetrated the mass public in terms of its thinking about the organization of society along ethnic lines, about individuals' own identities, and about their policy preferences in domains relevant to race and ethnicity. Central to this analysis is the question of whether a common national identity has been undermined by multiculturalism's emphasis on the validity of enduring ethnic differences, as many critics of multiculturalism maintain. Put simply, we wondered whether the new ethnic reality of American society would have consequences that radically differed from those of earlier waves of immigration and, among other things, how this new and more complex pattern of ethnicity would interact with the long-standing racial divide that America is yet to overcome.

As with any long and ambitious study (and this one has taken longer than either of us ever expected), the authors owe much to the efforts of others along the way. First and foremost, we have relied on a number of surveys carried out principally by three different organizations, to which we owe great debts of gratitude. One is the American National Election Studies (ANES), the sine qua non resource of studies such as ours. Several of the questions on which we have relied were first developed in the 1991 ANES Pilot Study based on a proposal from Citrin. We were also fortunate enough to be able to include a Multiculturalism Module in the 1994 General Social Survey (GSS), for which we are grateful to the GSS's then Board of Overseers, on which Sears served, and especially to its chair, Peter Marsden. Thanks to the support of Tom Smith, the principal investigator of GSS, we were able to include these and other items in later surveys. We also are grateful to our colleagues who collaborated with Sears in designing the Los Angeles County Social Survey (LACSS), Franklin Gilliam, John R. Petrocik, and Jim Sidanius, for incorporating our themes in those studies. For the data collection itself, we owe special thanks to the late Eve Fielder, then director of the UCLA Survey Research Center; Michael Greenwell, then director of the CATI facility; Madelyn de Maria, assistant director of the UCLA Institute for Social Science Research; and the many paid and student interviewers who put in long hours telephoning residents of Los Angeles County. Subsequent to data collection, the LACSS data were skillfully and accessibly archived by Libbie Stephenson, head archivist at the UCLA Social Sciences Data Archive, making it possible for the data to be accessed by our analysts at both UCLA and UCB, as well as at other institutions.

At the data analysis stage, we benefited from a large number of truly gifted and loyal research assistants. They are Sharmaine Vidanage Cheleden, P. J. Henry, Jocelyn Kiley, Amy Lerman, Morris Levy, Michael Murakami, Chris Muste, Kathryn Pearson, Victoria Savalei, John Sides, Christopher Tarman, Nicholas A. Valentino, Colette van Laar, and Matthew Wright. Matt and Morris were especially instrumental in the home stretch of data analysis and presentation. We also owe a great debt to Marilyn Hart for many years of help with manuscript preparation and to Katherine Nguyen and Maria Wolf for pulling everything together in such organized fashion at delivery time. Finally, we are most grateful to Lewis Bateman of Cambridge University Press and to Dennis Chong, our series editor and valued friend, for their almost infinite patience and continuing support for this project.

Prologue

The monumental legislative changes of 1964 and 1965 that changed American history forever are the catalysts for this book. In 1964, as a response to the growing strength of the civil rights movement, Congress passed the Civil Rights Act. In 1965, the Voting Rights Act put a dagger in the heart of the two-caste racial system in the South, a system that had existed for the more than three centuries since African slaves were first imported to North America. In 1965, the Hart-Celler Immigration and Nationality Act, on the surface tinkering only modestly with prevailing immigration priorities, unexpectedly opened the flood-gates to massive influxes of non-European immigration over the course of the next half century.

The consequence of immigration reform has been a rapid rise in the cultural diversity of the nation, mimicking a similar surge a century earlier. Those changes reshaped an overwhelmingly white nation with relatively small minorities of African Americans and Native Americans deliberately kept largely out of sight of the mainstream. In 1965, the United States began on a path that will, a few decades from now, turn it into a nation with no majority racial or ethnic group.[1] Just as important, accompanying this demographic change have been new political movements demanding greater equality not only for African Americans but for Latinos and Asian Americans as well.

What is the consequence of these changes for national unity? Nations are defined by "common sentiment," by what members of a community think of

---

[1] Much that is written on the subject focuses on the famous ethnocultural pentagon of whites, African Americans, Latinos, Asian Americans, and Native Americans. It is sometimes the convention to differentiate the terms "racial" and "ethnic" in referring to these groups. We make no such distinction, given the social construction of all those categories, and use the two terms interchangeably.

themselves and what makes them belong together.[2] Nation building thus involves inculcating a sense of common identity. How to do this in a culturally heterogeneous society is the challenge of *e pluribus unum*. What, then, is the glue that holds America together? With historical answers as a backdrop, this book's purpose is to determine how the American public thinks about the linkages between ethnicity and the nation's identity in a society whose composition and political culture have changed radically in the past fifty years.

Our focus, then, is on the exacting task of balancing unity and diversity. But that task is not a new one for the United States but one that has faced the nation from its beginning. In the first census of 1790, those of English stock dominated, making up 49 percent of the total population and 60 percent of the whites. Blacks were 19 percent of the national total, and Germans, Scotch-Irish, Irish, Swedes, Dutch, and French made up the rest.[3] George Washington pronounced in 1783 that "America is open to receive not only the Opulent and respectable Stranger, but the oppressed and persecuted of all Nations and Religions."[4] Heeding the message, waves of immigration made a "settler" country ever more culturally and religiously diverse. Indeed, America has come to call itself "a nation of immigrants," treating the Statue of Liberty and Ellis Island as icons of national identity.

In practice, most of the early settlers were Protestants from the British Isles. Nevertheless, the founders rejected defining American identity in such ethnic terms. True, John Jay, Thomas Jefferson, and Benjamin Franklin believed in the importance of a common culture founded on British political values and English as a common language.[5] But they knew there would be other immigrants and simply assumed that newcomers would assimilate.

As a result, a normative conception of national identity, which we label *cosmopolitan liberalism*, was articulated. The core principle of cosmopolitan liberalism is the equal treatment of individuals. Everyone should be subject to the same rules and requirements. Discrimination on the basis of national origin was in principle anathema, but so too was the idea that membership in a particular ethnic group entitles one to special exemptions or rights.[6] The state should be difference-blind; that is, neutral to the ethnocultural identities of its members.[7]

---

[2] Wayne Norman, "Theorizing Nationalism (Normatively): The First Steps," in *Theorizing Nationalism*, ed. Ronald Beiner (Albany: State University of Press of New York, 1999), 53.

[3] This is the standard estimate based on the U.S. census's approximate calculations. See Peter Schuck, "Immigration," in *Understanding America*, ed. Peter Schuck and James Q. Wilson (Polity Press: New York, 2007), 361.

[4] Quoted from Daniel Tichenor, *Dividing Lines: The Politics of Immigration Control in America* (Princeton, NJ: Princeton University Press, 2002), 51.

[5] Summarized in Jack Citrin and Matthew Wright, "The Politics of Immigration in a Nation of Immigrants," in *New Directions in American Politics*, ed. Raymond J. La Raja (New York: Routledge, 2013), 238.

[6] Brian Barry, *Culture and Equality* (Cambridge, MA: Harvard University Press, 2002).

[7] Brian Barry, *Justice as Impartiality* (Oxford: Clarendon Press, 1995).

In principle, if not always in practice, then, this is an inclusive narrative that defines Americanism on the basis of a "civic creed" emphasizing democracy, constitutionalism, and individual rights. Immigrants would become Americans once they learned English and absorbed these values. The imagined national community of cosmopolitan liberalism embodied Ralph Waldo Emerson's credo: "America has no genealogy. Its family tree is not easily traced."[8]

With the first massive wave of immigration, however, an alternative set of norms about American identity emerged in the form of *nativism*. As Rogers Smith writes in *Civic Ideals*,[9] this ethnocentric tradition has waxed and waned, but in the nineteenth century its influence resulted in new and racist immigration and naturalization laws, culminating in the national origins system that lasted from 1924 until the civil rights era after World War II. The ideal immigrant for nativists was an Anglo-Saxon Protestant; if others were admitted, they should undergo a program of Americanization that could force them to shed their native customs.[10] Coercion, not just gradual change, would sustain the "*unum*."

Although nativism ostensibly was aimed at foreigners, its most glaring and enduring form of prejudice, of course, has been the ideologies and practices that assigned African Americans to a lower caste, first through slavery and then through the Jim Crow system. These institutions are incompatible with cosmopolitan liberalism, so their survival for more than a century and a half – what Gunnar Myrdal called the "American dilemma" – testifies to the limits of that original universalistic image.[11]

The long nativist moment ended with the pivotal 1960s legislation. Together, the end of racial discrimination in law and an ethnically neutral immigration regime can be viewed as the apogee of cosmopolitan liberalism. Nevertheless, in the sharply changed political context of the late 1960s, some, like the cultural nationalist faction of the civil rights movement, rejected cosmopolitan liberalism as a failure. Instead, they proposed what became the essential elements of *multiculturalism* as the normative foundation for justice and solidarity in a multiethnic nation-state.[12] As all commentators agree,[13] multiculturalism is a concept with a wide range of meanings. As a demographic concept, it refers to the presence of more than one cultural group within a single polity. This

---

[8] Quoted in Tichenor, *Dividing Lines*, 53.

[9] Rogers M. Smith, *Civic Ideals: Conflicting Visions of Citizenship in U.S. Public Law* (Chelsea, MI: Yale University Press, 1997).

[10] John Higham, *Strangers in the Land: Patterns of American Nativism, 1860–1925* (Brunswick, NJ: Rutgers University Press, 2002).

[11] Gunnar Myrdal, *An American Dilemma: The Negro Problem and Modern Democracy* (New York: Harper & Row, 1942).

[12] Two classic statements are Will Kymlicka, *Multicultural Citizenship* (Oxford: Oxford University Press, 1995) and Charles Taylor, "The Politics of Recognition," in *Multiculturalism: Examining the Politics of Recognition*, edited by Amy Gutmann (Princeton, NJ: Princeton University Press, 1994).

[13] Paul Kelly, "Introduction: Between Culture and Equality," in *Multiculturalism Reconsidered*, ed. Paul Kelly (Malden, MA: Polity Press, 2002), 4.

phenomenon is a feature of virtually all modern societies. As a normative ideology, multiculturalism is a theory of how states should deal with demographic diversity.

All versions of multiculturalism defend the equal recognition of ethnic cultures and the necessity of group-differentiated policies. They all regard the individual as formed in the crucible of a particular culture whose dignity and preservation is essential to his or her freedom in choosing how to live.[14] If the state does not prescribe rights and provide resources that sustain minority "ways of life," the privileges and power of the cultural majority will be reinforced, and minorities will be forced to choose between assimilation and marginalization. Multiculturalism thus endorses the maintenance and strengthening of group identifications and the equality of all cultural traditions, without necessarily embracing every cultural practice as acceptable.[15] It flatly rejects nativism as racist. But it also rejects some core precepts of cosmopolitan liberalism. It generally regards equal treatment as inadequate protection for cultural differences and, in some more extreme variants, as mere cover for de facto discrimination. So, at a practical level, the core thrust of multiculturalism is to promote the recognition of ethnic and racial groups, value their unique cultures, provide for their equal representation, and, as much as possible, work toward their equality, not merely before the law, but in access to the universal desiderata of modern life. It therefore promotes group-conscious policies instead of difference-blind equal treatment.

In sum, we distinguish cosmopolitan liberalism, nativism, and multiculturalism as alternative normative solutions to the problem of reconciling ethnic and racial diversity with the idea of a shared nation. Nativism's solution for the integration of increased diversity is an active program of Americanization. Cosmopolitan liberalism's solution relies on equal treatment, equal opportunity, and freedom of association. Multiculturalism's perspective on integrating new groups into a nation long dominated both culturally and politically by the descendants of northern Europeans is to reexamine the balance between ethnic and national identifications. As a result, as the title of this volume indicates, we ask whether the growing diversity of American society, and ideological responses to it, gnaw away at a common national identity and patriotic sentiments.

These normative debates pitting liberalism against multiculturalism form the background of our inquiry. But our primary concern is with the pattern of public support for these alternate ideological forms of the relationship between the nation and its racial and ethnic subgroups. We believe public opinion is an underexamined piece of the puzzle of *e pluribus unum*, a foundation for social cohesion and national unity that has received less scholarly attention than has the thinking of political elites.

[14] Kymlicka, *Multicultural Citizenship*.
[15] See Jeffrey Spinner, *The Boundaries of Citizenship* (Baltimore: Johns Hopkins Press, 1994), chapters 4 and 5 for a discussion of this issue.

We attend in particular to the political identities and attitudes of the mass public. On the one hand, we examine those that relate centrally to race and ethnicity, such as ethnic group consciousness, group-interested policy preferences, and opinions about multiculturalist norms and the policy positions that flow from them (although usually from other sources of support as well). On the other hand, we consider attachment to the nation in terms of patriotism and national identity. Then we look closely at whether ethnically oriented dispositions conflict with and compromise those that are nation-oriented. We examine each major ethnic group separately because the very essence of multiculturalism and identity politics is the disparate tendencies of diverse ethnic and racial groups.

In doing so, we try to understand the sources of the mass public's political thinking about race and ethnicity as it exists on the ground. We argue that academic discussions of cultural diversity in America are often oversimplified. Today's ethnic and racial groups are not static silos, destined to remain separate and unchanging, in a fixed racial hierarchy. Rather, diversity is dynamic. Moreover, America's historic black–white dualism may not be the most useful model for understanding the trajectory of incoming immigrant groups. In this vein, we empirically contrast three leading psychological models of how intergroup relations work in practice. Each is, of course, an ideal type, and so has some of the flavor of mythology as well as attempting to model reality.

One is the *assimilation* model best known through writings about the European immigrants of a century ago. These newcomers to the United States often faced resistance from the existing population and usually possessed fewer resources in terms of language, capital, education, job skills, and income. Initially, of course, true assimilation – either cultural or economic – was the exception, not the rule. Differences in national origin persisted for decades in the form of enduring hyphenated-American ethnic groups, frequently living in neighborhoods dominated by their own national group, maintaining some fluency in their original languages, marrying within the group, and often creating institutions parallel to those of the broader society. But a century later, much of that separateness has disappeared through pervasive residential dispersion, linguistic acculturation, waning ethnic identification, intermarriage, and upward mobility.

We examine whether or not today's immigrants – heavily from Latin America and Asia – are following the same path. In applying the assimilation model to the current era, we are cognizant that, relative to that heavy wave of European immigration of a century ago, the new immigrants are relatively recent arrivals. The heaviest immigration in that earlier era occurred over roughly a forty-four-year span, from 1880 to 1924. The current rush of immigration began in 1965, nearly fifty years ago as this is written. The two spans of time are similar in length. But at the comparable moment to the present, in the late 1920s, the Italians, Poles, Russian Jews, Greeks, and their brethren were quite distinctive and unassimilated. Applying the assimilation model should not assume that

Latinos and Asian Americans today look as assimilated as the descendants of those long-ago European immigrants do now, nearly a century after that wave of immigration slowed to a trickle.

The assimilation model does not account as well for the trajectory of African Americans as for the European immigrants across the past century. Realistically, blacks then and now have remained more separate from and more disadvantaged than the majority whites by such indicators as residential segregation, the level of intermarriage, and continuing gaps in socioeconomic status, education, morbidity, health, and other domains of well-being. Therefore, the assimilation model may work better for such heavily immigrant groups as Latinos and Asian Americans than it does for African Americans, suggesting a *black exceptionalism* model of ethnic group differences as an alternative. This presupposes a stricter and less permeable color line facing blacks than those immigrant groups, notwithstanding the common descriptions of Latinos and Asians as also people of color. It also presupposes the greater weight of centuries of disadvantage on the vast majority of African Americans than on new immigrants.

Finally, many social psychologists who specialize in intergroup relations are drawn to various elements of what we describe collectively as a *politicized group consciousness paradigm* of Americans' thinking about race and ethnicity, especially among minorities. This paradigm prioritizes such variables as categorization along group lines, group hierarchies, politicized in-group identity, antagonism toward out-groups, and intergroup competition as central elements of human psychology. This approach views racial and ethnic minorities as having especially strong ethnic identities, a sense of common fate with fellow group members, and perceptions of discrimination against their own group. These psychological foundations, we suggest, underlie the normative precepts of identity politics and multiculturalist ideology, particularly resonating with its emphasis on privileging ethnicity as a primary social identity.

We are interested not just in where the American public is today, but in the direction it may take in the future. As a result, we also test what we label a *vanguard* hypothesis. Here, we build on the literature identifying generational effects, stimulated by Karl Mannheim years ago.[16] He proposed that "generational units" of young people might be affected in common by "the times" (or, in German, the *zeitgeist*). Public and scholarly attention to cultural diversity and to multiculturalist ideologies has gained prominence only in the past thirty years or so. Exposure to these phenomena has been most widespread in our colleges and universities. The vanguard hypothesis proposes that there may be especially high levels of ethnic group consciousness, support for multiculturalism, and waning of national identity and patriotism among the young and college educated of all ethnic and racial groups.

---

[16] Karl Mannheim, "The Problem of Generations," in *Essays in the Sociology of Knowledge*, by Karl Manheim, ed. Paul Kecskemeti (Orlando, FL: Mariner Books, 1955).

Surveys underrepresent minorities

So, our study is a work of political psychology, focusing on public opinion. Our method is the sample survey. Much of our data is taken from representative national surveys such as the American National Election Studies (ANES) or General Social Survey (GSS). These surveys are excellent for tapping national opinion, especially that of whites. They are less useful for understanding the thinking of people of color, so central to our interests, because of the small numbers of such people generally interviewed in national surveys. For the opinions of African Americans, Latinos, and Asian Americans, we turn for the most part to the Los Angeles County Social Surveys carried out annually for almost a decade in a metropolitan area that ranks at the top in the nation, or very close to it, in cultural diversity. But we buttress this analysis of ethnic differences when possible with findings from the more recent 2008 or 2012 ANES studies, which have much larger numbers of African-American and Latino respondents than did previous ANES studies.

The data we present in this book are drawn from a variety of surveys conducted over a period of years rather than from a single survey, which, however well designed, constitutes a snapshot taken at a single point in time. Our approach thus resembles a kind of meta-analysis, searching for consistency in the results of many studies using multiple measures. In addition, we deliberately adopt a somewhat old-fashioned analysis, emphasizing description based on simple cross-tabulations before embarking on more rigorous multivariate tests. And even there we eschew the "kitchen sink" model of massive equations that present themselves as the Holy Grail with no omitted variables. Admittedly, this leaves us open to the charge of failing to establish genuine "causal" relationships, if such an achievement ever was possible through multiple regression analysis. We are convinced, however, that the simpler portrait we attempt to draw here – one that does, after all, insist on testing for the statistical significance of relationships – provides nuanced and accessible evidence of public opinion on the political challenges of multiculturalism in contemporary American politics.

To anticipate the results briefly, we have reassuring news about national attachment. Americans' patriotism remains strong and pervasive. We do find that whites are generally more devoted to the symbols of the nation than are minority groups. But African Americans, the most disadvantaged of America's racial groups, are highly patriotic by any standard. The patriotism of Latinos, also quite disadvantaged, is closely dependent on their immigration status. The American-born are considerably more patriotic than the foreign-born. That is true even of the Mexican Americans who Samuel Huntington worried were a threat to American unity[17] and who dominate the Latino population in the Southwest and California and increasingly are spreading throughout the nation.

---

[17] Samuel P. Huntington, *Who Are We?: Challenges to American Identity* (Cambridge, MA: Harvard University Press, 2004), chapter 8.

Perhaps most importantly, U.S.-born Latinos are just as patriotic as whites.[18] This suggests that, over time, Latinos' overall attachment to the nation will grow as their numerical center of gravity moves toward the U.S.-born and away from immigrants. Surprisingly, partisan cleavages overshadow ethnic divisions about patriotic sentiments, with white conservatives and Republicans substantially more enamored with symbols of the nation than white liberals and Democrats. Young whites, rather than minorities, stand out as the least patriotic, yielding partial support for the vanguard hypothesis. So if the American *unum* indeed is crumbling or breaking apart, it is due more to partisan and generational polarization than to ethnic diversity.

In surveying the literature, we distinguish between a liberal "soft" version of multiculturalist policies and a more radical "hard" variant. Both defend group-conscious policies. However, the scope and content of their proposals differ. Soft multiculturalism focuses on the symbolic recognition of different groups to affirm their value and acceptance of their differences and on modest adjustments of traditional policies to accommodate the special needs of minority groups along the road to integration, such as the use of bilingual ballots to allow heavily immigrant groups to achieve proportionate political representation. Hard multiculturalism, on the other hand, assumes that the differences among ethnic groups are stronger and more persistent and emphasizes the major costs of assimilation to those called upon to adapt. In that view, both justice and social peace require formal group representation, exemptions for cultural minorities in domains such as family law, and policy-making negotiations among parties resembling a quasi-confederation.[19]

To make a long story short, we find widespread acceptance of soft multiculturalism, even among whites. In contrast, we find general opposition to hard multiculturalism, even among ethnic minorities. Not surprisingly, then, the "harder" multiculturalist proposals advocated by some political theorists do not achieve much visibility in the mainstream political agenda in the United States.

What about our three political-psychological models? First, is there evidence of strong ethnic group consciousness in America's largest minority groups, driving separate policy agendas favoring their own ethnic interests? High levels of aggrieved group consciousness, as reflected in especially strong racial identity, a sense of common fate with fellow group members, and perceived discrimination and blocked opportunities against their group, are common only among

---

[18] This confirms earlier studies by De la Garza, Citrin, et al. See Rodolfo de la Garza, Angelo Falcon, Chris F. Garcia, and John A. Garcia, "Latino National Political Survey, 1989–1990" (ICPSR 6841); Jack Citrin, Amy Lerman, Michael Murakami, and Kathryn Pearson, "Testing Huntington: Is Hispanic Immigration a Threat to American Identity?," *Perspectives on Politics* 1 (March 2007): 31–48.

[19] Iris Marion Young, *Justice and the Politics of Difference* (Princeton, NJ: Princeton University Press, 1990); and Bhikhu Parekh, *Rethinking Multiculturalism* (Cambridge, MA: Harvard University Press, 2000).

African Americans. Each minority group does support public policies most congruent with its own presumed interests. But there is little sign of a "people of color" coalition that gives steady support to all minority groups' interests against whites.

Second, one fear swirling around debates over immigration is that new immigrants are not likely to gradually acculturate to America or assimilate to the mainstream. Mexican Americans, who dominate the Latino population, are sometimes especially targeted as likely to remain more separate than did those fabled European immigrants because of their large urban ghettoes, the proximity of Mexico, and the ease of moving back and forth across the border.[20] To repeat, we believe that the heaviest waves of Mexican immigration have come too recently to have reached any stable equilibrium level of assimilation as yet. Nevertheless, we find numerous indications of integration among southern California Latinos already. Nativity matters, as the assimilation model assumes. As noted earlier, U.S.-born Latinos are considerably more patriotic than are the foreign-born. They are more likely to identify as "just American" or as both American and ethnic than as purely ethnic. They show less group consciousness. They are less likely to see value in remaining separate as opposed to blending into the broader society. Such findings suggest some limits to the quasi-essentialist interpretation of American ethnic groups found in some politicized group-consciousness perspectives, portraying them as persistently inhabiting somewhat separate silos. Nevertheless, assimilation is a slow process, and, as our data confirm, it occurs across generations more often than within a new immigrant's lifetime.

Third, the black exceptionalism model hypothesizes that African Americans have always faced a uniquely powerful color line, one that is not completely impermeable but that continues to be difficult to crack. Despite their linguistic assimilation and their significant and ongoing contributions to a common popular culture, many blacks are excluded by the legacy of the past from the level of integration into the mainstream that voluntary immigrant groups have undergone, and, we argue, are continuing to undergo. Indeed, of all the major ethnic and racial groups blacks have, on average, by far the strongest levels of aggrieved ethnic group consciousness. Young blacks are especially likely to have strong group consciousness, suggesting enduring obstacles to interethnic cooperation.

What of the potential incompatibility of national and ethnic attachments? Does identity politics, based on high levels of ethnic consciousness and group-interested political preferences, constitute a centrifugal force, a kind of "divide-and-rule" form of politics that undercuts cooperation and mutual sacrifice on behalf of the nation as a whole? Hearteningly, we see only limited evidence of any such collision of identities, even among the most disadvantaged minority groups, blacks and Latinos. In fact, the correlation between their strength of patriotism and of ethnic identity is persistently nearly zero, rather than negative,

---

[20] Huntington makes this argument forcefully.

as might be expected from some versions of the politicized ethnic consciousness model. Immigrants generally favor hyphenated identities, which our evidence suggests appear to serve as transitional way stations in self-definition, positively associated with both patriotism and the strength of ethnic identity.

From a normative point of view, we find it encouraging that most Americans appear to be accepting of what we have called soft multiculturalism, encompassing recognition and tolerance of difference and support for policies that ease the integration of today's minority groups into the broader society. That acceptance should help dampen intergroup conflict and ease social cohesion in an increasingly diverse society. However, the commitment of the general public, including ethnic minorities, to cosmopolitan liberalism's principle of individual rather than group rights seems intact. Hard lines between ethnic groups, like the "one-drop" color line historically dominant in the United States, would seem to us to foster stereotyping, discrimination, and intergroup conflict.

Finally, despite the influx of so many immigrants, patriotism remains at a higher level in the United States, indeed higher than in most other advanced industrial democracies.[21] The fly in the ointment, as it has been for almost 400 years, is the persisting disadvantage experienced by African Americans. Their response is in some respects predictable: a high level of aggrieved group consciousness, as noted earlier, and high levels of support for government policies that aid blacks as a whole. In another respect, their response is more surprising and encouraging for the unity of the nation: high levels of national attachment and patriotism.

FORESHADOWING

We conclude this prologue by outlining what comes next. Chapter 1 introduces the history of earlier debates over national unity and the challenges posed to it by massive immigration in the contemporary era. Then it introduces our three normative models for offering alternative ways of accommodating diversity while maintaining public attachment to the nation as a whole: cosmopolitan liberalism, nativism, and multiculturalism. The writings of leading advocates and critics of multiculturalism are reviewed, going over some of the groundwork introduced here and laying out the distinction between hard and soft multiculturalism.

Chapter 2 introduces our three psychological models of race and ethnicity in America: politicized group consciousness, immigrant assimilation, and black exceptionalism. It also discusses the more general psychological issues surrounding the individual's management of plural identities. It concludes by laying out our basic empirical methodology, describing the surveys we rely on, and presenting some descriptive demographic statistics about the different racial and ethnic groups we compare.

---

[21] Tom W. Smith and Seokho Kim, "National Pride in Comparative Perspective: 1995/96 and 2003/04," *International Journal of Public Opinion Research*, 18 (2006), 127–36.

Each of the next seven chapters of the book addresses a separate central empirical question regarding public opinion. Chapter 3 presents our definition of national identity, distinguishing self-categorization, emotional attachment to the nation, and ideas about the nation's norms and boundaries. It poses three broad questions: How patriotic are Americans, what variations are there among them, and what does it mean to be an American? The first entails measuring patriotism and national pride. The second examines variation between ethnic groups and tests the vanguard and immigrant assimilation hypotheses. The third question entails an exploration of the content and character of American national identity and pride. Is American nationality defined in civic terms potentially achievable by all, such as citizenship and political beliefs, or in primordial ethnic terms such as race, religion, or nativity?

Chapter 4 examines ethnic consciousness. It begins by examining perceptions of the severity of ethnic group conflict within the nation. It then presents measures of politicized ethnic group consciousness in terms of its constituent parts: strength of ethnic identity, perceived common fate, and perceived discrimination. It estimates the prevalence of each in the four main American ethnic groups we examine in this study. It also offers a composite index of aggrieved group consciousness. The chapter concludes with an exploration of the sources of strong ethnic identities within each ethnic group, testing the politicized group consciousness, assimilation, black exceptionalism, and vanguard hypotheses.

Chapter 5 describes public opinion about multicultural norms concerning the role of ethnicity in American political life. We examine beliefs about ethnic essentialism and attitudes toward the official recognition of ethnicity, assimilation, and the basis for the political representation of racial and ethnic groups. We assess the prevalence of a coherent ideology about multiculturalist norms. Then we test for the psychological origins of support for multiculturalism. Does it stem from strong ethnic group consciousness among minorities? Does it wane with the assimilation of post-immigration generations of Latinos? Is it especially strong among the young and better-educated vanguards?

Chapter 6 takes up the possible collision of national and ethnic identities, especially among minorities. Does strong ethnic consciousness compromise national unity by weakening national identity, as some fear? Do hyphenated identities reflect in equal measure the intertwining of ethnic and national identity? Do post-immigration generations show assimilation in terms of increasing attachment to the nation in preference to ethnic identity? We test whether patriotism is positively associated with whites' ethnic identities and negatively associated with those of ethnic minorities. We conclude by examining whether support for multiculturalist norms compromises strong national identity.

Chapters 7 and 8 analyze opinion toward important policies that form elements of multiculturalism's agenda, defined in terms of race-targeted, immigration, and language policies. We first assess areas of consensus about both soft and hard multiculturalist policies across the main ethnic and racial groups. Then we turn to ethnic differences in attitudes toward those group-conscious policies,

examining the possible roots of such group cleavages in divergent group interests, intergroup competition, and differential assimilation. We examine the
coherence across domains of multiculturalist policy preferences as we did with
multiculturalist norms. Finally, we examine differences in the associations of
patriotism and ethnic identity with policy preferences across ethnic groups and
issue domains, focusing particularly on the dividing line between racial issues
and those relating to cultural unity.

Chapter 9 considers where contention about American identity and multiculturalism fits within the broader range of prevailing partisan and ideological
battle lines in American politics. In the general public, are beliefs about
American identity becoming increasingly polarized along party lines? Do preferences about group-conscious policies, such as affirmative action, immigration,
and language, align themselves with the standard major partisan cleavages on
economic and social issues?

Finally, Chapter 10 provides a summary and conclusion to the book. Of
particular relevance is the pattern of ethnic cleavages on the attitudes and beliefs
examined, for this indicates whether and when the politicized group consciousness, assimilation, and/or black exceptionalism perspectives best explain divisions of opinion. We also consider in each case the probable future trend in
popular outlook, as suggested by the vanguard hypothesis about differences
across generational and educational lines.

I

The Challenge of *E Pluribus Unum*

What does the ethnic diversity of the United States imply for its national identity? This question has been asked repeatedly since America's founding, but the ongoing demographic transformation of the country gives it renewed significance. What are the implications of this increased cultural diversity for *e pluribus unum*, the creation of one out of many in a nation of immigrants? Has it unleashed unmanageable centrifugal forces? Does the country need new psychological glue to hold a multiethnic polity together in the twenty-first century? In this chapter, we contrast the solutions for managing America's diversity given by three normative perspectives: cosmopolitan liberalism, nativism, and multiculturalism. We concentrate on how these conceptions strike the balance between group and national identities, how they view the role of the state in responding to the demands of a new array of minorities, and how the implications of their proposed policies may affect national solidarity.

THE LIBERAL CONSENSUS AND ITS CRITICS

Almost seventy years ago, a united nation emerged victorious from a great war. Commitment to a common culture seemed to be taken for granted. No political movement then seriously challenged the ideal of *e pluribus unum* symbolized by the image of the melting pot.[1] Published in 1955, Louis Hartz's *The Liberal Tradition in America* provided the dominant scholarly interpretation of American political culture for years to come.[2] This normative view, which we label *cosmopolitan liberalism*, emphasized that America's core identity is ideological, not ethnic, not limited to a particular people. For Hartz, as for de

[1] Louis Hartz, *The Liberal Tradition in America: An Interpretation of American Political Thought Since the Revolution* (New York: Harcourt Brace, 1955).
[2] Philip Abbott, "Still Louis Hartz after All These Years: A Defense of the Liberal Society Thesis," *Perspectives on Politics* 3, no. 1 (2005): 93–109.

I

Tocqueville and many other commentators, Americanism is a *civil* religion, a creed comprising belief in the values of democracy, individualism, liberty, equality, and property rights. Hartz, Seymour Martin Lipset, and others also argued that the firm grip of this liberal tradition helps explain the exceptionalism of the country's politics – the lack of a strong socialist party, the weakness of the labor movement, the acceptance of economic inequality, and the boundaries on government action that limited the development of the welfare state.[3] But the creedal definition of American identity implicitly was inclusive: anyone could belong to America if he or she embraced the civil religion, spoken in English.

In the past several decades, however, the idea of cultural unity in American politics has come under sustained attack. Looking backward, Rogers Smith holds that Hartz's characterization of a uniform, individualist American political culture is incomplete. He argues that a rival ethnocultural tradition long had widespread support, sustaining a racial hierarchy through Jim Crow laws and discriminatory immigration and naturalization policies.[4] Whereas Tocqueville and Hartz implied that adherence to the liberal American creed would be sufficiently strong cement to unify the country's diverse population, John Higham[5] showed that *nativism*, an ethnocentric response that held new waves of newcomers as unqualified to be true Americans, was a recurring response to nineteenth-century immigration. Nativism repudiated the inclusiveness of cosmopolitan liberalism in favor of a conception of American identity that limited full membership in the national community to white Anglo-Saxon Protestants. Smith concluded that this response to non-British immigrants, buttressed by restrictive laws, along with enslavement of blacks and eradication and segregation of Native Americans, belied the claim that cosmopolitan liberalism was hegemonic. Instead, it highlighted the coexistence of a potent inegalitarian tradition.[6]

Looking forward from Hartz, recent work from across the political spectrum projects an image of America as a splintering society.[7] Identity politics, culture

---

[3] Hartz, *The Liberal Tradition in America*; Seymour Martin Lipset and Gary Marks, *It Didn't Happen Here: Why Socialism Failed in the United States* (New York: W. W. Norton & Company, Inc., 2000).

[4] Rogers M. Smith, "Beyond Tocqueville, Myrdal, and Hartz: The Multiple Traditions in America," *The American Political Science Review* 87, no. 3 (1993): 549–66; Rogers M. Smith, *Civic Ideals: Conflicting Visions of Citizenship in U.S. History* (Chelsea, MI: Yale University Press, 1997).

[5] John Higham, *Strangers in the Land: Patterns of American Nativism, 1860–1925* (New Brunswick, NJ: Rutgers University Press, 1955).

[6] Ibid., Smith, *Civic Ideals*.

[7] Andrew Hacker, *Two Nations: Black and White, Separate, Hostile, Unequal* (New York: Charles Scribner's Sons, 1992); Arthur M. Schlesinger Jr., *The Disuniting of America: Reflections on a Multicultural Society* (New York: W. W. Norton & Company, 1998); Peter Brimelow, *Alien Nation: Common Sense about America's Immigration Disaster* (New York: Random House, Inc., 1995); Todd Gitlin, *The Twilight of Common Dreams: Why America Is Wracked by Culture Wars* (New York: Metropolitan Books, Henry Holt and Company, 1996); Gertrude Himmelfarb, *One Nation, Two Cultures* (New York: Alfred A. Knopf, 1999), 116–41.

wars, and party polarization are recurring catchwords in accounts of today's politics, drowning out depictions of national solidarity based on a consensual creed. Accounts of the centrifugal forces challenging an overarching sense of American national identity often begin, ironically, by pointing to the aftermath of the civil rights movement's successes.[8] To distill the argument, the end of legal segregation failed to eliminate the wide racial gap in economic and social circumstances, prompting support for cultural nationalism among some black activists in the late 1960s. Almost forty years after Hartz's assertion of liberal consensus, Andrew Hacker's review of the racial landscape was titled, *Two Nations, Black and White, Separate, Hostile, Unequal.*[9]

At the same time, the example of the civil rights movement catalyzed demands for greater equality by other groups, including ethnic minority groups enlarged by immigration, women, and the lesbian, gay, bisexual, and transgender (LGBT) community.[10] Increased assertiveness about such subnational identities fueled a style of thinking that judges public policies principally by how they affect the prestige, welfare, and survival of one's particular *group* rather than the country as a whole. Multiculturalism – in its political rather than demographic incarnation – emerged as an ideological defense of institutionalizing rights for minority groups, partly aiming to redistribute resources through group-conscious allocations but also to shore up the capacity of minority cultural norms and practices to survive the pressures of assimilation. Multiculturalist thinkers gave greater weight to the significance of group identities than did Hartz and his followers. Compared to both cosmopolitan liberalism and nativism, multicultur-alism places the ideal of *e pluribus unum* on the back burner, a less important goal than the representation and protection of minorities.

Multiculturalism is not without its critics, even on the left. A prominent example is Todd Gitlin, who worried that the political elevation of ethnic and gender identities has dimmed the prospects for "common dreams" and class-based redistribution.[11] In a similar vein, Arthur Schlesinger Jr. predicted the "disuniting of America" if identity politics made incursions into a common culture by fragmenting the content of public education.[12] Which groups deserve special protection, which policies should advance their interests, and whether group rights can override universal individual rights are questions about which policy makers in the United States and elsewhere differ.[13] This book does not review the full array of demands for group rights, bypassing, for example, those

---

[8] United States, Kerner Commission, *Report of the National Advisory Commission on Civil Disorders* (Washington: U.S. Government Printing Office, 1968).
[9] Hacker, *Two Nations: Black and White, Separate, Hostile, Unequal.*
[10] To this list, we might add advocates for the rights of the disabled, elderly, children, and animals.
[11] Gitlin, *The Twilight of Common Dreams.*
[12] Schlesinger Jr., *The Disuniting of America.*
[13] Paul Kelly, "Introduction: Between Culture and Equality," in *Multiculturalism Reconsidered*, ed. P. Kelly (Oxford: Polity Press, 2002), 5–13.

on behalf of women, the elderly, workers, and the deaf and disabled.[14] Instead, we focus on what we regard as the most important challenges to *e pluribus unum*, the enduring racial divide and the demographic transformation resulting from the opening of the door to non-European immigrants when Congress passed the Immigration and Nationality Act of 1965, sometimes known as the Hart-Celler Act.

The size and composition of the new wave of immigrants were unanticipated, but so too perhaps were the anxieties it aroused. The resulting influx of Hispanics and Asians raised alarms about the threat to a common sense of American nationhood similar to those expressed by the nineteenth-century nativists. In a widely publicized and controversial statement, Samuel Huntington asserted that "the single most immediate and most serious challenge to America's traditional identity comes from the immense and continuing immigration from Latin America, especially from Mexico."[15] Huntington believed that the sheer extent of immigration and high birth rates among Mexican migrants who share a language and are concentrated in a region of the United States close to their country of origin means that they will fail to acculturate like their European predecessors or Asian contemporaries. Whereas Hacker viewed race as the dividing line between two separate and hostile nations, Huntington's worst-case scenario for the future is that the United States will split into two language-based nations: an English-speaking "Anglo-America" and a Spanish-speaking "Mexamerica" that, like Quebec in Canada, regards itself as a distinct society deserving political autonomy.[16]

Huntington's response to the confluence of identity politics and Hispanic immigration rejected multiculturalism's support for cultural differences and called for the reinvigoration of American identity built on Anglo-American Protestant values. In his 1993 book *American Politics: The Politics of Disharmony*, Huntington invoked the Tocquevillian civic creed as the core of Americanism. A decade later, he deemed a commitment to political principles neither strong nor unique enough to bind a nation together and added a healthy dollop of the English language, work ethic, patriotism, and religiosity to comprise American identity. Accusations of nativism followed, but in principle one could envisage people of any national origin acculturating to these norms.

Many critics dismissed the vision of America breaking apart under the pressure of Hispanic immigration. From an empirical perspective, Alba and Nee, Barone, and Citrin et al. cite evidence showing that today's immigrants, including Hispanics, are following the same trajectory of incorporation taken by their

---

[14] Iris M. Young, *Justice and the Politics of Difference* (Princeton, NJ: Princeton University Press, 1990), is the most prominent proponent of guaranteed representation for these groups in most important social roles, but others also write of multiculturalism without culture being the sole criterion for assigning group rights.

[15] Samuel P. Huntington, "The Hispanic Challenge," *Foreign Policy* (March/April 2004): 32.

[16] For a more complete statement, see Huntington, *Who Are We?*.

European predecessors.[17] Predicting the future is a fool's game, perhaps, but the optimistic account of contemporary immigration is that newcomers from all over the globe generally choose to embrace America's democratic creed, learn English, and live its dream of hard work rewarded. They add complex flavors to the stew bubbling in the American melting pot without causing its main ingredients, the English language and self-reliance, to boil away. America "morphs newly arrived Koreans into NASCAR fans, transmogrifies Hmong into country and western addicts, and allows the children of illegal aliens to become PhD's, electrical engineers, and newspaper columnists."[18]

And, from a normative point of view, many liberals and multiculturalists alike reject Huntington's recommendation that immigrants *should* Americanize by embracing Anglo-American Protestant values. They regard the maintenance of diverse ethnic traditions as both morally valid and quite compatible with America's sense of itself.[19] Here, we examine evidence for the claim that ethnic diversity and cultural division gnaw from within at an overarching sense of attachment to the nation.

Not all possible threats to a common national identity come from within. A potential external threat to a strong sense of national identity is globalization. By this we mean a set of processes that boost the salience of larger transnational contacts and identifications. Economic interdependence has diminished the sovereignty of even the American superpower, fraying the connections between citizenship and personal welfare and increasing cosmopolitan commitment to international legal norms.[20] Self-interest in the global marketplace pushes American corporations to downgrade their "national" character. And the web of international travel communications fosters a growing similarity in cultural expression.

Theorists of globalization argue that the concept of citizenship no longer must be wedded to membership in a nation-state. The development of a cosmopolitan morality embedded in international law and the pervasiveness of migration give birth to notions of multinational, transnational, and postnational citizenship.[21]

---

[17] Michael Barone, *The New Americans: How the Melting Pot Can Work Again* (Washington, DC: Regnery Publishing, Inc., 2001); Richard Alba and Victor Nee, *Remaking the American Mainstream* (Cambridge, MA: Harvard University Press, 2003); Jack Citrin, Amy Lerman, Michael Murakami, and Kathryn Pearson, "Testing Huntington: Is Hispanic Immigration a Threat to American Identity?" *Perspectives on Politics* 5, no. 1 (2007): 31–48.

[18] Victor Davis Hanson, *Between War and Peace: Lessons from Afghanistan to Iraq* (New York: Random House, 2004), 170.

[19] Tamar Jacoby, "Rainbow's End," *The Washington Post*, May 16, 2004, p. BW03. Available online at http://www.washingtonpost.com/wp-dyn/articles/A25699-2004May13.html.

[20] Saskia Sassen, *Losing Control? Sovereignty in an Age of Globalization* (New York: Columbia University Press, 1996); Robert B. Reich, *The Work of Nations: Preparing Ourselves for 21st Century Capitalism* (New York: Simon & Schuster, 1993).

[21] See, e.g., Linda Bosniak, "Citizenship Denationalized," *Indiana Journal of Global Legal Studies* 7 (2000): 447–509; and Peter J. Spiro, *Beyond Citizenship: American Identity after Globalization* (New York: Oxford University Press, Inc., 2007).

Among the multiple layers of belonging, identification with the nation is receding in importance according to some theorists. But others emphasize the staying power of national attachment at an almost unconscious level. As Michael Billig puts it, in established states, identification with the nation becomes banal through daily reminders: seeing the national flag on public buildings, using the national coins and currency, celebrating national holidays, driving on streets named for political and military heroes, and even reading about international sporting competitions.[22]

But whatever the normative merits of global citizenship and a generalized love of humanity, the humanitarian ideal of "one world, one family" at present seems too thin an emotional gruel to satisfy most publics. For example, the banal habits of national attachment are among the many obstacles to the development of a strong sense of European identity despite the efforts of the institutions of the European Union. Indeed, perhaps because of the very diversity of the American population, patriotic rituals such as flying the flag in homes and stores, playing the national anthem at sporting events, and reciting the Pledge of Allegiance were more pervasive in the United States than in other countries well before September 11, 2001. But we show that despite political polarization and public divisions over important cultural issues, the national attachment of Americans remains pervasive and strong.

EARLIER DEBATES OVER NATIONAL IDENTITY

At the moment of American independence, a majority of the colonists were from Britain, but the population also included people from other European countries, African slaves, and native tribes. Early commentators held mixed views about the presence of variety. John Jay considered the hegemony of English or Anglo-American culture as the foundation of national progress, writing in *The Federalist* papers that "Providence had been pleased to give this one connected country to one united people, a people descended from the same ancestors, speaking the same language, professing the same religion, attached to the same principles of government, very similar in their customs and manners."[23] Benjamin Franklin was more explicit in demanding cultural uniformity, worrying that the influx of Germans into Anglicized Pennsylvania would result in "their" language and customs driving out "ours."[24]

Against this, Jean de Crevecoeur famously described America as a place where "individuals of all nations are blended into a new race of men."[25]

---

[22] Michael Billig, *Banal Nationalism* (London: Sage Publications, 1995).

[23] Quoted in Harold J. Abramson, "Assimilation and Pluralism," in *Harvard Encyclopedia of American Ethnic Groups*, ed. Stephan Thernstrom (Cambridge, MA: Belknap Press of Harvard University Press, 1980), 152.

[24] Quoted in Peter D. Salins, *Assimilation, American Style* (New York: Basic Books, 1997), 25.

[25] Philip Gleason, "American Identity and Americanization," in *Harvard Encyclopedia of American Ethnic Groups*, ed. Stephan Thernstrom (Cambridge, MA: Harvard University Press, 1980).

Almost two centuries later, John Steinbeck repeated the proclamation, including California Chinese and Alabama Negroes as well as Boston Irish and Wisconsin Germans as part of an interwoven new breed – Americans – who have "*more in common than they have apart.*"[26] The implication, for cosmopolitan liberals at least, was that anyone could become an American simply by accepting the country's fundamental ideals of liberty, democracy, and economic self-reliance; by learning English; and, above all, by proclaiming loyalty to their new nation rather than to their country of origin.[27] Emphasizing common values rather than shared ancestry as the foundation of American nationality had several strategic advantages. Because the cultural homogeneity of the United States was taken for granted, this formula for nationhood facilitated the psychic separation from their mother country among the citizens who were of British descent. Moreover, affirming that American identity was based on universal values rather than ancestry ultimately made it easier to incorporate immigrants of varying origins without fundamentally altering the nation's self-concept.

The inclusionary potential of the founders' civic credo was not realized in early practice. In fact, throughout American history one reaction to diversity has been to deem some groups – American Indians, blacks, Asians, and some European immigrants – biologically, intellectually, or culturally unqualified for full membership in the "circle of we." Notwithstanding egalitarian rhetoric, a racial hierarchy was the first American model for handling groups different from the settlers of British ancestry.[28] Skin color was the ultimate dividing line between full members of the national community and people outside or on the fringe. The native tribes and blacks were excluded from the outset. As early as 1835, de Tocqueville was convinced that the cultural survival of the Indian nations was doomed and prophesied that blacks would remain a subordinate and separate group.[29] The civic religion he extolled applied to whites only.

Viewed as savages, Native Americans were eradicated, segregated, or "civilized" through forced assimilation. The treatment of blacks was different. Forcibly imported to provide cheap labor, slaves were exploited and abused long after the Declaration of Independence proclaimed the equality of *all* men. And although the Civil War and Emancipation represented a victory for universal ideals, Jim Crow laws in the South and less formal modes of exclusion elsewhere long sustained the subordination of blacks. However, a formal racial and religious hierarchy was morally discredited and then legally outlawed by developments after World War II, so it is no longer a viable model for defining American nationality or managing the conflicts arising from ethnic diversity.

---

[26] Quoted in Salins, *Assimilation, American Style*, 43, emphasis in original.
[27] Ibid.
[28] George M. Fredrickson, "Models of American Ethnic Relations: A Historical Perspective," in *Cultural Divides*, ed. Deborah Miller and Dale Prentice (New York: Russell Sage Foundation, 1999), 24.
[29] Alexis de Tocqueville, *Democracy in America*, translated by Harvey C. Mansfield and Delba Winthrop (London: Penguin Books, 2002 [1835]).

A more relevant and culturally resonant model is the experience of nineteenth-century European immigrants over time. Beginning in the 1840s, the arrival of massive numbers of non-English and non-Protestant immigrants triggered a nativist movement demanding a more restrictive definition of national identity on the grounds that only Anglo-Saxons possessed the moral and intellectual qualities required for democratic citizenship, the hallmark of "true" Americanism.[30] At first, the nativist movement targeted Irish and German Catholics whose presumed obeisance to the pope would prevent their being fully loyal to their new country. Then, after the Civil War, Asians were targeted as being an "inferior" race. Later, immigrants from southern and eastern Europe took the brunt of nativist rejection, on the grounds that their radicalism and uncouth manners made them unsuitable for democratic citizenship.[31]

Confronting this wave of new immigration stretching from the middle of the nineteenth century to the early twentieth century, nativists sought to limit and then to subject those who did enter the country to a rigorous process of "Americanization." Buttressed by the rise of Social Darwinism in intellectual circles, nativists argued that since natural selection within the human species had produced a superior Anglo-Saxon culture, the laws of evolution validated banning the immigration of Chinese, denying essential rights to blacks, and limiting the use of languages other than English in schools.[32]

Theodore Roosevelt's thinking provides a good example of the nativist version of absorbing newcomers.[33] Roosevelt accepted European immigration and even acknowledged that new blood could add to the nation's vitality, although he drew the line at nonwhites. Nonetheless, in his eyes a single standard of conduct was required to complete the process of nation building, so immigrants would have to shed their original customs and "must learn to talk and think and *be* United States."[34] Citizenship required total identification with America itself: there was no room in his nation for hyphenated Americans or loyalty to any flag but one.[35]

Dedicated to Roosevelt, Israel Zangwill's 1909 play *The Melting Pot* presented an optimistic, even romantic picture of the relations among diverse cultural groups in America. But as historian Philip Gleason has shown, there are two variants of the metaphor of the melting pot for the acculturation of immigrants.[36] The nativists viewed assimilation as a process of *cleansing*, the melting-down of native customs to attain Anglo-conformity. Zangwill's own interpretation hearkened back to earlier predictions that the *blending* of

---

[30] Higham, *Strangers in the Land*.
[31] Ibid.
[32] Ibid.
[33] Noah Pickus, *True Faith and Allegiance: Immigration and American Civic Nationalism* (Princeton, NJ: Princeton University Press, 2005), 86–90.
[34] Theodore Roosevelt quoted in Pickus, *True Faith and Allegiance*, 90.
[35] Ibid.
[36] Philip Gleason, "American Identity and Americanization."

diverse groups would create a new, vital, distinctively American race.[37] New immigrants would learn English and adopt America's democratic political creed without much outside intervention. Yet they could retain elements of their original heritage, and this would help create a new and enriched common culture.[38]

Cultural pluralists like Horace Kallen, a precursor of contemporary multiculturalists, rejected the idea of the melting pot in either incarnation. Kallen called on immigrants to preserve their languages and traditions. He described the United States not as one nation but as a voluntary union of many (European) nations, each of which should have equal status.[39] America should be an orchestra in which each cultural instrument would have a permanent place. For Kallen, pluralism would result in a beautiful symphony; for his critics, the coexistence of many languages and traditions conjured up the biblical Tower of Babel.

One-way assimilation became the dominant approach of policy makers once World War I intensified concerns about national unity and insistence on Americanization. In 1921 and 1924, new legislation both restricted the total number of immigrants and established a system of visa preferences favoring people from northern Europe. Without replenishment, immigrants from other stocks could assimilate more readily. Their status improved through economic advancement, political involvement, and the decline of prejudice against them.[40] Earlier classifications of some Europeans as "Nordic and light" and others as "Mediterranean and dark" vanished.[41] In Michael Lind's words, between the Civil War and World War II the country was slowly transformed from white "Anglo-America" into white "Euro-America."[42] As World War II loomed, the assimilation model was the consensual explanation for the creation of a unified nation built on heterodox ethnic foundations.

This conception of assimilation refers to processes resulting in greater similarity among all the country's ethnic groups, whites included. In *Assimilation in American Life*, Milton Gordon distinguished between *structural assimilation*, involving the large-scale entry of minorities and immigrants into the economic, social, and political institutions of the host society and ultimately leading to intermarriage, and *cultural assimilation*, involving the adoption of dominant

---

[37] Ibid.
[38] Desmond King, *Making Americans: Immigration, Race, and the Origins of the Diverse Democracy* (Cambridge, MA: Harvard University Press, 2000); John Higham, "Multiculturalism and Universalism: A History and Critique," *American Quarterly* 45, no. 2 (1993): 195–219.
[39] Horace Kallen, *Cultural Pluralism and the American Idea: An Essay in Social Philosophy* (Philadelphia: University of Pennsylvania Press, 1956).
[40] Nathan Glazer, *We Are All Multiculturalists Now* (Cambridge, MA: Harvard University Press, 1997), 96.
[41] Roger Waldinger and Mehdi Bozorgmehr, eds., *Ethnic Los Angeles* (New York: Russell Sage Foundation, 1996).
[42] Michael Lind, *The Next American Nation: The New Nationalism and the Fourth American Revolution* (New York: The Free Press, 1995).

values and customs constituting the "American way of life."[43] Gordon believed that structural assimilation would inevitably lead to cultural unity. The power of assimilation would, over time, weaken ethnic identity, making it a largely symbolic, optional attachment. If this is so, then assimilation indeed is the antithesis of multiculturalism's emphasis on the importance of preserving cultural differences and strong ethnic attachments.

CONTEMPORARY CHALLENGES TO THE ASSIMILATION MODEL

We accept that European immigrants to the United States in the nineteenth and early twentieth centuries largely have assimilated – structurally, politically, and culturally. The big exception to this pattern of ethnic changes continued to be the lot of African Americans, the descendants of slaves, with most continuing to live under the oppressive Jim Crow system after legal emancipation. At the dawning of the twentieth century, W. E. B. Dubois wrote that "the problem of the twentieth century is the problem of the color line, and of the 'double consciousness' of blacks: they had no other country but America, yet had a distinct collective fate."[44] Indeed, in that era, a century ago, almost all white Americans would probably now be regarded as holding "racist" ideologies.

The fight against the Nazis and then the Cold War competition for the allegiance of decolonized new nations in Asia and Africa made racism less tenable in opinion and policy. During the years following World War II, moreover, the economic and political mobilization of black Americans accelerated, and the movement to end racial segregation strengthened. Support for the ethnocultural and racist versions of national identity began to dissolve. Martin Luther King Jr. dreamed of integration fueled by common American ideals. The chant "Jim Crow Must Go!" was a call for civic inclusion. Through the convulsive social changes precipitated by the civil rights movement, blacks gradually garnered the rights of full citizens. Despite dogged resistance in the South, predominantly white elites in America moved to extend equal rights to blacks and other minority groups. Legal embodiments of these rights, such as *Brown v. Board of Education*, the Civil Rights Act of 1964, and the Voting Rights Act of 1965, constituted a proclamation of equality for African Americans, a belated Declaration of Independence.

Those civil rights laws of the 1960s removed the final legal vestiges of racial segregation and provided voting rights to blacks throughout the country. Still, despite substantial economic and political progress in the last half of the twentieth century,[45] the residues of slavery and discrimination are

---

[43] Milton M. Gordon, *Assimilation in American Life: The Role of Race, Religion, and National Origins* (New York: Oxford University Press, 1964).

[44] W. E. B. DuBois, *The Souls of Black Folk* (New York: Cosimo, Inc., 2007 [1903]), iii.

[45] Stephan Thernstrom and Abigail Thernstrom, *America in Black and White: One Nation, Indivisible* (New York: Simon & Schuster, Inc., 1997). For a contrary view, see Douglas S. Massey and Nancy A. Denton, *American Apartheid: Segregation and the Making of the Underclass* (Cambridge, MA: Harvard University Press, 1993).

clear. Blacks remain more residentially isolated than other ethnic minorities, even more so than recent immigrants; are less likely to intermarry with other groups; and have been less upwardly mobile in economic and occupational terms.[46] This exceptional history and collective memory of group suffering sustain a distinctive political identity. More than members of other ethnic groups in America, blacks link their personal interests to the fate of the group as a whole and look to state action in the form of race-conscious policies rather than individual mobility as the path to collective progress.[47] The status and outlook of African Americans remain exceptional, as comparisons to the immigrant minorities, including those born in the United States, show.[48]

At almost the same time that historic civil rights legislation was enacted, the Immigration and Nationality Act of 1965 extended the principle of equality to a new domain. By replacing the discriminatory national origins system for visa preferences with a commitment to family reunification, this reform led to an unanticipated explosion of immigration, most of it from Asia and Latin America, particularly from Mexico.[49] The triumph of an ethnically neutral system of immigration was the kernel of Huntington's later nightmare. By the twenty-first century, according to Kenneth Prewitt, the director of the U.S. Census Bureau, the United States had become "the most demographically diverse nation in world history."[50] Between 1960 and 2010, the proportion of the U.S. population that was foreign-born more than doubled, growing from 5.4 percent (9.7 million people) to 12.9 percent (40 million people).[51] Due to their relative youth and higher fertility compared to the native-born, new immigrants and their offspring accounted for half of the U.S. population growth between 1990 and 2010.[52] In California, New York, and Florida, the favorite destinations of

---

[46] Nathan Glazer, "Black and White after Thirty Years," *National Affairs* 121 (Fall 1995); Jennifer Lee and Frank D. Bean, "America's Changing Color Lines: Immigration, Race/Ethnicity, and Multiracial Identification," *Annual Review of Sociology* 30 (2004): 221–42.

[47] Michael C. Dawson, *Behind the Mule: Race and Class in African-American Politics* (Princeton, NJ: Princeton University Press, 1994).

[48] *Brown v. Board of Education of Topeka*, 347 U.S. 483 (1954); David O. Sears and Victoria Savalei, "The Political Color Line in America: Many 'People of Color' or Black Exceptionalism?" *Political Psychology* 27, no. 6 (2006): 895–924.

[49] Aristide R. Zolberg, *A Nation by Design: Immigration Policy in the Fashioning of America* (New York: Russell Sage Foundation, 2006); Daniel J. Tichenor, *Dividing Lines: The Politics of Immigration Control in America* (Princeton, NJ: Princeton University Press, 2002).

[50] Kenneth Prewitt, "Demography, Diversity, and Democracy: The 2000 Census Story," The Brookings Institution (2002). Available online at http://www.brookings.edu/articles/2002/win ter_demographics_prewitt.aspx.

[51] Migration Policy Institute Data Hub, at http://www.migrationinformation.org/DataHub/charts/final.fb.shtml (accessed June 25, 2013).

[52] Migration Policy Institute Data Hub, at http://www.migrationinformation.org/datahub/acscensus.cfm# (accessed June 25, 2013).

new arrivals, by 2010 immigrants comprised 27 percent, 21 percent, and 19 percent of the population, respectively.[53]

The revolutionary immigration law passed in 1965 was a low-profile reform with little political visibility. It was a product of elite compromise and was viewed by its proponents, including President Johnson, as a largely symbolic action that would help reunite families separated by war without dramatically altering the number and origins of immigrants.[54] However, making family reunification rather than national origin the basis for visa preferences meant that the new immigrants would increasingly resemble those of their immediate predecessors. A father from a particular country sent for his wife, children, and parents. Once citizens, spouses used the next level of visa preferences to send for their siblings. A process of "chain migration" then allowed each sibling to spawn a new cluster of immigrants by bringing in their own spouses, children, and in-laws. So once the young Hispanic, Asian, and African immigrants began to arrive, the size of these ethnic groups in the United States grew exponentially.[55] Between 1970 and 2010, about 30 million immigrants came to the United States. Well more than half came from either Mexico or Central America. Asia contributed more than a quarter, whereas less than 15 percent of immigrants arriving after the passage of the 1965 act came from the previously most important originating sources, Europe and Canada, combined.[56] The Latino population jumped 58 percent, more than four times the nation's overall population growth, between 1990 and 2000 and an additional 43 percent between 2000 and 2010, constituting more than half the nation's total population growth.[57] Latinos in 2010 made up 13 percent of the U.S. population, compared to 9 percent in 1990,[58] and are increasingly widely distributed throughout the country.[59] The trend is continuing. Between 2000 and 2010, the Latino share of the population grew by another 3 percent in the country as a whole, by 6 percent in California, and 3 percent in Los Angeles County. More than half of America's foreign-born residents today are Latinos from Central and South America. More than 30 percent are from Mexico. Mexicans also are estimated to comprise 58 percent of the nation's illegal immigrants, a group of more than 11 million people.[60]

---

[53] Thomas A. Gryn and Luke J. Larsen, "Nativity Status and Citizenship in the United States: 2009," *American Community Survey Briefs*, October 2009. Available online at http://www.census.gov/prod/2010pubs/acsbr09-16.pdf.

[54] Daniel Tichenor, *Dividing Lines: The Politics of Immigration Control in America* (Princeton, NJ: Princeton University Press, 2002).

[55] Ibid.

[56] Migration Policy Institute, *supra* note 52.

[57] Jeffrey Passel, "Mexican Immigration to the U.S.: The Latest Estimates" (2011). Available online at http://migrationin.ucdavis.edu/cf/files/2011-may/passel-new-patterns-in-usimmigration.pdf.

[58] Ibid.

[59] Audrey Singer, "The Rise of New Immigrant Gateways," *The Living Cities Census Series* (Washington, DC: The Brookings Institution, 2004).

[60] Jeffrey Passel, "Mexican Immigration to the U.S.: The Latest Estimates" (2011). Available online at http://migrationin.ucdavis.edu/cf/files/2011-may/passel-new-patterns-in-usimmigration.pdf.

The nation's Asian population has also surged, doubling between 1970 and 2010. In fact, between 2000 and 2010, immigrants from Asia were more numerous than those of Hispanic background, as well as more educated and wealthier than even the average native resident.[61] The largest increase in this latter decade was among those from the Indian subcontinent, due in part to the influx of skilled immigrants to work in high-tech companies, but Chinese comprise the largest group of foreign-born residents of Asian origin.[62] Asians also have moved outside the traditional loci of immigration such as Los Angeles, San Francisco, and New York. In the meantime, whites and, to a lesser extent, blacks have moved away from states with high concentrations of immigrants – whites to the nation's hinterland and blacks to the South.[63]

Figure 1.1 summarizes the changes from 1980 to 2010 in the ethnic composition of the United States, California, and Los Angeles County, the populations whose attitudes we survey. In each case, the non-Hispanic white and the black shares of the population are declining, whereas the Latino and Asian segments are growing. In areas with a high concentration of recent immigrants like California, therefore, the politics of multiculturalism center as much on the terms of integrating these diverse newcomers into the national community as on the enduring problem of racial inequality.

THE EMERGENCE OF THE MULTICULTURALIST CHALLENGE

The twinned revolutions in racial and immigration policies represented the apogee of the cosmopolitan liberal image of America as the integrated political community of equal individuals. In law, at least, the racist and ethnocentric definitions of American nationality embedded in nativism were defeated. However, two major developments have occurred since then to challenge the idea that America had settled on outlawing discrimination as the solution for defining nationhood and treating its minority groups. Nativism had largely been eliminated in law and official policy, but it remained an active force in public opinion, albeit in modified form from that existing in the days of slavery and Jim Crow.[64] Second, although cosmopolitan liberalism may have triumphed in

---

[61] Pew Research Center, "The Rise of Asian Americans," June 2012.

[62] Jessica S. Barnes and Claudette E. Bennett, "The Asian Population: Census 2000 Brief," U.S. Census Bureau: C2KBR/01-16 (2002). Available online at http://www.census.gov/prod/2002pubs/c2kbro1-16.pdf.

[63] Ibid.

[64] David O. Sears, Jim Sidanius, and Lawrence Bobo, eds., *Racialized Politics: The Debate About Racism in America* (Chicago: University of Chicago Press, 2000); Donald R. Kinder and Lynn M. Sanders, *Divided by Color: Racial Politics and Democratic Ideals* (Chicago: University of Chicago Press, 1996); Michael Tesler and David O. Sears, *Obama's Race: The 2008 Election and the Dream of a Post-Racial America* (Chicago: University of Chicago Press, 2010).

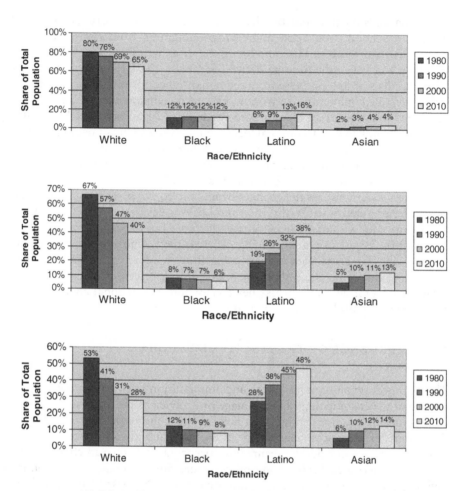

FIGURE 1.1. (A) Ethnic Change in the United States: 1980–2010. (B) Ethnic Change in California: 1980–2010. (C) Ethnic Change in Los Angeles County: 1980–2010. From U.S. Bureau of the Census (census.org) and the California Department of Finance (dof.ca. gov/research).

official policy, it soon faced an ideological challenge led by the very minority groups that had benefited from the decline of legal discrimination.

Triggered by persisting racial inequalities, intensifying ethnic consciousness, and the new demographic profile caused by immigration, multiculturalism emerged as a new prototype for treating racial, cultural, and religious diversity in the United States. It is critical at the outset to distinguish between multiculturalism as a descriptive demographic term referring to the presence within a single polity of many distinct religious, racial, or ethnic groups, and multiculturalism as an ideology, a set of propositions regarding the proper way to respond to this sociological diversity. In the descriptive sense, it is plain that America is and always has been a multicultural society. As an ideology, multiculturalism is a perspective that rejects not just nativism but also the liberal's position that mere toleration of group differences is a sufficient guarantee for treating members of minority groups as citizens with equal rights. As a body of thought, multiculturalism is closely associated with the politics of difference. It rejects the liberal principle of equal treatment before the law for everyone regardless of background as insufficient. It calls instead for group-differentiated rights to combat the dominant patterns of political and cultural power that marginalize certain groups, particularly ethnic minorities.[65]

In political philosophy, the battle over the legitimacy of group rights is at the center of the frequently bitter debates between defenders of multiculturalism and their liberal critics.[66] As political psychologists, we do not try to adjudicate the fierce debates between the two camps regarding the implications of their competing principles for justice.[67] Nor can we settle the ultimately empirical argument about whether assimilation or the preservation of cultural differences is more effective in achieving values such as national loyalty, social solidarity, or economic redistribution. Rather, our goal in this section is to identify those principles and prescriptions of multiculturalism that bear on the problem of *e pluribus unum* as a prelude to assessing in later chapters the extent of public support for them.

Multiculturalism is a protean and contested term. As a result, critics can easily be condemned for imposing a false unity on a variegated body of thought or cherry-picking to ridicule the most extreme proposals. In what follows, therefore, we try to speak to the unifying threads of a wide range of multiculturalist writings by political theorists and other elites. How tightly interconnected the core facets of multiculturalism turn out to be in public opinion is an empirical matter that we examine in a later chapter.

In our interpretation, multiculturalist ideology has these main components: a theory of political identity that affirms the enduring significance of group consciousness; a conception of the nation-state as a confederation of subnations with distinctive values, customs, and interests; and a set of government policies designed to recognize and accommodate the claims of minority groups.[68]

---

[65] We rely here on the excellent overview of Sarah Song, "Multiculturalism," *Stanford Encyclopedia of Philosophy* (Winter Edition 2010). The term "group-differentiated rights" comes from Will Kymlicka, *Multicultural Citizenship: A Liberal Theory of Minority Rights* (Oxford: Oxford University, 1995).

[66] Brian Barry, *Culture and Equality* (Cambridge, MA: Harvard University Press, 2002) provides perhaps the most trenchant criticism.

[67] Kelly, *Multiculturalism Reconsidered*, is a collection of commentaries on Barry's *Culture and Equality*, both critical and friendly. Among the most critical comments are the chapters by Bhikhu Parekh, "Barry and the Dangers of Liberalism" and Chandran Kukathas, "The Life of Brian, or Now for Something Completely Difference-Blind."

[68] Jack Citrin, David O. Sears, Christopher Muste, and Cara Wong, "Multiculturalism in American Public Opinion," *British Journal of Political Science* 31, no. 2 (2001); David Miller, *Citizenship and National Identity* (Cambridge, UK: Polity Press, 2000), 106–108.

Multiculturalism is an ideology of redistribution with two separable foci. One is the need to redress inequalities in economic and political power. Theorists emphasizing this goal propose proportional representation in most important institutions for a wide range of disadvantaged groups, including African Americans, women, the elderly, gays and lesbians, and the disabled, not all of which necessarily have distinct cultures.[69]

The second focus, dominant among political theorists, is to protect the rights of ethnic and religious minorities such as Latinos or Asians in the United States and Muslims in Europe, or self-declared minority "nations" such as the Quebecois or Catalan, to live according to their own "ways of life." Language policy, religion-based exemptions from generally applicable laws, and forms of political autonomy are among the proposed means for achieving this goal.[70] As we briefly describe later, multiculturalists differ in their justifications for group-differentiated rights, the scope of these rights, and the types of groups that should possess them.

In all its variants, however, multiculturalism calls for positive state action to enable members of cultural minorities to retain a strong subnational group identity and to affirm the equal value of their distinctive norms.[71] Accordingly, multiculturalism opposes policies of assimilation, just as the cultural pluralist Horace Kallen did.[72] Indeed, citing the spread of identity politics that multiculturalism facilitates, Nathan Glazer wrote in 1993 that assimilation has become a "dirty word" among many immigrant activists, a synonym for the enforced stripping away of one's original language and customs.[73] The sociological evidence seems strong that, among white Americans, the assimilation of immigrants is so widespread by the third generation that ethnicity has faded; what remains is mostly a symbolic ethnicity.[74] Multiculturalism seemingly seeks to forestall this from occurring for today's immigrants.

THE AMERICAN CASE

Canada coined the term multiculturalism and became the poster child of the movement by officially defining itself as a multicultural nation. The demographic catalyst again was immigration, which by the early twenty-first century had transformed the country such that the majority of the population no longer had the traditional British or French heritage and an increasing percentage

---

[69] Young, *Justice and the Politics of Difference*, makes this case and argues against viewing group cultures as permanently fixed.

[70] Song, "Multiculturalism," summarizes some of these proposals. A fuller list is in Jacob T. Levy, *The Multiculturalism of Fear* (Oxford: Oxford University Press, 2000).

[71] Kymlicka, *Multicultural Citizenship*, makes state action a core tenet of multiculturalism.

[72] Kallen's position is discussed in Jeff Spinner, *The Boundaries of Citizenship: Race, Ethnicity, and Nationality in the Liberal State* (Baltimore: Johns Hopkins University Press, 1994), chapter 4.

[73] Nathan Glazer, "Is Assimilation Dead?," *The Annals of the American Academy of Political and Social Science* 530: 122 (1993): 122–36.

[74] Spinner, *The Boundaries of Citizenship*, 67; and Herbert J. Gans, "Symbolic Ethnicity: The Future of Ethnic Groups and Cultures," *Ethnic and Racial Studies* 2, no. 1 (1979): 1–20.

identified as "visible" (i.e., nonwhite) minorities.[75] Beginning in 1971 with a pronouncement by Premier Trudeau, Canada breathed ideological and institutional life into its new demographic reality. It proclaimed that the country was committed to multiculturalist ideals of equality and mutual respect among the country's ethnic cultural groups and that cultural heterogeneity was beneficial and would be supported by the state. When Canada repatriated its constitution from Britain in 1982, the new Charter of Rights and Freedoms stipulated that the rights laid out in the document were to be interpreted in a manner consistent with multiculturalism.[76] In 1988, the Canadian Multiculturalism Act was passed, and federal funds began to be distributed to ethnic groups to help them preserve their cultures.[77] In 2002, June 27 of each year was designated as Canadian Multiculturalism Day.

The United States also has proclaimed its commitment to diversity in many ways – adding Martin Luther King Jr. Day as a national holiday; initiating ethnic history months; advertising diversity as a virtue in politics, the academy, and business; taking cultural sensitivity training seriously; and giving widespread media coverage to multiculturalism in politics, literature, food, music, and dance. There have been official apologies for slavery and for the incarceration of Japanese Americans during World War II, acts that do not establish minority rights but that belatedly endorse an inclusive conception of nationhood. More significantly, diversity has come to refer to the inclusion of women and minorities in important positions, as indicated by complaints early in his second term that President Obama's cabinet was deficient in this regard. But notwithstanding the recognition of diversity in rhetoric and policy, an official baptism of the United States as a multicultural country à la Canada seems unlikely.

Still, advocates of multiculturalism in the United States actually sound a lot like their Canadian counterparts. They reject the idea of "straight-line assimilation," preach respect for tolerance and celebration of cultural differences, and demand both representation and degrees of autonomy for certain racial and ethnic groups.[78] Keith Banting and Will Kymlicka surveyed the adoption of multiculturalist policies in the United States in 2010 and concluded that it ranked just below Canada and Australia in the implementation of measures they considered important, including affirmative action for minorities and immigrants, protections in electoral law, and bilingual education.[79]

---

[75] "2006 Census release topics" (http://www.12.statcan.gc.ca/census-recensement/2006/tr-td/indes-eng.cfm).

[76] Jonathan L. Black-Branch, "Making Sense of the Canadian Charter of Rights and Freedoms," *Canadian Education Association* (1995), 38.

[77] Ibid.

[78] Shana B. Bass, *The Multicultural Moment: The Politics of the Multiculturalism Movement in the United States*, unpublished PhD dissertation, UCLA Department of Political Science, 2005, is a fine summary of the varied proposals of the American multicultural "movement."

[79] Keith Banting and Will Kymlicka, "Introduction: Multiculturalism and the Welfare State: Setting the Context," in *Multiculturalism and the Welfare State: Recognition and Redistribution in*

Multiculturalism took hold in the United States for several reasons. First, the civil rights movement placed the issue of equality among subnational racial groups squarely on the national agenda. Second, when legal changes ending discrimination and nominally enhancing equality of opportunity failed to bring about equality of outcomes, grassroots ethnic empowerment groups formed and turned toward multiculturalist solutions such as Afrocentric education and community control of schools. Third, white elites, for a variety of reasons, took the lead in supporting the promotion of minority interests, in terms of the policies Banting and Kymlicka highlight in their cross-national comparisons: affirmative action policies for immigrants as well as native minorities, bilingual education, and electoral rules such as district rather than city-wide elections designed to overcome obstacles to the success of minority candidates. The many black protests and urban riots of the late sixties further pushed white elites to be accommodative, at least for a time. And burgeoning immigration later swelled the ranks of those who could make multiculturalist claims.

As in other countries, the proposals of multiculturalists in the United States have been varied and conflicted. Reviewing the rhetorical landscape, Vincent Parillo distinguishes among inclusionists, separatists, and integrative pluralists, with each faction disagreeing about the value of integration versus the rigid maintenance of separate ethnic cultures and institutions.[80] His classification fits quite neatly with the distinction we make between hard and soft versions of multiculturalism. We define the harder proposals as aiming at affirming and sustaining ethnic group differences, so that the nation is analogized to a mosaic of multicolored tiles separated by strong grout. We define softer proposals as making marginal changes in those policies that disadvantage minorities, proposing accommodations to minority groups that actually facilitate integration into the mainstream, and providing symbolic support for the inclusion of minority groups as part of the national community. Some hard multiculturalists disdain soft multiculturalism as a superficial, "festival" program with little real bite[81] and contrast this with hard multiculturalism's pursuit of social justice through more radical forms of redistribution. It should be said that even within a confined policy domain there are hard and soft versions of proposed policies. For example, soft bilingual education attempts to move non-English speaking children to English as quickly as possible, whereas the harder version teaches in Spanish or other non-English language through high school, with the intention of maintaining the student's original language and therefore his or her culture.

Contemporary Democracies, ed. Keith Banting and Will Kymlicka (New York: Oxford University Press, 2010).

[80] Vincent N. Parrillo, *Diversity in America* (Thousand Oaks: Pine Forge Press, 1996).

[81] Christian Joppke and Steven Lukes, "Introduction: Multicultural Questions," in *Multicultural Questions*, ed. Christian Joppke and Steven Lukes (Oxford: Oxford University Press, 1999).

MULTICULTURAL QUESTIONS

Cosmopolitan liberalism emphasizes inclusion and the divorce of ethnicity and the state. Multiculturalism takes the opposite tack, demanding state intervention to base policy on the accommodation of group differences. But three further questions have inspired much multiculturalist writing. What justifications are there for multiculturalism? Which groups should receive its special benefits? And what policies would address the goals of multiculturalism?

Justifications for Multiculturalism

Sarah Song delineates several distinct justifications for providing a minority group the right to act or not act in a certain way that is in accordance with its cultural obligations and commitments.[82] Such a right may give freedom to members of minorities to speak their own language or observe religious traditions regarding marriage or child-rearing. To the extent that these rights allow for self-government, they may also restrict the freedom of nonmembers, as in the case of English-speakers in Quebec.

One justification for multiculturalism is based on the idea that people are formed by their societal culture and that the value of this culture is a good in its own right. As spelled out in Charles Taylor's "politics of recognition," diverse cultural identities should be presumed to be of equal worth, and the protection of each is required to allow individuals to live a life that dignifies their identities.[83] Kymlicka agrees that there is a strong connection between a person's self-respect and the respect accorded to his or her cultural group. Although insisting that he is a liberal, he defends special protections for minority groups on the grounds that they provide the individual with the autonomy to choose a pattern of life from a set of choices that cultures provide. Multicultural policies are required to produce that choice; the state is never truly neutral, if only because the majority group's language is used at school and in state services.[84] For Kymlicka, cultural accommodations are instruments for reducing inequalities; without them, the majority group will have enduring access to more advantaged social roles.

Others adopt a different justification, which Song calls a "postcolonial" argument, and deny the automatic moral primacy of Western liberal norms. In a culturally diverse society, liberal values have no inherent right to prevail. Such theorists cite the conquest of aboriginal and other peoples as grounds for denying the state's authority over them. Instead, different cultural communities should deliberate and negotiate a system that may involve parceling out

---

[82] Song, "Multiculturalism."
[83] Taylor, "The Politics of Recognition."
[84] Kymlicka, *Multicultural Citizenship*, 111.

governance to different groups depending on the policy domain.[85] Bhiruck Parekh,[86] for example, questions the privileging of rights such as free speech when this may lead to insulting a cultural or religious group, and some are more willing to have the state share responsibilities with communal groups in the domains of welfare or family law. At its extreme, this justification of multiculturalism – holding all cultures equally valid – can defend such practices as genital mutilation of young women, tribal rules against dating, limiting educational opportunities, and other illiberal practices, even "honor killing".[87]

In contrast, Taylor and Kymlicka hold that multiculturalism should not tread on important individual rights that have been historically consensual in the West, such as freedom of speech or the right of a minority group member to exit his or her religious group and adopt mainstream values and practices. Moreover, the illiberal norms justified by the postcolonial defense frequently violate principles of gender equality, and this has led some feminists to ask whether multiculturalism is bad for women.[88]

What we have described here is the defense of a multiculturalism of "rights." Jacob Levy proposes another kind of justification. He defends a more flexible and pragmatic multiculturalism of "fear," which is not centrally concerned with preserving ethnic identities but with mitigating the threats to social peace and individual freedom stemming from interethnic conflict and attacks on those who may choose to leave their cultural community for the mainstream. This is self-evidently highly relevant to the African-American case.[89]

Which Groups?

Which groups deserve accommodation? Kymlicka's paradigm distinguishes indigenous peoples and "national minorities" from immigrants in developing a theory of multiculturalist citizenship.[90] Indigenous peoples are victims of conquest and dispossession. This, for Kymlicka, entitles them to "self-government rights" to assure the maintenance of their way of life. Along these lines, Native Americans in the United States have some claim to self-government rights such as the control of territory and some, often tenuous, freedom from the application of national laws regarding land ownership, child-rearing, smoking, and gambling.

The proposition that national minorities should have special rights is contingent on there being more than one "nation" in the state. If so, each should

[85] Bhikhu Parekh, *Rethinking Multiculturalism: Cultural Diversity and Political Theory* (Cambridge, MA: Harvard University, 2002).

[86] Parekh, "Barry and the Dangers of Liberalism."

[87] Susan Moller Okin, et al., *Is Multiculturalism Bad for Women?* (Princeton, NJ: Princeton University Press, 1999).

[88] Ibid.

[89] Levy spells this out in chapter 1 of the *Multiculturalism of Fear.*

[90] Kymlicka, *Multicultural Citizenship*; and Will Kymlicka, *Politics in the Vernacular: Nationalism, Multiculturalism, and Citizenship* (Oxford: Oxford University Press, 2001).

have a claim to self-rule. Quebec, the home of many descendants of the French military defeat at the hands of the British in Canada in the eighteenth century, is a clear current example. Secession is one option for these national minorities: a less drastic choice is being granted broad rights within a federation. In the case of Quebec, Kymlicka endorses the legal primacy of French, the right to force new immigrants to attend French schools, the right to shape its own immigration policy, and the possibility of carving out a special status with regard to the Canadian Charter of Rights.[91]

Kymlicka treats ethnic groups such as immigrants, refugees, and minority religions and races differently from indigenous peoples and national minorities for several reasons. These groups generally have come to their new country voluntarily. In doing so, they knowingly leave a life rooted in their original culture for a life in a different one. Moreover, they generally aspire to integration rather than separatism. Finally, the members of any given group of immigrants may be too small, scattered, and lacking in the resources to create the institutionally complete society required to sustain a separate societal culture.[92] Still, both to facilitate integration and fend off coercive assimilation, ethnic groups should have "polyethnic" and "special representation" rights.

America today defines diversity in terms of the pan-ethnic categories (African-American, Hispanic, Asian, and Native American) common in the post–civil-rights era. The critical issue for both theorists and policy makers is the difference between African Americans and immigrant groups. Clearly, most American immigrant groups have faced discrimination and prejudice in employment and the use of their native languages. Nevertheless, we argue that, over time, European immigrant groups have overcome these barriers and to a large degree have assimilated as "whites," with diminishing use of hyphenated ethnic labels such as Irish-Americans. The diverse European immigrants viewed by Horace Kallen as intrinsically different are now lumped together in political discourse and public policy as members of a homogeneous "white" category. Nonwhite groups comprising the other four sides of America's ethnoracial pentagon are similarly treated as internally homogeneous when it comes to qualifying for the benefits of diversity-based programs such as affirmative action and government contracts.[93]

The case of African Americans is more complicated. As we have noted, they are exceptional in their lack of similar levels of assimilation, in most respects. African Americans were legally prevented, first by slavery, and then by Jim Crow and many analogous formal and informal restrictions throughout the nation, from integrating into the mainstream society. They faced widespread institutional segregation – from residential neighborhoods, churches, schools, public

[91] Ibid.
[92] Kymlicka, *Multicultural* Citizenship, chapter 2; and *Politics in the Vernacular*, 155–60.
[93] David A. Hollinger, *Postethnic America: Beyond Multiculturalism* (New York: Basic Books, 2006).

parks, hospitals, and workplaces – and were forced in numerous respects to develop a parallel and separate society.[94]

Does this separateness make African Americans fit the colonized, conquered, national minority pattern like the Puerto Ricans or Quebecois, which might, according to some versions of multiculturalism, give them the right to a quasi-sovereign state alongside the majority nation? Kymlicka argues against this on the grounds that the slaves did not have a common language, culture, or national identity. Moreover, their separateness was imposed, not intentionally adopted or desired. And the whites of European origins who uprooted African Americans from their cultural homeland strove to prevent the maintenance of previous languages and customs, much as in the case of coercive assimilation of immigrants.[95]

Kymlicka admits that African Americans, as largely descended from involuntarily enslaved immigrants from Africa, and as a group so central to American multiculturalism and to our empirical analyses, are a gray area in his typology. Nathan Glazer, once a noted opponent of affirmative action, had hoped that the end of legal discrimination would launch African Americans on the integrative path of immigrant groups. But by 1997 he recognized that this hope had not been realized. So he began searching for special measures targeted at improving the circumstances of the African-American population.[96]

The separateness of blacks and pessimism about overcoming it has fueled occasional advocacy of separatism and secession. Indeed, in a recent article Andrew Valls[97] argues, against Kymlicka, that African Americans should indeed be considered a national minority deserving of self-government rights. He describes African Americans as an intergenerational community with a set of shared memories and values, common institutions, and common practices.[98] Moreover, like national minorities and unlike ethnic groups whose origins lay in voluntary immigration, African Americans were incorporated into the United States involuntarily. It may be true that African Americans do not have a distinct language and have culturally assimilated in many ways, but this ignores the *racial* barrier to integration. Moreover, the strong senses of racial identity and shared fate among blacks are akin to the sentiments that commonly underlie a sense of national identity.

So Valls calls for "community control" of separate black institutions as a "home" for African Americans, not secession – which territorial dispersion, if nothing else, makes impractical. This "community control" would have to be adequately funded through redistribution from whites, a problematic outcome

---

[94] Andrew Valls, "A Liberal Defense of Black Nationalism," *American Political Science Review* 104, no. 3 (August 2010): 467–81.
[95] Kymlicka, Politics in the Vernacular, chapter 9.
[96] Glazer, *We Are All Multiculturalists Now.*
[97] Valls, "A Liberal Defense of Black Nationalism."
[98] Ibid., 470.

at best. Clearly, this is a step back from integration, if not outright rejection of it. Such a system would also have to protect those African Americans who choose to opt out of the broader nation-oriented political system. Community control, then, is seen as a legitimate counterpart to the institutional arrangements and group rights multiculturalists defend for cultural minorities.[99] These proposals fall into the hard category of multiculturalism.

Rogers Smith has made a related proposal about Mexican Americans. He argues that the United States owes a special obligation to immigrants of Mexican descent because of having "coercively constituted their identities."[100] He calls for giving priority to Mexicans in immigration and facilitating dual citizenship. He contends that, by insisting on Mexican Americans' assimilation, America has failed to abide by multiculturalism's principle that their cultural identities are untouchable. In his view, that becomes a legitimate basis for reparations and special treatment.[101]

Finally, American courts also have struggled with the claims of various religious groups for special treatment: yarmulkes in the military, yes; peyote as a legitimate religious practice, no; withdrawal from public education for Amish youth, yes; refusing a transfusion to a sick Jehovah's Witness child, no. Doubtless as the population continues to diversify, new claims for group benefits and cultural exemptions will arise. And we reiterate that the variants of multiculturalism that focus on culture as the criterion for official recognition pay scant attention to formulations that concentrate on economic disadvantage more than different language and customs as the basis for special treatment.

Which Policies?

What are the concrete policies that leading multiculturalists have proposed? Kymlicka and Levy propose two overlapping inventories.[102] Kymlicka's suggestions range from the harder proposals for quotas in the allocation of political and economic positions to the softer proposals of promoting ethnic festivals and teaching tolerance and sensitivity. Among these are adopting affirmative action programs and reserving seats in the legislature to increase the representation of immigrants (or the women and disabled), exemptions from dress codes and Sunday closing legislation for certain religions, providing government funding for ethnic studies and festivals, antiracism and diversity training, and bilingual education programs for immigrant children. He argues that these measures are all designed to make it easier for immigrants to enter mainstream society with a sense of dignity and, in fact, undermine a potential imperative to separate.

---

[99] Ibid., 476–78.
[100] Rogers M. Smith, "Living in a Promise Land?: Mexican Immigration and American Obligation," *Perspectives in Politics* 9, no. 3 (September 2011), 545–557.
[101] Ibid., 552–55.
[102] The examples cited here are drawn from lists in Kymlicka, *Politics in the Vernacular*, 163; and Levy, *The Multiculturalism of Fear*, 127.

Levy's list similarly includes some religion-based exemptions to dress codes, general rules such as the right of members of certain groups to keep one's children from attending school after a certain age or to wear religious headgear in the military and public schools, and the official recognition of minority legal codes, which multiculturalism regards as needed defenses against the majority group's opposition. Levy also includes what he calls "assistance claims," such as affirmative action, multilingual ballots, and funding of ethnic associations and symbolic claims such as the naming of national holidays. Multiculturalism regards exemptions as needed defenses against the majority group's opposition to minority customs and assistance as required to overcome obstacles to participation due to culturally specific disadvantages or discrimination.[103]

These policies can be located on the continuum of soft to hard multiculturalism. Soft policies view the recognition and preservation of cultural differences as compatible with and even functional for integrating immigrants. Harder policies go further and seek parity of power and resources for minority ethnic groups through redistributive policies and communal representation. In our analysis of public opinion, we are careful to record how the hard and soft versions of multiculturalism differ in their level of support and in the pattern of ethnic consensus and cleavage.

Although there are differences between the perspectives of cosmopolitan liberalism and soft multiculturalism, they share an acceptance of the mingling of cultures in the sense of a process of two-way assimilation. Advocacy of multiculturalism in American politics tends to be the softer variety. So, looking at a decline in racial discrimination and prejudice and the increased readiness to acknowledge the value of minority cultures through public ceremonies and reforms in education, it is easy to see why Nathan Glazer wrote that "we are all multiculturalists now."

Nevertheless, multiculturalism's defense of preserving cultures has been criticized by a range of scholars for conceiving of cultures as static wholes rather than overlapping and evolving bodies of customs, for eroding the principle of equal treatment before the law, for diverting attention from economic redistribution, for failing to protect the rights of weaker members within minority groups, and for dividing rather than unifying society as a whole.[104] In this work, we only address the last of these charges, exploring whether multiculturalism's emphasis on sustaining ethnic identifications and loyalties undermines a common sense of American identity and attachment to the nation.

MULTICULTURALISM AND NATIONAL IDENTITY

Why should integrating ethnicity and nationality pose dilemmas that often lead to political strife? Both collective identities extend the individual's sense of

---

[103] Levy, *The Multiculturalism of Fear*, 128, 133.
[104] Song, "Multiculturalism," has summarized these objections, most of which are made by Barry in *Culture and Equality*.

belonging to a group to the adoption of its norms and goals as one's own.[105] When the goals and standards of two groups are incompatible, the problem of identity choice or prioritization arises. One reason that this choice can be so fateful is that ethnic and national identities often have enormous emotional significance; people are willing to make great sacrifices for their ethnic group or country.

Donald Horowitz writes that ethnic conflict is both ubiquitous and often deadly and that the emotive power of ethnic affiliations tends to dominate ties based on class or professional memberships.[106] The potency of ethnic ties, according to Horowitz, rests on the idea of a common provenance, the subjective belief in a common descent.[107] Ethnicity has a resemblance to family and draws strength from the belief that blood is thicker than water. Kallen's remark about not being able to change one's grandfather is a clear assertion of this principle. In such views, compared to the ideas of territorial proximity or a common legal status as the basis of loyalty and mutual obligation, ethnicity may have a psychological advantage. Indeed, multiculturalism takes the enduring strength of ethnic identities as axiomatic. Advocates of the politics of difference argue that group recognition will assuage ethnic rivalries and facilitate peaceful coexistence in a multiethnic polity. Critics of multiculturalism fear that the opposite will occur – that reinforcing ethnic identities in the political domain will foster balkanization rather than comity. But the intensity and scope of ethnic divisions – and whether loyalty to "us" is accompanied by hostility toward "them" – may depend in part on how issues are framed, especially whether outcomes are cast in a winner-take-all manner.

We define a nation as a group of people with a sense of "we-feeling" seeking political autonomy. The concept of national identity refers to the criteria for membership in the nation; these attributes are varied and malleable but generally include a cultural component.[108] In the modern world, national self-determination is the dominant principle of political legitimacy. In Benedict Anderson's famous phrase, the nation is an imagined community in which strangers are converted into kin through a shared sense of identity.[109] Ernest Gellner wrote that in today's world "a man must have a nationality as he must have a nose and two ears."[110] In other words, in a world of nations, everyone takes it for granted that he or she has a nationality. Patriotic references to one's

---

[105] Marilynn B. Brewer, "The Many Faces of Social Identity: Implications for Political Psychology," *Political Psychology* 22, no. 1 (2001): 115–25.

[106] Donald L. Horowitz, *Ethnic Groups in Conflict* (Berkeley: University of California Press, 1985).

[107] Ibid.

[108] Ernst B. Haas, *Beyond the Nation-State: Functionalism and International Organization* (Stanford: Stanford University Press, 1964); Anthony D. Smith, *National Identity* (Reno: University of Nevada Press, 1991); Norman, "Theorizing Nationalism (Normatively)."

[109] Benedict R. O'Gorman Anderson, *Imagined Communities: Reflections on the Origin and Spread of Nationalism* (New York: Verso, 1983).

[110] Ernest Gellner, *Nations and Nationalism* (London: Oxford University Press, 1983), 6.

fatherland or motherland illustrate that ideas of nationhood, like those of ethnicity, also evoke the emotional force of family ties.

All nationalist ideologies insist that one's national identity should have priority over all other group memberships. In most established nation-states, this nation-first outlook is nurtured through a process of socialization that involves parents, schools, media, and repeated civic rituals. Historically, the formation of modern nation-states included the triumph of a core ethnic group over peripheral minorities. The English incorporated the Scots, and the Spanish absorbed the Catalan, albeit with mixed success in imposing cultural homogeneity in both cases. Not surprisingly, then, multiculturalists complain that control of socialization by dominant ethnic groups is precisely what marginalizes minority cultural groups. But that complaint begs the question of what set of beliefs unite a society committed to the preservation of differences.

It is when nationality and ethnicity are not completely overlapping that the problem of *e pluribus unum* arises. In these contexts, the critical issues are (1) whether the majority ethnic group accepts minorities as equal citizens and (2) whether minority groups seek to promote their own identities at the expense of a shared allegiance to the nation. When the claims of subnational communities do not give way to what the majority perceives as a nation's common values and purposes, then national unity and multiculturalism can be on a political collision course.

What is the case for prioritizing a sense of national identity in a multiethnic society? True, history, including current history, is littered with examples of bitter religious and ethnic conflict founded on subnational ties. But nationalism also has fueled catastrophic bloody episodes. World Wars I and II, wars between nations seeking or defending international hegemony, were the most destructive in human history. An ethnic civil war such as that in Syria or Kosovo or Rwanda is conflict on a small scale when compared to the clash between Nazi Germany and the USSR. And a strong sense of national identity readily can be directed at "others" within, as manifested in intolerance toward and an unwillingness to help fellow citizens who are deemed atypical and hence not true members of the national community.

Yet there are positive arguments for prioritizing a sense of national identity. David Miller, a self-styled "liberal nationalist," writes that without it, "There is nothing to hold citizens together, nothing to motivate people without personal ties to participate in common projects for nonstrategic reasons."[111] Miller compares a nation to a team. It may be formed by formal criteria such as legal nationality, but the real indicator of a team is that its members are committed to a common purpose and recognize their mutual obligations and the need to put team spirit above personal ambition.[112] Of course, the idea of nation as team

---

[111] David Miller, *Market, State, and Community: Theoretical Foundations of Market Socialism* (Oxford, UK: Clarendon Press, 1989), 245.

[112] David Miller, *On Nationality* (New York: Oxford University Press, 1995).

does not mean that it always is a fighting unit with an enemy. The nation might also be seen as a work team, mobilized on occasion not against outsiders but to respond to a natural disaster such as a hurricane or oil spill or to sacrifice in order to pay for dams and bridges or to join in remembering an admired national leader. From this conception of nationhood, the bases for team membership or entry into what David Hollinger has called the national "circle of we" matters for drawing the boundaries of tolerating, helping, sharing, protecting, and sacrificing.[113]

We have presented multiculturalism as a leading new proposal for the historical problem of accommodating America's varied ethnic makeup. A central concern of this book is whether, given America's new demographic reality, there is a tension between patriotism and social solidarity at the national level and support for multiculturalism and social solidarity at the subnational level. Do Americans of diverse origins still share a distinctive sense of peoplehood? Do the country's dominant Anglo-Americans conceive of the national community in ways that include its diverse minorities? Do ethnic minorities give priority to a common national identity or prefer to define themselves as members of separate cultural communities? Put differently, are psychological commitments to country and ethnicity competing or complementary? And does this vary across ethnic groups?

National identities have *normative content*, designating the criteria for belonging to the nation.[114] Most scholars agree that these conceptions of nationhood are crafted or constructed by elites rather than springing forth spontaneously from mass publics. Beliefs about American nationality were forged in the crucible of the War of Independence and then remade in the wake of crises such as the Civil War and World War II. Reinforced by socialization at home and in school, and buttressed by the repeated performance of civic rituals like the Pledge of Allegiance, honoring the flag, and singing the national anthem, national identities tend to be sticky. But, as described earlier, their contents are sometimes contested, and the official interpretation derived from laws, the pronouncement of leaders, literature, and song may diverge from the conceptions of ordinary citizens.[115] In this regard, we can examine whether American identity is cosmopolitan liberal in the abstract but nativist in segments of public opinion.

In the literature on nationalism, a familiar contrast is between ethnically inclusive "civic" nations founded on belief in political principles or "constitutional patriotism" and "ethnic" nations based on ancestry or blood. But it is generally agreed that these categories refer to ideal types and that there are no purely civic or

---

[113] David A. Hollinger, *Postethnic America*.
[114] Rogers Brubaker, *Citizenship and Nationhood in France and Germany* (Cambridge: Harvard University Press, 2002); Jack Citrin, Ernst B. Haas, Beth Reingold, and Christopher Muste, "Is American Nationalism Waning?," *International Politics Quarterly* 38, no. 1 (1994): 1–31.
[115] Rogers M. Smith, *Civic Ideals*.

ethnic nations.[116] Both types of nations have a cultural component, usually including a common language and a set of shared experiences and practices that undergird the sense of belonging to the same political community. Moreover, even civic nations typically have an ethnocultural core, even if they redefine themselves to embrace ethnic diversity both demographically and ideologically. This is what Huntington insisted on in stressing the Anglo-Protestant fundament of American national identity and worrying that it may crumble in the wake of Hispanic immigration. Still, even if national identities are an amalgam of civic and cultural attributes, which ones are weighted more heavily may determine the dominant conception of nationhood and who is likely to feel the strongest sense of national attachment. Indeed, it has been argued that conceiving of American identity in terms of support for highly generalized political symbols and values should make it easier to bind people of different races, regions, or cultures together.[117] The flag may symbolize military victories for some Americans and racial justice for others, but as long as either interpretation is legitimate, both groups can rally around and defend it.

Multicultural proposals differ in the extent to which they ostensibly are directed at integrating minority groups, particularly immigrants, but it is fair to say that all variants of multiculturalism are opposed to assimilation to the majority group's culture. Yet assimilation clearly has been successful in forging a sense of common American identity. Just are there hard and soft variants of multiculturalism, assimilationist strategies also vary. Assimilation in contemporary America is "thin," requiring relatively little of newcomers. In *Assimilation, American Style*, Peter Salins denies that assimilation and cultural diversity are incompatible.[118] He argues that all that immigrants are expected to do to become American is to learn English, to adopt the fundamental values of the nation's political creed, and to place loyalty to America ahead of any residual identification with one's original homeland.[119] But this need not mean giving up all one's prior habits or traditions. Indeed, critics of multiculturalism complain that not enough is being done to reinforce Salins's minimalist version of Americanism.

Nevertheless, it does seem plausible that as long as America is tolerant and welcoming, the new immigrants from Latin American and Asia may follow the largely assimilationist path of their European predecessors. The civil rights legislation of the 1960s places considerable legal obstacles in the way of discrimination against new immigrants. With the hegemony of English as the international language of science and commerce and the penetration of American popular culture into every global nook and cranny, substantial Americanization of immigrants living in the United States at some minimal level seems inevitable.

---

[116] Bernard Yack, "The Myth of the Civic Nation," and Kai Nielsen, "Cultural Nationalism, Neither Ethnic nor Civic," in *Theorizing Nationalism*, ed. Ronald Beiner.
[117] Billig, *Banal Nationalism*.
[118] Salins, *Assimilation, American Style*.
[119] Ibid.

American politics today could be described as Janus-faced. One face is an emphasis on identity politics that elevates the significance of ethnic loyalty as the guide to behavior. The second face stresses patriotism and national pride, as exemplified in the post-9/11 United States. In the chapters that follow, then, we assess the pattern of identity choices among America's main ethnic groups and how they respond to the leading alternatives for coping with the problem of *e pluribus unum*: cosmopolitan liberalism, nativism, and variants of multi-culturalism.

The Political Psychology of Identity Choice

Demographic change clearly has complicated prevailing patterns of ethnic relations in the United States. Immigration and differential fertility rates have greatly increased the numbers of Latinos and Asians, and the challenge of their cultural, economic, and political integration is layered on the historic and entrenched racial divide. Nationalism, in the sense of prioritizing a common national identity, and multiculturalism, in the sense of elevating the particular identities of each ethnic group, are based on particular assumptions about human psychology. A driving purpose of our book is to draw on psychological theories to explain patterns of public opinion confronting the search for solidarity in a multiethnic society. We believe that making explicit the psychological assumptions embedded in alternative solutions and testing for them will illuminate the political dilemmas as well. In particular, we argue that the relatively recent political term *multiculturalism* in fact builds on a much broader and historically quite general social psychological approach to racial and ethnic divisions.

THE PSYCHOLOGY OF AMERICAN INTERGROUP RELATIONS

We begin by presenting and contrasting three broad social-psychological conceptions of how Americans form and utilize their ethnic identifications in the context of contemporary ethnic diversity. In subsequent chapters, we apply these alternative characterizations of ethnic relations to understanding public opinion regarding national identity and multiculturalist ideology.

Politicized Group Consciousness

Contemporary trends in social psychological theory have increasingly focused on group categories as powerful determinants of behavior. Cognitive

categorization theories suggest that people automatically and even uncon-
sciously categorize individuals (themselves as well as others) into social groups,
particularly on the basis of salient perceptual dimensions such as race, gender,
and age.[1] Social identity theory[2] takes a further step, suggesting a basic need for
a specifically *social* identity, and thus explains universal tendencies to form
solidary groups and allocate resources along group lines, even in the absence
of any especially self-interested reason to do so. This generates systematic "in-
group favoritism" or "group-serving biases" favoring the in-group at the
expense of out-groups. Although social identity theory assumes that humans
are innately predisposed to define themselves in terms of group identity, it does
not claim that any particular identity is inherently preferred or psychologically
required. Indeed, people can have multiple group identities. Presumably, social
context has much to say about the salience of any particular identity. Political
mobilization is often a key player in that process, as the modern cases of the
Basques, Quebec, Yugoslavia, Scotland, Belgium, Catalonia, Iraq, and Syria
illustrate.

Social identities refer to the dimensions of one's self-concept defined by
perceptions of similarity with some people and difference from others. They
develop because people categorize themselves and others as belonging to groups
and pursue their goals through membership in these groups. They have political
relevance because they channel feelings of mutuality, obligation, and antagonism, delineating the contours of one's willingness to help others as well as the
boundaries of support for policies allocating resources based on group membership. Indeed, the intimate connection between the personal and the social bases
of self-regard becomes clear when one recalls how quickly an insult to the dignity
of one's group can trigger ethnic violence.[3]

Theories of group competition, such as realistic group conflict theory[4] and
power theory,[5] also assume the ubiquity of group formation based on a need for
social identity. But they go further, emphasizing the role of intergroup competition
over valued resources in intergroup conflict. Social structural theories of group

[1] Susan T. Fiske and Steven L. Neuberg, "A Continuum of Impression Formation, from Category-Based to Individuating Processes: Influences of Information and Motivation on Attention and Interpretation," in *Advances in Experimental Social Psychology*, ed. Mark P. Zanna (New York: Academic Press, 1990).

[2] Henri Tajfel, "Social Categorization, Social Identity, and Social Comparison," in *Differentiation between Social Groups: Studies in the Social Psychology of Intergroup Relations*, ed. Henri Tajfel (London: Academic Press, 1978).

[3] Horowitz, *Ethnic Groups in Conflict.*

[4] Lawrence Bobo, "Whites' Opposition to Busing: Symbolic Racism or Realistic Group Conflict?" *Journal of Personality and Social Psychology* 45 (1983): 1196–1210.

[5] Hubert M. Blalock, *Toward a Theory of Minority-Group Relations* (New York: John Wiley and Sons, 1967); Michael W. Giles and Kaenan Hertz, "Racial Threat and Partisan Identification," *American Political Science Review* 88, no. 2 (1994): 317–26; V. O. Key, Jr., *Southern Politics in State and Nation* (New York: Alfred A. Knopf, Inc., 1949).

hierarchies, such as sense of group position theory,[6] social dominance theory,[7] and color-blind racism theory[8], assume stable hierarchies of status and power based on inherent conflicts of interest between groups. Exactly which group divisions display the sharpest conflicts presumably depends on the particular historical and social contexts. However, all these theories view the racial hierarchy in the United States as largely impervious to change. Social dominance theory departs somewhat from these others by stipulating that, through various mechanisms, intergroup competition may be stifled. Subordinate groups may not even be fully aware that they are being oppressed. System justification theory focuses particularly on the psychological mechanisms by which dominant and subordinate groups alike justify the status quo.[9] Power theory adds that social contexts that include large subordinate groups should be politically threatening to the dominant group, motivating it to make choices that protect its own power.[10]

---

[6] Herbert Blumer, "Prejudice as a Sense of Group Position," *The Pacific Sociological Review* 1, no. 1 (1958): 3–7; Lawrence Bobo and Vincent Hutchings, "Perceptions of Racial Group Competition: Extending Blumer's Theory of Group Position to a Multiracial Social Context," *American Sociological Review* 61 (1996): 951–72.

[7] Jim Sidanius and Felicia Pratto, *Social Dominance: An Intergroup Theory of Social Hierarchy and Oppression* (New York: Cambridge University Press, 1999). Social dominance theory departs somewhat from these others by stipulating that dominance hierarchies may be quite stable and through various mechanisms intergroup competition may be stifled. Subordinate groups may not even be fully aware that they are being oppressed.

[8] Eduardo Bonilla-Silva, *Racism without Racists: Colorblind Racism and the Persistence of Racial Inequality in the United States*, 2nd ed. (Lanham, MD: Rowman & Littlefield Publishers, 2006).

[9] John T. Jost, Mahzarin R. Banaji, and Brian S. Nosek, "A Decade of System Justification Theory: Accumulated Evidence of Conscious and Unconscious Bolstering of the Status Quo," *Political Psychology* 25 (2004): 881–919.

[10] Some more anthropologically oriented theorists go still further, privileging race and ethnicity as essentialist dimensions of categorization, such as in the notion of primordial attachments or the competition between national identity and communal, tribal, or other subnational groupings; e.g., Clifford Geertz, "Ideology as a Cultural System," in *Ideology and Its Discontents*, ed. David Apter (New York: Free Press, 1964); Donald Horowitz, *Ethnic Groups in Conflict*. Even if these categories are only socially constructed, they may nonetheless be taken by ordinary people to be psychologically essential or genotypic (Douglas L. Medin and Andrew Ortnoy, "Psychological Essentialism," in *Similarity and Analogical Reading*, ed. Stella Vosniadou and Andrew Ortony [New York: Cambridge University Press, 1989]; Deborah Prentice and Dale Miller, "Some Consequences of a Belief in a Group Essence: The Category Divide Hypothesis," in *Cultural Divides: Understanding and Overcoming Group Conflict*, ed. Deborah Prentice and Dale Miller [New York: Russell Sage Foundation, 1999]; K. Anthony Appiah and Amy Guttmann, *Color Conscious: The Political Morality of Race* [Princeton, NJ: Princeton University Press, 1996]). This perceived essentialism of racial categories may stem from a natural tendency for children to form categories about kinds of humans (Lawrence A. Hirschfield, *Race in the Making: Cognition, Culture, and the Child's Construction of Human Kinds* [Cambridge, MA: The MIT Press, 1996]; although see Jennifer L. Eberhardt and Jennifer L. Randall, "The Essential Notion of Race," *Psychological Science* 8 [1997]: 198–203). Still, such essentialist assumptions are not required to view ethnicity and race as central dimensions of group categorization in contemporary American society because the prevailing sociopolitical context has long given them ample attention.

Highly politicized forms of ethnic group identification are the most relevant to our discussion. At the most basic level, Phinney has usefully distinguished four aspects of ethnic identity: the label that one applies to oneself, a sense of belonging to the group, positive and negative attitudes toward it, and participation or involvement in the group.[11] Crocker and Luhtanen[12] argue that favoring one's own group (in-group favoritism) is more closely associated with collective than with personal self-esteem. Simon and Klandermans talk about a politicized collective identity that is engaged when people perceive themselves as "self-conscious group members in a power struggle on behalf of their group."[13]

Whatever the nuanced differences among these theories, they all generally share the view that group categories, group hierarchies, politicized in-group identity, antagonism toward out-groups, and intergroup competition are central elements of human psychology. For convenience, we label the common core of these theories, as applied to contemporary American ethnic and race relations, a *politicized group consciousness* paradigm. We argue that it is a view that provides the psychological underpinnings of multiculturalist ideology. The increased ethnic diversity of recent decades in the United States should have heightened the salience of ethnicity. Greater diversity should strengthen ethnic group boundaries and intergroup cleavages, provoking both the dominant whites to protect their own privileges and subordinate ethnic minority groups to demand more resources in their own group's interests. From this perspective, increased diversity is likely to stimulate ethnic polarization over resource allocations.

Organizing a society along multiculturalist lines and providing group-based entitlements, even if only out of fear of civil strife, might seem to be a natural political solution to such conflicts. In such a society, ethnic groups might be treated as if they were subnations with their own group rights and kept pacified by binding 'treaties' that ensure more equitable allocations of resources among groups. Cosmopolitan liberalism, in contrast, normally interprets disadvantage in more individualized terms and so would look first to solutions targeting disadvantaged individuals, such as supplying financial aid to the poor or disabled or allowing individuals to sue if they believe they have been discriminated against. A potential danger of the multiculturalist solution, to repeat a central thrust of the first chapter, is that legitimating the recognition and strengthening of subnational ethnic identities may undermine the foundation of national unity built on a common identity.[14]

---

[11] Jean S. Phinney, "Ethnic Identity in Adolescents and Adults: Review of Research," *Psychological Bulletin* 108, no. 3 (1990): 499–514.

[12] Jennifer Crocker and Riia Luhtanen, "Collective Self-Esteem and Ingroup Bias," *Journal of Personality and Social Psychology* 58 (1990): 60–67.

[13] Bernd Simon and Bert Klandermans, "Politicized Collective Identity: A Social Psychological Analysis," *American Psychologist* 56, no. 4 (2001): 319.

[14] Huntington, *Who Are We?*, Brian Barry, *Culture and Equality*, and Todd Gitlin, *The Twilight of Common Dreams* make this argument.

IMMIGRANT ASSIMILATION AND BLACK EXCEPTIONALISM

Symbolic politics theory offers an alternative view of the psychology of race and ethnicity in America. Its theoretical core gives greater weight, it gives significant weight to variations in historical and cultural contexts rather than assuming a static racial hierarchy.[15] It recognizes the historical tendency toward *assimilation* of voluntary immigrants to America and the fact that African Americans have had unusual difficulty in being integrated into the mainstream of the society – *black exceptionalism*. This account differs from that of the politicized group consciousness paradigm in several respects. We argue that many of the differences stem from the former paradigm's occasional overgeneralization from the idiosyncratic, specific historic case of African Americans to all racial and ethnic minorities. That is, the politicized group consciousness paradigm often models the psychology of whites on the same group-centered variables as the psychology of blacks and generally proposes that all other "people of color" resemble blacks.[16]

Why do we argue that this theory overgeneralizes from that specific case? For one thing, most whites today may not have a high level of racial group consciousness. The United States has always been overwhelmingly composed of whites of European ancestry. White hegemony has rarely been seriously challenged, even with the growth of cultural diversity in recent decades. For most whites today, being white may be no more noteworthy than the air they breathe. Of course, there have been exceptional moments and contexts in which white identity has been highly salient. Most obviously, the historical evidence is clear that whites' racial consciousness was very high in the Old South, especially in areas where whites were not overwhelmingly numerically dominant.[17] Being of the white race was perhaps the single most important marker of social status in that context. Many, if not most, social practices were deeply affected by race. Some parallels no doubt occur in large urban areas outside the South that received extensive black in-migration earlier in the twentieth century. But even in large metropolitan areas today, strong racial consciousness among whites is generally likely to be less common than it was in the Old South, where day-to-day life was pervasively organized by race.

Second, the situation of African Americans has always been fundamentally different from that of other non-European people of color. African Americans, we argued earlier, are not just another immigrant group. Contemporary African Americans are mostly descendants of those brought involuntarily to America

---

[15] David O. Sears, Jack Citrin, Sharmaine Cheleden, and Colette van Laar, "Is Cultural Balkanization Psychologically Inevitable?" in *Cultural Divides*, ed. Deborah Prentice and Dale Miller (New York: Russell Sage Foundation, 2000); Sears and Savalei, "The Political Color Line in America."

[16] Note that Marilynn Brewer argues that there are systematic inherent differences between majority and minority groups. See her "The Importance of Being We: Human Nature and Intergroup Relations," *American Psychologist* 62, no. 8 (2007): 728–38.

[17] See, e.g., V. O. Key Jr., *Southern Politics in State and Nation.*

centuries ago as slaves and forced to live a separate, inferior existence. The extensive legal guarantees of equal rights followed by redistributive affirmative action policies in recent decades have significantly opened greater opportunities to blacks. The racial gaps in domains such as income and educational attainment have narrowed in the past half century, the language of race has become less demeaning, and white support for formal racial discrimination and segregation has virtually vanished. Racial tolerance has grown, especially among young and better educated whites. To cite the most dramatic recent example, the election of a black president would have been unimaginable a few decades ago.

Nevertheless, the black exceptionalism perspective argues that African Americans remain subject to uniquely high levels of prejudice and discrimination. Key to this view is the notion of the inertial power of history. Even as laws change, fundamental social practices and the mentalities of ordinary people typically follow only slowly, as in the classic contrast of "stateways" with "folkways." The residues of racial prejudice in the behavior and attitudes of ordinary Americans have persisted long after the Emancipation Proclamation and 1960s-era civil rights legislation eliminated formalized racial inequality from the law books.[18] Indeed, underlying the extraordinary outcome of the election of a black president is much evidence that the public's response to the election campaign was the most racialized in recent history, with racial attitudes playing a considerably more powerful role in determining presidential preferences than in prior elections.[19] Despite considerable progress in many areas in the past half century, the reality is that even today blacks are not as socially integrated into the broader society as are other nonwhite groups, including immigrants. For example, blacks continue to be more residentially segregated and to intermarry less often with other ethnic groups than are other people of color. Moreover, blacks continue to suffer higher levels of disadvantage than any other ethnic and racial groups in such widely dispersed domains as longevity, health, income, wealth, and education.[20]

It would not be surprising if these enduring disadvantages in power and resources and lack of integration with other groups have elevated blacks' racial consciousness beyond that of other ethnic and racial groups. Having been treated distinctively solely because of their race for several centuries, blacks might well have stronger racial identities than other groups do, along with a

---

[18] David O. Sears and P. J. Henry, "Over Thirty Years Later: A Contemporary Look at Symbolic Racism," *Advances in Experimental Social Psychology* 37 (2005): 95–150; Nicholas A. Valentino and David O. Sears, "Old Times There Are Not Forgotten: Race and Partisan Realignment in the Contemporary South," *American Journal of Political Science* 49, no. 3 (2005): 672–88.

[19] Tesler and Sears, *Obama's Race.*

[20] Michael A. Stoll, "Job Sprawl and the Spatial Mismatch between Blacks and Jobs" (Washington, DC: The Brookings Institution, February 2005); David O. Sears, John J. Hetts, Jim Sidanius, and Lawrence Bobo, "Race in American Politics: Framing the Debates," in *Racialized Politics: The Debate about Racism in America*, ed. David O. Sears, Jim Sidanius, and Lawrence Bobo (Chicago: University of Chicago Press, 2000).

stronger sense of common fate with their fellow group members, and they might well perceive that they are subject to more racial discrimination than other groups are. Similarly, it would not be surprising that blacks might be especially likely to base their political attitudes on racially relevant matters on their group consciousness and perceived group interests.[21]

What about the other nonwhite minorities that comprise the large majority of recent immigrants into the United States? The politicized group consciousness paradigm, emphasizing ethnic identification and interethnic competition, might well lead us to expect especially strong group consciousness among Latinos and some Asian national groups as well. After all, they too share differing skin color and lesser numbers, and most have fewer economic resources than the native-born white majority group. Indeed, Latino and Asian identity movements modeled on the black civil rights movement did develop in the 1960s, with similar demands for redress for past discrimination and for group-conscious policies to improve their conditions.[22]

However, the black exceptionalism perspective argues that the color line applied to Latinos and Asians is considerably more flexible than the relatively impermeable color line surrounding blacks, allowing them easier integration into the broader society. Indeed, a number of scholars[23] argue that today's Latino and Asian immigrants are following in the wake of earlier European immigrants in gradually experiencing structural and cultural integration. Those Europeans may be a more relevant model for Latino and Asian groups given the more entrenched separation and inequality experienced by African Americans. Finally, adding to the gap in the experiences of blacks as opposed to Latinos and Asians is the fact that most of the latter two groups immigrated to or were born in the United States after formal discrimination on the grounds of race or ethnicity had been rendered illegal.

It is important not to overstate the scope of the claims made by the assimilation perspective. Ethnic consciousness has not entirely disappeared among the descendants of European immigrants. For example, it remains more important among Americans descended from the mainly southern and eastern European waves of immigrants of a century ago than among those of western and northern European ancestry who had arrived in earlier waves of immigration.[24] But the subjective importance of ethnic identity among descendants of the later waves of immigration has declined across generations to a level much lower than it was

---

[21] Robert A. Brown and Todd C. Shaw, "Separate Nations: Two Attitudinal Dimensions of Black Nationalism," *The Journal of Politics* 64, no. 1 (2000): 22–44; Dawson, *Behind the Mule*; Sears and Savalei, "The Political Color Line in America"; Lawrence Bobo and Devon Johnson, "A Taste for Punishment: Black and White Americans' Views on the Death Penalty and the War on Drugs," *Du Bois Review: Social Science Research on Race* 1, no. 1 (2004): 151–80.

[22] Joseph Tilden Rhea, *Race Pride and the American Identity* (Cambridge, MA: Harvard University Press, 1997).

[23] Alba and Nee, *Remaking the American Mainstream*; Barone, *The New Americans*.

[24] Alba and Nee, *Remaking the American Mainstream*.

several decades ago. Alba estimated that even in a sample drawn in the 1980s, only about one-fifth of those with European ancestry held their own ethnic identity with substantial intensity.[25] Given the erosion of objective ethnic differences and behavioral manifestations of ethnic identity, he uses Herbert Gans's description of the residues of ethnicity in the great majority of descendants of European immigrants as being primarily "symbolic."[26]

The black exceptionalism model highlights the uniqueness of African Americans in U.S. history, from the earliest days of slavery through the formalized discrimination of Jim Crow to the more ambiguous mixture of formal equality with substantial informal discrimination and segregation today. The very term *exceptionalism* implies that the path toward acceptance and integration may be easier for other groups. Assimilation means becoming similar to and denotes the erosion and ultimate disappearance of social and cultural differences among ethnic groups. The so-called straight-line path toward assimilation assumes that each generation after immigration will be more likely to speak English, more likely to climb the social ladder, and more likely to intermarry.

The black exceptionalism and assimilation models of ethnic group relations are therefore linked, because the black population would not be exceptional if other groups were as restricted by the color line and as blocked from social mobility or, more positively, if the progress toward equality for African Americans were more rapid and complete. Both paradigms clearly challenge the psychology underlying multiculturalism, which assumes the enduring significance of ethnic identity as part of one's self-concept and leads naturally to support for policies that allow for the preservation of this cultural basis of self-definition.[27]

From a psychological perspective, then, both national and ethnic identities can be considered among the social categories that can define people based on their sense of commonality and shared destiny. History suggests that both modes of identification have strong emotional significance. Accordingly, although the boundaries for the two types of identities and the specific "them" contrasted with "us" differ, the consequences of these politicized group memberships can be similar in that group members express a preference toward the members of their own group and a dislike for those of the out-group.[28] When a strong sense

---

[25] Richard Alba, *Ethnicity in America: The Transformation of White Ethnicity* (New Haven, CT: Yale University Press, 1990), 294.

[26] Gans, "Symbolic Ethnicity."

[27] Indeed, there is good evidence that immigrants to the mainland United States who have discernible African ancestry have more difficulty assimilating than those without it. Those with origins in the Caribbean provide such comparisons. See Massey and Denton, *American Apartheid*; Alejandro Portes and Ruben Rumbaut, *Immigrant America: A Portrait* (Berkeley: University of California Press, 1996).

[28] Ashley W. Doane, "Dominant Group Ethnic Identity in the United States," *Sociological Quarterly* 38, no. 3 (1997): 375–97; Arthur H. Miller, Patricia Gurin, Gerald Gurin, and Olga Malanchuk, "Group Consciousness and Political Participation," *American Journal of Political Science* 25 (1981): 494–511; Michal Shamir and Alan Arian, "Collective Identity and Electoral Competition in Israel," *American Political Science Review* 93 (1999): 265–77.

of ethnic consciousness is directed against other members of the same nation, it can become a powerful wedge that shatters national unity, much as envisaged by Huntington in his provocative statement about the dangers of the high rates of Mexican immigration.

MANAGING PLURAL IDENTITIES

The existence of multiple social identities, including nationality and ethnicity, means that the contrasts invoked – the relevant "we" and "they" – vary according to the context or situation. In time of war, national identities are salient, whereas in an election period, partisan and ideological identities are more likely to govern behavior. Some group memberships are completely embedded or nested in others, resembling the Russian *matryoshki*, a set of increasingly small dolls, with each fitting into a larger sibling. In objective terms, all Berkeleyans fit into the category of Californians who in turn fit into the more comprehensive category of Americans. But the more encompassing national identity includes people whose other group identities are not the same.

In the United States and other culturally plural societies, national and ethnic identities do not completely overlap. Many psychologists emphasize the fluidity of self-categorizations in which group memberships are not fixed. Instead, they are viewed as emergent, context-specific outcomes of both the individual and the specific situation.[29] Of course, some group boundaries are more rigid than others. One can choose whether or not to become a parent or to change professions. Republicans can become Democrats, and New Yorkers can move to Silicon Valley and eventually feel like Californians. But it is difficult for Americans to become Japanese and almost impossible for a white to become black (although light-skinned blacks have "passed" in the sense of being accepted, unknowingly, by whites as one of them).

The choice of identities is often regulated by politics. In the relatively recent past, women could not join the military, and most Asians were denied access to American citizenship. And even when one meets the formal and emotional criteria for group membership, others may refuse to validate that subjective choice. The native-born daughter of Chinese immigrants may have a strong sense of American identity yet be told by fellow citizens of different origins that she is not "truly" American. German Jews considered themselves German; Hitler taught them otherwise.

Like all political ideologies, multiculturalism rests on certain psychological assumptions. As it happens, the implicit psychology of multiculturalist philosophers parallels the propositions of many contemporary American social psychologists specializing in the study of intergroup relations. These psychologists emphasize the predominance of consensual and stable ethnic group boundaries,

---

[29] Penelope Oakes, "Psychological Groups and Political Psychology: A Response to Huddy's 'Critical Examination of Social Identity Theory,'" *Political Psychology* 23, no. 4 (2002): 809–24.

strong ethnic identities, the politicization of group identities and interests, and thus the expectation of intergroup conflict.[30] For our part, we regard these assertions and the implicit corollary that strong ethnic identities indicate reciprocal hostility as hypotheses, not facts. Indeed, the weakening of ethnic identities among earlier waves of immigrants to the United States as a result of upward mobility, intermarriage, and acculturation might make one question the idea that today's ethnic group boundaries are fixed.

The clear exception is the case of the African Americans, whose relative isolation makes the image of rigid group boundaries largely accurate. The multiculturalist assumption seems to be that the exceptionally rigid black–white divide will extend to the new immigrant groups of today, denying the permeability that characterized the experience of earlier immigrants to America, even though Germans, Italians, and Irish were once thought to constitute different races. As an ideology, multiculturalism worries about the success of the assimilation paradigm, the reality of which much current sociological research continues to affirm.[31] And the policy agenda of multiculturalism includes elements that resist assimilation, out of concern that if the state did not act, the ethnic loyalties of immigrants to their original cultures would erode. Still, many social psychologists seem to assume that the inherent strength of ethnic ties among today's minorities will persist.

In addressing the issue of multiple allegiances, the philosopher Amartya Sen distinguishes between competing and noncompeting identities.[32] Competing identities typically arise when one belongs to two or more groups categorized in the same terms. People with dual citizenship, for example, may be unable to avoid choosing in which country's army to serve. But when the groups to which one belongs are classified on different bases, such as profession on the one hand and religion on the other, their claims need not collide.

Are nationality and ethnicity competing identities in Sen's sense of the term? And when does it matter if the ethnic group rather than the nation is one's primary psychological habitat? Generally speaking, political psychologists have debated whether the two are largely irrelevant to each other or white ethnicity is essentially equivalent to American national identity.[33]

[30] David O. Sears, "Experimental Social Psychology, Broader Contexts, and the Politics of Multiculturalism," in *Political Psychology of Democratic Citizenship*, ed. Eugene Borgida, Christopher M. Federico, and John L. Sullivan (New York: Oxford University Press, 2009), 326.

[31] Alba and Nee, *Remaking the American Mainstream*.

[32] Amartya Sen, "Beyond Identity: Other People," *The New Republic* (December 18, 2000), 23–30.

[33] Jim Sidanius and John Petrocik, "Communal and National Identity in a Multiethnic State: A Comparison of Three Perspectives," in *Social Identity, Intergroup Conflict, and Conflict Reduction*, ed. Richard D. Ashmore, Lee Jussim, and David Wilder (New York: Oxford University Press, 2001); Jack Citrin, Cara Wong, and Brian Duff, "The Meaning of American National Identity: Patterns of Ethnic Conflict and Consensus," in *Social Identity, Intergroup Conflict, and Conflict Reduction*, ed. Richard D. Ashmore, Lee Jussim, and David Wilder (New York: Oxford University Press, 2001); Sears, "Experimental Social Psychology, Broader Contexts, and the Politics of Multiculturalism"; Mahzarin R. Banaji and Thierry Devos, "American = White?" *Journal of Personality and Social Psychology* 88, no. 3 (2005): 447–66.

Cheering for the home team in an international sporting contest is perhaps a symbolic act of national loyalty but failing this "rooter's test" hardly means that immigrants are reluctant to meet the demands of American citizenship, support American political institutions, or fight for America.[34] Most domestic political issues, such as taxation, health, or environmental policies, do not pose a choice between national and ethnic identities. Yet there are counterexamples, as when ethnic interests divide people over trade, military aid, or immigration policies. And sometimes, as the example of the Japanese Americans after Pearl Harbor shows, strong national and ethnic identities are irreconcilable. In that case, loyalty to the United States overwhelmingly prevailed. More generally, Americans need not regard nationality and ethnicity as an either/or proposition and may describe themselves in hyphenated terms as Mexican-Americans, Italian-Americans, African-Americans, and so on. One can ask, of course, whether the emotional emphasis is on the term *before* or *after* the hyphen and whether the ethnic modifier of American identity simply designates a country of origin or whether it is intended to signify membership in a subculture with a unique configuration of interests.

Here, we examine the compatibility of national and ethnic identifications across America's diverse groups and take a hard look at the empirical backing for multiculturalism's ideas about the emotional significance of ethnicity and also whether minorities prioritize this dimension of self over their nationality. Do most Americans naturally categorize themselves along one side of the ethno-cultural pentagon, so that the terms white, black, Latino, and Asian capture a primary self-identification? A large study of University of California, Los Angeles (UCLA) students, doubtless accustomed to hearing about the value of ethnic and racial diversity as customarily defined in pan-ethnic terms as "Latinos" or "Asians," found that, instead, most Latino and Asian respondents used a wide variety of their original nationality categories to describe themselves, rather than lumping themselves into the pan-ethnic groups.[35] And when Cara Wong presented a long list of group (including ethnic) categories to respondents and asked them to indicate their primary identifications, party, locality, ideology, age, and class categories were chosen more frequently than race or ethnicity.[36]

As noted earlier, much social-psychological writing about intergroup relations reports findings consistent with multiculturalist ideology. These findings, based largely on artificial experiments with small groups of college students, downplay data from surveys insisting that enduring in-group/out-group

---

[34] Ibid.

[35] David O. Sears, Mingying Fu, P. J. Henry, and Kerra Bui, "The Origins and Persistence of Ethnic Identity among the 'New Immigrant' Groups," *Social Psychology Quarterly* 66, no. 4 (2008): 419–37.

[36] Cara J. Wong, *Boundaries of Obligation in American Politics: Geographic, National, and Racial Communities* (New York: Cambridge University Press, 2010).

distinctions imply that only members of a particular ethnic group can articulate and defend its interests. A recent essay by Pamela Conover hearkens back to the language of the philosophers Charles Taylor and Will Kymlicka.[37] Conover writes that minority groups must have presence and voice in shaping their preferences and identities, a phrase that on the surface seems compatible with the fundamental democratic principle of individual autonomy. Her point, though, is that unless minority organizations speak for the group, the group's interests will be misunderstood and its members' identities will become inauthentic. Only when people are convinced that their ethnic identities and interests are inextricably tied will political issues become relevant to the self and produce a group-centered point of view. The political necessity for ethnic self-realization, then, is a politics of recognition, produced perhaps by a system of descriptive recognition. The psychological justification for abandoning the principle of liberal individualism in favor of group rights is that constitutive or identity-based preferences induce more attention to politics, more stable attitudes, and more assertive actions on behalf of the group.[38] Transforming rights in this way is intended to produce greater social equality, as well as the ability of minority groups to live their inherited "way of life." But critics assert that this emphasis on group differences may harden divisions and make politics a negotiation among separate communal groups with little sense of a common interest.[39]

Those psychologists sympathetic to multiculturalism tend to downplay the value of a common national identity for minorities. In this vein, Marilynn Brewer argues that majority and minority groups have very different identities. The superordinate American identity is not a lubricant or salve that permits the recategorization of an out-group as an in-group.[40] Rather, America is essentially owned by the white majority group, and their national identity is more salient to its members than their ethnic identity. Minorities, it is implied, recognize and resent this "America equals white" credo and thus are alienated from the national identity. For subordinate minority groups, ethnic and national

---

[37] Pamela Johnston Conover, "The Politics of Recognition: A Social Psychological Perspective," in *The Political Psychology of Democratic Citizenship*, ed. Eugene Borgida, Christopher M. Federico, and John L. Sullivan (New York: Oxford University Press, 2009); Charles Taylor and Amy Gutmann, *Multiculturalism: Examining the Politics of Recognition* (Princeton, NJ: Princeton University Press, 1994); Kymlicka, *Multicultural Citizenship*.

[38] Pamela Johnston Conover, Donald D. Searing, and Ivor M. Crewe, "The Deliberative Potential of Political Discussion," *British Journal of Political Science* 32, no. 1 (2002): 21–62.

[39] Schlesinger Jr., *The Disuniting of America*; Richard Rodriguez, *Hunger of Memory: The Education of Richard Rodriguez* (New York: The Dial Press, 1982).

[40] Samuel L. Gaertner, John F. Dovidio, et al., "Across Cultural Divides: The Value of a Superordinate Identity," in *Cultural Divides: Understanding and Overcoming Group Conflict*, ed. Deborah Prentice and Dale Miller (New York: Russell Sage Foundation, 1999); Marilynn B. Brewer, "Social Identity and Citizenship in a Pluralistic Society," in *The Political Psychology of Democratic Citizenship*, ed. Eugene Borgida, Christopher M. Federico, and John L. Sullivan (New York: Oxford University Press, 2009).

identities thus are in conflict, and the stronger one focus of affiliation, the weaker the other.

The core of our empirical analysis is a comparison of the interplay of national and ethnic identities and the implications of these identifications for opinions about multiculturalism. In theorizing about intergroup and intragroup differences, we draw on a number of familiar psychological categories, some more prominent in the politicized group consciousness paradigm and others in the black exceptionalism perspective. And although we have noted the resonance between the politicized group consciousness perspective and multiculturalism's emphasis on strong ethnic identities, we should note that ethnic differences in political preferences might simply reflect calculations of group interest in specific cases rather than a more generalized commitment to maintaining group differences. However, both the psychological and political theories imply that within each ethnic group, intensity of *group consciousness* will increase intergroup differences.

Because national and ethnic identities are established through a process of socialization encompassing both direct experience and social learning, we also consider the associations of age and education to these attitudes and, later, their linkages to opinions about multiculturalism. We noted earlier that younger Americans are more likely to have been socialized during the era of demographic change ushered in by immigration and also are more likely to have been exposed to the celebration of diversity and dampening of overt expressions of patriotism among segments of the media, political, and academic elites.[41] Finally, multiculturalism is a relatively recent ideology often espoused in the nation's universities, so exposure to its norms and policy proposals might be greater among the relatively young college-educated population. For all these reasons, socialization processes may result in what we label a "vanguard" effect, in which younger and better educated citizens will be less likely to have strong national identities and more likely to have positive views about multiculturalism. With the new generation of "Millennials" born after 1980 experiencing all this and the impact of globalization, confirmation of the vanguard effect might portend increasing support for the multiculturalist image of nationhood in the future.

In examining the dual effects of recent immigration and group consciousness on minorities' identities, we contrast three alternative predictions. One version of a politicized group consciousness hypothesis, the *segmented assimilation* idea, states that some members of the new immigrant groups quickly become relegated to a subordinate niche in America's rigid racial hierarchy. They then begin to identify with the urban underclass and may display political behavior resembling that of African Americans'.[42] A *classical assimilationist* view, by contrast,

---

[41] Huntington, *Who Are We?*

[42] Portes and Rumbaut, *Immigrant America*; Alejandro Portes and Min Zhou, "The New Second Generation: Segmented Assimilation and its Variants," *Annals of the American Academy of Political and Social Science*, 530 (1993): 74–96.

is that recent immigration produces strong attachment to ethnic identities (i.e., original nationalities), but that strong ethnic consciousness may be largely a transitional state among those of Latin American and Asian origins, weakening over time with longer time in the United States, naturalization, and especially nativity. The closely related *black exceptionalism* view expects that the strong group consciousness found among African Americans, in part a function of the greater extent of discrimination they experience, will be less common among the new immigrant groups and particularly among the native-born.

POLITICAL MODELS OF AMERICAN NATIONHOOD

This book probes public opinion about American national identity and how to address the problem of *e pluribus unum*. It uses national and Los Angeles County surveys to determine the nature and psychological underpinnings of the strength of national and ethnic attachments, beliefs about how national and ethnic identities should be prioritized, and preferences regarding the role of government in promoting cultural unity and sustaining cultural differences, respectively.

What do the images of nationhood embodied in cosmopolitan liberalism, nativism, and multiculturalism imply for the relationship between national and ethnic identities? To repeat, cosmopolitan liberalism envisages the United States as a community of autonomous individuals with equal rights, accepting cultural diversity within the national community but denying that government has a responsibility for preserving cultural differences and regarding identity politics as divisive. When push comes to shove, cosmopolitan liberals are likely to prioritize the nation over the ethnic group. Nativism also rejects the official recognition of multiple cultures, but fuses American national identity with a particular Anglo-American way of life. Hence, nativism insists on the assimilation of immigrants, elevating nationality over ethnicity as the basis for political identity and striving to make identity politics obsolete.

Multiculturalism, by contrast, construes ethnicity as a vital and enduring foundation for one's personal social, and political identity, so that the perceived common fate of "our" group becomes the touchstone of political thinking, the mental shortcut employed to decide issues relevant to the group's identity or interests. Accordingly, the dilemma for multiculturalists is to find a place for the *unum* in American life, to furnish some unifying ideological cement for a diverse society.

These normative views are plainly in evidence among elites. But the extent of agreement between political leaders and the general public about how to cope with diversity has obvious political relevance. Without denying the power of political and media elites to shape popular attitudes, we believe that the opinion of rank-and-file citizens about how to balance unity and diversity is potent in its own right. At a minimum, the public's views limit the actions elected officials can safely contemplate without fear of reprisal. At their maximum, popular preferences can have full directive powers when policies engage strong group cleavages and cherished values.[43] A good example is California, where policies designed to benefit ethnic minorities galvanized opponents to use the initiative process to overturn well-established affirmative action and bilingual education programs.[44] An important subtext to that cautionary California tale is, of course, that whites were overrepresented in the electorate and their preferences dominated those of minority groups who were, in varying degrees, more in favor of these programs. This cleavage anticipates our focus throughout much of our study on the extent to which the majority whites and ethnic minorities share the same views about multiculturalism and the tradeoff between national and ethnic identities or offer competing preferences.

Among elites, both advocates and detractors of policies that give special support to minority groups try to make their case in terms of the general welfare rather than solely on the basis of particularistic group interests. The claim that multicultural policies generate *public goods* holds, for example, that affirmative action increases economic efficiency by expanding the pool of available talent or reducing the social tensions created by blocked opportunities; immigration imports needed workers and self-reliant individuals determined to fulfill the "American dream"; and bilingual education speeds the mobility of newcomers who contribute to the general economic well-being of the society. The brief for the opposition argues that affirmative action undermines the merit principle that promotes efficiency and innovation and that it is unfair to qualified individuals, that immigration of culturally dissimilar people threatens social solidarity and the capacity for collective action, and that bilingualism erodes the mutual understanding and tolerance that democracies need.

In addressing these questions, we go beyond the pronouncements of politicians, activists, and intellectuals to concentrate on what ordinary people think about American national identity and multiculturalism. To do so, we rely on a series of representative national surveys conducted between 1992 and 2012 and a complementary set of surveys from Los Angeles County. The extraordinary ethnic heterogeneity of Los Angeles, in particular the rapid growth of its Latino and Asian communities, and the constant salience of race and ethnicity in its politics make it a useful case study of how the interactions between demographic diversity and identity politics may affect the country as a whole.[45]

---

[43] Key Jr., *Southern Politics in State and Nation.*

[44] See, e.g., Andrea Louise Campbell, Cara Wong, and Jack Citrin, "'Racial Threat,' Partisan Climate, and Direct Democracy: Contextual Effects in Three California Initiatives," *Political Behavior* 28, no. 2 (2006): 129–50; and Peter Schrag, *Paradise Lost: California's Experience, America's Future* (New York: New Press, 1998).

[45] See, e.g., Nicholas Vaca, *Presumed Alliance* (New York: Harper Collins, 2004); and Lawrence Bobo and Devon Johnson, "Racial Attitudes in a Prismatic Metropolis: Mapping Identity, Stereotypes, Competition, and Views on Affirmative Action," in *Prismatic Metropolis: Analyzing Inequality in Los Angeles*, ed. Lawrence Bobo, Melvin Oliver, James Johnson, and Abel Valenzuela (New York: Russell Sage Foundation, 2000), 81–163.

ANALYTIC STRATEGY AND DATA SOURCES

We reserve most of our methodological discussion for Appendix 2.1, where the interested reader can turn for the details of our data sources and measures. However, here, we outline our general strategy of analysis, which is of three general kinds.

One focus is on the overall general public's political identities and attitudes toward multiculturalism. For this purpose, we examine national surveys, which tend to provide useful, generally valid, and representative estimates of aggregate opinion. Naturally, these surveys mostly reflect the dominant white majority's views because whites constitute more than three-quarters of the adult general public.

A second general purpose is to understand the sources of the dominant white majority's opinions about diversity and multiculturalism. This requires subgroup analyses that uncover the determinants of such attitudes, and the national surveys provide sufficient numbers of white respondents to allow for quite reliable analyses of those determinants. However, the measures relating to multiculturalism in these national surveys are usually quite limited because most typically focus on a number of other issues as well. Therefore, we rely heavily on the annual Los Angeles County Social Survey (LACSS) conducted from 1994 to 2002 because multiculturalism was a primary focus of inquiry in those surveys.

Our third purpose is to examine the same identities and attitudes among ethnic and racial minorities because it is from their ranks that most of the political pressure for multiculturalism emanates. This poses a more difficult methodological dilemma, since representative national surveys tend to provide only small subsamples of these minority groups, given their small numbers in the general population (see Figure 1.1). Also, the diversity of ethnic, national, and class origins within those groups complicates the analysis of small numbers of respondents still further.[46] The Hispanics in the national samples represent a mix of some quite different groups that vary in important characteristics including citizenship, time of immigration, social class, political preferences, and English-language proficiency. The Asian subsamples are so small that they cannot be taken to be fully representative.

As a result, although we do present some data from these national surveys on Hispanic and Asian aggregate opinion, we have considerably less confidence in

---

[46] For example, the national surveys we use do provide enough blacks (about 13 percent) to provide reasonable estimates of aggregate black opinion, but for the most part only minimally adequate numbers of black respondents to provide for internal analyses. National survey samples typically contain only 4 to 8 percent who are Hispanic, and even they are divided among groups that are quite different politically and socioeconomically, such as Mexican Americans, Puerto Ricans, and Cuban Americans. And the Asian subsamples constitute only 1 to 2 percent of these national samples.

most of them. (Replication across surveys does enhance that confidence somewhat, as we will show.) Because internal analyses of such small and doubtfully
representative subsamples are quite unreliable, we again turn mainly to the
LACSS for that purpose. When we pool the eight available surveys from 1994
to 2002, the number of blacks and Hispanics does increase enough to make for
more reliable analysis of ethnic minorities. The size of the pooled Asian subsample approaches reliability, at least for aggregate purposes, although its
representativeness still raises concerns.

NATIONAL SURVEYS

Two sets of national surveys provide somewhat different sets of items relevant to
our inquiry. The American National Election Studies (ANES) have been carried
out every two years since 1952 as a study of presidential and congressional
elections. In presidential years, these studies have generally involved national
samples of 2,000 cases or more, interviewed once face-to-face in the respondents' homes between September 1 and Election Day and then again in the two
months after the election. In off years, the samples have been similar in size but
respondents were interviewed only once, after the election. The response rates
have typically averaged around 65 percent, which means that two-thirds of all
respondents initially targeted for an interview ultimately were actually interviewed. The remainder either could not be contacted or refused to be
interviewed.[47]

The ANES samples represent the ethnic breakdown of the United States
rather well. These surveys are best equipped to examine the opinions of whites
and blacks because of the fairly substantial numbers of each group who were
interviewed. The main exception is the selective use of the 2012 ANES surveys,
which had large numbers (952 and 922) of African-American and Latino
respondents, with all being citizens. About two-thirds of the Latinos were
native-born. Still, we generally are cautious about making strong claims about
the minority groups in the national surveys.

The second set of national surveys are the General Social Surveys (GSS),
which have typically been conducted on an annual or biennial basis since
1972, focusing especially on sociologists' interests in social indicators. They
repeat a standard core of demographic and attitudinal items in each survey
and then usually add one or more modules of items in a targeted area. In
1994, one of the major modules was on multiculturalism, for which we served
as principal investigators. Many of the questions included in this module were

---

[47] The ANES reports response rates for each survey, using as the response rate denominator for
cross-section nonpanel surveys all age-eligible citizens randomly selected among individuals living
in simple households. This involves individuals who for multiple and varied reasons did not give
an interview. As an example the response rate for the pre-election survey in the 2000 ANES survey
was 64.8 percent for the face-to-face interviewing and 57.2 percent for the telephone interviewing.

repeated in the 2004 GSS. The response rates tend to be about the same or a little better than those of the ANES, but both are at the high end of those for academic surveys and should not give us serious concern.

LOS ANGELES COUNTY SOCIAL SURVEYS

The sample frame for the LACSS consists of all adults in Los Angeles County. According to the U.S. census, Los Angeles County had a total population of 8,863,164 in 1990, 9,519,338 in 2000, and by 2010 it had grown to 9,818,605. It now represents about 25 percent of the population of the state of California. Los Angeles County, even more than the United States as a whole, has undergone remarkable ethnic diversification over the past four decades, since the liberalization of immigration law in 1965.[48]

Earlier, we compared the ethnic composition of Los Angeles County with that of the nation as a whole, in Figure 1.1. To review, according to the 2010 census, Los Angeles County is less than half white (28 percent of the Los Angeles County population versus 65 percent of the U.S. population), is comparably African American (8 percent vs. 12 percent), and is far more Latino (48 percent vs. 16 percent) and Asian (14 percent vs. 4 percent). Moreover, Los Angeles, San Antonio, and Miami are by far the most heavily Latino metropolitan areas in the nation.[49] And, although the margin is less dramatic, those were the only three areas to have a non-Hispanic white minority as early as 1990.[50] So, by moving from national to local surveys, we move to a far more ethnically diverse environment – not only collecting larger samples of ethnic and racial minorities, but also moving to a context in which ethnic issues are more likely to be salient

---

[48] Los Angeles County should not be confused with the city of Los Angeles, a smaller political unit entirely confined within its boundaries. The city contained 39 percent of the population of the county in the 2000 census. Describing the differences between the two units is no easy task. Geographically, the city primarily includes the areas to the south and west of downtown Los Angeles, as well as the San Fernando Valley to its northwest. It includes such familiar areas as Hollywood, Brentwood, Pacific Palisades, West Los Angeles, South Los Angeles and Watts, San Pedro and Los Angeles Harbor. Politically, the county includes many other cities within the Los Angeles basin itself, including predominantly white, affluent cities such as Santa Monica, Malibu, Culver City, Beverly Hills, Pasadena, and the South Beach cities such as Manhattan Beach and Redondo Beach. It also includes the large and diverse city of Long Beach and the many culturally diverse cities in the San Gabriel Valley to the east of downtown Los Angeles, such as Monterey Park, Pomona, Claremont, and West Covina, and the vast and lightly populated Antelope Valley to the north, beyond the mountains framing downtown Los Angeles, including the cities of Lancaster and Palmdale, as well as many nonincorporated areas. For our purposes, among the most important of the latter are the heavily Hispanic areas of East Los Angeles, as well as the heavily Hispanic cities of Pico Rivera, Huntington Beach, and Bell to its immediate south. Demographically, the county is somewhat more heavily Hispanic and somewhat less black than the city.

[49] U.S. Census Bureau, State & County QuickFacts. Accessed online August 20, 2013 at http://quickfacts.census.gov/qfd/states/06/0644000.html.

[50] Ibid.

and politicized. As will be seen, however, not only are the larger ethnic samples a major advantage, but carrying out an assessment of public opinion about multi-culturalism in a highly diverse context also turns out to be a conservative test. Moreover, population projections all assume that the Los Angeles region will become increasingly ethnically diverse over time.[51] Since the same is to be expected of the nation as a whole, by examining Los Angeles here we are in some ways examining the nation of tomorrow.

This ethnic diversity of metropolitan Los Angeles is a relatively new develop-ment. Throughout most of its history, Los Angeles was an overwhelmingly white metropolitan area. As recently as 1960, non-Hispanic whites constituted 81 percent of the population of Los Angeles County, Latinos only 10 percent, and Asians only 2 percent.[52] Nevertheless, racial politics have been strikingly impor-tant in recent decades, especially revolving around conflict between blacks and whites. Intense political conflicts over race began in 1965 with the Watts riot.[53] Dramatic race-based confrontations continued over the next few decades: the mayoral elections in 1969 and 1973, in which a moderate black city councilman, Tom Bradley, ran for mayor of Los Angeles;[54] the highly contentious policy of busing for school integration in the Los Angeles Unified School District in the mid-1970s; the deadly and costly rioting in 1992 following the acquittal of police officers involved in a racial beating;[55] the passage in 1994 of Proposition 187, a statewide ballot proposition that proposed an end to the provision of many government services to illegal immigrants; and the statewide ballot Propositions 209 in 1996 and 227 in 1998 mandating an end to official affirmative action and bilingual education, respectively. In all these cases, race and ethnicity were at the forefront of political contention and proved to be the central cleavages in the public's response.[56] So, by examining Los Angeles, we are studying a case in which race and ethnicity have already created considerable tension.

[51] See, e.g., Georges Sabagh and Mehdi Bozorgmehr, "Population Change: Immigration and Ethnic Transformation," in *Ethnic Los Angeles*, ed. Roger Waldinger and Mehdi Bozorgmehr (New York: Russell Sage Foundation, 1996).

[52] James P. Allen and Eugene Turner, *The Ethnic Quilt: Population Diversity in Southern California* (Northridge: Center for Geographical Studies, California State University, Northridge, 1997).

[53] David O. Sears and John B. McConahay, *The Politics of Violence: The New Urban Blacks and the Watts Riot* (Boston: Houghton Mifflin, 1973).

[54] Donald R. Kinder and David O. Sears, "Prejudice and Politics: Symbolic Racism versus Racial Threats to the Good Life," *Journal of Personality and Political Psychology* 40 (1981): 414–31; Raphael J. Sonenshein, *Politics in Black and White: Race and Power in Los Angeles* (Princeton, NJ: Princeton University Press, 1994).

[55] Mark Baldassare, *The Los Angeles Riots: Lessons for the Urban Future* (Boulder, CO: Westview Press, 1994).

[56] David O. Sears, "Black-White Conflict: A Model for the Future of Ethnic Politics in Los Angeles," in *New York and Los Angeles: Politics, Society, and Culture: A Comparative View*, ed. David Halle (Chicago: University of Chicago Press, 2003).

The LACSS employed random-digit-dial telephone interviews conducted annually during the years 1994 to 2002, typically during the first six months of each calendar year.[57] In most years, the LACSS samples aimed to represent the adult population of Los Angeles County, with the variety of ethnic groups more or less as they came. The most straightforward test of representativeness involves educational level because telephone surveys usually overrepresent the well educated. Appendix 2.1 compares the pooled LACSSs with 2000 census data (the year closest to our surveys) for Los Angeles County in terms of most advanced educational level attained for each ethnic group. There is a slight bias in that direction, but it does not seem terribly serious. Among whites, there is something of an overrepresentation of those with some college but no BA, but the less educated are well represented. Among Latinos and blacks, those with moderate levels of education are overrepresented at the expense of the least educated. By and large, then, we conclude that, in terms of educational level, the data are not seriously biased.

However, we do note three qualifications about the LACSS samples. First, during this period, the proportions of whites and Latinos in Los Angeles County were sufficiently large that random-digit-dial sampling collected sufficient numbers of both groups to provide reliable estimates of the aggregate opinion of each group and to make internal analysis possible. However, as will be seen, large numbers of Latinos in Los Angeles County are relatively recent immigrants and not fluent in English, and so are not comfortable with being interviewed in English. Pooling all the LACSSs, 71 percent of the Latinos said they were not born in the United States, and 61 percent said that at home they spoke either no English or mostly a language other than English. As a result, in all years, the LACSS employed a Spanish-language interview schedule for those respondents who preferred to be interviewed in Spanish. About half the Latino interviewees, on average, took advantage of that opportunity. This allows us to have confidence that the Latino subsamples were not self-selected for English language fluency.

Second, the proportion (although not the absolute numbers) of county residents who were African American had been dropping somewhat in the LACSS years (to 10 percent in 2000). To get sufficient numbers of blacks to provide reliable estimates, blacks were oversampled in the 1994 and again in the 2000 through 2002 surveys by oversampling telephone exchanges known to contain disproportionate numbers of blacks. Given the considerable residential segregation of blacks, this proved to be a generally successful strategy.

Third, the Asian population in Los Angeles also was relatively small (about 12 percent in the 2000 census), which poses similar problems. In addition, many are recent immigrants, and the variety of Asian languages they use (various dialects of Chinese, Vietnamese, Hindi, Tagalog, etc.) ruled out Asian-language interviews. We suspect this introduces some biases into the Asian subsample, which of

---

[57] The 1996 LACSS was conducted with Professor Jim Sidanius as principal investigator, and its content focused primarily on affirmative action, so it contains few of the measures we need for our study.

necessity was selected by English-language fluency. We have no way to estimate precisely the magnitude of bias, but our best guess is that these LACSSs probably succeeded in interviewing only the most English-fluent half of their potential Asian subsamples.[58] For example, 70 percent of our Asian respondents said they were born outside the United States, a number very similar to the proportion of foreign-born Latinos. But 64 percent said they spoke only English or mostly English at home, far higher than the proportion of Latinos who only or mostly spoke English (39 percent). For this reason, we present the Asian data somewhat more hesitantly and cautiously than the data from the other three ethnic groups.

Each LACSS by itself had from 600 to 800 respondents, approximately (see Appendix 2.1). Those are sufficient cases for some purposes, but usually the number is too small for desired comparisons. As a result, we decided to pool the surveys into a cumulative file, enabling us to internally analyze a larger number of black and Latino cases (652 and 1,380, respectively). The pooled Asian subsample approaches the size required for reliability (268), but for the reasons indicated earlier, we are cautious in our use of it. In general, the pooling does no great violence to the data. Generally speaking, the marginal frequencies are similar across surveys when the items are the same, and the relationships among items are similar. In a couple of instances, changes did occur across time, and we discuss these cases where relevant.

The ethnic breakdown of respondents in the eight LACSSs is also shown in Appendix 2.1. When compared to the census estimates shown in Figure 1.1, the full sample falls short of the Asians in Los Angeles County and oversamples blacks, for reasons already given. Our objective in using the LACSS is, however, not to provide full-population estimates because we utilize national surveys for that purpose. Rather, its primary utility is in developing in-depth understandings of the separate ethnic and racial subgroups.

DEMOGRAPHIC DESCRIPTION OF LOS ANGELES RACIAL AND ETHNIC GROUPS

Our central focus is on contemporary American ethnic groups. For convenience, we use the conventional pan-ethnic labels – whites, blacks, Latinos,[59] and Asians. Our work is a piece of political psychology, so we focus on perceptions and attitudes rather than group position in the social stratification system.

---

[58] Note that our objective in using the LACSS is not to provide full-population estimates because we utilize national surveys for that purpose. Our purpose is to develop in-depth understandings of the separate ethnic and racial subgroups. The oversampling, or even undersampling, of specific ethnic subgroups should not compromise that purpose if the subsamples of those groups continue to be representative of the groups in question. In the case of blacks, but possibly not Asians, we believe it is an apt source for that analysis.

[59] For the most part we use the term "Latino" rather than "Hispanic," in recognition of the Latin-American rather than Iberian origins of our respondents. However, most survey questions use the term "Hispanic," so we use the term used in the particular item when quoting item wording.

Nevertheless, these groups differ socially and economically in some important ways, and we need to make those demographic characteristics clear. We use the cumulative file of the LACSS to do this, both because it is the one source of data that contains reasonable numbers of each group and because we depend on it heavily in the analysis that follows.

Table 2.1 shows the demographic characteristics of the four main ethnic groups in these pooled data. As can be seen, the white and Asian populations

TABLE 2.1. *Demographic Composition of Ethnic Groups in Los Angeles County*

	Whites (%)	Blacks (%)	Hispanics (%)	Asians (%)
Education				
College degree	38	26	9	45
Some college or 2-year degree	38	37	22	37
High school or GED degree	18	24	33	13
Some high school	5	9	11	4
8th grade or less	2	4	25	1
Income				
More than $70,000	35	16	6	28
$50,000–70,000	14	14	6	13
$30,000–50,000	23	25	21	25
$20,000–30,000	12	18	22	16
$10,000–20,000	11	16	30	10
Less than $10,000	5	12	15	8
Subjective Class				
Upper	2	1	1	2
Upper middle	28	11	9	24
Middle	39	31	26	42
Working	31	57	64	32
Age				
18–29	15	19	35	41
30–39	23	22	32	27
40–49	23	23	19	17
50–59	18	15	8	7
60 and above	21	21	6	8
Gender				
Male	46	37	44	44
Female	54	63	56	56
Marital Status				
Married or living as married	51	30	59	43
Widowed	9	10	3	2
Divorced	14	16	7	6
Separated	2	6	6	1
Never married	23	36	26	48

Source: Pooled Los Angeles County Social Surveys (LACSS), 1994–2002.

are the best educated, and the Latino subsample, the least. The whites also have the highest income levels, whereas blacks are generally middle income, with Latinos tending to concentrate in the lower income brackets. Not surprisingly, then, whites tend to describe themselves as upper middle or middle class, whereas blacks and Latinos tend to identify with the working class. Both Latinos and Asians are distinctly younger than whites or blacks. In part, this reflects heavy recent immigration, which usually is more common among younger adults, but in part it probably reflects the absence of older non–English-speaking Asians from our samples. The gender distribution is similar across groups except that, among blacks, females far outnumber males. This is a fairly standard finding in sample surveys and presumably results from a variety of circumstances (including the predominance of female-headed households and thus male transience, black males' suspicion of interviewers, the incarceration of many black males, and even differential mortality rates). The differences in marital status reflect a number of circumstances as well: the low marriage rate among blacks; the youthfulness of our Asian respondents, who are disproportionately never-married; and the traditional family structure of Latino families.

One of the phenomena triggering our interest in multiculturalism is the high rate of immigration that has occurred in the past four decades. A key focal point for our analysis is to examine the psychological and political integration of these immigrants as they enter the United States. In Los Angeles, the immigration has disproportionately come from Latin America, most especially from Mexico, and from Asia.

A key variable turns out to be the individual's immigration status. By this we mean the extent to which the individual is an immigrant at all, and if so, how recently an immigrant. To analyze this variable we developed a composite typology out of four individual variables, as shown in Table 2.2: whether or not the individual's parents were born in the United States; whether or not the individual was; if not, whether or not the individual has become a naturalized citizen; and, if an immigrant, for how many years the individual has been in the United States.

Combining these variables yields five distinctive categories of a variable we call *immigration status*. As shown in Table 2.2, the natives are those who are at least third-generation Americans, with both parents as well as themselves having been born in this country. The second generation includes those born in the United States, but with parents who were born elsewhere. The new citizens are those born elsewhere, as were their parents, but who have become naturalized U.S. citizens. The long-term noncitizens were born elsewhere, as were their parents, and they have not become naturalized, but they have resided in the United States for at least ten years. Finally, the recent immigrants were themselves and their parents born elsewhere; they have not become naturalized, and they have lived in the United States fewer than ten years.[60]

---

[60] Most of our analyses do not use the full immigration status scale because of insufficient cases in all categories.

TABLE 2.2. *Classification of Ethnic Groups by Immigration Status and Language Spoken at Home in Los Angeles County*

Immigration Status	Whites (%)	Blacks (%)	Latinos (%)	Asians (%)	Total (%)
Native	74	90	12	10	52
Second generation	15	5	20	21	15
New citizens	8	4	23	40	14
Long-term noncitizens	2	1	31	9	12
Recent immigrants	1	<1	15	19	7
N	2,002	1,012	1,668	334	5,016
Language Spoken at Home					
English only	78	87	11	29	53
Mostly English	14	12	28	36	21
Mostly another language	4	1	59	39	22
No English	1	0	11	7	5
N	1,478	715	1,341	253	3,787

Source: Pooled Los Angeles County Social Surveys (LACSS), 1994–2002.
Note: The five-category immigration status variable incorporates 5,548 respondents to the 1994–2002 LACSS (96 percent of all respondents), with only 237 cases (4 percent) missing.

Almost all respondents in our surveys fit this classification. As shown in Table 2.2, the black population of Los Angeles County is almost entirely native-born: 90 percent are at least third-generation Americans. As often observed, blacks are now the oldest American ethnic or racial group (excluding, of course, the now relatively small Native American category). Our data show that many more whites are relatively recent immigrants: 26 percent are second-generation Americans or even more recent. The Latino population is much newer still. Only 12 percent are natives, 69 percent are immigrants, and only half are citizens. Of our Asian sub-sample, too, only 10 percent are natives and 68 percent are themselves immigrants.

Table 2.2 also shows the stark differences across ethnic groups in language fluency. Almost all whites and blacks speak mostly English at home, and the vast majority of these groups use no foreign language at home at all. Most of the Latinos, on the other hand, speak mostly Spanish at home; very few speak only English. Our Asian subsample is mostly English-speaking; for the reasons given earlier, we suspect that we have under-sampled the immigrant Asian population, especially those who are not English-fluent.

Because so much of our analysis of immigrant groups focuses on Latinos, it would be well to look more closely at the characteristics of those who fall into these five categories. Table 2.3 shows the demographic characteristics of Latinos in each of these categories of immigration status. The natives give evidence of much demographic assimilation to the mainstream of the population. Their predominant language is English, and half have attended college, either a four-year or a community college. Very few are high school dropouts. They are

TABLE 2.3. *Characteristics of Latinos in Los Angeles, by Immigration Status*

	Natives (%)	Second Generation (%)	New Citizens (%)	Long-Term Noncitizens (%)	New Immigrants (%)	Total (%)
Language at Home						
English only	57	13	6	3	0	12
Mostly English	38	47	33	22	6	30
Mostly another language	4	36	54	62	72	49
No English	1	5	8	13	21	10
N	143	251	300	359	145	1,198
Education						
College degree	12	10	11	7	5	9
Some college or 2-year degree	38	40	23	10	17	23
High school or GED degree	36	32	32	31	39	33
Some high school	10	11	10	11	7	10
8th grade or less	4	7	24	41	32	25
N	196	330	377	519	242	1,664
Income						
More than $70,000	17	10	7	2	1	7
$50,000–70,000	16	8	7	3	1	6
$30,000–50,000	32	29	27	15	7	22
$20,000–30,000	17	22	23	24	18	22
$10,000–20,000	12	22	24	36	44	29
Less than $10,000	7	9	11	19	30	15
N	180	307	340	465	198	1,490
Age						
18–29	30	58	23	22	58	37
30–39	24	21	31	43	31	33
40–49	29	10	19	24	10	18
50–59	9	5	16	7	<1	7
60 and older	8	6	11	4	1	6
N	195	328	36	7	514	1,645

Source: Pooled Los Angeles County Social Surveys (LACSS), 1994–2002.

middle income, on average. And, like most of the Latino population, they tend to be quite youthful. The second generation looks similar, but less so: they tend to be bilingual rather than English-only, they too have graduated from high school and often attended some college, but their income is not as great and they are much younger. We look for them to be part way on the assimilatory road that the natives seem to be traveling, especially given their youth (most are under thirty).

The new citizens as a whole do not seem to be as assimilated in either language or socioeconomically, nor does it seem likely that they personally ever will be. They mostly speak Spanish, although with some English fluency; they are much more likely never to have gone beyond eighth grade, they are lower income, and many are older. They would appear to be permanently working class and very likely often unskilled workers. The long-term noncitizens resemble them demographically quite closely: predominantly Spanish-speaking, usually high school dropouts, lower income (on average, below $20,000 per year), and beyond the age when socioeconomic mobility is likely to occur very often (median age over thirty). The new immigrants are younger but otherwise quite similar: mostly Spanish-speaking, rarely with college experience, low income, and quite young (median age under thirty). These latter three categories seem destined to be relatively unassimilated, and it will be up to their offspring to move closer to the mainstream of American society.

Each of the next seven chapters of the book addresses a separate main empirical question regarding public opinion. Our usual procedure is to begin with national surveys and to describe ethnic group differences and internal variation within ethnic groups. As noted, those analyses deal primarily with white respondents. We then turn to the LACSS data for more sustained comparisons of ethnic groups. These comparisons allow us to explore the assimilation, black exceptionalism, and politicized group consciousness paradigms. The statistical approach generally is straightforward, beginning with simple bivariate comparisons and then moving on to more complex multivariate modeling based on regression analysis.

3

Contours of American National Identity

All nationalist doctrines insist that allegiance to the nation should override affiliations to less inclusive groups, such as those based on race, religion, language, or class. Writing about the aftermath of colonialism in *From Empire to Nation*, Rupert Emerson wrote that the nation is "the largest community which, when the chips are down, effectively commands men's loyalty, overriding the claims both of the lesser communities within it and those which cut across it or potentially enfold it within a still greater society."[1] Whether this claim about the strength and pervasiveness of identification with the nation and the unique importance of this identity still holds in the United States is the subject of this chapter.

Has the conflation of demographic change, due largely to immigration, and identity politics prompted an overall weakening of Americans' national identity and a widening of ethnic fault lines in patriotic sentiment? Pessimistic observers highlight distinctive threats to national attachment in all the country's main ethnic groups. Samuel Huntington singles out Hispanic immigration, arguing that the mass entry and geographic concentration of these newcomers close to their countries of origin may short-circuit the development of loyalty to the United States that occurred among earlier immigrant waves.[2] If Huntington is correct about the future attitudes of American Latinos, then the fact that they are the fastest growing segment of a projected majority-minority society is a significant challenge to the traditional meaning of *e pluribus unum*.

Alarms also are raised about the trajectory of patriotic feeling among the white majority. Huntington, echoing Arthur Schlesinger Jr.'s earlier plaint, argues that the disillusionment with American virtue catalyzed by the Vietnam War, the convulsions of the sixties, and the subsequent embrace of multiculturalism by

---

[1] Rupert Emerson, *From Empire to Nation: The Rise to Self-Assertion of Asian and African Peoples* (Boston: Beacon Press, 1960).

[2] Huntington, *Who Are We?*

academic and cultural elites is eroding the strength of national identification among young, well-educated whites.[3] Finally, scholars argue that the gains of the civil rights movement have stalled and that the historical oppression and continuing marginalization of blacks as a group leads many to believe that America remains white and to feel less emotionally attached than whites to the nation.[4]

In assessing the contemporary status of American patriotism, we concentrate on evidence of ethnic differences and change over the past two decades. Is there more ambivalence and negative feeling about America among blacks, or do they express strong patriotism despite recognition of their past mistreatment? Is the heavily immigrant Latino population remaining attached to its countries of origin or gradually embracing and prioritizing an American identity? Is national attachment declining among the vanguard of the future, the young and/or well-educated "GenXers" and "Millennials?" And with regard to beliefs about the *content* of American national identity, is there a national consensus or a pattern of contestation based on ethnic divisions? In particular, in drawing the boundaries of the so-called "circle of we," does the public generally use the inclusionary *civic* standard of common values and political principles or the exclusionary *ethnic* criterion of common descent in which the prototype of an American is based on race, religion, and place of birth? How American identity is defined and the extent to which this meaning is consensual or contested across ethnic lines has obvious relevance for contemporary political debates about immigration, language, and citizenship policies.

In interpreting the evidence about the patterns of ethnic differences in national attachment, we apply the three broad psychological paradigms described in the preceding chapter. If the traditional straight-line *assimilation* paradigm holds, immigrants and their offspring should, over time and generations, begin to identify themselves first and foremost as Americans, and differences in patriotism based on country of origin or ancestry should be minor, mainly reflecting an immigrant group's length of tenure in the United States. Although the assimilation paradigm does not presume the full extinction of ethnic pride among minority groups, it does suggest that the country's diverse immigrant groups prioritize their national identity when competing loyalties force them to choose. The politicized group consciousness paradigm, by contrast, projects large and enduring ethnic differences in national attachment. Proponents of this perspective often portray American society as a rigid racial hierarchy, with whites of European ancestry zealously guarding their place at the top of the social and political pyramid and people of color, whether immigrants or native-born, arrayed on lower rungs of the

---

[3] Schlesinger Jr., *The Disuniting of America*.

[4] Hacker, *Two Nations*; Gitlin, *The Twilight of Common Dreams*; Himmelfarb, *One Nation, Two Cultures*; Sidanius and Petrocik, "Communal and National Identity in a Multiethnic State."

ladder.[5] By this way of thinking, Americans, in reality if not in rhetoric, may hold to an ethnic definition of nationhood. In the words of Jim Sidanius, the politically dominant whites will claim "ownership of the nation."[6] For them, nationality and ethnicity are complementary because their power has enabled whites to successfully define the prototypical American in their own image.[7] But because of past discrimination and present marginalization, members of subordinate groups such as blacks, Latinos, and Asians see themselves as *in* but not *of* the American nation. If an ethnocultural definition of nationhood indeed prevails among whites, undermining the motivation of minorities to fully belong, then increased ethnic diversity would threaten social cohesion and national unity.

The black exceptionalism paradigm modifies this description of ethnic divisions, emphasizing the distinctiveness of the experiences and outlook of African Americans. This theoretical perspective accepts the proposition that assimilation may engender patriotism and unalloyed American identity among later generations of Latino and Asian immigrants. But blacks, who confront a less permeable color line, might express a uniquely enduring lower level of national attachment than whites.

IDENTITY AND PATRIOTISM

One facet of national identity is emotional attachment to one's fellow citizens and country – in a word, patriotism. If one asks about the beliefs underlying patriotism or why we love our country, the answer is likely to vary both within and across peoples. Still, the frequent portrayal of the nation as an extended family, reflected in the use of terms like "mother country," "fatherland," and "band of brothers" makes patriotism seem to be a natural human sentiment. And if the analogy with family ties holds, patriotism implies a willingness to sacrifice for one's fellow countrymen, even to kill and die for them.

Peter Karsten writes that during and following the Glorious Revolution in England, "patriot" and "patriotism" entwined the defense of fundamental democratic liberties and rights with a place and way of life.[8] In the eighteenth

---

[5] Jim Sidanius, et al., "The Interface between Ethnic and National Attachment: Ethnic Pluralism or Ethnic Dominance?" *Public Opinion Quarterly* 61, no. 1 (1997): 102–33. See also Sidanius and Pratto, *Social Dominance*; Lawrence Bobo and Mia Tuan, *Prejudice in Politics: Group Position, Public Opinion and the Wisconsin Treaty Rights Dispute* (Cambridge, MA: Harvard University Press 2006); Eduardo Bonilla-Silva and Karen S. Glover, "We Are All Americans: The Latin Americanization of Race Relations in the United States," in *The Changing Terrain of Race and Ethnicity*, ed. Maria Krysan and Amanda E. Lewis (New York: Russell Sage Foundation 2004); John Jost, Christopher M. Federico, and Jaime L. Napier, "Political Ideology: Its Structure, Function, and Electoral Affinities," *Annual Review of Psychology* 60 (2009): 307–37.

[6] Ibid.

[7] Ibid.

[8] Peter Karsten, *Patriot-Heroes in England and America* (Madison: University of Wisconsin Press, 1978).

century, this image of the patriot as a potential martyr in the struggle against undemocratic authorities dominated the rhetoric of the American rebels.[9] Yet by the late nineteenth century patriotism had become synonymous with an emotional attachment to national symbols such as the anthem and flag that could be channeled into a blank check for whomever is in power. The slogan, "my country right or wrong," converts patriotism into blind faith and an overweening sense of superiority rather than just a willingness to fight for the nation's founding principles and established way of life. Bemoaning this possibility, George Kateb has called patriotism "the most deadly form of group attachment," arguing that it makes the love of an abstraction – the country – into a self-preference that licenses destructiveness toward other countries and punitive treatment of fellow citizens who warn against this behavior.[10] On the same lines, Oscar Wilde demeaned patriotism as "the virtue of the vicious." Patriotism comes to the fore when the nation is under attack. But even then patriotism can represent either the vigilant defense of national institutions or a toxic attack on imagined enemies. So, is love of country noble and unselfish, merely signifying a sense of mutuality with one's fellow nationals, or intolerant, conveying belief in one's superiority to both foreigners and domestic minorities?

To cut through this moral ambiguity and linguistic confusion, writers commonly distinguish patriotism from chauvinism, or, alternatively, "constructive" from "blind" patriotism.[11] De Tocqueville described the more reflective form of patriotism as a state of mind in which "citizens grapple with various aspects of America which are not so rose-colored."[12] The constructive patriot recognizes and decries the gaps between American ideals and reality without turning his back on his country. By contrast, love of country is more uncritical in the blind, or instinctive, version of patriotism.[13] This harder edged, chauvinistic outlook reflects an unquestioning faith in whatever is done in the country's name and in the moral ascendancy of American values and customs.[14]

Using the language of social identity theory, patriotism denotes in-group pride without out-group hostility whereas chauvinism is usually defined as combining the two attitudes. However, both patriotism and chauvinism presume the psychological significance of a positive national identity and

---

[9] Ibid.

[10] George Kateb, *Patriotism and Other Mistakes* (New Haven, CT: Yale University Press, 2006).

[11] See, e.g., Ervin Staub, "Blind versus Constructive Patriotism: Moving from Embeddedness in the Group to Critical Loyalty and Action," in *Patriotism in the Lives of Individuals and Nations*, ed. Dani Bar-Tal and Ervin Staub (Chicago: Nelson-Hall and Schatz, 1997), 213–28; Robert T. Schatz et al., "On the Varieties of National Attachment: Blind vs. Constructive Patriotism," *Political Psychology* 20, no. 1 (1999): 151–74.

[12] de Tocqueville, *Democracy in America*.

[13] Robert T. Schatz, et al., "On the Varieties of National Attachment."

[14] Ibid.

imply that where there are multiple allegiances, a strong American identity is the constitutive element in one's overall sense of political self-definition.[15]

To assess the breadth and durability of Americans' emotional attachment to their country, its history, and its symbolic representations such as the flag, we rely on three kinds of survey questions: items that tap diffuse feelings of closeness, pride, and love; items that ask about pride in specific national institutions and achievements; and items that go beyond patriotism to express chauvinism, a sense of America's superiority.

ATTACHMENT TO THE NATION

We first assess the absolute level of attachment to the nation. We present the data separately by ethnic group. We start with whites. But since they represent the overwhelming majority of all Americans, their aggregated attitudes are very close for the population as a whole in the surveys we analyze. Then we turn to the thesis that ethnic diversity weakens patriotism, considering whether minority groups are estranged from the national community, both by comparison to whites and in terms of their absolute level of attachment. We also examine evidence of trends over time, although with less confidence on this point given the gaps in relevant data.

Table 3.1 presents responses to an array of questions assessing patriotism and chauvinism. Each survey is just a snapshot in time, of course. And it also must be noted that the distribution of public attitudes recorded here may be sensitive to the wording of the questions and to the response categories offered. (The precise wording for the questions used is provided in Appendix 3.1.) Nevertheless, the consistent pattern of answers from surveys conducted over two decades is telling.

There is overwhelming evidence that white Americans have a strong emotional connection to their country and its official symbols. Some examples, shown in the top of Table 3.1, illustrate the substantial number of people willing to endorse the strongest of words to convey their level of patriotism. Fully 73 percent of whites in the 1996 General Social Survey (GSS) strongly agreed that they would rather be a citizen of America than any other country in the world, and 83 percent said they felt close to America (with 36 percent saying very close). In the 1992 American National Election Study (ANES), 92 percent of white respondents said their love for country was extremely or very strong; twelve years later the number was essentially unchanged. And in a 2009 ANES survey conducted after President Obama was inaugurated, respondents were asked whether they loved America, felt neutral about it, or hated the country. Virtually no one expressed hate. Among whites, 75 percent chose the most positive option, "love America a great deal." White respondents also expressed overwhelmingly favorable feelings toward the American flag from the pre-9/11 era to the present. Enduringly strong patriotism among whites is again confirmed in the 2012 ANES results, in which 69 percent

---

[15] Ibid.

TABLE 3.1. *Percent with Strong Affective Attachment to America, by Race and Ethnicity*

Patriotism: Positively Worded Items:		Whites (%)	Blacks (%)	Latinos (%)
National Data				
1996	Rather be citizen of	73[a]	66[a]	–
2004	America? (% strongly agree)[1]	78	65	
1996	Closeness to America	36[a]	31[a]	–
2004	(% very close)[1]	56	35	
1992	Strength of love for country	92	70	–
2004	(% extremely, very strong)?[2]	91[a]	81	91[a]
2009	Extent of love/hate for the United States (% love a great deal)[2]	75	57[a]	64[a]
2012	Extent of love/hate for the United States (% love)[2]	69	59[a]	58[a]
1992	Feelings about American	83	53	–
2004	flag (% extremely, very good)[2]	86[a]	61	88[a]
2009	Feelings about American flag (% extremely good)[2]	71	45	59
2012	Feelings about American flag (% extremely, very good)[2]	76	59	73
Los Angeles Data				
1997–99	Have great love for America (% strongly agree)[3]	72	62[a]	57[a]
1994–97	Pride to be an American (% extremely or very)[3]	80[a]	75[a]	53
1997–00, 2002	Sight of the American flag very moving (% strongly agree)[3]	53	43[a]	48[a]
Deny Criticism				
1998	America is not a particularly wonderful country (% strongly disagree)[3]	61[a]	49[a]	35
1998	Other countries are better places to live than the United States (% strongly disagree)[3]	51[a]	54[a]	30
1998	Flag should not be treated as sacred object (% strongly disagree)[3]	30[a]	36[a]	21

(continued)

TABLE 3.1 *(continued)*

Patriotism: Positively Worded Items:		Whites (%)	Blacks (%)	Latinos (%)
Chauvinism				
1996	America is better country	40[a]	38[a]	–
2004	than most others (% strongly agree)[1]	42	34	–
1996	World better if others more	15[a]	17[a]	–
2004	like Americans (% strongly agree)[1]	17[a]	14[a]	–
1996	America should follow	12[a]	15[a]	–
2004	interests, even if conflicts result (% strongly agree)[1]	13[a]	10[a]	–
1996	People should support	10	16	–
2004	country even if it's wrong (% strongly agree)[1]	10[a]	15[a]	–
2009	How strongly support country, right or wrong (% extremely, very strongly)?[2]	50[a]	48[ab]	41[b]
2009	Should there be more criticism of the United States, less, or the same (% great deal less)[2]	15[a]	20[a]	11[a]
Negative Emotions about America				
"Some things about America today make me feel...)				
2004	Angry about America (% agree)[2]	52[a]	60[a]	40[a]
2004	Ashamed about America (% agree)[2]	57[a]	60[a]	43[a]
1996	Ashamed about America	16[a]	20[a]	–
2004	(% strongly agree)[1]	18[a]	21[a]	

Survey Citations: 1, General Social Survey (GSS); 2, American National Election Studies (ANES); 3, Los Angeles County Social Survey (LACSS)

All entries in a given row are significantly different ($p < .05$) unless they share the same superscript. A "neither agree nor disagree" option was also provided in the ANES emotions items. Minimum N's, by race/ethnicity: 1992 ANES: 1,863 white, 282 black; 2004 ANES: 876 white, 180 black, 81 Latino; 2009 ANES: 1,775 white, 273 black, 171 Latino; 2012 ANES: 3,256 white, 952 black, 922 Latino; 1996 GSS: 797 white, 109 black; 2004 GSS: 953 white, 155 black; LACSS (positive items): 548 white, 288 black, 462 Latino; LACSS (negative items): 273 white; 71 black; 210 Latino.

The precise wordings for these items and those in the remaining tables in this chapter are in Appendix 3.1.

said they "loved" the United States (the top two options were "love" and "like") and 76 percent said seeing the American flag made them feel "extremely" or "very" good.

As elsewhere in this volume, we present parallel data from both national and Los Angeles surveys when possible. Respondents in the Los Angeles County Social Surveys (LACSS) were asked whether they were proud to be Americans, how much they loved their country, and whether they typically felt moved when they saw the American flag. Strong patriotism was also very high among whites in Los Angeles. As shown in the second panel of Table 3.1, 72 percent of the white Los Angeles respondents strongly agreed that they loved the United States, 80 percent said they felt "extremely" or "very proud" to be an American, and (53 percent strongly agreed that) said they found the sight of the American flag moving.

In both the national and Los Angeles surveys, the survey questions yielding overwhelmingly positive sentiments among whites were typically worded such that any agreement with plausible assertions is keyed as reflecting patriotism. A long history of survey research has shown that people are more likely to agree than disagree with any plausible assertions, everything else being equal.[16] To check on whether these very positive sentiments were inflated by such a bias, we asked three items in the 1998 LACSS on which expressing attachment entailed active disagreement with derogatory statements about America. As can be seen in the third panel of Table 3.1, the majority of whites evince strong patriotism on these items as well, with 81 percent disagreeing that America is not a particularly wonderful country and 70 percent disagreeing that there are other countries better to live in. Whites split evenly over the controversial assertion that the flag is a sacred object. Calling an object sacred, of course, is a more extreme statement than indicating mere love. These results showing strong national attachment conform to the findings reported by Elizabeth Theiss-Morse, although based on just a single survey, the American Peoples Survey conducted in 2002.[17] Overall, in her national sample, there was a stronger sense of positive attachment to one's fellow Americans than to other groups defined by race, gender, religion, or region.

There also is ample evidence of the racial differences that the politicized group consciousness and black exceptionalism paradigms would predict.[18] However,

---

[16] Howard Schuman and Stanley Presser, *Questions and Answers in Attitude Surveys* (San Diego: Academic Press, 1981). Herbert Hyman and Paul Sheatsley, "The Authoritarian Personality: A Methodological Critique," in *Studies in the Scope and Method of the Authoritarian Personality*, ed. Richard Christie and Marie Jahoda (Glencoe, IL: The Free Press, 1954).

[17] Elizabeth Theiss-Morse, *Who Counts As an American? The Boundaries of National Identity* (New York: Cambridge University Press, 2009). She constructed a four-item measure of American identity comprising questions about whether respondents saw themselves as members of a particular group, felt that membership in that group was important to their personal self-image, expressed strong ties to other members in the group, and evaluated others in the group positively on a series of traits such as honesty and political interest.

[18] Theiss-Morse also reports a lower level of American identity among blacks than whites. See Theiss-Morse, *Who Counts As an American?*, 48.

it is equally or perhaps more important to add that a strong sense of national identification remains pervasive even among African Americans. In the national data, a majority of blacks almost always falls on the positive side of questions about closeness to, love for, and pride in America. Nevertheless, their sense of national commitment is usually less passionate and more subdued than that of whites. On many of the items listed in Table 3.1 there is a gap of 10 percent or more between the two racial groups. The percentage of blacks and whites choosing the most patriotic or chauvinistic response option differed significantly in 44 percent of the thirty-two items (both national and Los Angeles surveys) included in the table. However, it is important to underline that such differences usually are due to the greater reluctance of blacks to choose the most positive of the response options available, not widespread preferences for manifestly negative positions.

Specific examples make both points. The 2004 ANES had a fairly substantial number of blacks ($N = 180$) and so presumably yields reasonably reliable estimates. This survey shows a racial gap to leading symbols of nationhood. Whereas 91 percent of whites had felt extremely or very strong love for their country, 81 percent of blacks did. In the 2009 ANES, 75 percent of whites said they loved their country a great deal, compared to 57 percent of blacks ($N = 273$ in the sample), and in the 2012 ANES the 59 percent of blacks ($N = 952$ in the sample) saying they loved their country was 10 points lower than the figure for whites ($N = 3,256$ in entire sample).[19]

There is a more noticeable and consistent racial gap in patriotic sentiment when the flag is the symbolic representation of national attachment than when respondents are simply asked about feelings of closeness, love, or pride. In the 1992 ANES, whites were 30 percent more likely to say they felt extremely or very good when they saw the American flag flying (83 to 53 percent); in 2004 the margin was 86 to 61 percent; and in 2009, where the second warmest response option was the more tepid moderately good rather than very good, the racial gap among those choosing only extremely good was 71 to 45 percent. These gaps showed up again in the 2012 ANES, where 76 percent of whites and 59 percent of blacks said that seeing the flag made them feel extremely or very good, a difference of 17 points. We speculate that the more measured response of blacks may partly reflect the partisan connotations of the flag. Since at least the 1950s, the political right has sought to appropriate the use of the flag as a symbol of national attachment and loyalty. Republicans and conservatives were also later enraged by the denigration of the flag by anti-Vietnam protestors and were the leading proponents of a constitutional amendment to ban flag burning. From the Reagan elections on, Republican campaigns have forced Democratic presidential candidates on the defensive, most recently prodding candidate Obama to wear an American flag in his lapel as testimony to his patriotism.

---

[19] The 1996 GSS had a relatively small subsample of blacks ($N = 111$), and one must be cautious about estimates based on so few respondents.

Given the wide racial gap in party affiliation, it is worth asking whether the difference in feelings about the flag disappears if one compares only black and white Democrats. Controlling for party identification, however, diminishes but does not eliminate the racial divide in this domain: in the 2012 ANES, the overall racial gap of 17 percent in love for the flag is reduced to 8 percent among Democrats. For the question regarding love for America, the racial gap narrows from 10 to 5 percent when only Democrats are considered. This both indicates the presence of partisan differences in patriotism among whites and reaffirms the distinctiveness of black feelings about the flag, a symbol of a nation whose founding depended on the acceptance of slavery.[20]

In Los Angeles, as in the nation as a whole, blacks are nearly as likely as whites to express positive feelings about most symbols of American nationhood. For example, as can be seen in the second panel of Table 3.1, blacks in the Los Angeles surveys tend also to be proud of America: 75 percent said either "extremely proud" or "very proud," compared to 80 percent of the whites. This high level of attachment among blacks recurs on most of the LACSS items, with the single exception that a rather large minority of blacks (34 percent, compared to 17 percent of whites) agree that America is not a uniquely wonderful country. Still, just as in the national data, the Los Angeles surveys reveal less intense patriotism among blacks than whites. Significant racial differences also emerge on most of the LACSS items in respondents' opting for the most extremely patriotic position (strongly agree, extremely proud, strongly disagree). In terms of love for America and finding the flag moving, the races differ by 72 to 62 percent, and 53 to 43 percent, respectively.

The racial gap in national identity seems quite durable, but so too is the high level of overall patriotism among both blacks and whites over the past two decades. Responses to identical 1992 and 2004 ANES items showed little change among whites, with a movement of only 91 to 92 percent in expressions of love of country and 83 to 86 percent in warm feelings for the flag. In 1992, blacks' patriotism had been more tepid than whites'. But movements in black attitudes over this period on these two items were quite sharply in the direction of greater, not less, patriotism. Differences in question wording notwithstanding, the latest 2012 ANES shows evidence of continued high levels of patriotism for both whites and blacks, compared to the 1992 ANES study, as can be seen in Table 3.1. So, as for trends in popular feeling, there is no systematic support for the hypothesis of declining patriotism over time.

Rather than showing steady erosion, patriotism surged after the terrorist attacks on America on September 11, 2001. Symbolic attachment to the country clearly strengthened in the aftermath of this tragedy.[21] Naturally, on indicators

---

[20] Randall Kennedy, *The Persistence of the Color Line: Racial Politics and the Obama Presidency* (New York: Pantheon, 2011).

[21] See, e.g., Deborah J. Schildkraut, "The More Things Change ... American Identity and Mass and Elite Responses to 9/11," *Political Psychology* 23, no. 3 (2009): 511–35.

that previously had recorded almost universal identification with America, ceiling effects precluded much post-9/11 change. In the 2002 ANES, conducted a year after 9/11, 91 percent of the sample said their love for the United States was either extremely or very strong, quite similar to the 1992 89 percent ten years earlier. But on indicators originally yielding less extreme levels of attachment (not show in Table 3.1), more change occurred. A post 9/11 poll, conducted in June 2003, found that 70 percent of a national sample felt either extremely or very proud to be an American, compared to 55 percent in January 2001. In addition, the proportion denying that there are aspects of America to be ashamed of jumped from 18 percent in 1996 to 40 percent in late 2001.[22] Clearly, events can greatly increase the salience of patriotic sentiment and raise (or presumably lower) the scope and intensity of national attachment.

PATRIOTISM OR CHAUVINISM?

Does the strong emotional identification with their country among most Americans extend beyond a patriotic love of one's own country and its way of life to chauvinism, an aggressive sense of superiority to other nations? There is no logical connection between identification with the in-group and hostility toward others – patriots need not be bigots.[23] But there may be a general psychological link. The GSS questions recorded in Table 3.1 allow comparison of the level of love for one's country to the level of support for chauvinistic sentiments.

White Americans do have a pervasively strong belief that America is a better country than most: 40 percent of whites in 1996 and 42 percent in 2004 strongly agreed that America is superior, as shown in Table 3.1. But that admiration of the nation does not translate into an equally universal belief that other countries should change to be just like America: only 15 percent of whites in 1996 and 17 percent in 2004 agreed strongly that the world would be a better place if people from other nations were more like Americans. Nor does it indicate a consensus that America should try to dominate other nations: only 12 percent of whites in 1996 and 13 percent in 2004 agreed strongly that America should follow its own interests, even if this leads to conflicts with other countries. And only 10 percent of whites in each year concurred strongly with the diagnostic indicator of blind patriotism, the statement that people should support their own country even if it is in the wrong. A 2009 ANES question asked how strongly people felt they should support the country, regardless of whether it is right or wrong. Asked this way, whether one's country actually was in the wrong is left

---

[22] These are results from a national survey conducted by the National Opinion Research Center.

[23] Rui J. P. De Figuereido Jr. and Zachary Elkins, "Are Patriots Bigots? An Inquiry into the Vices of In-Group Pride," *American Journal of Political Science* 47, no. 1 (2003): 171–88; Leonie Huddy and Nadia Khatib, "American Patriotism, National Identity, and Political Involvement," *American Journal of Political Science* 51, no. 1 (2007): 63–77.

somewhat ambiguous, and a larger proportion, 50 percent of whites, expressed the need to give seemingly unquestioning support (24 percent extremely strongly and 26 percent very strongly). However, although some Americans do link pride in their own country to a belief in its supremacy, this group remains a minority. For the majority, the nearly universal love of country does not lead to a jingo-istic, blind version of patriotism.

The 1996 and 2004 GSS included a sufficient number of items to allow for a more systematic analysis of the relationship between national pride and chauvinism. These surveys asked respondents about their level of pride in 10 specific political, economic, and cultural considerations about the United States: democratic performance, global influence, the economy, the Social Security system, science and technology, sports, arts and literature, armed forces, history, and fairness to social groups. Asking about specific aspects of the nation's political and social life produces more refined and complex responses than simply eliciting diffuse emotional reactions to abstract symbols of nationhood such as America, the flag, or our country. These single-item measures tend to crowd responses to the most positive category, which compresses estimated differences between groups. This tendency is reduced by the greater concreteness of the objects of these indicators of pride and by the fact that the list includes elements such as the military and Social Security that appeal to different ideo-logical perspectives and to both constructive and "blind" patriots.[24]

In Figure 3.1, we compare pride in specific domains of American life between 1996 and 2004 and between white and black respondents. We contrast the unmistakably positive "very proud" responses with the two combined negative "not very proud" and "not at all" answers, leaving out the more ambiguous if often well-populated "somewhat proud" category. This approach better captures the intensity of patriotic feelings across domains and over time. Showing the balance of opinion by computing the differential in the percentages of prideful respondents records the trend in patriotism among each racial group.

Large majorities of whites say they are very proud of the history of America as a whole, of the country's scientific and technological achievements, and the armed forces. In these domains, almost no critical feelings were expressed. Pluralities of whites also said they were very proud about domains of national life that are either subjects of partisan debate, such as the quality of democracy and economic achievement, or narrower subdomains that arguably engage less than the entire society, such as sports and arts and literatures. In two instances, each related to politically charged policies or racially tinged outcomes, the consensus is more negative. In both 1996 and 2004, less than 15 percent of whites said they were very proud of the country's Social Security system, pre-sumably because of its well-publicized fiscal difficulties in the future. And slightly more than 20 percent said they were very proud of the nation's record in terms

---

[24] Smith and Kim, "National Pride in Comparative Perspective."

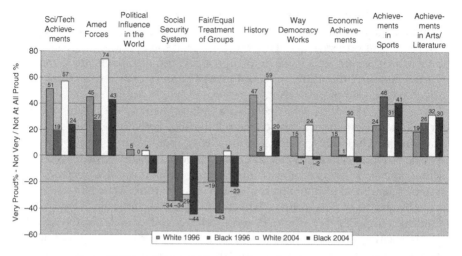

FIGURE 3.1. Foci of National Pride in America, by Ethnicity. Figures are for "net pride" created by subtracting the proportion of respondents who say they are "not very" or "not at all" proud from those who say they are "very proud" of America's achievement in a particular domain in response to: "How proud are you of America in each of the following? Very proud, somewhat proud, not very proud, or not proud at all? The items are as follows: its scientific and technological achievements; America's armed forces; its political influence in the world; its Social Security system; its fair and equal treatment of all groups in society; its history; the way democracy works; its economic achievements; its achievements in sports; its achievements in the arts and literature."

Note: All black–white differences are significant at $p < .05$ except the following: Armed Forces 1996; Political Influence in the World 1996; Social Security System 1996 and 2004; Achievements in Sports 2004; Achievements in the Arts and Literature 1996 and 2004.

of fair and equal treatment of all groups, perhaps thinking of the nation's troubled history of the treatment of black Americans. Indeed, negative feelings outnumbered expressions of pride when it came to Social Security (in both 1996 and 2004) and fairness toward all groups (in 1996). In all other cases, the balance of white opinion tilted, sometimes heavily, toward pride (as shown by the percentage difference between "very proud" and "not proud" answers).

Figure 3.1 sharpens the evidence of racial differences cited earlier. Blacks and whites expressed a substantially different pattern of judgments about specific domains of American political and cultural life. Whites tended to express pride in most of the ten areas evaluated. Blacks were generally positive about such universalistic domains as the armed forces and science and technology. As with responses to diffuse measures of patriotism, however, the balance of opinion among blacks generally was much less one-sided than among whites. They were slightly more proud than whites of the nation's achievements in sports and, in 1996, in the arts and literature, perhaps because these are domains to which blacks now have access and where they are well represented. More notably, however, many more blacks than whites are not proud of the history of America. They held distinctively negative attitudes about the nation's record in the area of equal treatment and have obviously ambivalent assessments about the closely related domains of democratic performance and economic achievement. Where the balance of opinion among blacks tilts toward pride, it is a more muted statement of positive opinion than the collective outlook of whites. And among blacks there were more cases where the balance of opinion actually is negative – political influence in the 2004 GSS, Social Security in both 1996 and 2004, fairness and equality in both years, the way democracy works in both years, and economic achievements in 2004 only. In six out of ten cases in 1996 and seven out of ten in 2004, the racial differences in pride are statistically significant, and in only one case – sports in 1996 – were blacks significantly more positive than whites.

Looking at change between 1996 and 2004, any shifts in opinion tended to be small, although there generally were more positive responses in 2004, which again can perhaps be attributed to 9/11 and its aftermath. The clearest evidence of this dealt with pride in the nation's armed forces, newly engaged in the wars in Afghanistan and Iraq; the proportion of white respondents saying they were very proud jumped from 53 to 78 percent. The trends in black and white opinion between 1996 and 2004 were quite similar, and blacks also become noticeably more proud of America's armed forces.

These indicators of pride in diverse domains of national life confirm that the sense of national attachment among blacks, although positive overall, is less consistent and less passionate than that of whites. Their more muted expressions of pride are especially clear in areas that relate most directly to blacks' disadvantaged status in the society. Their positive views of many mainstream institutions is tempered by a critical assessment of the country's practices and history from the perspective of a distinctive racial group, as both the politicized group consciousness paradigm and multiculturalist ideology would suggest. But the persistent evidence that blacks and whites share a strong emotional attachment to the country means that it would be misleading to interpret these differences as a sign of pervasive black alienation or the dangerous presence of an ethnically based unpatriotic group in the country.

We constructed composite measures of national pride and chauvinism in the 1996 and 2004 GSSs.[25] Aggregate levels of both national pride and chauvinism are high, with mean scores of 70 and 76 for patriotism in 1996 and 2004, respectively,

[25] See Tom W. Smith and Lars Jarkko, "National Pride: A Cross-National Analysis," *GSS Cross-National Report No. 19* (Chicago: NORC, 1998); and Tom W. Smith and Seokho Kim, "National Pride in Comparative Perspective." The national pride index gave responses to each of ten items as 1 (no pride at all) to 4 (very proud) score, summed these, and then rescored the total, standardizing for the number of items, to create a measure ranging from 0 (low pride) to 100 (high pride). The same procedure was used to create a chauvinism index comprising five items: "I would rather be a citizen of the United States ...;" "there are some things about the United States that make me ashamed ..." (reverse scoring); "the world

and slightly lower mean scores of 61 and 63 for chauvinism for the full sample of respondents in 1996 and 2004. Both the "constructive" and "blind" versions of patriotism rose during the period that encompassed 9/11, a finding that parallels the rise in generalized affect toward the country revealed in survey questions about the country and the flag discussed in connection with Table 3.1. Whites, averaging 71 on the pride scale in 1996 and 77 in 2004, displayed more pride by conventional statistical standards in both years than blacks, who averaged 66 in 1996 and 69 in 2004. Although both groups showed significant increases in national pride between 1996 and 2004, whites may have been more moved by 9/11 and also less disaffected by the behavior of the Bush administration and thus maintained a larger increase over 1996 than blacks. Whites' 64 mean chauvinism score in 2004 was also higher than blacks' 59, indicating a gap that had not existed in the 1996 survey, where the group means were a nearly identical 61.

The International Social Survey Program (of which the GSS is a part) administered the same national pride and chauvinism items to respondents in twenty different national samples in Europe, Australia, Canada, New Zealand, Japan, and the Philippines. Those who worry that patriotism in the United States is declining should be reassured by these comparative data. In 1996, even before 9/11, the United States ranked second in patriotism to Ireland and second in chauvinism to Austria. In 2004, the United States ranked first on both dimensions, registering the largest aggregate shift in the positive direction of any country. In the 2004 study, the United States ranked first in its citizens' assessment of the specific domains of democratic performance, political influence, economic achievement, and the armed forces. It ranked second with regard to its history, third in the fair treatment of all groups, and seventh with respect to pride in the Social Security system. It appears, then, that even when American respondents are critical and disappointed with their country's achievements or behavior in particular domains, their overall attitudes toward their country are generally more positive and forgiving than those of citizens of most other countries.

The generalized feeling of emotional attachment to America recorded in Table 3.1 carries over to judgments about most specific features of national experience. For example, in the 2004 survey, the correlation between the question asking about felt closeness to America is correlated .38 (Pearson's r) with the ten-item national pride index. National pride and chauvinism also are positively correlated (.50 in 1996 and .45 in 2004), a further reflection that a common emotional thread runs through these diverse measures of attachment to the nation.

would be a better place if people from other countries were more like Americans"; "generally speaking the United States is a better country than most ..."; and "people should support their country even if the country is in the wrong." The internal consistency of these scales is more robust for national pride than for chauvinism, perhaps because of the more similar response alternatives on the former items: alpha for national pride is .81 in the 1996 and .80 in 2004, and alpha for chauvinism is .58 in 1996 and .65 in 2004.

THE ASSIMILATION OF NEW IMMIGRANTS

Among the leading issues in debates about contemporary immigration is whether the newcomers from Latin America and Asia are assimilating. To answer this, of course, means asking assimilation to "what." In the context of this chapter, the "what" refers to attachment to the United States. The criterion for full assimilation would be the point at which an immigrant stream has the same level of affection for and loyalty to America as groups with long histories in the country. But assimilation is a process that takes place over time, and no one should expect the newly arrived immigrant to adopt new values and identifications immediately upon arrival. Rather, the assimilation paradigm assumes that predictors of integration such as length of time living in the United States, being born in the United States, and naturalization, to mention just a few, will be associated with a stronger sense of American identity.

Unfortunately, the data required to test this assimilation hypothesis are not plentiful. The national surveys we are analyzing typically have too few respondents of either Latino or Asian origin to generate reliable estimates. The exceptions in Table 3.1 are the Latino data in the 2009 ($N = 171$) and 2012 ($N = 922$) ANES surveys, and they do not include noncitizens. Moreover, the available national surveys targeted for Latinos and Asians specifically have limited relevant items. Neither the 2000 or 2008 national surveys of Asian-origin respondents nor the 2006 National Latino Survey, both now available for secondary analysis, included questions about patriotism or emotional attachment to the United States, apart from a question asking strength of American identity and another asking primacy of American identity relative to national origin or pan-ethnic identification. However, we should note that the earlier 1989 Latino National Political Survey concluded that Latinos are as patriotic as whites once differences in background and nativity are taken into account, a finding that comports with the assimilation paradigm.[26]

The data reported in Table 3.1 do suggest that, when immigrants are included, Latino respondents in the aggregate are consistently less strongly attached to the United States than are whites. In the 2009 ANES, 64 percent of Latino respondents, all citizens, reported they loved the United States a great deal, and 59 percent said that seeing the American flag generally made them feel extremely good. In 2012, 58 percent of Latinos reported loving the United States, and a higher 73 percent said seeing the American flag made them feel extremely or very good. The 2009 proportions are about 12 percent less patriotic than whites but slightly more positive (7 percent and 14 percent, respectively) than blacks. The white–Latino

---

[26] Rodolfo O. De la Garza, Angelo Falcon, and Chris F. Garcia, "Will the Real Americans Please Stand Up: Anglo and Mexican-American Support of Core American Political Values," *American Journal of Political Science* 40, no. 2 (1996): 335–51. This is largely confirmed in a later study with a 2004 national survey. See Deborah J. Schildkraut, *Americanization in the Twentieth Century: Public Opinion in the Age of Immigration* (New York: Cambridge University Press 2011).

TABLE 3.2. *Patriotism: Latinos by Immigration Status, and All Whites*

	Latinos			Whites
	Noncitizens (%)	Naturalized (%)	U.S.-Born (%)	(%)
Patriotism: Positively worded items				
I have great love for America (percent strongly agree)	52	66[a]	61	72[a]
How proud are you to be an American? (percent extremely or very)	35	64	79[a]	80[a]
I find the sight of the American flag very moving (percent strongly agree)	44	52[a]	51[a]	53[a]
Minimum *N*	241	91	129	548
Deny Criticism				
America not particularly wonderful country (percent strongly disagree)	18	33	61[a]	61[a]
Flag should not be treated as a sacred object (percent strongly disagree)	11[b]	13[b]	41[a]	30[a]
Other countries are better places to live than United States (percent strongly disagree)	17[b]	26[b]	51[a]	51[a]
Minimum *N*	100	39	71	273

Entries within any given row that share the same superscript are not significantly different ($p < .05$).
Source: Positive assertions: Los Angeles County Social Survey (LACSS) cumulative file (1997–2000); negative assertions: 1998 LACSS.

gap on the love of country item persisted in 2012, but Latinos were only minimally lower than whites in good feelings toward the flag.

The LACSS data we collected beginning in 1994 include Latinos and Asians, citizens and noncitizens alike. These data also show that as a whole Latinos and Asians (data not shown), like blacks, were consistently less patriotic than whites. For example, only 53 percent of the Latinos and 59 percent of the Asians said they were extremely or very proud to be an American, compared to 80 percent of the whites. On five of the six LACSS items measuring attachment to America, Latinos were less positive than whites, as can be seen in Table 3.2.

However, when one takes immigration status into account, support for the assimilation paradigm among Latinos is clear, and their apparent lower attachment to the nation essentially disappears. U.S.-born Latinos achieve the criterion for complete assimilation cited earlier, averaging about the same attachment to America as do whites on all six LACSS questions.[27] Across the but one of the six questions, U.S.-born Latinos show significantly more attachment to America than do naturalized citizens. They in turn show more attachment than do noncitizens. Most of these latter differences are also significant. Relatively new arrivals to the country unsurprisingly do not immediately reorient their ingroup attachments, but later generations increasingly endorse patriotic sentiments and soon are indistinguishable from whites.

We developed a patriotism scale, running from a minimum of zero to a maximum of 100, from the LACSS data based on agreeing with three positive assertions: I am proud to be an American, I have great love for America, and I find the sight of the flag very moving. The differences between racial and ethnic groups in scores on this scale confirm what was shown by the frequency distributions of Table 3.2. Although whites (mean patriotism = 87) again express significantly more patriotism than blacks (mean patriotism = 80), the more important fact for present purposes is that the psychological incorporation of immigrants is clearly ongoing. Native-born Latinos (mean patriotism = 85) express almost exactly the same level of attachment to the United States as whites, and the patriotic outlook of even naturalized Latinos (mean patriotism = 84) in the Los Angeles County samples is very similar to of that of those born in the United States. In contrast, noncitizen Latinos (mean patriotism = 77) are significantly less patriotic than blacks, as well as than the other Latino groups. These noncitizens tend to have spent less time in the United States, are less fluent in English, and understandably are more likely to think of themselves as still belonging to their country of origin and hoping to return there. Although the small number of cases ($N = 94$) makes assertions about Asian Americans (mean patriotism = 79) tentative at best, 54 percent of those born in the United States versus 14 percent of the recent immigrants were above the median in patriotism on this three-item measure, paralleling the Latino data.

IS PATRIOTISM SLIPPING IN THE VANGUARD OF THE FUTURE?

Racial conflict and the failure of new immigrants to assimilate are two of the putative causes of a fragmented American future in which attachment to the nation as a whole will have declined. Another oft-cited reason for the weakening of American national identity is the changing content of political socialization – that is, the flow of communications from family, schools, and mass media – that mold the political values and identifications of people from childhood on. Critics

---

[27] Only one of the differences between whites and native-born Latinos is statistically significant.

of multiculturalism have argued that new norms of political discourse consider the open expression of national pride as somewhat unseemly.

Moreover, attention to diversity and the role of minority groups in American political history – central aspects of soft multiculturalism – have become increasingly universal in the curricula of America's schools and universities.[28] Promoting positive views of diversity has an especially prominent place on many college campuses. College websites often have a link outlining their multifaceted contributions to diversity; many have freshman orientation programs that highlight race and ethnicity and promote intergroup tolerance rather than conflict, and some colleges, such as the University of California, Berkeley, require a course about diversity in America as a graduation requirement.[29] At the high school level, battles over the history curriculum generally have resulted in a movement to revise history textbooks to include a multicultural emphasis on race, class, and gender and to develop standards that highlight both the mistreatment of minorities and their contributions.[30]

Not surprisingly, this movement to modify the standards for teaching American history was controversial and became involved in the "culture wars" of the 1990s. Gary Nash, a prominent historian and leader of a professional task force to recommend national history standards, was attacked in 1994 by Lynne Cheney, wife of the future vice president, for proposing a "grim and gloomy" version of American history that downplayed the achievements of heroes like George Washington and Ulysses Grant to accentuate the negative and embrace political correctness.[31] Nevertheless, some years later, Nash pointed out that whereas resistance was ongoing, textbooks embodying the new standards were widely used throughout the country.[32]

To the extent that media and academic elites have embraced multiculturalism's emphasis on ethnic identity and devaluation of a common national culture, as conservative critics have charged, the impact on public attitudes should be most pronounced among the young and highly educated, the groups most likely to have been exposed to these ideas. Indeed, a study by Dennis Chong based on the 1994 GSS argues that those educated at elite colleges after 1986 are more likely than their peers to favor policies promoted by multiculturalists, among others, such as bilingualism and the maintenance of minority cultures.[33] This is part of a more general generational shift that has seen young and better educated whites become more liberal in their racial attitudes and in their attitudes about

---

[28] Nathan Glazer, *We Are All Multiculturalists Now*.

[29] Ibid.

[30] For an overview of the diverse variants of "multicultural education," see Joe Kincheloe and Shirley Steinberg, *Changing Multiculturalism* (London: Open University Press 1997).

[31] Lynne Cheney, "The End of History," *Wall Street Journal*, October 20, 1994.

[32] Gary B. Nash, Charlotte Crabtree, and Ross E. Dunn, *History on Trial: Culture Wars and the Teaching of the Past* (New York: Alfred A. Knopf, 1997).

[33] Dennis Chong, "Free Speech and Multiculturalism In and Out of the Academy," *Political Psychology* 27, no. 1 (2006): 29–54.

sexual orientation.[34] However, Chong also finds that such recent college graduates are less likely to endorse strong patriotic sentiments. To the extent that there has been a fundamental, generational change in the content of political socialization and the development of new norms that regard the frank expression of national pride as misguided, then the replacement of patriotic older cohorts by more skeptical youngsters and the continuing spread of higher education may indeed result in diminishing the collective strength of American national identity, much as Huntington predicted.[35]

A White Vanguard?

To test what we term this "vanguard" hypothesis of declining patriotism, we compare age and education groups. Once again, we conduct this analysis *within* racial and ethnic groups. Looking first at whites, then, is there evidence for declining patriotism among the so-called vanguard of the American public? An array of national surveys and the LACSS polls show that young whites do attach less emotional significance to their American identity than do older whites. The generational differences are sometimes quite large, and sometimes more modest. Table 3.3 summarizes these differences for questions about emotional attachment to the country and feelings about the flag in the national surveys. For example, 55 percent of the white respondents in the 1996 GSS over the age of 60 said that they felt very close to America, compared to just 24 percent of those less than 30 years old. In the 2004 GSS, the comparable figures were 69 percent and 34 percent. The comparable age differences on the GSS chauvinism and national pride scales average only 9 percent, though most are significant. On the ANES items regarding love of country and attachment to the flag, all eight age differences are significant, averaging 27 percent. So the generational differences are quite consistent and very large on the items measuring generalized emotional attachment to the nation.

The vanguard hypothesis about the lower national attachment of the college-educated whites receives some support in the national surveys, but at a considerably weaker level. The GSS closeness and chauvinism measures yield significant differences between the college educated and those without a college degree, but the pride measure does not. Overall, the educational differences average only 6 percent. In the ANES, half the education differences are significant, but they average only 7 percent.

A more telling test of the vanguard hypothesis would examine the joint effects of youth and higher education, that slumping levels of patriotism should be most pronounced among the young who have college degrees because of the spread of multiculturalist ideologies in today's colleges and universities. We had sufficient

---

[34] Pew Research Center for the People and the Press, "In Gay Marriage Debate, Both Supporters and Opponents See Legal Recognition as 'Inevitable.'" June 6, 2013.

[35] Huntington, *Who Are We?*

numbers of such white respondents only in the national surveys. Accordingly, we cross-tabulated three age categories by having a college degree or not, yielding a typology with six categories. The key group included whites aged eighteen to twenty-nine with college degrees. Then we compared those six categories on the measures of national attachment shown in Table 3.3.

To make a long story short, we continued to see strong main effects of youth and little impact of higher education. But we found little that was distinctive about the key group, youths with college degrees. The education effects were no larger among the under-thirties than among those aged thirty to fifty-nine; the age differences between those two categories were the same among the college educated as among those with less education; and, among those aged eighteen to twenty-nine, the college-educated differed only minimally from those without college degrees, averaging just 3.9% less patriotic over the fourteen indicators shown in Table 3.3. So we conclude that generational differences in patriotism among whites are quite stable, but the expected role of multiculturalist-influenced higher education does not materialize.

Age differences remain robust among whites in the Los Angeles County surveys, although here too the educational differences are less pronounced, statistically significant only regarding feelings about the flag. Of those sixty and older, 86 percent strongly agreed that they had great love for the country, and 73 percent said that the flag stirred patriotic feelings in them. These fell to 53 percent and 38 percent, respectively, among the young.

So there is consistent evidence of a post-1960s countercultural norm showing weakened attachment to America among younger whites across almost all surveys, as Huntington had gloomily suspected. Remarkably, this less patriotic outlook remained intact in surveys conducted in an era far after Vietnam and before the unpopular disputed war in Iraq, suggesting that a new direction in political discourse indeed may be having an effect. However, there is little evidence of the hypothesized role of institutions of higher learning in damaging patriotism.

Black and Latino Vanguards

Among racial and ethnic minorities, do the youngest and best educated also show the least patriotism? In analyzing minority attitudes, we briefly look at the 2012 ANES, which included more than 952 black and 922 Latino respondents, and the Los Angeles data, which critically includes Latino noncitizens who were not sampled in the ANES. In the 2012 ANES, the sample of blacks under thirty was consistently less patriotic than their older counterparts. Perhaps the most telling datum is that only 44 percent of the black respondents in that survey said they loved the United States compared to 66 percent of those older than sixty. Younger blacks also were also considerably less enthusiastic about the flag. In the LACSS sample, younger blacks, like younger whites, were less likely to express pride in being an American or have strong positive feelings about the flag than older cohorts. However, as with whites, there is much less evidence of

TABLE 3.3. *Affective Attachment to America: The White Vanguard Hypothesis*

		Age			Education	
		18–29	30–59	60+	College+	< College Degree
GSS						
Close to America	1996	24%	34%	55%	32%	38%
(% very)	2004	34	58	69	48	60
Chauvinism (scale mean)	1996	57[a]	60[a]	67	54	63
	2004	58	64	68	58	67
Pride (scale mean)	1996	66	70	79	72	69
	2004	75[a]	77[ab]	79[b]	77[a]	78[a]
Minimum N		176	549	226	273	640
ANES						
Love for country	1992	47[a]	50[a]	70	50	58
(% extremely strong)	2004	50	64[a]	68[a]	60[a]	63[a]
	2009	48	74	89	71[a]	76[a]
	2012	48	69	81	68[a]	69[a]
Patriotic feelings for flag	1992	35[a]	42[a]	62	39	51
(% extremely good)	2004	44	60[a]	62[a]	54[a]	59[a]
	2009	51	71	81	63	75
	2012	30	43	57	36	49
Minimum N		125	321	148	175	318
LACSS						
Love for America	1997–99	53	72	86	68[a]	74[a]
(% strongly agree)						
Proud to be an American	1994, 1997	35	44	59	37[a]	34[a]
(% extremely proud)						
Feelings about the flag	1997–02	38	49	73	46	57
(% strongly agree)						
Minimum N		95	348	99	201	345

Notes: For the specific items, see Table 3.1. Age or education differences in a given row differ significantly ($p < .05$), unless entries share the same superscript. Chauvinism and Pride are additive indices consisting of five and ten items, respectively, standardized and rescored to vary between zero and one and then multiplied by one hundred. Data shown are scale means for indicated groups.
Sources: General Social Survey (GSS) 1996 and 2004; American National Election Studies (ANES) 1992, 2004, and 2009; proud to be American item 1994, 1997 Los Angeles County Social Survey (LACSS); love for the country item 1997, 1998, 1999 LACSS; feelings about the flag item 1997–2002 LACSS. Note that the second-most patriotic response to the flag item in the 2009 ANES was "moderately good" rather than "very good," as in the 1992 and 2004 ANES, and the second-most patriotic response to the love of country item in the 2009 ANES was "a moderate amount" rather than "very good," as in the 1992 and 2004 ANES. In 2012, the highest response category for the "love of country" item was "love it" with next most patriotic response being "like it." Response categories for the flag item were the same as those in 1992 and 2004.

differences consistent with the educational component of the vanguard hypothesis among blacks: college graduates expressed nearly identical feelings about the flag and were in fact slightly more likely than those who did not finish college to say they loved the country.

For the Latino citizens sampled in the 2012 ANES, large age differences again appear: 44 percent of those under thirty said they loved the United States, compared to 68 percent of those older than sixty. Among those under thirty, 26 percent said they felt extremely good when they saw the American flag while among those over sixty this percentage more than doubled to 54 percent. Differences by one's level of education once again ran counter to the hypothesis that vanguards would manifest lower levels of patriotism. Those with a college degree expressed, if anything, slightly warmer feelings about the flag and love for the country.

The LACSS data, collected about a decade earlier, show a more mixed pattern of results. Latinos younger than thirty were no less likely than their older counterparts to express great pride in being an American. Education made no difference in feelings about the flag. In fact, among Latinos, education seems to push slightly in the direction of a greater attachment to America. Again we warn about small sample sizes, but this is further, if tentative, evidence that Latinos seem to be following the model of assimilation experienced by earlier European immigrants rather than tracking the more victimized and disaffected historical experience of blacks.

To test whether both youth and higher education independently erode Americans' identification with the nation, and to summarize these findings succinctly, we created a patriotism scale from the pride and flag items and estimated a multiple regression equation on the ANES and LACSS data within each ethnic group, as shown in Table 3.4. The age effects are very similar for all ethnic groups, with younger Americans consistently less patriotic. The education effects are consistently small and rarely significant, indicating little impact on patriotism among both whites and blacks, and education actually increases patriotism among Latinos in the Los Angeles sample, although only among the foreign-born.

This is an interesting departure from the vanguard hypothesis we began with: that longer immersion in the formal American educational system tends to weaken national attachment. There is little evidence for that proposition in any of the major ethnic groups. There is some reversal among Latinos, but only in the Los Angeles data and only among the foreign-born, of whom few attend four-year colleges. True, young Latinos are subject to the same cultural streams that erode patriotic sentiment as their black and white counterparts. But, overall, growing up in America seems to end up in the feeling of belonging to America, contrary to the politicized group consciousness paradigm.

Huntington's concern about challenges to national attachment in America may not have been hollow, but the group he should have worried about is not only, at present, the Latino immigrants but rather the younger cohorts of all ethnic groups. One possible interpretation of the results is that the zeitgeist of modulated feelings about the country has diffused throughout the entire younger generation rather

TABLE 3.4. *The Vanguard Hypothesis: Predictors of Patriotism*

			Latinos			
	Whites	Blacks	All	U.S. Born	Foreign Born	Asians
2012 ANES						
Age	.07***	.09***	.07***	.09***	.02	–
Education	−.02***	.02	.02	.02	.03	–
Adjusted R^2	.07	.08	.05	.07	.00	–
N	3,209	939	898	613	282	–
LACSS						
Age	.04***	.04***	.04***	.03**	.05***	.05***
Education	−.01	−.02	.03***	.02	.02**	−.02
Adjusted R^2	.07	.07	.05	.04	.06	.08
N	938	410	839	262	571	143

Each column is a separate regression equation. Entries are standardized regression coefficients. The dependent variable is the two-item patriotism scale. Age is the 3-category variable described in Table 3.3 and education a dummy variable (college degree vs. no college degree). All foreign-born Latinos in the 2012 ANES are naturalized citizens.
*** $p < .001$ ** $p < .01$ * $p < .05$
Source: 2012 American National Election Studies (ANES) and Los Angeles County Social Survey (LACSS), 1998, 1999, 2000, 2002.

than just the college-educated through the influence of the media and other modes of popular culture. Further research will be required to determine whether this is a recent development affecting current youthful generations who have grown up in an era of greatly increased cultural diversity. Alternatively, it may be the continuation of longer-standing trends, such as the waning influence of the patriotism inspired in earlier generations by World War II and/or the erosion of patriotism among the young that accompanied the Vietnam War.

WHAT DOES IT MEAN TO BE AN AMERICAN? BOUNDARIES OF NATIONHOOD

A strong sense of national identity indicates solidarity with other Americans and implies a willingness to act on their behalf. This sense of fraternity, however, rests on more than a legalistic response to the question, "Are you an American?" or a love of the abstract "our country." Identities have normative content. They attain meaning through the qualities – physical image, social characteristics, personal habits, character traits, or values – that define group membership.[36]

[36] Rogers Brubaker, "The Manichean Myth: Rethinking the Distinction between 'Civic' and 'Ethnic' Nationalism," in *Nation and National Identity: The European Experience in Perspective*, ed. Kriesi Hanspeter et al. (Zurich: Ruegger, 1999), 55–71. See also Michael Walzer, *What It Means to Be an American* (New York: Marsilio Publishers, 1992).

Political cohesion and feelings of mutual obligation among group members are more likely to emerge when the subjective meaning of a group's identity is shared.

"What does it mean to be an American?" is a recurring question for historians, in part because the country has remade itself through successive waves of immigration and in part because beliefs about the attributes of American nationhood have been varied, malleable, and contested. So it is possible for people who love their country and prioritize their national identity above all others to use different criteria for establishing the subjective and legal boundaries of nationhood, for dividing "us" from "them." The "circle of we" can be more or less permeable, and this feature plus the extent to which normative conceptions of American identity are widely shared should have implications for group relations and public policies relating to immigration, citizenship, and access to social rights.

We began by contrasting two normative prototypes for American national identity: cosmopolitan liberalism, which emphasizes commitment to egalitarian democratic political values and individualism as the traits defining a true American, and nativism (or ethnocultural nationalism), which holds that only people with certain ethnic characteristics can become acculturated to American values and fully belong.[37]

The liberal and nativist images of America dovetail with the analytic distinction between civic and ethnic nations that remains the dominant theoretical distinction in the literature on nationalism. The ethnic nation, exemplified by Germany and Japan, defines membership on the principle of descent. In those cases, the nation is a marriage of blood and soil; primordial criteria determine whether one is deemed a national, and citizenship is based on your parents' ancestry, not simply on being born in the country. The boundaries of the civic nation, by contrast, are permeable. In principle, anyone can belong provided he or she accepts the prevailing values and institutions. A civic identity thus is voluntarist in nature and far more open to immigration. Writing about American identity, historians often refer to it as an ideology or creed.[38] In the civic nation, birthright, *jus soli*, provides legal status as a citizen.

The ethnic and civic models of nationhood must be viewed as ideal types rather than accurate descriptions of particular national identities.[39] Rhetoric and reality often diverge when it comes to policies governing nationhood. For example, supposedly civic nations like the United States and France have had quite restrictive immigration and citizenship policies at various points in their history and still do.[40] As we commented in Chapter 1, most nations have a core ethnic group whose language and customs shape expectations of what it

---

[37] Ibid.
[38] Ibid.
[39] Yack, "The Myth of the Civic Nation."
[40] Smith, *Civic Ideals*, documents this for the United States.

means to act like a "national." Huntington[41] argues further that, for ordinary people, commitment to highly abstract civic principles is not engaging enough to create deep feelings of national solidarity; a common cultural code that quickly identifies "we" and "they" is necessary. For him, then, a common culture, an amalgam of religiosity, language, and political values, is required to unify the increasingly diverse American nation. Huntington argues that America's common culture rests on the values of the Anglo-Protestant ethnic "core" of the United States at its founding. This conception of nationhood can be inclusive, in that ethnicity does not preclude acculturation, or exclusive, in that certain ethnic groups are deemed too culturally dissimilar to adopt the dominant cultural code. Which conception of national identity prevails should have implications for a range of public policies.

The classification of countries as either civic or ethnic, just as the characterization of American identity as either liberal or nativist, generally is based on the content of laws, literature, official statements, and the writings and speeches of politicians, intellectuals, and publicists. Whether these alternative conceptions of national identity recur in mass public opinion is a separate question. The methodological approach for gauging the subjective conceptions of nationhood among ordinary citizens was pioneered by Citrin, Reingold, and Green in 1990, in a study catalyzed by ethnic change in California.[42] Distilling the themes animating the historical literature on the core of American identity, they developed a series of items asking people whether particular attributes were important for making someone a true American. The values of equal treatment, economic self-reliance, and political participation embodied the civic, creedal conception of nationhood described by observers from de Tocqueville to Huntington and Rogers Smith.[43] By contrast, being born in America and believing in God are particularistic characteristics that define a narrower, ethnic, and nativist definition of Americanness. The results of that survey showed that Californians believed that a wide range of attributes, both civic and ethnic, defined a true American but that the criteria of religion and nativity were the least likely to be endorsed.[44]

---

[41] Huntington, *Who Are We?*
[42] Jack Citrin, Beth Reingold, and Donald P. Green, "American Identity and the Politics of Ethnic Change," *Journal of Politics* 52 (1990): 1124–54.
[43] De Tocqueville, *Democracy in America*; Huntington, *Who Are We?*; Smith, "Beyond Tocqueville, Myrdal, and Hartz."
[44] Three fine recent books already cited have used this method to create similar measures of American identity. Schildkraut (*Americanization in the Twenty-First Century*) analyzes a 2004 national survey to develop indicators of liberal, ethnocultural, and civic republican conceptions of national identity and uses these to assess current attitudes about immigration. Theiss-Morse, *Who Counts as an American*, distinguishes between soft (civic) and hard (ascribed or ethnic) boundaries or nationhood and analyzes the antecedents and consequences of these outlooks. Wong, *Boundaries of Obligation in American Politics*, uses the GSS items to create a Traditional Americanism Index and asks how this conception of national identity relates to feelings of obligation to fellow citizens and opinions about foreigners. Clearly, some of their concerns overlap with our own, and we comment on their findings at several points. Nevertheless, the

A June 1991 California Poll asked 80 percent of a statewide cross-section of respondents an open-ended question about whether there are unique American qualities that make us different from citizens of other countries. Respondents were permitted to mention up to two specific qualities and by an overwhelming margin freedom and equality were named most often. The vast majority (85 percent of all the comments) described American uniqueness in favorable terms. Their cognitive content mostly invoked ideological themes familiar to any reader of de Tocqueville's classic *Democracy in America*. The dominant image portrays America as a locus of personal liberty and individual equality and opportunity. These responses to an open-ended question of a largely white sample reflect the dominance of the civic or creedal conception of Americans rather than an ethnic conception based on being Christian, white, or of Anglo-Saxon origins.

The 1991 and 1992 ANESs and the 1996 and 2004 GSSs used those earlier models to ask national samples to rate the importance of a set of specific qualities for being a true American. The qualities presented to them were drawn from both competing conceptions of American national identity linked to the civic–ethnic distinction. Virtually everyone interviewed accepted that prototypically American qualities do exist. The 1996 GSS sample rated seven attributes, and fully 43 percent of the respondents named at least five as very important for making someone a true American. Only 1 percent of this sample viewed all seven as not at all important. What this indicates is that people simultaneously can and do endorse multiple traditions of nationhood, viewing American nationality as an amalgam of civic values and ethnic attributes.

Figure 3.2 points to the normative primacy among whites of the civic conception of American identity emphasizing social equality, freedom of speech, political participation, and self-reliance. In the 1996 and 2004 GSSs, broadly inclusive civic aspects of American identity, such as American citizenship or simply feeling American, were more widely viewed as more important attributes of the true American than such ethnically exclusive qualities as being born in America, living most of one's life in America, or being a Christian. The 1992 ANES (results not shown in Figure 3.2 in part because the items and response categories differed from the GSS) affirms this conclusion: civic definitions such as treating people of all backgrounds equally, voting, freedom of speech, and trying to get ahead on one's own were more likely to be cited as extremely or very important for making someone a true American (average agreement of 76 percent and 86 percent) than were the more ethnicity-laden criteria of believing in God or speaking English (average agreement of 55 percent).

Figure 3.2 also shows that, between 1996 and 2004, there was a general shift in the direction of naming most of the listed attributes as important. We are tempted to explain this by the greater salience of national identity and unity in

main foci of this book – the management of plural identities and the impact of multiculturalism, especially within the major ethnic groups – are different and distinctive.

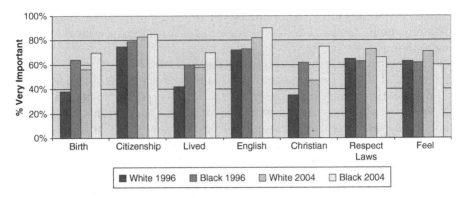

FIGURE 3.2. Normative Content of American Identity, by Ethnicity. The precise question wording is as follows: "Some people say that the following things are important for being truly American. Others say they are not important. How important do you think each of the following is?... to have been born in America; to have American citizenship; to have lived in America most of one's life; to be able to speak English; to be a Christian; to respect America's political institutions and laws; to feel American."
Note: All black–white differences are significant at the .05 level except the following: Citizenship 1996 and 2004, English 1996, Respect Laws 1996 and 2004, and Feel 1996.
Source: 1996 and 2004 General Social Surveys.

the aftermath of 9/11. Nevertheless, it is clear that from 1996 to 2004 more people named speaking English, being an American citizen, having been born in America, and living here all one's life as more important in making one a true American. This increase in the importance of qualities that immigrants are less likely to possess occurred among whites and the relatively small number of blacks in these surveys. This change, too, might most plausibly be explained by the increased suspicion of foreigners following 9/11.

In addition to the ANES and GSS results, the recent studies of Theiss-Morse and Schildkraut[45] confirm that Americans define national identity far more often in terms of the American creed, such as valuing the vote, civil liberties, equal opportunity, and individualism, than in ascriptive terms, such as being U.S.-born, white, English-speaking, and/or Christian. For example, Theiss-Morse reports that being white is named by less than 20 percent of respondents as a criterion of being a true American.[46] In her 2002 national survey, belief in equality was universally considered very important (93 percent), followed by respect for the law (73 percent) and speaking English (72 percent).[47] And although knowing the national language may appear to be an ascribed characteristic, in reality English is generally mastered in school by the offspring of

[45] Theiss-Morse, *Who Counts As an American?*; Schildkraut, *Americanization in the Twentieth Century.*
[46] Ibid.
[47] Ibid.

immigrants and is not a rigid boundary.[48] Indeed, comparative studies show that a common language is almost everywhere considered a critical aspect of nationhood.[49]

The fact that so many respondents name both civic and ethnic traits as attributes of Americanism suggests that many ordinary citizens do not sharply distinguish the multiple traditions or alternative conceptions of national identity in the nation's history.[50] Indeed, when one constructs indices of civic (respect laws and feel American) and ethnic (born in America and being a Christian) national identity in the 2004 GSS, they are positively correlated (.35).[51] Nevertheless, the data in numerous studies suggest that characterizing the United States as a civic nation reverberates in public opinion, as well as in elite behavior.

Although overall differences between blacks and whites regarding the traits making one a true American were slight, meaningful racial differences did emerge in three areas. Blacks felt considerably more intensely than whites that treating all equally was an extremely important attribute of a true American. In the 1992 ANES sample (not shown in Figure 3.2), blacks (65 percent) were more likely than whites (52 percent) to say that equality was extremely important. But the overwhelmingly native-born blacks also showed a surprisingly strong attraction to exclusionary and ethnocultural qualities, perhaps because that differentiates their own long-standing claim to Americanness from such claims made by more recent immigrants. Blacks were especially likely to emphasize the importance of being native-born (64 percent, as opposed to 38 percent for whites in the 1996 GSS) and of having lived in the United States for most of one's life (60 percent, as opposed to 42 percent for whites). Interestingly, blacks were also more inclined to impose the religious criterion of being a Christian (59 percent, compared to 34 percent for whites).

This pattern of demographic difference is confirmed by multiple regression analyses that estimate the effects of black and Hispanic ethnicity, age, and formal education on answers to the four-point questions about the importance of particular qualities for making someone a true American, using the 1992 ANES and the 1996 and 2004 GSS studies. After adjusting for the age and education of respondents, blacks and Latinos remain more likely than whites to ascribe great importance to the value of treating minorities equally. Interestingly, Latinos also are not more likely than whites to downplay the need to speak English well to be a true American, a fact we interpret as a commonsense understanding that, to become fully accepted in America and to get ahead, speaking English is essential. Finally, the multivariate analysis

---

[48] Jack Citrin, et al., "Testing Huntington."
[49] Gellner, *Nations and Nationalism*.
[50] Jack Citrin and Matthew Wright, "Defining the Circle of We: American Identity and Immigration Policy," *The Forum* 7, no. 3 (2009). Available online at http://www.bepress.com/forum/vol7/iss3/art6
[51] Ibid.

confirms the tendency of blacks to be more likely than whites to consider nativity, Christianity, and living in America as important for making one a true American.

Theiss-Morse also confirms that blacks are more likely than whites to cite being a Christian (69 to 33 percent), being born in America (56 to 32 percent), and speaking English (84 to 71 percent) for making one a true American. More generally, the ethnic criteria of national identity are more prevalent among people with less formal education and also are more matters of partisan contention than deep division between the white majority and racial minorities.[52] Whites themselves are sharply divided about the nativist criteria rather than acting as a unified group trumpeting their superior ethnic qualities and greater Americanness over those of ethnic and racial minorities.

An additional test of the vanguard hypothesis of weaker national identities among the young and well educated comes from analysis of how these groups conceive of American identity. An initial finding is that those younger than thirty and those with a college education are simply less likely to agree that there are distinctively American traits, qualities that are important for defining a true American. We created a measure comprising the number of times a respondent named one of the seven items proposed as attributes of true Americanism as very important. In every case, those younger than thirty and the college educated were significantly less likely to name any proposed criterion of American identity as important. The implication is that the underlying nationalist idea of Americans as a distinctive people, whether civic or ethnic, has less resonance among the young and well educated. Indeed, this result holds even when the criterion of Americanism is the innocuous civic notion of respect for laws and institutions, although the differences were greater for ethnic items such as Christianity and nativity, consistent with much other data showing greater nativism among the older and less educated.[53]

Is national attachment, defined as feelings of closeness to America, national pride, or chauvinism, more closely tied to liberal (civic) or nativist (ethnic) conceptions of national identity? The 2004 GSS study shows that those who express a strong sense of national attachment, whether measured by their feelings of closeness to America, their national pride score, or their chauvinism score, are more likely to say that *every* proposed criterion for being of a true American, civic or ethnic, is important. In contrast, chauvinism is more strongly related to believing that the ethnic traits of nativity, religion, living in the United States, and speaking English are more important attributes of nationhood than are national pride or simply feeling close to America. Overall, four aspects of national attachment – feelings of closeness, national pride, chauvinism, and a tendency to weigh ethnic features of Americanism more heavily than civic

---

[52] This is documented later.

[53] For example, Howard Schuman, et al., *Racial Attitudes in America: Trends and Interpretation*, Revised Edition (Cambridge, MA: Harvard University Press, 1997).

attributes – are positively correlated. However, the differences in the strength of these relationships do suggest that *how* nation is imagined as well as the *strength* of national attachment may matter for people's policy preferences, a topic addressed in Chapter 8.

CONCLUSION

This chapter explored various prognoses for declining national attachment in America – prognoses shared, interestingly, both by advocates of multiculturalism and their conservative critics who envisage an increasingly fragmented society. However, for the most part, our findings do not support these expectations. First, it is true that whites are more highly attached to symbolic representations of America than are other groups. However, we find, using a variety of indicators, that Americans of all ethnic and racial groups express very high levels of patriotic attachment to their country. In the aggregate, this attachment comes closer to constructive than blind patriotism in several respects. All groups are critical of America's shortcomings in providing equality to all. Most important, the ethnic and racial differences in patriotism are quite limited, although African Americans are somewhat more lukewarm than whites and more critical of America in domains to which they are historically attuned as salient to their group's status. But, to repeat, the majority outlook among blacks remains one of pride in most aspects of national life.

Second, there is some support for the black exceptionalism paradigm. Blacks, despite their overall positive attitude toward America, are less strongly patriotic than whites. And the LACSS data showed native-born Latinos also were more patriotic than blacks, almost all of whom were born in America. This suggests that the relatively impermeable color line that surely has mitigated patriotism among blacks is not perceived as a similar barrier for native-born Latinos.

Third, this chapter shows that the claim that Latino immigrants are not assimilating is belied by the evidence of how citizenship, nativity, and speaking English promotes patriotism among Latinos. The ongoing influx of Latino immigrants does mean that, at any given time, in the aggregate, Latinos will be less likely to define themselves as Americans and have the same level of patriotism as whites. But, over time, assimilation clearly is occurring, with the level of national attachment increasing as they spend more time in the United States and become culturally and socially integrated. Evidence of the stronger attachment to America of native-born as compared to foreign-born Latinos buttresses the superior explanatory power of the assimilation paradigm.

Fourth, there is mixed support for the vanguard hypothesis, the proposition that the young and/or college educated are less patriotic and more supportive of multiculturalism than their older and/or less-educated counterparts. This group is less likely to acknowledge that there is something unique about Americans as a people. Critics of multiculturalism are especially concerned that exposure to multiculturalist dogma in institutions of higher education will weaken a strong sense of American identity. We do find that patriotism is considerably weaker among the young than older Americans. But the college educated are only slightly less patriotic than the less educated. The lower level of national attachment among the young appears in all ethnic groups. Moreover, the young are less attached to America irrespective of their levels of education. So the segment of the vanguard hypothesis that looks to exposure to multiculturalist teaching in colleges and universities to explain lagging levels of patriotism among the youngest generation is not sustained. As a result, if the observed assimilative patterns persist, fears that more ethnic diversity in the United States will undermine patriotism seem overblown. If anything, the greater challenges are the greater disaffection of blacks and the detached outlook of the young in all groups.

Finally, this chapter explored the public's conceptions of what it means to be an American – the normative content of national identity. Here, the politicized group consciousness paradigm would expect group interests to dominate public attitudes. Whites would define a true American in self-promoting terms such as their race, nativity, or religion; blacks would emphasize equal treatment along with nativity and speaking English; Latinos and Asians would emphasize citizenship. The dominant finding in our data, however, is that all ethnic groups primarily define a true American in terms of the civic American creed, stressing the importance of treating people equally, working hard to get ahead, respecting American laws and institutions, and speaking English, rather than in purely ethnocultural terms.[54] Black exceptionalism does not extend to conceptions of the prototypical American. True, blacks tend to emphasize being born in America and a long history here as important for being a true American more than other groups. But this outlook, to some degree a reflection of group interest and history, differentiates them from recent immigrants more than from whites. Overall, the ethnic and racial differences in normative conceptions of American identity are quite small. In virtually every respect, the specter of ethnic balkanization in national attachment and beliefs about American identity is far more a chimera than an imminent reality. What remains a consistent cleavage is the greater reluctance of young and well-educated Americans to endorse the idea that there is a unique American identity automatically worthy of embrace.

---

[54] True, social desirability may be at work in limiting the number of people willing to say that being white defines the true American, but this kind of sensitivity surely cannot account for differences of more than 70 percent from the frequency of "civic" responses.

4

The Ethnic Cauldron and Group Consciousness

This chapter turns from patriotism to ethnic consciousness, the other side of the dialectic of nationality and ethnicity. Multiculturalism, in the sense of demands for group-conscious policies, was pushed onto the American political agenda by continuing racial inequalities, even after legal discrimination was ended, by the appearance of two new and growing "visible minorities" that had entered the United States because of immigration reform, and by the sense among many minority leaders that whites continued to resist strong government efforts aiming at compensatory redistribution of political and economic resources. Presumably, if the white majority readily accepted minorities' grievances, then there would be less pressure for group-based rights and other multiculturalist policies.

In Chapter 2 we suggested that the psychological platform or image of human nature embedded in ideological multiculturalism is the set of assumptions we described as a generic politicized group consciousness paradigm, specifying that people possess strong in-group loyalties that dominate political reactions when ethnic interests are engaged. But American public opinion has generally not been closely examined to determine how common those assumed psychological foundations are.[1]

The purpose of this chapter, therefore, is to determine the pervasiveness of the proximal subjective orientations that presumably are necessary to convert the realities of racial discrimination, demographic change, and white resistance into support for multiculturalism as a political ideology. That is, to what extent does the American public, particularly ethnic and racial minorities, possess the group-related orientations that would lay the psychological groundwork for the support of multiculturalism's emphasis on preserving cultural differences and subnational identifications? In this regard, Wong finds that ethnicity generally is not at the

---

[1] Wong, *Boundaries of Obligation in American Politics*, is a notable exception.

top of people's self-definition when they are given a choice among multiple social identities. Still, when in-group identities based on ethnicity are strong, do they spill over into negative feelings toward out-groups and in this way breed intergroup conflict?[2]

We begin by examining the extent to which Americans see ethnicity as an inherent and indelible source of cleavage and conflict. Do they perceive today's more culturally diverse America as an ethnic cauldron, bubbling over with group antagonism? If ethnic groups are widely seen as very different and in constant conflict, perhaps multiculturalism would provide welcome treaty-like agreements that allow all groups to peacefully, if somewhat uneasily, coexist.

Second, we assess the levels of ethnic and racial consciousness in America within the major ethnic groups, both absolute levels and the relative levels across groups. Are ethnic loyalties now so powerful, especially within minority groups, that they potentially threaten the unifying attachment to the nation examined in the preceding chapter? We examine group consciousness in terms of four components: self-categorization, strength of ethnic identity, sense of common fate, and perceived discrimination.

Third, we examine the sources of ethnic differences in-group consciousness in terms of the psychological hypotheses that we introduced in Chapter 2. To review, the politicized group consciousness paradigm generally views all ethnic and racial minority groups as relegated to subordinate niches in a rigid American hierarchy, and the resulting discrimination leads them to identify more powerfully with their own in-group. A contrasting assimilation paradigm suggests that immigrants may indeed enter the nation with dominant ethnic identities centering on their nations of origin. But that form of group consciousness may be transitory, as many of their native-born descendants gradually become integrated into the broader society. A partially overlapping approach, the black exceptionalism hypothesis, similarly predicts a tendency for immigrant groups to trend toward the white majority over time. But it would expect that the strongest racial group consciousness is to be found among African Americans, as a result of the pervasive prejudice and discrimination they have experienced over the past four centuries in America. The vanguard hypothesis looks for differences within ethnic groups in the strength of ethnic group consciousness, arguing that younger and better educated minorities may have become increasingly attached to their racial and ethnic in-groups as their primary social identities under the growing influence of multiculturalist ideology in educational and media institutions.

As will be seen, we find that some social psychological perspectives on intergroup relations present a somewhat overblown account of the extent of intergroup conflict in contemporary America, at least as seen through the eyes of

---

[2] For an account of the relationship between in-group identification and out-group hostility, see Marilynn B. Brewer, "Identity and Conflict," in *Intergroup Conflicts and Their Resolution: Social Psychological Perspectives*, ed. Daniel Bar-Tal (New York: Psychology Press, 2011).

ordinary Americans. We find evidence for both the assimilation and black exceptionalism views of ethnic group consciousness: whites have little, blacks have the most, and among Latinos, group consciousness wanes over later generations in America. Contrary to the generational differences we found with patriotism in the preceding chapter, there is little evidence of increased ethnic consciousness in the vanguard. Extrapolating from these data, gloomy predictions of greater ethnic cleavages in the future seem unwarranted.

AMERICA AS AN ETHNIC CAULDRON

The premise of the politicized group consciousness paradigm is that the differences among American ethnic and racial groups are essential, enduring, and inherently in conflict.[3] Do Americans generally accept that portrait of an ethnically fraught society as a factual premise? Put another way, how widespread is the perception of America as an ethnic cauldron? In this section, we describe the perceptions of intergroup relations held by each racial and ethnic group along several different dimensions.[4]

First of all, do Americans perceive our ethnic and racial groups as essentially different from one another?[5] Such perceptions might pave the way for public acceptance of multiculturalist policies that help adjudicate differences among ethnic groups by promoting greater equality among them but without trying to force integration on them. Table 4.1A, based on 2000 General Social Survey (GSS) national data, shows that most members of each major ethnic group, about 60 percent, did agree that ethnic minority groups in the United States are very distinct and very different from one another. Almost as many, around half, agreed that whites as a group are very distinct and different from ethnic minority groups. So the first brick of a psychological foundation for ideological multiculturalism is indeed in place for many Americans: the widespread perception that ethnic minority groups are distinctively different from each other and from whites.

---

[3] See Bobo, "Whites' Opposition to Busing"; Lawrence Bobo, "Prejudice as Group Position: Micro-Foundations of a Sociological Approach to Racism and Race Relations," *Journal of Social Issues* 55 (1999): 445–72; Lawrence Bobo and Mia Tuan, *Prejudice in Politics*; David O. Sears and Donald Kinder, "Whites' Opposition to Busing: On Conceptualizing and Operationalizing Group Conflict," *Journal of Personality and Social Psychology* 48 (1985): 1141–47; Sidanius and Pratto, *Social Dominance*; Jost, et al., "A Decade of System Justification Theory." These latter two theories argue that social peace in the sense of stability in the hierarchical ordering of ethnic groups can persist because minority groups do not challenge their subordinate statuses due either to risk aversion in a kind of "self-handicapping" or to the belief that the prevailing system is legitimate.

[4] For simplicity of interpretation, we present the proportion perceiving ethnic cleavages on any given item out of all those responding to the item: when the item has a middle, noncommittal category (e.g., neither agree nor disagree), we include it in the denominator.

[5] Jennifer L. Eberhardt and Jennifer L. Randall, "The Essential Notion of Race"(cited in *Cultural Divides: Understanding and Overcoming Group Conflict*, ed. Deborah Prentice and Dale Miller [New York: Russell Sage Foundation, 1999]).

TABLE 4.1. *Perceptions of Ethnic Group Distinctiveness and Conflict, by Ethnicity*

	Whites (%)	Blacks (%)	Latinos (%)
A. Ethnic Distinctiveness			
Ethnic minority groups in the United States are very distinct and very different from one another (2002 GSS) (% agree)	61[a]	59[a]	59[a]
Whites as a group are very distinct and different from ethnic minority groups (2002 GSS) (% agree)	49[a]	53[a]	55[a]
B. Extent of Ethnic Group Conflict			
Are ethnic groups in conflict in Los Angeles and Southern California, or are ethnic groups getting along these days? (LACSS 1994, 1997, 1999–2002) (% "in conflict")	66	55[a]	58[a]
Has the wide variety of ethnic groups in LA helped or hurt the quality of life here? (LACSS 1994–2002) (% "hurt")	38[a]	35[a]	33[a]
In the next five to ten years, would you say that relations among LA's different racial and ethnic groups will improve a lot, improve, stay about the same as they are now, get worse, or get a lot worse? (LACSS 1994–2000) (% "get worse" or "get a lot worse")	34[a]	32[a]	33[a]
C. Ethnic Conflict Is Not Inevitable			
Ethnic minority groups will never really fit in with mainstream American culture (GSS 2002) (% agree)	15[a]	17[a]	16[a]
Is conflict among ethnic and racial groups just part of life, or is most of it unnecessary? (LACSS 2001–02) (% just part of life)	17[a]	13[a, b]	12[b]
D. Source of Group Conflict			
Too many ethnic, racial, business, and religious groups are only interested in what benefits them (LACSS 1998–99) (% agree)	69	61	52
Are Americans of different ethnic groups united or divided about the most important values? (LACSS 1994–95) (% divided)	57	76	69
Minimum Base *N* (GSS 2002)	2,156	398	85
Minimum Base *N* (LACSS Cumulative)	518	294	445
Minimum Base *N* (LACSS 2001+2002)	214	221	240

For agree–disagree items, base includes "neither agree nor disagree."
Superscripts denote results of independent samples t-tests. All entries in a given row are significantly different ($p < .05$) unless they share the same superscript.
Sources: 2002 General Social Survey (GSS); Los Angeles County Social Survey (LACSS) cumulative file, 2001 and 2002 individual year files.

Do most people view those ethnic cleavages as generating great social conflict within the society and perhaps enough conflict to warrant group-conscious policy solutions? Here, we must rely on the Los Angeles County Social Surveys (LACSS) in the absence of directly relevant national data. This database should, if anything, *over*estimate the level of perceived ethnic conflict relative to the rest of the nation because southern California is one of the most ethnically diverse regions in the United States, with a considerable history of racial and ethnic conflict, as noted in Chapter 2. Indeed, Huntington described southern California as a poster child for diversity-driven fragmentation.

Most residents of Los Angeles County in recent years did indeed perceive considerable ethnic conflict, as shown in Table 4.1B. The most direct question asked was, "Are ethnic groups in conflict in Los Angeles and southern California or are they getting along?" Clear majorities in each ethnic group selected "in conflict" rather than "getting along."[6]

However, two other findings qualify this initial portrait of a tense and fragile metropolis. Only about one-third in each ethnic group said that the wide variety of ethnic groups in Los Angeles had hurt the quality of life there. And only a minority was pessimistic about the future. When asked whether relations among Los Angeles's different racial and ethnic groups will improve or get worse in the future, only about a third in each group said worse. In terms of perceived conflict, then, residents of Los Angeles were of divided minds rather than holding a uniform image of a society splintered by intergroup rivalries and conflicts. Most saw some conflict but most also saw benefits of diversity and were optimistic about the future.[7]

Second, this is a rare instance in this study in which pooling surveys across years can mislead. In 1991, several Los Angeles police officers were videotaped beating a black motorist, Rodney King. Four were later charged with police brutality and sent to trial. However, in the spring of 1992, the jury acquitted all four. When news of the verdict spread, a major civil disturbance broke out in South Los Angeles, the area with the densest concentration of blacks and Latinos. The police quickly lost control of the streets, and the rioting lasted for almost a week. More than a thousand businesses were damaged and more than 400 completely destroyed. More than 5,000 individuals were arrested and more than fifty were killed.[8]

Not surprisingly, ethnic conflict was perceived to be at an extremely high level in Los Angeles in the years immediately after the rioting, as shown in

---

[6] Also see Bobo and Hutchings, "Perceptions of Racial Group Competition."

[7] In addition, we created a scale of perceived ethnic conflict out of the three items shown in Table 4.1B. On this scale, whites showed the strongest perception of ethnic conflict, followed by foreign-born Latinos, blacks, and U.S.-born Latinos, in order. All the differences between adjacent groups were significant ($N = 5,201$), with the exception of blacks and U.S.-born Hispanics. Still, the differences are not large, as can be seen by scanning the results for the individual items shown in Table 4.1B.

[8] Baldassare, *The Los Angeles Riots*.

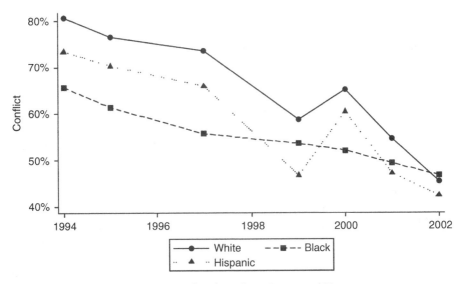

FIGURE 4.1. Ethnic Groups in Conflict, by Ethnic Group and Year
Source: Los Angeles County Social Survey (LACSS) Cumulative.

Figure 4.1. But as the memories of the rioting faded, perceptions of ethnic conflict dropped sharply in all ethnic groups. Consider the opinions of whites. In 1994, 81 percent thought ethnic groups in LA were in conflict, whereas by 2002, only 45 percent thought they were; 48 percent thought the wide variety of ethnic groups in the area hurt the quality of life there in 1994, but only 36 percent felt this in 2002, and the proportions believing intergroup relations would worsen over the next five to ten years fell from 42 percent in 1994 to only 24 percent in 2002.

An even more dramatic increase over time in perceived harmony and optimism occurred among ethnic minorities. The percent of blacks viewing ethnic groups as getting along rather than as in conflict rose from 34 percent in 1994 to 53 percent in 2002; among Latinos the rise was from 27 percent to 58 percent. Both groups were almost evenly split in 1994 about whether diversity had helped or hurt the quality of life in Los Angeles, but two-thirds of each group responded "helped" in 2002. Similarly, in 1994, both minority groups had been evenly split about what to expect in the future, but by 2002, optimists were far more numerous, by a four-to-one margin among blacks and by more than two-to-one among Latinos. *2001?!*

These increasing perceptions of harmony among ethnic groups occurred as memories of violent rioting receded. Such changes seem inconsistent with the subtext of most versions of the politicized group consciousness paradigm, which arguably implies that ordinary people chronically view ethnic group relations as trapped in a persistent pattern of conflict. Rather, the data seem to reflect a more dynamic portrait of intergroup relations. Yes, there always is the potential for conflict, even violent collective conflict on occasion – but for the most part people seem to be saying that different ethnic groups *can* get along.

We might therefore expect that most Americans would *not* think that either the differences between ethnic groups or intergroup conflicts are etched in stone. Indeed, Table 4.1C shows that overwhelming majorities in each ethnic group in a national sample believe minority groups will ultimately fit in with mainstream American culture, reflecting a widespread popular acceptance of the assimilation prototype described in Chapters 1 and 2. Nor were most residents of Los Angeles deeply pessimistic that ethnic tensions are ineradicable. Few in any ethnic group thought intergroup conflict was inevitable; rather, the great majority believed most such antagonism is unnecessary.

Multiculturalism assumes that minority groups need protection from the natural tendency of the majority to impose its own cultural norms on them and to resist redistribution. Similarly, the politicized group consciousness paradigm assumes that whites are pursuing their own interests and in this way shoring up the established ethnic hierarchy. The implication is that both the reality and perceptions of ethnic conflict revolve around material group interests, such as differences in wealth, income, schooling, housing, and so on. But that is not the only possibility; they might well center on more symbolic cultural values instead. The Los Angeles data presented in Table 4.1D show that both dimensions are involved. A majority in each ethnic group believes that too many ethnic, racial, business, and religious groups are motivated by group interest, that they are "only interested in what benefits them." But strong majorities in each group also believe that different ethnic groups are divided about important values.

Minorities do diverge from whites to some extent here. It seems that whites are more likely to perceive ethnic and racial groups as driven by parochial interests than are blacks or Latinos. Conversely, blacks and Latinos are more likely than whites to perceive such conflicts as produced by divisions over important values. As will be seen, whites tend not to think of their group as a racial or ethnic group, so perhaps the question is generally interpreted as referring to ethnic and racial minorities. Finally, the data regarding perceptions of interethnic conflict give us another hint of black exceptionalism. One premise of that perspective is that long-established patterns of behavior and thinking may have great inertial power even when societal reality changes, a phenomenon we might call the "burden of history." Blacks have until recently been the largest and occasionally the most restive racial minority group, and so they presumably pose the greatest threat to whites' privileged group position. But other groups have joined the challenge in immigration-rich southern California. The rapid population growth of Latinos has made them the numerical majority in some locales, increasing both the demand for public services and infrastructure and their political power. Asian Americans have rapidly become more competitive economically, as reflected in, among other things, their sudden and dramatic overrepresentation in higher education, which has displaced whites in particular. One could therefore imagine that blacks might no longer be seen as the group most threatening to whites' privileged group position.

Yet whites' perceptions do not reflect such changes. The LACSS asked the respondent which ethnic group was most in conflict with his or her own. Whites by a large margin saw blacks as the group most in conflict with them, as shown in Table 4.2. Asians also focused on conflict with blacks, despite the fact that in many contexts they are competing more with whites than blacks for positions that provide for upward mobility and integration into the broader society. Conversely, by large margins blacks and Latinos saw each other as their greatest antagonists. Foreign-born Latinos especially pinpoint blacks as their opponents in conflict over desired resources. Most observers would find these latter perceptions quite realistic. The two groups do in fact share sometimes conflicted neighborhoods, compete for working- and middle-class jobs, and rely more than whites on public services.

Such perceptions of ethnic distinctiveness, conflict, and group-interested behavior would presumably need to reflect a coherent set of beliefs if they were to serve as a strong psychological foundation for the broad acceptance of multiculturalism. Ideally, we could test for such ideological coherence in the standard

TABLE 4.2. *What Group Is Your Ethnic Group Most in Conflict With? (Los Angeles Data)*

	Black	Latino			Asian	White
		Total	Foreign-Born	U.S.-Born		
Ethnic Group Respondent Perceives Own Group as Most in Conflict with:						
Hispanics	54%	10%	12%	7%	21%	32%
Blacks	5	66	70	54	33	61
Asians	7	7	6	12	17	3
Whites	27	15	10	25	21	1
Other	7	2	3	2	8	3
Total	100%	100%	101%	100%	100%	100%
N	197	222	163	59	24	185

Source: 2001 Los Angeles County Social Survey (LACSS).

way of looking at interitem correlations.[9] But we cannot because no survey contains all the items we have just reviewed. We can only test for small areas of coherence. In the 2002 GSS, the two ethnic distinctiveness items shown in Table 4.1A were significantly correlated among whites ($r = .41$) and among blacks ($r = .47$); too few Latinos were identified as such to provide a confident estimate. That may overestimate coherence because the item wordings are very similar. Four LACSSs contained at least two of the other items shown in Table 4.1. We computed their intercorrelations within each ethnic group. The six resulting correlations were rather weak (ranging from $r = .13$ to $.15$) and showed no obvious pattern (although four were statistically significant at $p < .05$). We would conclude that perceptions of ethnic differences and conflict do not show a great deal of coherence.

Overall, then, most people in all groups seem united in the core belief that ethnic minority groups are distinct, different from each other, and different from whites; that ethnic groups are generally in considerable conflict with each other; that minorities are pushing too hard for their own interests; and that the values held by American ethnic groups differ across groups. In these respects, Americans of all ethnic groups do seem to share the assumption that there are inherent group conflicts. This politicization of group consciousness may engender support for multicultural proposals aimed at protecting minority group interests and identities.

But this portrait of a public primed for ethnic conflict may be too one-sided. The data also point to the traditional American optimism that ultimately minorities will fit in with the mainstream culture. There is also a broad consensus that cultural diversity is a positive value, that diversity does not inherently produce ethnic conflict, and that, over time, ethnic relations are likely to improve. That is, few Americans seem to believe that their ethnic differences are so essential to their being that group conflict is so inevitable – and likely to be so severe – that walls need to be constructed between groups. It is noteworthy that neither the historically oppressed blacks nor the largely immigrant Latinos differ from the historically dominant whites in these respects.

We have argued that the psychological subtext of most versions of the politicized group consciousness paradigm and of hard multiculturalism is that America, or at least its highly diverse metropolitan areas, potentially resembles a collection of volatile communities riven by ethnic divisions. However, this outlook appears not to be shared by the majority of ordinary Americans, whatever their race or ethnicity. The general consensus seems to be that ethnic group differences can be mitigated and that conflict is not inevitable, as the assimilationist ethos of cosmopolitan liberalism implies. Yes, there is a general recognition of ethnic group differences and perhaps of differing interests, but a

---

[9] Philip E. Converse, "The Nature of Belief Systems in Mass Publics," in *Ideology and Discontent*, ed. David E. Apter (London: Free Press of Glencoe, 1964).

majority of Americans in all racial and ethnic groups still believe that such differences can be overcome and that attaining a common culture is possible.

ETHNIC GROUP CONSCIOUSNESS

We turn next to another key feature of multiculturalism – but, crucially, not of cosmopolitan liberalism: the proposition that ethnic group consciousness is an especially central feature of the personal identities of Americans. Our main empirical focus here is to assess the strength of group consciousness in each main ethnic group.

Definition and Theories of Ethnic Group Consciousness

To start with, what do we mean by ethnic or racial group consciousness? Previous research has generally defined the concept in terms of four components. The first is *self-categorization* as a member of an ethnic in-group.[10] This is the ethnic identity version of the "What is the circle of we?" question we asked about national identity in the preceding chapter. As will be seen, however, we are cautious about assuming that individuals' preferred ethnic identities invariably match the conventional American pan-ethnic pentagon of white, black, Latino, Asian, and Native American used by the U.S. Census. A second component is *strength of identification* with that group. This construct has a long historical pedigree, being central to reference group theory as well as warranting a mention in theorizing about personal identity and social identity.[11] A third component is a *sense of common fate*, or linked fate as it is sometimes described: individuals' perceptions that their own outcomes will be affected by how their ethnic group as a whole fares. This too has a long heritage in social psychology and has appeared more recently in theories of intergroup relations.[12] The fourth component is *perceived discrimination* against one's own ethnic group and more generally feeling it is not being treated fairly. We consider each of these components in turn and then develop a typology that involves all of them.

---

[10] See, e.g., Miller, et al., "Group Consciousness and Political Participation."

[11] Philip E. Converse and Angus Campbell, "Political Standards in Secondary Groups," in *Group Dynamics*, ed. Dorwin Cartwright and Alvin Zander (New York: Harper Row, 1968); Angus Campbell, et al., *The American Voter* (New York: Wiley, 1960); Herbert Hyman, "Problems in the Collection of Opinion-Research Data," *American Journal of Sociology* 55, no. 4 (1950): 362–70; Harold H. Kelley, "Two Functions of Reference Groups," in *Society for the Psychological Study of Social Issues, Readings in Social Psychology*, ed. Guy Swanson, Theodore Newcomb, and Eugene Hartley (New York: Holt, 1952), 410–14; Erik H. Erikson, *Childhood and Society* (New York: W. W. Norton & Company, 1993 [1950]); Henri Tajfel and John C. Turner, "The Social Identity Theory of Inter-Group Behavior," in *Psychology of Intergroup Relations*, ed. William Austin and Stephen Worchel (Chicago: Nelson-Hall, 1986).

[12] John W. Thibaut and Harold H. Kelley, *The Social Psychology of Groups* (New York: John Wiley & Sons, 1959); Bobo and Johnson, "Racial Attitudes in a Prismatic Metropolis"; Dawson, *Behind the Mule*.

What would different psychological theories predict about ethnic differences in-group consciousness? As noted in Chapter 2, many contemporary social psychologists share the basic elements of a politicized group consciousness paradigm, stressing that attachment to an in-group identity, antagonism toward out-groups, and intergroup competition are central elements of human psychology. Linking these underlying psychological processes to social contexts in which inequality among groups prevails, a number of theorists posit the persistence of stable group hierarchies of status and power, as well as the inevitability of intergroup competition. Dominant groups rule and subordinate groups struggle.[13]

In the contemporary United States, these theories imply that intergroup relations revolve around the struggle among racially conscious groups competing to maximize their own interests. Minority groups may be expected to have especially strong group consciousness because of the disadvantages they face in a racial group hierarchy that has whites ensconced at the top. But whites, too, might be expected to have strong racial group consciousness because of the threat to their privileges chronically posed by less advantaged challengers of color.[14]

In Chapter 2, we contrasted this view with the black exceptionalism model. It argues that African Americans are fundamentally different from other non-European people of color, given the embedded one-drop rule that has long separated those with any discernible African ancestry from everyone else. In this view, the color line applied to Latinos and Asians is considerably more flexible, particularly in later generations further removed in time from immigration. As a result, the subjective importance of ethnicity for them might fade just as it has among descendants of the earlier waves of immigrants from Europe.[15]

---

[13] Bobo, "Whites' Opposition to Busing"; Robert A. Levine and Donald T. Campbell, *Ethnocentricism: Theories of Conflict, Ethnic Attitudes and Group Behavior* (New York: Wiley, 1972); Blumer, "Prejudice as a Sense of Group Position"; Lawrence Bobo, "Race, Public Opinion and the Social Sphere," *Public Opinion Quarterly* 61 (1997): 1–15; Sidanius and Pratto, *Social Dominance*; Bonilla-Silva, *Racism without Racists*. Social dominance theory is included here as a racial hierarchy theory because it is predicated on the inherent tendencies of groups like ethnic groups to compete in their own interests. However, it also assumes that dominance hierarchies are usually quite stable and through various mechanisms are able to suppress those competitive pressures.

[14] Bobo, "Prejudice as Group Position"; Bobo and Tuan, *Prejudice in Politics*. Again, social dominance theory departs somewhat, making allowance for a form of group-based false consciousness on the part of some minorities who support the racial group hierarchy.

[15] Indeed, Portes and Rumbaut (*Legacies: The Story of the Immigrant Second Generation* [Berkeley: University of California Press, 2001], 165) find that identification with one's national origins is more common among foreign-born than U.S.-born children and that identities such as American or hyphenated-American are more common among U.S.-born children. Also see Phinney, "Ethnic Identity in Adolescents and Adults"; and Aida Hurtado, Patricia Gurin, and Timothy Peng, "Social Identities – A Framework for Studying the Adaptations of Immigrants and Ethnics: Mexicans in the United States," *Social Problems* 41, no. 1 (1994): 129–51.

This contrast of our three psychological paradigms leads to some specific empirical comparisons. First, the politicized group consciousness paradigm generally expects substantial ethnic group consciousness among all groups, although higher levels among minorities. Second, it treats African Americans as not qualitatively different from other subordinate minority groups, although perhaps at the bottom of the racial hierarchy. In contrast, the idea of black exceptionalism emphasizes the distinctiveness of the enduring discrimination against blacks and predicts that they will experience substantially higher group consciousness than will other people of color. Because today's blacks are overwhelmingly American born, the appropriate comparison group in our data would be U.S.-born Latinos.[16] Third, the politicized group consciousness paradigm would expect that past discrimination against all people of color in America should have produced strong group consciousness among Latinos and Asians. Perhaps it would be even stronger in later generations among the native-born disillusioned with continuing discrimination and economic inequality. However, the assimilation prototype would distinguish between any new immigrants at entry who for some period of time might feel like and be treated as part of an alien group and later generations who may have succeeded in becoming integrated into the broader society and as a result have a weakened sense of group consciousness.

Ethnic Self-Categorization

The politicized group consciousness paradigm, as we have argued earlier, tends sometimes to overgeneralize the African-American case to all people of color. In contrast, black exceptionalism suggests that the color line may be most impermeable for those with discernible African ancestry. Because being African American is unusually stigmatizing, by this view, one might expect other people of color to shy away from a social identity as black.

One direct test comes from the separate questions in recent U.S. Censuses asking about race and Hispanic background. That is, Latinos were also given an opportunity to select a racial identity, from white, black, American Indian, Asian, Native Hawaiian, or some other race. In 2000, of those with Hispanic background, 48 percent described themselves on the race question as white, only 2 percent as black, and 42 percent as some other race. The movement of Latinos toward self-identification as white was even more pronounced in the 2010 census, when 53 percent of those with Hispanic background identified as white, 2.5 percent as black, and 37 percent as some other race (giving more

---

[16] In the pooled LACSS surveys, only 6.5 percent of the blacks were foreign born. Latinos also have the advantage of being similar to blacks in key demographic indicators of socioeconomic status, making this a relatively conservative test of the hypothesis. We do not use Asians here because of sampling concerns about the foreign-born versus U.S.-born comparison in the absence of Asian-language interviews.

than one identity was allowed, and another 6 percent chose two or more identities). This reluctance of Latinos to identify themselves as black is underlined by the fact that only 1.1 percent of the Latinos who said they were of some other race also said they were black or African American.[17]

A similar finding about the relative looseness of the color line surrounding Latinos and Asians and the stricter one surrounding blacks comes from data on the identities chosen by interracial couples for their children. In the 2000 census, individuals were allowed to categorize themselves as having more than one racial or ethnic identity. Fifty-six percent of parents with children under eighteen years of age chose just one racial identity for their children. Among those, most black–white couples described their children as black, whereas most Asian–white and Latino–white couples chose white rather than Asian or Latino.[18] Analogous findings were reported in data collected on immigrant children and their parents. The overwhelming majority of those from the Caribbean nations with the most African ancestry, such as Jamaica and Haiti, described themselves as black, whereas at most 1 percent did so among those from nations dominated by those with Spanish or Indian ancestry, such as Cuba, Mexico, and Nicaragua. They preferred to describe themselves as white, Hispanic, Latino, or Mexican.[19]

Another question that might be raised about the politicized group consciousness paradigm concerns the response categories it typically uses for self-categorization. This perspective typically assumes that Americans self-categorize into the major pan-ethnic categories of the American pentagon used over the years in many U.S. Censuses: whites, blacks, Latinos (or Hispanics), Asians, or Native Americans.[20] This ought to be especially common among those born and brought up in an America primarily composed of only two racial groups. But, of course, the country's demography has changed, and the alternative assimilation model might suggest that many immigrants would prefer to identify more with their own original nationality group than with such Americanized pan-ethnic categories. That is, the pan-ethnic category label such as Asian or Asian American may not always reflect the ethnic self-identification preferred by the individual but may arbitrarily lump together people who do not share meaningful cultural roots.[21] For example, Korean and Japanese immigrants may

---

[17] For these data, see tables 2 and 10 in U.S. Census Bureau, 2011. "An Overview: Race and Hispanic Origin and the 2010 Census."

[18] Sonya M. Tafoya, Hans Johnson, and Laura E. Hill, "Who Chooses to Choose Two?" in *The American People: Census 2000*, ed. Reynolds Farley and John Haaga (New York: Russell Sage Foundation, 2005). Also see Jennifer Lee and Frank D. Bean, *The Diversity Paradox: Immigration and the Color Line in Twenty-First Century America* (New York: Russell Sage Foundation, 2010).

[19] Alejandro Portes and Ruben G. Rumbaut, *Legacies: The Story of the Immigrant Second-Generation* (Berkeley: University of California Press, 2001).

[20] For a nuanced exception, see Bonilla-Silva, *Racism without Racists*.

[21] Nazil Kibria, "The Concept of 'Bicultural Families' and Its Implications for Research on Immigrant and Ethnic Families," in *Immigration and the Family. Research and Policy on*

feel more like members of their own nationality groups than like Asians, especially given the historic enmity between those nations.

To test this idea requires an open-ended question to elicit the respondent's own spontaneous ethnic self-categorization, rather than forcing people into pan-ethnic categories by using the fixed response alternatives of the standard closed-ended census question. In the 2000 LACSS, respondents were asked at the outset of the interview, "Which ethnic or racial group do you most closely identify with?" We divided these responses into those giving the standard pan-ethnic labels versus those using labels referring to national origins (e.g., Mexican, Romanian). Our most reliable data on predominantly immigrant groups come from Latinos: 79 percent of the Latinos used a pan-ethnic label, whereas 99 percent of the blacks and 93 percent of the whites did so.

An earlier study collected such spontaneous self-categorizations in a study of more than 2,000 incoming freshmen at the University of California, Los Angeles (UCLA) in 1996, prior to their actual enrollment or residence at the university. The students were asked at the outset, "What racial or ethnic group do you most closely identify with?" Almost all the largely nonimmigrant blacks and whites did indeed choose the familiar pan-ethnic categories: of the blacks, 98 percent chose African American, Afro-American, or black, and, of the whites, 93 percent said white, Caucasian, or Anglo-Saxon.[22]

However, the Asian and Latino students, overwhelmingly the products of recent immigration, presented a sharp contrast.[23] National origin identities were more common than American or pan-ethnic identities. Among the Asian students, more than half (58 percent) cited only their nation of origin (e.g., Chinese), and another 5 percent did so in hyphenated form (e.g., Chinese-American). Only a minority used the conventional pan-ethnic labels Asian American (11 percent) or Asian or Southeast Asian (25 percent combined). Among Latinos, the same pattern held, although not quite as dramatically. Half referred to specific nationalities, split between the nations themselves (e.g., Mexican) and the hyphenated version (e.g., Mexican-American). The other half used the conventional American pan-ethnic labels (25 percent Hispanic, 14 percent Latino/a, 11 percent Chicano/a). That is, most of those from the new immigrant groups rejected the standard pan-ethnic identities, instead choosing identities within the narrower categories of their recent national origins.

U.S. Immigrants, ed. Alan Booth, Ann C. Crouter, and Nancy Landale (Mahwah, NJ: Lawrence Erlbaum Associates, 1997); Michael Omi, "Shifting the Blame: Racial Ideology and Politics in the Post-Civil Rights Era," *Critical Sociology* 18, no. 3 (1999): 77–98; Alejandro Portes and Dag MacLeod, "What Shall I Call Myself? Hispanic Identity Formation in the Second Generation," *Ethnic and Racial Studies* 19, no. 3 (1996): 523–47; Sears, Fu, Henry, and Bui, "The Origins and Persistence of Ethnic Identity among the 'New Immigrant Groups.'"

[22] Sears, Fu, Henry, Bui, "The Origins and Persistence of Ethnic Identity among the 'New Immigrant' Groups."

[23] Ninety percent and 62 percent, respectively, had no parents or grandparents born in the United States.

Additional data on the self-categorizations of Americans of Asian descent come from the 2008 National Asian American Survey.[24] Respondents were allowed to check more than one alternative. In total, 87 percent checked either their nationality group or a hyphenated nationality-American group, whereas 40 percent checked Asian or Asian American. An earlier (2001) national survey found that 64 percent of Asians chose either a pure nationality identity or the hyphenated nationality-American identity, whereas 15 percent selected Asian American.[25] Finally, studies based on national samples by the Pew Research Center found that both Hispanics and Asian Americans overwhelmingly preferred to identify themselves with their country of origin rather than adopting pan-ethnic labels.[26]

In other words, the assumption that all "people of color" fit the African-American model oversimplifies the self-categorizations of ethnic minorities in two ways. By our argument, the color line in self-categorization primarily applies to those of any discernible African ancestry. Classifying Latinos and Asians as people of color ignores the desires of many to distance themselves from, rather than be categorized with, the more stigmatized African Americans. Second, it ignores the greater psychological closeness of many to their national roots than to the conventional American pan-ethnic groupings. Presumably, that is especially true of those whose families immigrated to America quite recently. Indeed, the same may be true of recent black immigrants from Africa or the Caribbean who, in the first or second generation, may identify more with their nations of origin than with African Americans.[27]

Strength of Ethnic Identity

A second component of group consciousness is the strength of ethnic identity. Our primary measures consist of three items in the LACSS, on the strength of identification with fellow ethnics, the importance of the individual's ethnicity to his or her sense of identity, and how often the person thought of him- or herself in terms of ethnicity. Each question provided four response alternatives. Table 4.3 gives the exact wording and the marginal frequencies for each item by ethnic group.

Most versions of the politicized group consciousness paradigm, perhaps especially group position theory, would expect whites' racial consciousness to

[24] Janelle Wong, et al., *Asian American Political Participation: Emerging Constituents and Their Political Identities* (New York: Russell Sage Foundation, 2011), 162.

[25] Pei-te Lien, M. Margaret Conway, and Janelle Wong, "The Contours and Sources of Ethnic Identity Choices among Asian Americans," *Social Science Quarterly* 84, no. 2 (2003): 461–81; also see Wong, et al., *Asian American Political Participation*, 155.

[26] Pew Research Center, "The Rise of Asian Americans."

[27] Mary Waters, *Ethnic Options: Choosing Identities in America* (Berkeley: University of California Press, 1990); and Mary Waters, *Black Identities: West Indian Dreams and American Realities* (Cambridge, MA: Harvard University Press) 2001.

TABLE 4.3. *Ethnic Differences in Group Consciousness (Los Angeles Data)*

		Ethnicity of Respondent				
	Black	Latino			Asian	White
		Total	Foreign-Born	U.S.-Born		
Strength of Ethnic Identity						
How strongly do you identify with other (ethnicity) people? (% "very strongly")	59%[a,b]	55%[a]	60%[a,b]	44%[c]	38%[c]	25%
How important is being (ethnicity) to your sense of identity? (% "very important")	66[a]	68[a]	72	58	46	15
How often do you think of yourself as a (ethnicity) person? (% "very often")	55[a]	69	75	56[a]	44	11
Range of n's	192–715	688–1,340	474–943	214–397	157–254	808–1,470
Common Fate						
Do you think what happens generally to [ethnicity] people in this country will have something to do with what happens in your life? (% "a lot")	39%	22%	23%[a]	19%[a,b]	16%[a,b]	16%[b]
N	377	439	313	126	75	431
Face Discrimination because of Ethnicity						
I experience discrimination because of my ethnicity. ("always" or "frequently")	19%	29%	30%[a]	26%[a]	11%	4%
Other members of my ethnic group experience discrimination. (% "always" or "frequently")	52[a,b]	51[a]	55[b]	42	26	11
Range of n's	226–608	258–712	193–516	65–193	45–123	300–764

(*continued*)

TABLE 4.3 (continued)

	Black	Ethnicity of Respondent			Asian	White
		Latino				
		Total	Foreign-Born	U.S.-Born		
Opportunity for Ethnic Group						
American society owes people of my ethnic group a better chance in life than we currently have. (% "strongly agree" or "agree")	72%[a]	74%[a]	82%	54%	38%	18%
American society provides my group fair opportunity ("disagree strongly" or "disagree")	56	25	23[a]	32[b]	28[a,b]	10
Range of N's	227–589	266–709	200–518	66–191	46–121	280–744

Superscripts denote results of independent samples t-tests. All entries in a given row are significantly different ($p < .05$) unless they share the same superscript. The "Total Latino" column is not compared to the foreign- or U.S.-born Latino categories.

Source: Los Angeles County Social Survey (LACSS), drawn from the following years: Strength of ethnic identity = 1997–99; both importance of ethnicity and how often R thinks of self as ethnicity = 1997–2002; common fate = 2001–02; discrimination against self = 1994; group discrimination and American society owes group a better chance = 1994, 2001–02; American society provides group fair opportunity = 1994.

be fairly well developed.[28] A white person's sense of *group* privilege could scarcely be threatened by minorities' demands without the individual being self-conscious of his or her whiteness. However, as can be seen in Table 4.3, whites were far less likely to express strong ethnic identities than were any of the minority groups. Indeed, members of minority groups were usually three or four times as likely to express strong ethnic identities. This low salience of whites' racial identity is perhaps not remarkable. Whites of European origin have been by far the dominant group in America for the past three centuries, numerically and in almost every other way, so why would they generally feel very racially distinctive? Nevertheless, whites in the Los Angeles metropolitan area live in a region that is among the most ethnically diverse in the world. Whites' original numerical dominance has eroded swiftly over the past few decades. Whites are now in the minority in Los Angeles County and are outnumbered by Latinos. One might think that they would feel threatened by their rapid fall and highly attached to their privileged status. Yet ethnic identity was far less important to whites.

The black exceptionalism hypothesis suggests that blacks' racial identities in particular should be stronger than those of other ethnicities. Indeed, Table 4.3 shows that blacks had considerably stronger ethnic identities than did other U.S.-born minorities. For example, 59 percent of the blacks identified very strongly with their own ethnic in-group, whereas only 44 percent of the U.S.-born Latinos did. Similarly, 66 percent of blacks said their own racial identity is very important, as against 58 percent of the U.S.-born Latinos. Both differences are statistically significant. For some reason, there was no difference in how often they think of themselves in terms of their ethnicity.

Finally, the assimilation hypothesis would expect new immigrants to have especially distinctive senses of ethnic identity compared to those born in America, even those sharing their country of origin. As noted earlier, our test of this idea in the Los Angeles data focuses especially on Latinos because the Asian subsample is likely to underrepresent the less assimilated, given the absence of Asian language interviews. Accordingly, we divided the Latinos into immigrants and those born in the United States. As can be seen in Table 4.3, foreign-born Latinos had a far stronger sense of ethnic identity (e.g., 60 percent felt very strongly identified with other Hispanics) than do those who were U.S.-born (44 percent did). On each of the three items, foreign-born Latinos had significantly stronger ethnic identity than did the U.S.-born, consistent with the assimilation hypothesis.

---

[28] Bobo and Tuan, *Prejudice in Politics*. Social dominance theory would not necessarily expect most whites to be so self-conscious of their biases toward maintaining their group's dominance. See Sidanius and Pratto, *Social Dominance*.

Perceptions of Common Fate

A third component of ethnic consciousness is a sense of common or linked fate with other members of one's own ethnic group. We included such a measure in the 2001 and 2002 LACSSs: "Do you think what happens generally to [ethnicity] people in this country will have something to do with what happens in your life?" Contrary to some versions of the politicized group consciousness theories, however, whites had very little sense of linked fate with other whites, significantly less than either blacks or Latinos, as shown in Table 4.3.

The black exceptionalism hypothesis again receives strong support. Blacks were far more likely to perceive common fate with others of their own racial in-group than were members of any other group. In the most direct test of the hypothesis, blacks (39 percent) were twice as likely to feel "a lot" of common fate as did U.S.-born Latinos (19 percent). Similar findings emerged from an earlier extensive survey of Los Angeles County, the 1994 Los Angeles Study of Urban Inequality (LASUI). Based on the same common fate item as used in the LACSS, blacks were much more likely to feel a lot of common fate with other members of their racial group (40 percent) than were Latinos (25 percent) or Asians (20 percent).[29]

The assimilation hypothesis is seemingly not supported in the LACSS. Foreign-born Latinos were only slightly higher in their sense of common fate with their co-ethnics than were the U.S.-born, and not significantly so. This may be misleading, though. Note that the wording of the item casts the respondent's perspective well into the future, asking if the in-group's fate *"will have something to do with what happens in your life"* [emphasis added]. This future orientation contrasts with the ethnic identity items, all of which focus on the present. Perhaps even foreign-born Latinos accept the conventional assimilation narrative about immigration to America and expect that over time their ethnicity will have decreasing influence over their lives. However, the assimilation hypothesis was supported in the LASUI. There, the foreign-born Latinos were substantially more likely than U.S.-born Latinos to feel a sense of common fate with their fellow group members.[30] So, with respect to common fate, we have some indication that ethnic group consciousness is greater for immigrant Latinos than for the U.S.-born, but the evidence is more mixed than with strength of ethnic identity.

Perceived Discrimination

The fourth leg of group consciousness is a sense of grievance about how one's own ethnic in-group is treated, as reflected in indices of perceived discrimination.

---

[29] That survey included door-to-door interviews with approximately 1,000 respondents in each of the four major ethnic groups. See Bobo and Johnson, "Racial Attitudes in a Prismatic Metropolis," 95.

[30] Bobo and Johnson, "Racial Attitudes in a Prismatic Metropolis," 96.

We have several measures of such feelings. One set involved estimates of the amount of discrimination against themselves or other members of their group because of their ethnicity. A second set focused on a broader sense of ethnic grievance, the belief that American society owes their ethnic group a better chance in life and that American society has (not) provided their ethnic group a fair opportunity to get ahead.[31] The frequencies of aggrieved respondents in each ethnic group are shown at the bottom of Table 4.3.

Not surprisingly, whites felt much less likely to be the target of discrimination than did any of the ethnic minority groups. For example, only 11 percent of whites said members of their group always or frequently experienced discrimination because of their ethnicity compared to 52 percent of blacks and 51 percent of Latinos. Only 18 percent of the whites felt that American society owed their group a better chance, whereas 72 percent of the blacks and 74 percent of the Latinos did so.[32] Whites were significantly less aggrieved than all minority groups on each item.

Again, the black exceptionalism hypothesis suggests that blacks should show stronger group consciousness than other people of color who were born and brought up in the United States. All four items indeed show that blacks perceived significantly greater discrimination against their own group than did U.S.-born Latinos. In some cases, the difference is quite striking. For example, more than half the blacks felt that American society does not provide their group with a fair opportunity to get ahead, compared to only one-third of the U.S.-born Latinos.

Finally, the assimilation hypothesis is that perceived discrimination should drop in the later generations of the new immigrant groups. Indeed, U.S.-born Latinos are lower in perceived discrimination than are the foreign-born on three of the four items significantly so on two. The difference is most dramatic in terms of being "owed ... a better chance." Oddly, the difference is reversed on the last item: the foreign-born were more likely than were the U.S.-born to agree that American society provides Latinos a fair opportunity to get ahead.

Group Consciousness Typology

Truly strong ethnic group consciousness would seem to depend on the confluence of all three of these last components: strong group identity, perceptions of common fate, and perceived discrimination.[33] The general thrust of the politicized

---

[31] The first and last were available in 1994 only; the others in 2001 and 2002 as well.

[32] Similar differences between whites and minorities emerged from the 2002 Pew National Survey of Latinos (see Pew Hispanic Center, "2002 National Survey of Latinos: Summary of Findings" [Washington, DC, December]. Accessed online at http://www.pewhispanic.org/files/reports/15.pdf). Only 13 percent of the whites said they, a family member, or a close friend had experienced discrimination due to race or ethnicity in the last five years, against 31 percent of Latinos and 46 percent of blacks (p. 74).

[33] We exclude self-categorization here because, in all but one of our surveys, the only measure of it is choice of one of the conventional pan-ethnic identities.

group consciousness paradigm appears to suggest that having all these beliefs is quite common, which is one reason why multiculturalism advocates ethnic-based entitlements as a necessary means for keeping the peace among warring tribes. The black exceptionalism and assimilation theories suggest that they might be more common among blacks and new immigrants, respectively, than in other groups. Their implication would be that extending multiculturalist solutions to the entire society may presuppose a more enduring and grievance-based ethnic consciousness among the descendants of immigrants than is actually the case.

So, how many Americans in each ethnic group strongly identify with their own racial or ethnic group, *and* feel a sense of common fate with fellow ethnics, *and* believe that their ethnic group is frequently discriminated against? To assess this, we created a typology ranging from the strongest level of group consciousness, consisting of people high in all three components, to the weakest, who are low in all three. The percentages of people in each ethnic group who fell into each level of ethnic group consciousness are shown in Table 4.4.

The items measuring these three dimensions were not included in all surveys, so we are limited to just those mounted in 2001 and 2002. The level of strongest group consciousness ("strongly aggrieved ethnic consciousness") included those who were high on all three dimensions: (1) above the full-sample median on the two-item scale of strength of ethnic identity; (2) felt that what happens to their fellow ethnics will have "a lot" to do with what happens in their own lives; and (3) were above the full-sample median on a two-item perceived discrimination scale based on perceptions of how often other members of their ethnic group experience discrimination and the extent to which American society owes "people of my own ethnic group" a better chance in life.

Only 1 percent of the whites attained this high level of aggrieved group consciousness, as shown in Table 4.4. This level of white group consciousness would seem to be too low to generate the potential sense of threat from ethnic minority groups generally presumed by the politicized group consciousness theories. More surprising, only a limited number of ethnic minorities showed this highest level of ethnic group consciousness: 25 percent of blacks, 14 percent of Latinos, and 5 percent of Asians. This suggests that only a relatively small constituency possesses the psychological prerequisites for supporting multiculturalist ideology.

Are these apparently low levels of strongly aggrieved ethnic consciousness merely an artifact of setting too high a threshold? We tried setting a more relaxed standard, insisting only that the respondent be above the sample median in perceived discrimination, presumably necessary for a sense of ethnic grievance, but without insisting on such a tight psychological connection to one's ethnic group. Thus, we included all those who were also above the median on either group identity *or* perceived common fate. But when we pool the original highest level with this more moderate group, we again see far more group consciousness among minorities than among whites. Only 5 percent of the whites meet this more relaxed standard, far lower than the 55 percent of the blacks, 57 percent of Latinos, or even the 23 percent of Asians.

TABLE 4.4. *Ethnic Group Consciousness Typology (Los Angeles Data)*

		Ethnicity of Respondent				
	Black	Latino			Asian	White
		Total	Foreign-Born	U.S.-Born		
Aggrieved Ethnic Consciousness						
Strongly	25%	14%	16%	7%	5%	1%
Moderately	30^a	43	49	29^a	18	4
Symbolic Ethnicity Only						
Discrimination, But Not Group Conscious	16$^{a,\,b}$	16$^{a,\,c}$	16^b	14$^{b,\,d}$	11$^{a,\,b,\,c}$	11$^{c,\,d}$
Contented						
Little Discrimination, Some Group Consciousness	14^a	18^b	14^a	31	42	19^b
No Ethnic Group Consciousness	15^a	10	6	19^a	24^a	65
Column N	363	437	310	127	76	431

The composite group consciousness typology is based on three dimensions: (1) strength of ethnic identity (2-item scale: "how important is being [ethnicity] to your sense of identity" and "how often do you think of yourself as a [ethnicity] person?"); (2) sense of common fate with ethnicity (single item); (3) perceived discrimination against R's ethnicity (2-item scale: "Other members of my ethnic group experience discrimination" and "American society owes people of my ethnic group a better chance in life than we currently have").

"Aggrieved-strongly" respondents were higher than the full sample median response on all three dimensions; "aggrieved-moderately" respondents are higher than the full sample median on (3) and either (1) or (2); "symbolic ethnicity only" respondents are higher than full sample median only on (3); "contented" respondents are higher than full sample median on (1) or (2) but not on (3); "no ethnic group consciousness" respondents are lower than the full sample median on all three dimensions. Superscripts denote results of independent samples t-tests. All entries in a given row are significantly different ($p < .05$) unless they share the same superscript. The "Total Latino" column is not compared to the foreign or U.S.-born Latino categories.

Source: 2001–02 Los Angeles County Social Surveys (LACSS).

Next, we turn to testing our theoretical hypotheses using this typology. The results again show strong support for black exceptionalism. Blacks (25 percent) were almost four times as likely as U.S.-born Latinos (7 percent) or Asians (5 percent) to show the highest level of aggrieved group consciousness. Applying the more relaxed standard supports black exceptionalism as well: 55 percent of the blacks, as against 36 percent of the U.S.-born Latinos and 23 percent of the Asians, were at least moderately high in-group consciousness.[34]

---

[34] We had insufficient Asians to divide them into U.S.- and foreign-born, but in the pooled LACSS sample, 70 percent were foreign born, and 64 percent at least mostly spoke English.

There is also strong support for the assimilation hypothesis. Foreign-born Latinos (16 percent) were more than twice as likely to be high in strongly aggrieved group consciousness than were U.S.-born Latinos (7 percent). Applying the more relaxed standard still supports the assimilation hypothesis among Latinos: 65 percent of the foreign-born, as against 36 percent of the U.S.-born, show at least moderately aggrieved group consciousness. If we extrapolate this finding into the future, when an increasing proportion of Latino families will have been in the United States for more generations since immigration, Latinos' ethnic consciousness should decline, contrary to Huntington's speculations.

These two top categories of the typology together constitute the outer boundary of what we would consider strong ethnic group consciousness. All the respondents meeting these criteria perceive considerable unfair treatment of their own group and associate themselves personally with their ethnic group to some degree. Both seem to us to be essential elements in most versions of the politicized group consciousness paradigm. So this represents our best effort at estimating how frequently people possess the subjective beliefs sufficient to provide psychological fuel for strong support among minorities for multiculturalist ideas. Very few whites or Asians and relatively few U.S.-born Latinos or Asians do. Even moderately aggrieved ethnic group consciousness seems to be common only among blacks and foreign-born Latinos.

The third level of our measure of group consciousness is one that we describe as symbolic only, following Gans. These respondents see their group as being treated unfairly but do not see much *personal* connection between themselves and their groups (defined as being above the sample median in perceived discrimination, but low in both strength of ethnic identity and in common fate). That is, they make political judgments about their group's treatment, but such judgments have little personal relevance. Of course, the absence of a strong personal connection to the group would not prevent engagement in political action on its behalf. But we see generally low levels of symbolic ethnicity in all groups, ranging from 11 to 16 percent, and few ethnic differences.

We identify the fourth level of our measure as "contented" because it includes people who perceive little discrimination against their own group but do feel some personal connection to it (defined as being above the full sample median in ethnic identity and/or common fate). The ethnic differences in this category again support the black exceptionalism hypothesis. Only 13 percent of the blacks are contented, against 31 percent of the U.S.-born Latinos and 42 percent of the Asians. They also support the assimilation hypothesis. Only 14 percent of the foreign-born Latinos, as against 31 percent of the U.S.-born Latinos, fall into this contented category. This reinforces one of our central messages: blacks' racial consciousness remains a potentially powerful political force, whereas the ethnic consciousness of the new immigrant groups seems to wane among later generations in the United States.

Finally, the lowest level includes those with no ethnic political consciousness (defined as being below the sample median on each dimension: ethnic identity, common fate, and perceived discrimination). Not surprisingly, whites are most likely to fall into this category. But perhaps more surprising is how pervasive this lack of group consciousness is among whites: 65 percent have no discernible racial group consciousness by this standard.

GRADUAL ASSIMILATION

But there is a still more nuanced story to be told about this process of gradual assimilation. Most immigrants do arrive with high hopes. The 2002 Pew survey shows that 89 percent of all Latinos felt that the opportunity to get ahead was better in the United States than in their country of origin. There was very little difference between foreign-born and U.S.-born Latinos in this respect (90 percent to 87 percent, respectively). Most Latinos believed their children would get a better education, hold better jobs, and earn more money than they would. This suggests that neither new immigrants nor Latino ethnics born in this country expect the extreme level of blocked opportunity that arguably would build support for a system of group rights.[35]

The Pew survey, like our surveys, reports that the foreign-born Latinos are much more likely than the U.S.-born to report that discrimination is a major problem in preventing them from succeeding in the United States (52 percent to 30 percent, respectively), in schools (45 percent to 26 percent, respectively), and in the workplace (48 percent to 29 percent, respectively). Moreover, the nature of the discrimination seems to change markedly among later generations. Foreign-born Latinos experience discrimination more because of their language (46 percent) than their physical appearance (13 percent), whereas the reverse is true for U.S.-born Latinos (14 percent to 43 percent, respectively). Moreover, the foreign-born Latinos are more likely to experience discrimination at the hands of other Latinos (89 percent report that it is a problem) than are native-born Latinos (73 percent).[36] This presumably occurs most commonly because of differences in income, education, and countries of origin. This replication of our findings with a national survey reassures us about the generality of our findings.[37]

Finally, we can say something further about how quickly over generations in the United States Latinos lose the high level of ethnic consciousness they show at

---

[35] Pew Hispanic Center, "2002 National Survey of Latinos: Summary of Findings," 38–40.

[36] These data yield traces of the deterioration Portes and Rumbaut (*Immigrant America*) describe as "segmented assimilation" among some in later generations who have immigrant origins. The foreign-born are more hopeful and optimistic, even though they experience the most discrimination. The U.S.-born begin to experience some skin color issues. And foreign-born Latinos are more likely than U.S.-born Latinos to expect upward mobility for their children, but it may be that the latter had already accomplished some of that expected assimilation (see Pew Hispanic Center, "2002 National Survey of Latinos: Summary of Findings," 40).

[37] Pew Hispanic Center, "2002 National Survey of Latinos: Summary of Findings," 70–81.

TABLE 4.5. *The Effects of Immigration Status on Strength of Latinos' Ethnic Group Consciousness (Los Angeles Data)*

		Latinos' Immigration Status				Blacks
	Natives	Second Generation	New Citizens	Long-Term Noncitizens	Recent Immigrants	
Strength of	43%	70%	77%[a]	78%[a]	81%[a]	58%
ethnic identity	(144)	(251)	(297)	(446)	(169)	(703)
(percent high)						
Common fate	21[a]	18[a]	19[a]	28[a]	20[a]	39
(percent high)	(38)	(89)	(121)	(129)	(60)	(377)
Perceived	39	58	70[a]	82[b]	88[b]	70[a]
discrimination	(67)	(129)	(171)	(221)	(119)	(606)
(percent high)						

Base n's in parentheses. "Percent high" refers to that respondent scoring higher than the overall median value of the relevant item. Superscripts denote results of independent samples t-tests. All entries in a given row are significantly different ($p < .05$) unless they share the same superscript. The "Total Latino" column is not compared to the foreign- or U.S.-born Latino categories.
Source: Los Angeles County Social Survey (LACSS) cumulative file. Ethnic identity scale taken from 1997–2002; common fate item taken from 2001–02 surveys; 2-item perceived discrimination scale taken from 1994, 2001–02 surveys.

entry. Table 4.5 presents a more refined test of the assimilation hypothesis using the full immigration status variable. It can be seen that only in the third generation do Latinos' levels of ethnic consciousness fall below the those of blacks. But even in the second generation, Latinos' perceived discrimination has already fallen below that of blacks. So the process of integration or assimilation in terms of lessened ethnic group consciousness is a gradual one. But over the generations following immigration, it seems inexorably to set Latinos apart from African Americans.

THE VANGUARD HYPOTHESIS

We turn now to the vanguard hypothesis. In the context of this chapter's primary focus, this suggests that the greater attention to and value placed on diversity in the culture at large and in the educational system particularly may have led to especially strong ethnic consciousness among the young and better educated. To test this at the bivariate level, we cross-tabulated both age and education separately by the ethnic group consciousness typology presented in Table 4.5, within each ethnic group.[38]

---

[38] Age was cut into eighteen- to twenty-nine-year-olds; thirty- to fifty-nine-year olds, and sixty-year-olds and older; education into those without any college and those with some college or more. We did not have sufficient cases to test the more refined version of the vanguard hypothesis that we

To make a long story short, there is little support for the vanguard hypothesis in any group. As a result, we do not show these somewhat lengthy analyses in the tables. Among whites, the range across age groups of aggrieved group consciousness, even using the more relaxed standard for that category, was 4 to 5 percent; of none at all, 65 to 70 percent. Among Latinos, the range across age groups was 56 to 57 percent (although too few were older than age sixty to yield a stable estimate). Among blacks, there was a little more indication of generational differences, with 62 percent of the eighteen- to twenty-nine-year-olds, 56 percent of the thirty- to fifty-nine-year-olds, and 47 percent of those sixty or older meeting that standard.

In terms of education, 1 percent of the college-educated whites met that standard, as did 7 percent of those without college. For Latinos, the comparable figures are 56 percent and 52 percent, respectively. For blacks, they are 52 percent and 57 percent, respectively. Perhaps hard multiculturalism and identity politics are more common among the young and on college campuses, but if so (we will see in Chapter 5), such effects do not extend to the conception of ethnic group consciousness articulated here.

ORIGINS OF STRONG ETHNIC IDENTITY

This volume is centrally concerned with the question of whether racial and ethnic loyalties threaten to divide the nation, perhaps by promoting support for ethnic group rights and other aspects of hard multiculturalism. Assessing how Americans perceive and feel about their ethnicity is the central purpose of this chapter. To this point, we have treated ethnic group consciousness as a unitary construct reflected in ethnic identity, perceived common fate, and perceived discrimination. But from a theoretical perspective, there may be important differences among these components. A final piece of the puzzle is to determine the conditions that produce strong ethnic identities, especially among disadvantaged minorities of color, presumably the natural constituency for multiculturalist policies.

The family of theories that we have collected under the rubric of the politicized group consciousness paradigm are founded on the assumption that a broad sense of discrimination and disadvantage among people of color generate particularly strong ethnic identities. The black exceptionalism and assimilation perspectives would argue instead that strong ethnic identities among minorities have their origins in two quite different historical circumstances: the peculiar history of blacks in America, with their centuries-long experience of slavery and formal discrimination, and the transitions faced by immigrants as they come to a new nation and, for some period of time, both feel and are treated as part of an alien group. The differences among these theories therefore revolve particularly

tested in Chapter 3, that the young *and* college educated in each ethnic group are the most distinctively group conscious.

TABLE 4.6. *Explaining Strength of Ethnic Identity: Regression Equations (Los Angeles Data)*

	Blacks		Latinos			Whites	
				I	II		
	r	b	r	b	b	r	b
Group Consciousness							
Perceived discrimination	.24**	.16*	.12*	.08	.06	−.04	−.08
		(.07)		(.05)	(.05)		(.06)
Common fate	.32***	.26***	.14**	.09*	.10**	.16**	.15***
		(.05)		(.04)	(.03)		(.05)
Perceived ethnic conflict	.02	−.03	.05	.02	.02	.04	.02
		(.03)		(.02)	(.02)		(.03)
Immigration Status							
Naturalized citizen	–	–	.06*	–	.11***	–	–
					(.03)		
Noncitizen	–	–	.13**	–	.10***	–	–
					(.03)		
Vanguards							
Youth	.13**	.07	.03	.01	.03	.07**	.05
		(.04)		(.02)	(.02)		(.04)
Higher education	.03	.01	−.01	.02	.02	.00	.00
		(.04)		(.04)	(.04)		(.03)
Controls							
Income	−.02	−.01	−.12**	−.02*	−.01	−.07*	−.01
		(.01)		(.01)	(.01)		(.01)
Female gender	.02	.01	.06*	.02	.03	−.01	−.01
		(.03)		(.02)	(.02)		(.03)
R^2 (adjusted)		.12		.03	.06		.02
N		336		408	408		376

Dependent variable is 2-item strength of ethnic identity scale where strong is high. "Perceived ethnic conflict" and "Common fate" are single items. Pairwise deletion. In the case of Latinos, a second regression equation is added to include immigration status, based on dummy variables for being U.S.-born or a naturalized citizen, with the reference category being foreign-born noncitizens. Entries are bivariate correlations (r) and unstandardized regression coefficients (b with standard errors in parentheses).
*$p < .05$ **$p < .01$ ***$p < .001$
Source: 2001–02 Los Angeles County Social Surveys (LACSS).

around the roles, respectively, of perceived discrimination and recent immigration in stimulating strong racial and ethnic identities.

The final step is to pit these hypotheses against each other in a more formal manner. Table 4.6 presents the bivariate correlations and regression equations linking the strength of ethnic identity to the core predictors we have been working with. We use perceived discrimination, common fate, and perceived ethnic conflict (perceptions of an ethnic cauldron) as the central variables emphasized by the politicized group consciousness paradigm. From that theoretical perspective, they should strengthen ethnic identity for all groups. According to the black exceptionalism hypothesis, that should be true primarily for blacks.

We used a two-item scale based on perceptions of discrimination against oneself and one's own group. We indexed the latter two variables with single items (the specific items are shown in Table 4.3). In the case of Latinos, we present two regression equations. The first uses the same regressors as for whites and blacks, so the coefficients can be compared across ethnic groups. In the second, we add dummy variables for naturalization status and noncitizenship, with U.S.-born as a reference category, to test the assimilation hypothesis. For all groups, we include age and educational level to test the vanguard hypothesis, and we control for income and gender.

Consistent with the black exceptionalism hypothesis, perceived discrimination is more strongly correlated with a strong sense of racial identity among blacks ($r = .24, p < .01$) than among Latinos ($r = .12, p < .05$) or whites ($r = -.04$, n.s.). Both perceived discrimination and sense of common fate continue to have significant effects among blacks, with all demographic controls included in the equation. The coefficients are far higher for blacks than for Latinos. As seen throughout the chapter, the emphasis on group conflict and competition in the politicized group consciousness paradigm fits pretty well with how blacks think about their own racial group. But it is a poorer fit for Latinos, for whom perceived discrimination is not significant in the regression equation. Finally, the data for whites also give minimal credence to that paradigm. White identity is quite unaffected by perceived discrimination or perceived conflict, although the regression coefficient for sense of common fate is significant, as can be seen in Table 4.6.

The story for Latinos has more to do with recent immigration than with group conflict. Both indicators of recent immigration are significantly associated with strong ethnic identities, as the assimilation hypothesis would suggest. The U.S.-born have the weakest ethnic identities, consistent with our hypothesis that strong Latino consciousness is largely a transitional consequence of recent immigration. In other words, the group consciousness variables do not have much resonance among Latinos who are not recent immigrants.

Finally, at the bivariate level, the vanguard hypothesis also received some support among blacks, in that the young have somewhat stronger racial identities. With the subjective elements of group consciousness considered, however, the young are no longer distinctive. It might be expected from the vanguard hypothesis that the young have stronger racial identities because they have a greater sense of common fate and being discriminated against. However, these data do not allow us to disentangle an aging from a generational interpretation of age differences. It is possible that older blacks have learned to accommodate to the American racial system, whereas more hot-blooded youths have not as yet. Alternatively, it is possible that today's generation of young blacks is less willing to accommodate than their elders were, even at the same age. The vanguard hypothesis does not get much support among Latinos or whites.

In short, in this final section, we tested for the origins of strong ethnic group identity. In several ways, we found that the dynamic underlying most versions of the politicized group consciousness paradigm held better for blacks than for whites or Latinos, consistent with the black exceptionalism hypothesis. Even in multivariate equations with other variables controlled, perceived discrimination strengthened ethnic identity among blacks, but rather little among Latinos or whites.

CONCLUSION

This chapter has taken up the question of ethnic group consciousness, a dimension that some hypothesize may stand in dialectical relation to the national identity discussed in the preceding chapter. We are guided in part by the social psychological theories of intergroup relations dominant in the current era, which postulate the ubiquity of group competition and conflict, group-interested motivation, discrimination against groups, and group-based hierarchies. Such theories, we argue, are the psychological substrate underlying hard multiculturalist ideology. We challenge the universality of such phenomena, instead viewing American ethnic and race relations as more conditioned by historical context, in particular the long and unique history of African Americans, and the heavy current waves of immigration from Latin America and East Asia. We argue that the essential elements of the politicized group consciousness paradigm over-generalize the black experience in America to other ethnic groups, and we offer the black exceptionalism and assimilation models as alternatives.

We first question the degree of group conflict in our society: is America now widely perceived as an ethnic cauldron? We do find evidence for considerable perceived intergroup conflict but at the same time note the widespread value placed on diversity, the view of most that interethnic conflict is not inevitable, and optimism that intergroup conflict is likely to decline in the future and that minorities ultimately will join the societal mainstream. We also note that perceptions of interethnic conflict have waxed and waned over time rather than remaining at a constant high pitch. We find little evidence of differences between whites and minorities in the perception of interethnic conflict.

Then we examined ethnic differences in the nature and strength of ethnic group consciousness. In several ways, our data challenge the generalization from African Americans to other ethnic groups. Blacks describe their racial identities using the conventional American pan-ethnic labels, but Latinos and Asians, with heavy immigrant compositions, do not, with many preferring to identify with their national origins, thus suggesting weak identification with the ethnic classification assigned to them in America. Blacks are unique in having the highest group consciousness of any primarily native-born ethnic group. Latinos actually show declining ethnic group consciousness in later postimmigration generations presumably more familiar with the American ethnic system. Most whites have very little racial group consciousness, rather than being hypersensitive to racial threats to their privileged position.

What are the implications of these findings? Most important for our purposes, they suggest that the psychological wherewithal necessary to produce a strong grassroots base for a multiculturalist group rights movement seems to be rarer among minorities than the common elements of politicized group consciousness theories would suggest. These seem to oversimplify the psychological dynamics of America's ethnic relations in three ways. Their explanation of white resistance to multicultural redistribution as being based in a widespread sense of threat among ethnically self-conscious whites seems off the mark. Most whites today have little ethnic group consciousness as whites. Second, they tend to presuppose that all people of color have strong ethnic group consciousness. That does seem to be the case for African Americans and immigrants, but not for U.S.-born minority groups without discernible African origins. Third, the level of aggrieved ethnic group consciousness is quite low except among African Americans, probably too low to be a firm basis for widespread adherence to ideologies of hard multiculturalism or for weakened national unity.

The strong evidence that the assimilation paradigm fits the pattern of identifications among Latinos provides further support for this surmise. All of the components of group consciousness and the composite typology based on them yield the same three general findings. First, whites express little ethnic group consciousness, far less than any of the ethnic minority groups do. This seems inconsistent with the implied subtext in the politicized group consciousness paradigm that many whites experience threat from ethnic and racial minorities.[39] Racially based backlash has a substantial white constituency, as indicated by evidence such as white opposition to black mayoral candidates, President Obama and his policies, school integration, and affirmative action.[40] But white racial backlash seems not to be based very often on a shared and aggrieved sense of whiteness.[41] In other words, the psychological underpinning for racially

---

[39] This theme is most apparent in the "sense of group position" theory (see Blumer, "Prejudice as a Sense of Group Position"; and Bobo and Tuan, *Prejudice in Politics*) that whites' self-conscious perceptions of threat to their privileged ethnic position are the primary engines for their resistance to political efforts to promote racial equality.

[40] Zoltan Hajnal, *Changing White Attitudes toward Black Political Leadership* (New York: Cambridge University Press, 2006); Kinder and Sears, "Prejudice and Politics"; Donald R. Kinder and Allison Dale-Riddle, *The End of Race? Obama, 2008, and Racial Politics in America* (New Haven, CT: Yale University Press, 2012); Tesler and Sears, *Obama's Race*; David O. Sears, Carl P. Hensler, and Leslie K. Speer, "Whites' Opposition to 'Busing': Self-Interest or Symbolic Politics?" *American Political Science Review* 73 (1979): 369–84; David O. Sears, Colette van Laar, Mary Carrillo, and Rick Kosterman, "Is It Really Racism?: The Origins of White American Opposition to Race-Targeted Policies," *Public Opinion Quarterly* 61 (1997): 16–53.

[41] See David O. Sears, and P. J. Henry, "Over Thirty Years Later."

based backlash among whites is less a distinctive in-group identification as white than anti-minority animus.

Second, the black exceptionalism idea hypothesizes that blacks continue to show unusually high levels of aggrieved racial consciousness and thus form a potentially strong base for group-conscious policies.[42] It receives consistent support in these analyses. Perhaps the most telling comparison is between blacks and U.S.-born Latinos, who are on average similarly economically disadvantaged but, we argue, less likely to be trapped on the wrong side of the color line. Blacks generally have stronger ethnic identity, a sense of common fate, and more often feel victimized by discrimination. This is contrary to Huntington's gloomy view of a future society with increasing numbers of U.S.-born Latinos adding to the politically alienated. Still, the persistence of this gap between blacks and U.S.-born Latinos would surely be bad news for American unity, perhaps because of mutual resentment between these two groups, something at which our data do hint. And, unfortunately, there seems to be some agreement that the impressive gains made by blacks after World War II have slowed or stopped in the past three decades, a structural factor that can bolster the sense of grievance described earlier.[43]

Third, these findings also support the assimilation hypothesis, suggesting that the current high level of ethnic consciousness among Latinos as a whole is coming more from immigrants than from native-born Hispanic Americans. The clearest indicator is that foreign-born Latinos are far higher than U.S.-born Latinos on the composite ethnic consciousness typology. One implication is that the current strong group consciousness of Latinos may be somewhat transitional, just as ethnic politics had been in earlier generations of European ethnics, and may wane as they assimilate into the broader society. Again, the gap in-group consciousness between blacks and Latinos as a whole may grow with time as the proportion of the native-born Latinos increases relative to immigrants and assimilation processes such as residential integration and intermarriage affect more of them.

This suggests, as Nathan Glazer has said, that the pressure for multiculturalist solutions to ethnic and racial issues stems largely from the unique black experience in the United States.[44] We go beyond Glazer in noting the distinctive group consciousness of foreign-born Latinos, suggesting that it may be a transitional phase as successive generations of Latino immigrants assimilate into the mainstream of the society. Only about a third of U.S.-born Latinos fell into even the moderately aggrieved group consciousness category, far fewer than the more

[42] Sears and Savalei, "The Political Color Line in America"; Glazer, *We Are All Multiculturalists Now*; Lee and Bean, *The Diversity Paradox*.

[43] Sears, Hetts, Sidanius, and Bobo, "Race in American Politics: Framing the Debates"; Michael A. Stoll, "African Americans and the Color Line," in *The American People: Census 2000*, ed. Reynolds Farley and John Haaga (New York: Russell Sage Foundation, 2005); Thernstrom and Thernstrom, *America in Black and White*.

[44] Glazer, *We Are All Multiculturalists Now*.

than half of the black respondents who did. We also note that even immigrant Latinos, at least those in the national sample interviewed by the Pew Trust, feel they are better off than they would be in their native lands. This too sustains Glazer's view that one crucial difference between the black experience and that of today's Latinos and Asians lies in the voluntary nature of nonblacks' immigration. Another we would add is the relative impermeability of the color line confronted by African Americans. As Glazer has said, multiculturalism is the product, ultimately, of America's failure to realize its ideals of equality, most particularly in the case of African Americans. Black exceptionalism would seem to explain the politics of race and ethnicity in America today better than do models focusing on more widespread perceptions of intergroup conflict and universal group-based hierarchies.

5

Public Opinion and Multiculturalism's Guiding Norms

In the preceding chapter, we saw that only a small minority in each ethnic group viewed America (or Los Angeles) as a cauldron in which irreconcilable ethnic conflicts boiled and bubbled. However, in establishing the general acceptance of the feasibility and desirability of *e pluribus unum*, we did not directly assess public opinion about the main principles of multiculturalism as a political ideology. In reviewing the many variants of multiculturalism in the scholarly literature, we distinguished among three components: a theory of personal identity, an image of the political community, and a set of policies designed to implement the normative commitment to the official recognition, representation, and protection of minority groups and their cultures.

In this chapter, we turn to public opinion about these core commitments to group-conscious principles. First, should society recognize an official responsibility for sustaining ethnic diversity, in the sense of government support for the maintenance of cultural differences in the face of the ongoing pressures toward acculturation? We describe this domain as *social multiculturalism*. Second, should these underlying ideas about the value of preserving ethnic identities and supporting the maintenance of particular cultures on a basis of equality dictate a policy regime based on descriptive representation in domains ranging from politics and professional occupations to the content of education and other cultural areas? We describe this outlook as *political multiculturalism*.

We earlier laid out a dimension that cuts across the contrast between the social and political domains. There are hard and soft multiculturalist versions of each. In our view, only the hard version's insistence on formal ethnic preferences and the equal status of all languages and cultural practices in a multiethnic policy constitutes a radical departure from America's historical openness to absorbing into the mainstream culture many of the customs and traditions of new immigrants. Institutionalizing these norms of communal representation and equality of results would be a striking departure from America's historical emphasis on individual achievement and advancement.[1] Americans have generally proclaimed the virtue of self-reliance, usually saying that people should be admitted to select educational programs and achieve professional success as a result of their own efforts and not because of their Caucasian, Cuban, Chinese, or other ethnic backgrounds.[2] Hence the pervasive support for equality of opportunity when the civil rights movement pitted that individualistic principle against the Jim Crow system of group-conscious racial discrimination.

The multicultural movement challenges this tradition of self-reliance, with many of its advocates claiming that a "neutral" merit principle is just a convenient cover for a system that continues to privilege economically, politically, and socially dominant groups at the expense of minorities. Even more radical versions of multiculturalism dismiss the idea of a perfectly fair color-blind process of allocating rewards as not just unrealistic but undesirable. For multiculturalists who focus on the need for redistribution of power and wealth, the reality of discrimination, even if subtle, and the natural advantages of the majority group justify affirmative action and other modes of redistribution. They argue that society would be better off by honestly acknowledging the enduring differences and conflicts among ethnic groups and the inevitable conflicts of interest between them, recognizing and accepting the prioritization of their group identities, and institutionalizing group representation through law.

Power-sharing arrangements and group rights are a familiar approach to keeping the peace in ethnically divided societies such as Lebanon, Belgium, Malaysia, Nigeria, Sri Lanka, and Canada. To varying degrees, the conflicts among linguistic, religion, and racial groups in these countries necessitated arrangements based on separate identities as the price of keeping them from breaking apart.[3] In the United States, echoes of Horace Kallen's description of the United States as a confederation of separate ethnic nations began to be heard in the late 1960s after the color-blind agenda of the civil rights movement was perceived by black activists and others on the political left as insufficient to produce true racial equality. However, those echoes were clearly faint and did not resonate sufficiently to engage pervasive political attention or reaction.

This chapter examines public opinion about multicultural norms. It has three main foci. First, we assess the extent of support among their presumed beneficiaries – ethnic and racial minorities. Second, we consider the constraint among beliefs about multiculturalist norms to probe the extent to which these ideas have been absorbed as a coherent ideology among ordinary citizens as opposed to intellectuals and political activists. Finally, through both

---

[1] A good example of the advocacy of such norms is given in Iris Young's *Justice and the Politics of Difference.*

[2] Data from the cumulative National Election Study 1960–2008 file show that, since 1986, Americans have opposed affirmative action by approximately four to one when it is defined in terms of racial preferences.

[3] See, e.g., Deborah Prentice and Dale Miller, eds., *Cultural Divides: Understanding and Overcoming Group Conflict* (New York: Russell Sage Foundation, 1999), 23–34.

simple bivariate comparisons and multivariate analysis, we test the fit of the data with the psychological perspectives described earlier: politicized group consciousness, immigrant assimilation, and black exceptionalism. To preview the most important results, we find substantial acceptance in all groups for the softer multiculturalist proposals that promote tolerance and the symbolic recognition of minority cultures. Conversely, we find little support for the hard multicultural principles of institutionalized group representation, even among the minority groups that they are intended to benefit.

SUPPORT FOR THE NORMS OF SOCIAL MULTICULTURALISM

The preceding chapter indicated that Americans do recognize the presence of persistent ethnic divisions in politics and accept the likelihood that ethnic groups will pursue their particular interests. Yet they are optimistic that, over time, ethnic conflicts, even if sometimes heated, will diminish in frequency and intensity. Given that most of the public does perceive American society as divided by ethnicity, do most also accept the multiculturalist view that ethnic differences as manifested in cultural diversity should persist and that state action to assure this is warranted?

What we label "social multiculturalism" embodies a commitment to the value of cultural diversity. Viewing ethnic and racial groups as enduring social entities, this viewpoint proposes the institutionalization of cultural differences. Accordingly, official efforts to promote assimilation to the white mainstream should be opposed. This contrasts with the nativist view that ethnic differences and conflict should be overcome through a program of Americanization, which is hoped to lead to one common culture. But given that we found in Chapter 4 that only a minority of our respondents regarded ethnic conflict as an inevitable feature of political life, it is plausible to expect that most Americans would regard cultural pluralism as quite compatible with social comity.

Consistent with this surmise, the top panel of Table 5.1 shows that the overwhelming majority in every ethnic group agrees that each group has the right to retain its own ethnic traditions, although the specific customs are not spelled out. Few Americans want to insist on the elimination of cultural differences between ethnic groups. Even among whites, 82 percent support such groups' rights to remain somewhat ethnically different, although ethnic minorities are much more likely to strongly agree with that view.

When it comes to official support for recognition of cultural differences, however, a sharper ethnic divide emerges. Whites are split over the question of how much attention to ethnic and racial history should be provided in the schools. A visible minority tilts toward believing too much attention is currently being paid to it, as would be expected from politicized group consciousness theories that focus on racial hierarchy and group-based conflicts of interest. Still, even whites do not endorse the more conservative position of actually *reducing* attention to minority groups in the curriculum. By contrast,

TABLE 5.1. *Support for Social Multiculturalism, by Ethnicity*

	Whites	Blacks	Latinos
Tolerance for and Recognition of Cultural Diversity			
... to help create a harmonious society, each ethnic group [should have] the right to maintain its own unique traditions[1]			
2002 GSS (% strongly agree)	28	41[a]	44[a]
(% agree)	54[a]	46[a,b]	44[b]
In history classes in high school and college, do the experiences of racial and ethnic minority groups in America receive too much attention now, too little Attention, or about the right amount?			
1994 GSS (% too little)	17	59	–
(% about right)	52	35	–
(% too much)	31	6	–
1994 LACSS (% too little)	28	60	44
(% about right)	48[a]	30	46[a]
(% too much)	24	11[a]	10[a]
Ethnic minorities should be given government assistance to preserve their customs and traditions.			
1996 GSS (% agree or agree strongly)[1]	11	44	–
2004 GSS (% agree or agree strongly)[1]	18	41	–
Overall Support for Cultural Assimilation			
People should think of themselves first and foremost as an individual American, rather than as a member of a racial, religious, or ethnic group			
1994–95 LACSS (% disagree)[1]	9	23[a]	24[a]
In order to have a smoothly functioning society, members of ethnic minorities must better adapt to the ways of American mainstream culture			
2002 GSS (% disagree)[1]	18[a]	32[b]	21[a,b]
Should different racial and ethnic groups maintain their distinct cultures and traditions, or adapt and blend into the larger society as in the idea of the melting pot?			

(continued)

TABLE 5.1 (continued)

	Whites	Blacks	Latinos
1992 ANES (% maintain distinctiveness)	35[a]	35[a]	40[a]
(% blend)	45[a]	56	40[a]
1994 GSS (% maintain distinctiveness)	30	41	–
(% blend)	39[a]	37[a]	–
1994–95 LACSS (% maintain distinctiveness)	26[a]	29[b]	30[a,b]
(% blend)	49[a]	50[a]	58
1996 GSS (% maintain distinctiveness)	29	33	–
(% blend)	45	35	–
2004 GSS (% maintain distinctiveness)	47[a]	45[a]	–
(% blend)	50[a]	53[a]	–

Little Support for Racial and Ethnic Separation Except for Latinos
We would have fewer social problems if people of the same
ethnic background lived and worked with people like themselves

	Whites	Blacks	Latinos
1994–95, 2000–01 LACSS (% agree)[1]	17[a]	20[a]	46
Minimum Base N (GSS 1994)	1,044	177	–
Minimum Base N (GSS 1996)	1,029	156	–
Minimum Base N (GSS 2002)	2,159	396	86
Minimum Base N (GSS 2004)	1,725	278	–
Minimum Base N (ANES 1992)	925	152	89
Minimum Base N (LACSS 1994)	247	220	243
Minimum Base N (LACSS 1994–95)	533	293	453

Entries for Latinos included only if $N > 80$. Entries show amount of support for social multiculturalism.
[1] Base includes all other responses.
Superscripts denote results of independent samples t-tests. All entries in a given row are significantly different ($p < .05$) unless they share the same superscript.
Source: American National Election Studies (ANES); General Social Survey (GSS); Los Angeles County Social Survey (LACSS).

a strong majority of blacks and a plurality of Latinos want more attention to their groups' histories. Indeed, blacks are by far the group most supportive of this change in how history is taught. This is another version of the theme introduced in Chapter 3; blacks are especially sensitive about the nation's history of racial inequality, and this influences their reactions to national institutions, symbols, and policies. In terms of the symbolic recognition of diversity, then, we again see evidence of black exceptionalism. Nevertheless, a national majority accepts the cultural differences present in America, at least in the abstract, an outlook compatible with at least what we have termed "soft multiculturalism."

Only a small minority of whites, around 15 percent or so, favor government assistance for preserving minorities' customs and traditions, however, signifying an overwhelming rejection among the majority group for a policy that is at the core of the multiculturalist agenda. Indeed, virtually every theorist of multiculturalism, including the self-labeled "liberal culturalist" Kymlicka, argues that official support is a necessary condition for the preservation of minority cultures.[4] We see much more substantial black support, more than 40 percent, for government action, however, so this is another issue on which cleavages between the races do surface.

More importantly, tolerance of some diversity in cultural traditions does not extend to elevating the status of ethnic identities above one's common national identity as an American. When given a simple dichotomous choice, wide majorities of all three main ethnic groups believe that people should think of themselves first and foremost as individual Americans rather than as a member of a subnational group, as shown in the middle panel of Table 5.1. This preference for American identity turns out to apply not merely to the respondent him- or herself, but to be a belief about what should be a general social norm for all Americans. The prioritization of a common national identity, even while recognizing the reality of ethnic differences in customs and preferences, runs counter to the tendency of hard multiculturalism to question the value of such superordinate identities.

Broad support is also expressed for the idea that minorities should adapt to the ways of the mainstream American culture in order to have a smoothly functioning society. In the general public, majorities in all ethnic groups believe that minorities "must better adapt" to mainstream culture. Similarly, Pew surveys of Hispanics and Asians have found general agreement that it was important to get along with other cultures and that learning English was essential for success in America.[5] A large majority of even the usually group-conscious blacks supports cultural assimilation, although here they may be

---

[4] See the account in Song, "Multiculturalism"; and Kymlicka, *Politics in the Vernacular*, chapter 2.
[5] Pew Hispanic Center, "National Survey of Latinos: Summary of Findings." See also, Pew Research Center, "The Rise of Asian Americans."

thinking of immigrants rather than of their own group.[6] Further confirmation comes from the 2006 Latino National Survey. More than 92 percent of those Hispanic respondents – more than 60 percent of whom preferred to take the survey in Spanish rather than English – indicated that it was very important for everyone in the United States to learn English. Only slightly more than 1 percent said it was not very or not at all important.

Moving *toward* the mainstream is one thing. But what are feelings about the possible *disappearance* of minority cultures? Are Americans more likely to support ethnic and racial groups' maintaining their distinctive cultures if the alternative is to blend into the broader society, as in the idea of the melting pot? We asked, "Should different racial and ethnic groups maintain their distinct cultures and traditions, or adapt and blend into the larger society as in the idea of the melting pot?" This dichotomous choice poses starkly the distinction between assimilationist and multiculturalist goals.

The data show a majority preference for adapting and blending in as the appropriate behavior for racial and ethnic groups. Admittedly, the content of both what would be abandoned by blending in and maintained by not adapting are unspecified in the question, leaving what is in the respondent's mind opaque. Thus, it is not clear whether the assimilationist option of the melting pot would actually mean the disappearance of cultural diversity in language use, voting preferences, child-rearing, dress, music, or food. Also, the fact that opinion about blending in versus maintaining distinctive cultures is relatively divided suggests that many Americans do not view cultural assimilation and cultural pluralism as incompatible. When respondents are given the middle choice that minorities should *both* blend and maintain, a substantial number gravitate to that option. Still, support for cultural assimilation always is the majority or plurality viewpoint.[7]

Finally, the civil rights movement carried forward a dramatic consensus on the desirability of racial integration. Has that momentum faltered in this era of ethnic change and identity politics, such that the emphasis on cultural differences and the intensification of ethnic pride have made minorities more supportive of separation?[8] In this respect our data again find little support among either whites

---

[6] The one-third of blacks who say minorities should retain their original cultures is approximately the same proportion we described in Chapter 4 as highly group conscious and also about the same proportion found in past research as sympathetic to black nationalism and separatism. Unfortunately, we do not have all these items in any one survey so this parallel cannot be explored further.

[7] No middle choice was offered in either the 1996 or the 2004 GSS question. Yet not shown in Table 5.1, a far higher share of respondents volunteered a "don't know" response in 1996 than in 2004. The questions were identical in structure and were part of the same module in both years, so the reason for the discrepancy is not clear. An analyst at NORC suggested that the decrease in "don't know" responses may be attributable to the fact that, in 1996, the module was completed by the respondent whereas in 2004 it was administered as a computer-assisted personal interview. However, decreases in "don't know" responses in other questions in the module between 1996 and 2004 were far more modest.

[8] Rhea, *Race Pride and the American Identity*.

or blacks for separatist tendencies that fit a preference for maintaining group differences. The bottom panel of Table 5.1 shows opinions about a society in which "people of the same ethnic background lived and worked with people like themselves." Racial and ethnic segregation, once widely supported among whites and more recently an occasional flirtation for some black intellectuals, is broadly unpopular among ordinary citizens in those groups. The somewhat surprising exception is that almost half the Latinos favored this notion of ethnic separation. This level of Latino approval for separation was quite steady; we found evidence for it in both the pooled 1994–1995 and the pooled 2001–2002 Los Angeles County Social Surveys (LACSSs). We return later to an interpretation for this departure from the norm in other groups.

SUPPORT FOR THE NORMS OF POLITICAL MULTICULTURALISM

Individual achievement based on the merit principle is the dominant norm in American culture, whatever the limits on the fulfillment of this ideal in practice. *What* you are rather than *who* you are should govern success. Rights, Justice Sandra Day O'Connor wrote in *Richmond v. Croson*, are individual rights and are to be enjoyed equally whether one is white or black. It seems most of the public agrees.[9]

The formal norms for political representation in the United States are similarly individualistic. There are no provisions for communal representation or for guaranteeing a share of seats in the legislature to women or minority groups such as have sometimes been instituted in other countries, plans that have often been described by political theorists as *descriptive representation*.[10] In principle at least, representation is organized in the United States on a geographical basis rather than according to group membership. In practice, of course, matters are more complex. Candidates are often selected to maximize a party's appeal to the ethnic make-up of a constituency, much as redistricting often uses geography to bias vote outcomes toward one party or the other.

The Voting Rights Act of 1965 can be viewed as a deviation from this individualistic principle. The law sought to overcome barriers against minority representation based on prejudice, but also puts a thumb on the scales in favor of electing minorities in majority-minority districts. It is a deviation that was justified at the time on the basis of the extraordinary obstacles historically placed in the way of African Americans' rights to vote, especially in the states of the former Confederacy. However, it took a heavy body blow from the U.S. Supreme Court in 2013, putatively on the grounds that the data regarding black voting

---

[9] *City of Richmond v. J. A. Croson and Co.* 488 U.S. 469 (1989). For a review of public opinion on facets of affirmative action and steady majority support for the merit principle, see Loan Le and Jack Citrin, "Affirmative Action" in Nathaniel Persily, Jack Citrin, and Patrick J. Egan eds., *Public Opinion and Constitutional Controversy* (New York: Oxford University Press, 2008).

[10] Hanna Pitkin, *The Concept of Representation* (Berkeley: University of California Press, 1972).

that presented one justification for federal oversight of redistricting plans and other electoral arrangement now were out of date.[11]

Cosmopolitan liberals and multiculturalists could agree that the specific history of infringements of African Americans' rights to vote, ongoing discrimination, and racial polarization in voting might warrant some guarantees that minorities had a fair chance to win elections. However, multiculturalism expresses a more deep-seated opposition to many of the standard individualistic arrangements for representation, and not just in electoral politics. Its advocates argue that ostensibly meritocratic systems often are biased and unfair. Historic shortcomings in terms of schooling, wealth, nutrition, power, social connections, and other factors have placed ethnic and racial minorities at a competitive disadvantage in most meritocratic systems. White elites tend to be in charge of organizing and administering the systems that define and measure merit, such as creating the tests that determine admission into college, conducting the job interviews, and controlling the political redistricting process. To return concretely to the example centrally relevant to the rise of multiculturalism, for many years, blacks were excluded from elective political office in the South through a variety of ostensibly meritocratic ruses imposed by white elites, such as literacy tests, poll taxes, at-large legislative districts, and so on.

To combat the biases introduced by nominally color-blind norms and so protect minorities from the self-interested drive of the majority group to remain dominant, some multiculturalists have proposed arrangements that guarantee increased representation of minorities. In its most extreme versions, this includes a call for proportional representation of specific ethnic and racial groups in important political, economic, and social roles, including in education.[12] By this principle, if 10 percent of Californians are black, then 10 percent of the students admitted to the University of California should be black, 10 percent of the faculty positions at state universities should be reserved for blacks, and 10 percent of the congressional seats in California should be set aside for blacks. The same principle of allocation should apply to other underrepresented minorities and, some argue, for women, gays, the disabled, and so forth. In a word, group rights are justified as a necessary response to the past disadvantages and current prejudices that lead to the underrepresentation of less powerful groups.

Underlying the defense of group rights and descriptive representation is the notion that someone sharing your own background – race, religion, gender, or ethnicity – can better know your true interests than someone of dissimilar background and can be trusted better to act on behalf of your interests as well as to protect your distinctive values and practices. Shared attitudes or policy preferences help but are not enough; a sense of common history, common experiences, and other similarities amounting to a form of kinship binds constituents and legislators,

---

[11] *Shelby County, Alabama v. Holder, Attorney General, et al.* 570 U.S. (2013).

[12] Lani Guinier, *The Tyranny of the Majority: Fundamental Fairness in Representative Democracy* (New York: Simon & Schuster, 1995).

students and teachers who share the same ethnicity or race. So, in assessing support for political multiculturalism (or group rights), a key indicator is the degree to which Americans, especially ethnic and racial minorities, favor the idea of descriptive representation, a principle historically opposed by cosmopolitan liberals.

Our survey data include two items measuring support for the idea of communal representation. One asked respondents whether people are best represented in politics by leaders from their own racial and ethnic background; a second probed whether one's own congressman should emphasize the concerns of "people like me" or those of "the country in general." As shown in Table 5.2, only a minority in each ethnic group chose the hard multiculturalist alternatives of descriptive representation. Clear majorities selected the standard individualistic alternatives, saying that the racial and ethnic background of political leaders doesn't make much difference in the quality of their representation and that congressmen should focus on helping the country in general rather than a narrowly defined ethnic group. Most tellingly, majorities of both blacks and Latinos do not favor this kind of descriptive representation. This is another example of the broadly based rejection of institutionalizing group rights that we report throughout this chapter.

A third item on ethnic representation in the abstract asked whether or not political organizations based on race or ethnicity promote separatism and make it hard for all of us to live together. Again, Table 5.2 shows that large majorities in all ethnic groups are seen to be unfavorable to organizational activity based mainly on race and ethnicity, although minority respondents are more sanguine about the effects of such organizations than are whites.

It is possible that people would respond more favorably to the idea of descriptive representation if asked about more specific situations than in the abstract. In the bottom panel of Table 5.2 we present the results for items asking about guaranteeing increased representation for minorities in several specific domains. However, in these concrete situations the principle of group rights is even more overwhelmingly rejected in favor of an individualistic norm. Descriptive representation for congressmen, teachers in public schools and universities, and admission to professional schools is accepted by only a small minority in all ethnic groups, with support among whites of less than 10 percent and typically of less than 20 percent among minorities. This is even less than the same level of support given government assistance for the maintenance of minority cultures that we showed in Table 5.1, the low water mark for support of social multiculturalism in this study. The one exception is that there is somewhat greater support, although still not a majority, for assuring that the history of a racial or ethnic minority group should be taught by a member of that group.

Despite the general consensus opposing proportional representation on ethnic lines, there are some predictable differences. Ethnic minorities are more likely than whites to accept the multiculturalist view, and sometimes the differences in opinion are large. Blacks in particular are more sympathetic to descriptive representation in the abstract than are other groups. For

TABLE 5.2. *Support for Political Multiculturalism, by Ethnicity*

	Whites	Blacks	Latinos
Descriptive Representation in the Abstract			
Are people best represented in politics by leaders from their own racial or ethnic background or doesn't the leader's background make much difference?			
1994 GSS (% own)	34	43	–
1994 LACSS (% own)	35[a]	41[b]	37[a,b]
I want my representatives in Congress to do things that help the country in general, or. . .to emphasize the concerns of people like me?			
1998–99, 2001 LACSS (% people like me)	26	41	30
Political organizations based on race or ethnicity promote separatism and make it hard for all of us to live together			
1994 GSS (% disagree)[1]	13	29	–
1994 LACSS (% disagree)	14	30[a]	28[a]
Descriptive Representation in Specific Domains			
Should congressmen have the same racial or ethnic background as their constituents or be considered purely on the basis of ability?			
1994 GSS (% ethnicity)	6	28	–
1994 LACSS (% ethnicity)	8	19	23
Should teachers in public schools and universities reflect students' ethnicity or be considered purely on the basis of ability?			
1994 GSS (% ethnicity)	6	18	–
1994 LACSS (% ethnicity)	6	13[a]	10[a]
Should students in professional schools have roughly the same ethnic and racial backgrounds as the people in their area or be considered purely on the basis of their ability?			
1994 GSS (% ethnicity)	4	15	–
The experience of a racial or ethnic minority group should be taught by a teacher from that group			
1994 GSS (% agree)[1]	22	45	–
1994 LACSS (% agree)	33	46[a]	47[a]
Minimum Base *N* (GSS 1994)	1,151	186	–
Minimum Base *N* (LACSS 1994)	269	222	247
Minimum Base *N* (LACSS 1998, 2001)	509	373	475

Data for Latinos not shown if *N* < 60. Entries show support for political multiculturalism.
[1] Base also includes "disagree" and "neither agree nor disagree."
Superscripts denote results of independent samples t-tests. All entries in a given row are significantly different ($p < .05$) unless they share the same superscript.
Source: General Social Survey (GSS), Los Angeles County Social Surveys (LACSS).

example, almost half the blacks in the national 1994 General Social Survey (GSS) agreed that people are best represented by people of their own background. Similarly, a substantial minority of blacks and Latinos do support descriptive representation in concrete situations, whereas this idea receives virtually no support among whites.

Our first conclusion, then, is that Americans of all racial and ethnic groups share a broad consensus on a particular middle-of-the-road version of soft multiculturalism. There is widespread tolerance for minorities' cultural traditions and distinctiveness, for the cultural "salad bowl," as it is sometimes described. But they also share a general consensus on a largely individualistic, assimilationist response to cultural differences in American society, rather than adopting the multiculturalist solution of organizing the society and polity around acknowledging ethnic and racial groups more formally and giving them specific group rights. Indeed, majorities in all three groups fall on the same side of twenty of the twenty-five questions shown in Tables 5.1 and 5.2. The main exceptions is that about half of the whites in a national sample and in Lose Angeles tended to believe that about the right amount of attention was being paid to the experiences of minority groups in history classes, whereas large majorities of blacks said too little attention is being paid to them. Otherwise the consensus across ethnic and racial groups is striking. Finally, we should reiterate that the acceptance of cultural pluralism does not extend to support for government aid to assure the persistence of minority cultures, a central tenet of multiculturalist ideology and practice in Canada and elsewhere.

Our second conclusion is that this cross-ethnic consensus regarding aggregate positions is subject to some qualifications. There is consistently more support for multiculturalism among minorities than among whites. Also, in some domains, blacks show the sharpest departures from that consensus, particularly in the recognition and appreciation of diversity, consistent with the theme of black exceptionalism introduced earlier. Finally, the one area in which Latinos seem to be distinctly different from both whites and blacks is in the acceptance or even preference for some separateness – to live and work among their own kind. This finding emerged in every LACSS and is consistent with Huntington's fear that Mexican Americans will not assimilate, especially those living near the Mexican border. One possible explanation for the black–Latino difference is that the history of slavery and Jim Crow has convinced blacks that the norms of assimilation and integration help prevent them from being sequestered in a lower caste position and shunted aside. Latinos, largely without that history, may not see integration as so valuable. Another possible explanation is that immigrant populations frequently integrate into the broader society through transitional communities of fellow immigrants, beginning their American lives in ethnic enclaves. The Latino population stems predominantly from relatively recent immigration, whereas the black population does not. If so, in this respect, too, Latinos would seem to be replicating the temporary desire for ethnic neighborhoods once so visible among the European immigrants of a century ago, now waning.[13] We test this possibility in the section titled "Assimilation of Immigrants" later in this chapter.

THE COHERENCE OF MULTICULTURALISM NORMS IN THE MASS PUBLIC

Among some political elites, multiculturalism appears to reflect a considered ideology, a well-connected set of beliefs, with one's opinion about the moral significance of group identities and differences guiding opinion formation across a range of specific issues. But does such structured thinking prevail in the mass public? In other words, among ordinary citizens, is multiculturalism a belief system whose overarching principles promote consistent thinking about public policies relating to ethnic group relations?[14]

Testing for the coherence of multicultural ideas poses something of a challenge for us because the questions about multicultural norms were asked in a number of different surveys rather than all being included in the same one. Additionally, these surveys varied considerably in ethnic composition. For that reason, sample-wide statistics would not have the same meaning in the ethnically complex Los Angeles surveys as in the nationally representative, predominantly white GSS. As a result, we tested for coherence within each survey that had sufficient numbers of multiculturalism items and large enough subsamples to conduct separate analyses for each ethnic group.

One approach was to create multi-item scales, which in most cases had rather low reliabilities in the samples as a whole. In the 1994 GSS, we found a high reliability for a three-item ethnic entitlements scale (alpha = .78) made up of the items asking about descriptive representation in Congress, teachers, and students in professional schools, but a very low reliability for a three-item scale made up of the more abstract questions about descriptive representation (alpha = .30). In the LACSS 1994, we found alphas of only .46 and .30 for two three-item scales focused on social multiculturalism and descriptive representation, respectively. In the 2002 GSS, we found that an "ethnic essentialism" scale comprised of the two questions about the distinctiveness of ethnic groups, including whites, had reasonable reliability (alpha = .59). A four-item social multiculturalism scale tapping attitudes about assimilation did not, however (alpha = .46). Other combinations of items tapping multicultural norms equally failed to produce scales with adequate reliabilities. So, only the ethnic essentialism and ethnic representation scales had significant reliabilities in the total samples. However, in each case, the wordings of the items making up the scale are so similar that we question whether they reflect a deep ideological consistency as opposed to superficial methodological artifacts.

A second approach adopted Converse's measurement of issue constraint and involved computing the average correlations across items in a particular

---

[13] Richard Alba, *Ethnicity in America*; Alba and Nee, *Remaking the American Mainstream*.
[14] Converse, "The Nature of Belief Systems in Mass Publics."

domain.[15] The outcome was not very different and failed to produce evidence of an overarching multicultural belief system in the mass public. We computed the average correlations across all the items in Tables 5.1 to 5.2 within each survey and each ethnic subsample. These average correlations are all quite small, except in the black subsample of the 1994 GSS, where the average correlation is $r = .27$, still modest at best. This relatively higher degree of constraint is mostly due to blacks' having more coherent attitudes about descriptive representation and about social multiculturalism. The other correlations range from $r = .15$ to $r = -.06$, and the median r is a paltry .07.

Given this substantial evidence of weak coherence *within* domains, is there any evidence of connective tissue *across* domains? The simple answer is no. Perhaps the clearest demonstration is the weak correlation between the ethnic essentialism and social multiculturalism scales in the 2002 GSS. In the total sample, the correlation was $r = .15$ ($p < .05$). Among whites, it was only slightly higher ($r = .18$, $p < .05$). In any case, these indices involve only a handful of the questions at our disposal on multicultural norms. As a result, they would seem to be of limited usefulness in the analyses to follow. So our inquiry into the underpinnings of support and opposition to multicultural norms is forced to use selected individual items rather than composite scales.

In sum, despite the voluminous literature about multiculturalism and the years of debates about diversity among political, academic, and media elites, it seems evident that the general ideas making up a multiculturalist ideology have not penetrated the mass public in ways that have produced a pervasive system of interconnected beliefs about the politics of difference in the American public.[16]

EXPLAINING ATTITUDES TOWARD MULTICULTURALIST NORMS

Adaptation to the mainstream remains the majority ideal in the surveys we have analyzed, along with a soft multiculturalist tolerance for ethnic differences. Hard multiculturalism's emphasis on group rights clearly is unpopular. Still, in the

---

[15] Ibid., 230.

[16] To say something about our overall strategy in testing the limits of coherence, we did factor analyses in the available surveys within each ethnic group and for the full samples using both orthogonal (varimax) and oblique (oblimin) rotations; scale reliabilities, again both within ethnic groups and for the full samples; average correlations within ethnic groups and for full samples; and average correlations both within and between attitude domains. Our conclusion is that attitudes toward multicultural norms do not show the same coherence as even the policy issues that usually are the focal points of partisan debate, which generally show only modest constraint (see Converse, "The Nature of Belief Systems in Mass Publics"; Donald R. Kinder, "Attitude and Action in the Realm of Politics," in *Handbook of Social Psychology*, ed. Daniel Gilbert, Susan Fiske, and Gardner Lindzey (Boston: McGraw-Hill, 1998), 778–867; Kinder, "Belief Systems after Converse," in *Electoral Democracy*, ed. Michael McKuen and George Rabinowitz. Ann Arbor: University of Michigan Press, 2000; Michael S. Lewis-Beck, et al. *The American Voter Revisited* (Ann Arbor: University of Michigan Press, 2008).

remainder of this chapter, we explore the limited variation in support for such ideas that we have found. In doing so, we concentrate on the survey questions close to the core of multiculturalism's emphasis on group recognition and representation and which generated significant ethnic differences in the simple cross-tabulations presented in Tables 5.1 and 5.2. Due to the limited numbers of minorities in national samples, we again use the LACSS for evidence about these groups. We consider the same four sets of factors in probing the determinants of support for multiculturalism as we pursued in earlier chapters: minority group consciousness, the assimilation of immigrants, the vanguard hypothesis, and the possible incompatibility of multiculturalism with strong feelings of national identity.

Minority Group Consciousness

We have repeatedly emphasized that multiculturalism is a redistributive ideology, seeking to enhance the societal position of minority groups through a program of official recognition and representation that reallocates both tangible and symbolic benefits to them away from the dominant white ethnic group. Identity politics, exemplified by a strong sense of group consciousness, should foster support for multiculturalism among minorities. More support for group-based rights, even at some expense of the cosmopolitan liberal ideal of equality of opportunity for individuals, should be particularly likely when perceptions of discrimination fuel strong group identification. Hence, strong ethnic group consciousness should function as the psychological foundation for the balkanized America most pungently attacked by Schlesinger and Huntington.[17]

The politicized group consciousness hypothesis suggests that group consciousness should contribute to support for multiculturalism, an ideology intended to promote minorities' group interests, enhancing their power and status. Our test begins with cross-tabulations of blacks' and Latinos' group consciousness by support for multiculturalism. Group consciousness was indexed by the strength of their ethnic identity and by perceived discrimination. Support for multiculturalism was indexed by the items shown in Tables 5.1 and 5.2. We rely mostly on the Los Angeles surveys for this purpose, both because few group consciousness measures were available in the GSS, and because there were usually too few blacks and Latinos in the GSS to allow for reliable subgroup analyses.

The top panel of Table 5.3 presents cross-tabulations of the importance of one's own ethnic identity by the multiculturalism items appearing in the same surveys. Among blacks, stronger racial identity was consistently and significantly associated with more support for multiculturalism. However, the differences tend to be modest, averaging 8 percent. No particular pattern seems to hold among Latinos, and the differences are quite small on average (3 percent more favorable to multiculturalism).

---

[17] Schlesinger Jr., *The Disuniting of America*; Huntington, *Who Are We?*

TABLE 5.3. *Support for Multiculturalism: The Ethnic Minority Group Consciousness Hypothesis*

	Blacks		Latinos	
Importance of Own Ethnic Identity:	High	Low	High	Low
Social Multiculturalism				
Each ethnic group has the right to maintain its own traditions				
2002 GSS (% agree)	90	78	89[a]	88[a]
Minorities must adapt				
2002 GSS (% disagree)	32	21	24	14
Better off if live and work with own				
1998–99 LACSS (% agree)	22	17	39[a]	40[a]
Political Multiculturalism				
Representatives represent country in general or people like me?				
1998–99 LACSS (% people like me)	44	38	32[a]	30[a]
Perceived Discrimination against Own Group:	High	Low	High	Low
Social Multiculturalism				
Attention to ethnic history?				
1994 LACSS (% too little)	66	54	53	37
Should think of selves as individual Americans, not ethnics				
1994–95 LACSS (% disagree)	29	16	28	20
Melting pot?				
1994 LACSS (% maintain distinct cultures)	38	19	28[a]	27[a]
Better off if live and work with own?				
1998–99 LACSS (% agree)	20[a]	21[a]	43[a]	43[a]
Ethnic organizations separatist				
1994 LACSS (% disagree)	31	27	27[a]	29[a]
Political Multiculturalism				
People best represented by own?				
1994 LACSS (% agree)	48	34	39[a]	34[a]
Representatives represent country in general or people like me?				
1998, 2001 LACSS (% people like me)	38[a]	51[a]	34[a]	35[a]
Minority experience should be taught by minorities?				
1994 LACSS (% agree)	54	39	47[a]	47[a]
Minimum Base N (GSS 2002)	272	121	58	28
Minimum Base N (LACSS 1994)	100	118	112	127
Minimum Base N (LACSS 1994–95)	102	119	138	117
Minimum Base N (LACSS 1998–99)	172	73	307	150
Minimum Base N (LACSS 1998, 2001)	123	100	142	109

In the 2002 General Social Survey (GSS), importance of ethnic identity measured as "importance of own ethnicity": "very" versus "moderately," "slightly," "not at all." In the Los Angeles County Social Survey (LACSS), "how important is your own identity?": "very" versus "somewhat," "not very," "not at all." Perceived discrimination against own group in LACSS reflects responses to "other members of my ethnic group experience discrimination" either "always" or "frequently" (both high) versus "occasionally," "seldom," or "never" (low). Entries are percentages in each ethnic group, and among those either high or low in-group consciousness (strength of ethnic identity in top panel, and perceived discrimination in bottom panel) who support multiculturalism on the index shown. Superscripts denote results of independent samples t-tests. Entries for each racial group in a given row are significantly different (*p* < .05) unless they share the same superscript.

The second panel of Table 5.3 shows similar cross-tabulations, but presents the relationship of perceived discrimination against one's own ethnic group to support for multiculturalism. All these data come from the LACSS because the GSS had no measure of perceived discrimination. Among blacks, greater perceived discrimination is associated with more support for multiculturalism in six of eight cases (and statistically significant in those six). In contrast, among Latinos, perceived discrimination also had no consistent association with support for multiculturalism, yielding significantly more support on just two of the eight items.

For both strength of ethnic identity and perceived discrimination, the dominant pattern is consistent with black exceptionalism. As seen earlier in Chapter 4, blacks had a stronger sense of group identity and were more likely to perceive discrimination against their group than was the case for other groups. Here, we add that blacks were more likely to tie these feelings of group consciousness to support for multiculturalism's promise to enhance their group's standing. No such consistent association was held among Latinos. Rather, in the period of our study, our public opinion data largely conform to Nathan Glazer's observation that multiculturalism in the United States flowed from the harsh experiences and disappointed aspirations of African Americans.[18]

Assimilation of Immigrants

The assimilation hypothesis should be tested primarily among Latinos in our datasets, given the reservations we have about our small Asian subsamples. This hypothesis states that the more assimilated members of this group – the native-born, naturalized citizens, and/or those who speak English – will be less supportive of multiculturalism than more recent arrivals. Americanization, we argue, encompasses increased support for mainstream cultural and political values, which are dominated by liberal individualism rather than group rights. By this logic, with greater assimilation in terms of citizenship and English language fluency, Latinos should develop more opposition to multiculturalist norms as they move toward the more individualistic, less ethnically separate posture that most whites share.

The Los Angeles data generally support that expectation, as shown in Table 5.4. In six of the eight comparisons, the native-born were less likely than noncitizen Latinos to support multiculturalism. In two cases, the differences are statistically significant. The differences are greatest with respect to items about self-segregation, as indexed by support for living and working with co-ethnics and approval of ethnically based organizations. Very few of the U.S.-born Latinos opted for self-segregation, contrary to Huntington's bleak prognosis.

These data indicate that the similar levels of approval for multiculturalism among blacks and Latinos, and the greater support among Latinos than whites, are both due in large part to the opinions of the more recent Latino

[18] Glazer, *We Are All Multiculturalists Now.*

TABLE 5.4. *Support for Multiculturalism: The Latino-Immigration Status Hypothesis*

	Latino Immigration Status		
	Noncitizen	Naturalized Citizen	U.S.-born
Social Multiculturalism			
Attention to ethnic history?			
1994 LACSS (% too little)	48[a]	35[a]	40[a]
Should think of selves as individual Americans, not ethnics?			
1994–95 LACSS (% disagree)	27[a]	24[a]	19[a]
Melting pot?			
1994–95 LACSS (% maintain distinct culture)	57[a]	61[a]	58[a]
Better off if live and work with own?			
1994–95, 2001–02 LACSS (% agree)	60	40	23
Ethnic organizations separatist?			
1994 LACSS (% disagree)	30[a]	41[a]	17
Minority experience taught by minorities?			
1994 LACSS (% agree)	49[a]	45[a]	46[a]
Political Multiculturalism			
People best represented by own?			
1994 LACSS (% own background)	38[a]	38[a]	33[a]
Representatives represent country in general or people like me?			
1998, 2001 LACSS (% people like me)	25[b]	32[ab]	39[a]
Minimum Base N (LACSS 1994)	133	46	67
Minimum Base N (LACSS 1994–95)	256	75	124
Minimum Base N (LACSS 1994–95, 2001–02)	459	195	249
Minimum Base N (LACSS 1998, 2001)	217	106	140

Only the multiculturalism items are shown that yielded significant ethnic differences in Tables 5.1 and 5.2. Superscripts denote results of independent samples t-tests. All entries in a given row are significantly different ($p < .05$) unless they share the same superscript.
Source: Los Angeles County Social Survey (LACSS) cumulative file.

immigrants. In particular, the surprising support for "living and working with people like themselves" among Latinos is entirely due to foreign-born noncitizens. Among blacks only 20 percent supported such separatism, as did only 23 percent of the U.S.-born Latinos, whereas 60 percent of the noncitizen Latinos favored residential separation. In general, U.S.-born Latinos fall partway between whites on the one hand and blacks and foreign-born Latinos on the other (compare Table 5.4 with Tables 5.1 and 5.2). This pattern of group differences suggests that, over later generations, Latinos are likely to assimilate toward the white mainstream in terms of attitudes about multicultural norms, assuming this trajectory holds in the future.

Vanguards

The vanguard hypothesis predicts that the young and better educated will be more favorable to multiculturalist norms. To repeat, optimally we would examine those who are *both* young and college-educated, and we do so in the minority of instances in which we have sufficient cases to do so. We began with simple cross-tabulations of the social and political multiculturalism items by age and education within each ethnic group. Also, because of differences in the age and educational distributions of the ethnic groups in these surveys, we had to use slightly different cutting-points within each ethnic group in order to achieve sufficient numbers of respondents. As indicated earlier, the number of Latinos in the GSS was insufficient to carry out such cross-tabulation analyses. To save space, we do not present these analyses, but merely comment on those that reflect systematic patterns.

Among whites, the generational half of the vanguard hypothesis gained considerable traction in the national GSS data. Whites younger than forty years consistently supported key elements of social multiculturalism more than did older whites. Younger whites also tended to approve of political multiculturalism more than did older whites in seven of nine comparisons, but these differences did not attain conventional levels of statistical significance. So, overall, if we look at the direction rather than the strength of age differences among whites, the generational piece of the vanguard hypothesis receives fairly consistent support.

The effects of college education among whites are somewhat less clear, as was also true in Chapter 3 regarding patriotism. College graduates did tend to be significantly more tolerant of sustaining cultural diversity and opposed to the idea that minorities must blend into the mainstream than were those with less formal education. But in the case of political multiculturalism, the college-educated whites were significantly more favorable only on the proposals for ethnic quotas for congressmen and teachers, and even here their support hovered around only 10 percent.

Strictly speaking, as we saw earlier in Chapter 3, the vanguard hypothesis predicts an interaction of age and education such that the greatest support for multiculturalism should emerge among those who are both young and college educated. In supplemental cross-tabulations, we tested the interactive effect of youth and college education among whites in the 1994, 1996, 2002, and 2004 GSS samples on the various multicultural norms and policy items. Specifically, we calculated the percent of respondents supporting each multiculturalist norm or policy for those with and without a college degree in each of our three age categories (under thirty, thirty to fifty-nine, and sixty and older). Due to the small numbers of college educated respondents under thirty years old (98, 86, 134, and 140, respectively) we interpret the results with caution and do not test for statistical significance.

In most cases, there was no evidence that age had a more pronounced positive effect on support for multiculturalism among college graduates than among nongraduates. One minor exception is worth noting: among those in the 2002 GSS with a college degree, the young were especially likely to express a tolerant view of nonassimilation. Of those who have a college degree, 27 percent of those between thirty and fifty-nine, and 42 percent of those under thirty, disagreed that "In order to have a smoothly functioning society, members of ethnic minorities must better adapt to the ways of American mainstream culture." The age gap was considerably smaller among those without a college degree (16 percent of those thirty to fifty-nine-years old versus 22 percent of those under thirty). However, the overall picture remains: low levels of support for multiculturalist norms among all groups.

Table 5.5 pursues the vanguard hypothesis among whites with the Los Angeles data, employing a multiple regression analysis with age and education as predictors (with gender as a control) of the selected social and multiculturalism items. On all but one of the eight items, younger whites remained more positive about multiculturalism than were those over the age of forty, significantly so half the time. The somewhat mixed effects of a college education among whites are essentially eliminated with controls for age and gender. Only two items yielded significant regression coefficients, in opposite directions from each other. We would conclude that the youth piece of the vanguard hypothesis is supported among whites, but the college-educated piece is not.

Turning now to blacks and Latinos, we find less consistent and weaker effects of age (or generation). Among blacks, there was a significant ($p < .05$) age effect on only one of the multiculturalism items, the belief that ethnic experiences should

TABLE 5.5. *Are White Vanguards Supporting Multiculturalism?*

	Youth	Education (Higher)	Gender (Female)	R^2
Attention to ethnic history? (too little)	.33**	.10	.08	3.5%
Should think of selves as individual Americans (agree)	.32**	.11	.13	2.3%
Melting pot? (maintain distinct cultures)	.09	.17	.20	1.0%
Better off if live and work with own (agree)	−.04	−.37***	−.18*	2.9%
People best represented by their own (agree)	.18*	.10	.03	2.8%
Represent country as a whole or people like me? (people like me)	.06	−.03	.05	1.0%
Ethnic organizations separatist? (disagree)	.03	.23***	−.04	1.0%
Minority experience taught by minorities? (agree)	.10	−.14	.35*	2.6%

Entries are unstandardized regression coefficients.
* $p < .05$ ** $p < .01$ *** $p < .001$
Source: Los Angeles County Social Survey (LACSS) cumulative file.

be taught by minorities.[19] Nevertheless, such generational differences as there are bend in the direction of the vanguard hypothesis: in all but two of fifteen comparisons younger blacks were more tolerant of diversity, opposed to wholesale cultural assimilation, and more supportive of descriptive representation than were older blacks. However, they were also more opposed to separatism in all four such comparisons. In other words, younger blacks noticeably gave more support to multiculturalism's devotion to maintaining cultural differences than did older blacks, although with modest numbers of black respondents in our surveys the differences typically were not statistically significant.

A similar pattern emerges when we compare blacks with different levels of educational attainment; college-educated blacks tended to be the most supportive of sustaining cultural differences. They were consistently both more tolerant of diversity and less insistent on cultural assimilation – but more opposed to real separatism – than were less educated blacks. The college-educated showed no consistent pattern of greater support for political multiculturalism. Overall, however, just two of the twenty-three education comparisons yielded statistically significant differences.

The data on Latinos from the LACSS yield few statistically significant differences. However, there was a modest trend for younger and better educated Latinos to be the most opposed to multiculturalism, perhaps because they were more likely to have been born in the United States. These simple bivariate results remained intact in regression analyses, run separately for blacks and Latinos, with age and education as predictors and gender as a control. If we confine our attention to just blacks and Latinos, then, these data support the black exceptionalism paradigm, with younger and better educated blacks relatively more likely to support maintaining a strong racial identity, sustaining cultural differences, and descriptive representation; whereas, if anything, their Latino counterparts seem slightly more favorable to assimilation, contrary to Huntington's thesis.

FULLER MODELS

In this chapter, we have mostly presented cross-tabulations to test our hypotheses about the sources of attitudes about multiculturalist principles and norms. In some cases, we have proposed different explanatory factors for minority groups and whites, although in the case of the vanguard hypothesis, the expectation is for a similar impact among all groups. In this penultimate section of this chapter, we consolidate the analyses focused on each individual hypothesis into fuller multivariate models that consider them all at once.

In the cross-tabulation analyses, we considered all the available social and political multiculturalism items. That would be cumbersome here, so we confine our attention to a select few, representing each domain of multiculturalist ideology and emphasizing items where bivariate analyses had indicated some

---

[19] For this reason, we have not presented the figures in tabular form.

link to our hypothesized explanatory factors. We focused on five: attention to ethnic history in schools and colleges, norms about political identification as either Americans or as ethnics, norms of maintaining distinct cultures or blending in, political representation by those with their own background, and whether ethnic organizations promote separatism. We conducted these analyses separately within each ethnic group (to test the black exceptionalism hypothesis). As predictors, we employed perceptions of discrimination against one's group (testing the politicized group consciousness hypothesis), age and education (the vanguard hypothesis), and gender (as a control). For Latino subjects, we employed dummy variables for noncitizens and naturalized citizens (with native-born as the omitted category) and English-language use (the assimilation hypothesis).

We hesitate to place too much reliance on what turn out to be somewhat scattered findings.[20] So, here, we mainly mention those that seem to be consistent with earlier data, organized in terms of our main hypotheses. Consistent with the general thrust of Chapter 4, we find that group consciousness, as indexed by perceived discrimination, has fairly consistent effects among blacks, significantly increasing the desire for more teaching of ethnic history and increasing discernibly (although not significantly) the norm of thinking of oneself in racial terms and supporting ethnic organizations. The few (see Table 4.3 earlier) whites who reported substantial antiwhite discrimination were significantly more opposed to giving more attention to ethnic history, suggesting that this is one multicultural issue that has had some salience in the context of the nation's racial conflicts. Among Latinos, perceived discrimination promoted support for thinking of oneself as an ethnic, but again this seems mainly to be due to the most recent immigrants; the coefficient is no longer significant with citizenship controlled. Oddly, perceived discrimination actually reduced support for ethnic organizations with citizenship controlled.

Among Latinos, the assimilation hypothesis continues to have a visible impact. U.S.-born Latinos, more than the foreign-born, continue to believe that people should favor personal identities as an American over ethnic identities and to be suspicious of ethnic organizations.

Support for the vanguard hypothesis continues to be spotty, aside from age differences among whites. Compared to older whites, the young are significantly more sympathetic to ethnic history and to norms of thinking of oneself as an ethnic, but age has no association with the other three items. More-educated blacks seem to have been less insistent on assimilation, in terms of both commitment to an American identity and blending in (as in the melting pot) than were less-educated whites.

---

[20] Only a dozen of the seventy-three coefficients we obtained in these analyses attain conventional levels of statistical significance ($p < .05$). Only a few less than that would be expected by chance, of course.

To test whether these findings hold up with our other main explanatory variables controlled, we added patriotism to these regression models. The results were actually somewhat stronger with controls included. Not surprisingly, patriotism among Latinos was more strongly associated with believing that one should identify as an American rather than as a member of an ethnic group, that minority groups should blend into mainstream society rather than maintaining their original customs, and that ethnic organizations contribute to separatism. These findings contribute further to our conclusion that Latinos, at least, are moving toward some greater identification with the broader society and away from ethnic separatism.

CONCLUSION

This chapter examined public support for multiculturalism's guiding principles and norms. Clearly, this was not a comprehensive review, necessarily bounded as it was by the array of questions included in the surveys at our disposal. We grouped these items into two broad domains: *social multiculturalism*, which focused on the tolerance for and recognition of cultural diversity and the elevation of cultural pluralism at the expense of assimilation, and *political multiculturalism*, which focused on support for group-conscious measures in the political realm. It must be noted that the opinions surveyed ranged along the continuum from soft to hard multiculturalism and that several of the harder proposals, such as an ethnic quota system in legislative representation, have never achieved the status of a concrete proposal seriously debated by political candidates and parties in the United States.

Our first conclusion is that Americans of all racial and ethnic groups share a broad consensus on a particular version of a soft multiculturalism, reflecting substantial acceptance of cultural pluralism and the value of ethnic minorities' retaining ties to their original cultures. The great majority in each group is willing to recognize and tolerate the persistence of ethnic difference, supporting the right of ethnic and racial groups to maintain their own unique traditions and wanting to give significant attention to ethnic and racial history. A considerable number eschew calling on minorities to blend into the larger society as in the metaphor of the melting pot.

By contrast, our second conclusion is that a majority of Americans in all the main ethnic groups also repudiate the proposals of hard multiculturalism for allocating positions based on ethnic background, not wanting to prioritize ethnicity or race in this way. They prefer that members of ethnic and racial minority groups should think of themselves as individual Americans rather than as members of specific ethnic groups, that minorities should adapt better to the mainstream, that they should integrate themselves into the broader society rather than living and working separately among their own, and that racially based organizations may lead to dangerous levels of separatism. All groups are less likely to support descriptive representation in specific domains than in the abstract.

Perhaps a salad bowl metaphor best fits the consensus: retain some distinctiveness, but the vegetables of diverse colors should all be mixed with the same dressing. In this sense, the majority of Americans of all ethnicities and races adhere to the traditional liberal precepts that were most prominent during the civil rights movement: integrate and acculturate rather than maintain separate racial and ethnic enclaves, but accept cultural pluralism rather than force its disappearance.

In the context of such broad opposition to hard multiculturalism, however, predictable ethnic differences did emerge. The minority groups who are the intended beneficiaries of multiculturalist policies were in general more likely to support them. This was most strongly the case among African Americans, consistent with the idea of black exceptionalism. For example, blacks were far more supportive of greater attention to ethnic and racial history than were whites or Latinos. Such differences in preferred norms are consistent with the evidence presented in Chapter 4 that blacks share a relatively high *personal* level of racial group consciousness. This chapter adds the point that blacks are more supportive of a *general* societal norm of racial group consciousness than are other groups. This falls in line with a considerable literature showing that, if given a choice, blacks usually prefer black political candidates, everything else being equal.[21] We hasten to add that this persistent black–white difference coexists with the fact that only a minority of blacks support hard multiculturalism in any of the numerous guises that we have examined.[22]

Testing this theory of black exceptionalism further also required us to compare blacks with the new immigrant groups, Latinos and Asians. We have less evidence on Latinos and present none here on Asians. But we find that Latinos, too, generally support multiculturalism more than do whites and often at a level approaching that of blacks. But among Latinos we also found evidence for the assimilation hypothesis over generations in the United States, in terms of reduced support for prioritizing ethnic over American identity and for living in ethnic enclaves. So Latinos' similarity to blacks erodes when we separate out the more assimilated U.S.-born or even naturalized citizens. They have already moved partway toward whites.

Having found some meaningful patterns consistent with the assimilation and black exceptionalism hypotheses, we then turned to other possible explanations for such support for multicultural norms as emerged. Perhaps because of the limited salience of abstract multiculturalist principles, we found a lack of coherence and ideological structure in the opinions of the general public. Very

---

[21] Jennifer Hochschild, *Facing Up to the American Dream: Race, Class, and the Soul of the Nation* (Princeton, NJ: Princeton University Press, 1995); Earl Black and Merle Black, *The Rise of Southern Republicans* (Cambridge, MA: Harvard University Press, 2002); Warren E. Miller and J. Merrill Shanks, *The New American Voter* (Cambridge, MA: Harvard University Press, 1996).

[22] See also Michael C. Dawson, *Black Visions: The Roots of Contemporary African-American Political Ideologies* (Chicago: University of Chicago Press, 2003).

likely as a result, the explanatory power of our hypothesized predictors was quite limited. Still, among blacks a politicized sense of group identity mattered: those who perceived more discrimination against their group were significantly more likely to favor many of the multicultural proposals. Among Latinos, however, this was only an occasional result.

The generational part of the vanguard hypothesis also received support: younger respondents were more favorable toward multicultural norms than were those older than forty. This divergence was larger and more consistent among white respondents, a finding that in some ways is consistent with Huntington's warning of the future erosion of belief in the assimilationist norm for immigrants to America.[23] At the same time, however, significant differences between the college-educated and less educated were rare, although the established tendency of education to be associated with support for racial integration rather than ethnic separatism recurs in our data. The generational differences in support for multiculturalism may simply reflect the greater exposure of younger whites to these ideas, whether through their educational experiences or media consumption or the embrace of diversity by many elites in the past several decades. Younger generations usually have less entrenched political predispositions, including in this case attitudes about the nation and group relations. Perhaps for that reason, too, they may be more willing to accept the ideas about recognizing and representing ethnic diversity that multiculturalism advances.

But should these results buttress the fears that an embrace of multiculturalism will gradually erode support for a common American culture and identity? We take this matter up in the next chapter. But here we note that the age differences generally are modest in size and that the majority of the younger cohort generally opposes the harder versions of multiculturalism. So we are hardly watching a seismic generational shift. And we consistently find little support for the second leg of the vanguard hypothesis, the effects of higher education in promoting multiculturalist ideology among whites. Rather, our findings are consistent with the traditionally greater support for the integrationist mentality of the civil rights movement among college-educated whites and rejection of the cultural nationalism that gained some support among black activists in the later 1960s. This is strong and reassuring evidence of the enduring impact of education in reducing racial prejudice and promoting support of antidiscrimination policies and integration in housing, employment, and schooling.[24]

[23] Huntington, *Who Are We?*

[24] Robert Levine and Donald T. Campbell, *Ethnocentricism*; Herbert H. Hyman and Paul B. Sheatsley, "Attitudes toward Desegregation," *Scientific American* 211 (1966): 16–23; Schuman, et al., *Racial Attitudes in America: Trends and Interpretation*.

6

When Do Ethnic and National Identities Collide?

Adopting a social identity inevitably requires drawing boundaries between "us" and "them." Nevertheless, in a complex society, individuals usually belong to several overlapping groups, forming multiple social identities that contrast with varied sets of others.[1] The modern person is made up of a mixture of loyalties and identifications: national, regional, linguistic, religious, social, and professional – identities that expand or contract as people's lives change. The ingredients in one's mix of social identities thus shift over time, often expanding as one acquires an occupation and plants roots in a specific community or disappearing, as when one leaves a church or emigrates.

The existence of multiple identities raises the problem of prioritization, and in this chapter we examine the balance between nationality and ethnicity. Which takes precedence, loyalty to nation or pride in ethnic group? In the limiting case of an ethnically homogeneous society, nationality and ethnicity completely overlap, and the possibility that national and ethnic identities clash is moot. They are one and the same, so patriotism and feeling close to your own ethnic group are bound together. Japan is Japanese, and so the idea of a loyal, but hyphenated, Japanese identity has no meaning.

In multiethnic societies such as the United States, though, the matter of reconciling one's national and ethnic identities is more complex. Ethnic identities often have great emotional significance, particularly in diverse societies, and in some contexts this may pose a challenge to claims of attachment to the nation, raising the question of prioritization. A poignant example concerns the choice of loyalties faced by Japanese Americans after Pearl Harbor, between the ethnicity of their family's country of origin and their nation of residence. Overwhelmingly,

---

[1] Sen, "Beyond Identity: Other People"; Marilynn B. Brewer and Sonia Roccas, "Individual Values, Social Identity, and Optimal Distinctiveness," in *Individual Self, Relational Self, Collective Self*, ed. Constantine Sedikides and Marilynn B. Brewer (Philadelphia: Psychology Press, 2001), 219–37.

and despite a harsh regime of internment imposed by their current government, they demonstrated the primacy of their allegiance to the United States.

Multiculturalist theorists have varied positions, as described in Chapter 1, about how to balance the claims of nationality and ethnicity. If multicultural norms are fused with conceptions of national identity, as in Canada, the potential tensions are minimized. If the nation is viewed as a confederation of co-equal entities, as in America's years under the Articles of Confederation, then even nationalists may concede that subnational state or ethnic identities can predominate. So in this chapter we consider whether a strong sense of ethnic identification among America's minority group members (see Chapter 4) competes with affective attachment to the nation (see Chapter 3), weakening their national identities. In the 1940s, many, including the president of the Unites States, seemed to fear that would be the outcome of the rival tugs on the loyalties of Japanese Americans after Pearl Harbor.

Some of the politicized group consciousness theories we discussed earlier suggest that such competition among bases of identification is likely. The argument is that in culturally diverse countries, one racial, linguistic, or religious group typically constitutes the nation's ethnic core because of its historical role in creating the state, its larger size, and its political and cultural dominance.[2] In America, presumably whites of European origin form that ethnic core. The result may be that minorities then feel estranged from a nation controlled by others and in which they feel disadvantaged.[3]

The same theories suggest that the affective linkage between ethnic and national identities in America's white majority may differ from that among ethnic minorities.[4] Because people tend to live and interact with others like themselves, the majority group is likely to perceive most other citizens as sharing their physical characteristics and values. So there might be a simple perceptual basis for the majority whites to conflate their ethnic and national identities. This might be especially true in the current era, when the structural integration of the massive wave of white immigrants from a century ago has virtually been completed.[5] In addition, the majority group has an interest in the dominance of its own cultural norms. In this view, then, for whites the nation and their ethnic group may be cognitively fused, and attachments to the two entities should be complementary.

Conversely, minority groups should be more likely to identify in ethnic terms if they both perceive themselves as different and are treated as such. As we saw in Chapter 4, African Americans, who themselves face an often impermeable color

---

[2] Mahzarin R. Banaji and Thierry Devos, "American = White?"; Conover, "The Politics of Recognition."

[3] Brewer, "Social Identity and Citizenship in a Pluralistic Society."

[4] Sidanius and Petrocik, "Communal and National Identity in a Multiethnic State."

[5] Alba, *Ethnicity in America*; Alba and Nee, *Remaking the American Mainstream*; Glazer, *We Are All Multiculturalists Now*.

line, do feel the strongest sense of ethnic identity, common fate, and of being discriminated against because of their race. Such theories might then expect blacks, Latinos, or Asians to define themselves exclusively in terms of their national identity less often than do whites. Blacks, however, also exhibit strong patriotic feelings and a strong sense of American identity. And as the structural integration of immigrants begins, a hyphenated identity, expressing both national and ethnic identity simultaneously, may be a common mode of accommodating multiple identities for minority group members.

The psychological tensions created in nations with minorities harboring strong ethnic identities can lead to at least three outcomes. The civic nation envisions a common identity founded on political ideals as the best guarantor of national unity. Accordingly, France today is insisting on imposing the republican values of egalitarianism and secularism on an increasingly diverse society by banning religious symbols such as the Islamic veil, Jewish yarmulke, or Christian cross from being worn in public schools. The French mock American multi-culturalism for pandering to ethnic diversity in a way that undermines the meanings of a common sense of nationhood and the equal responsibilities of citizenship.[6]

Alternatively, separation of church and state in the United States has resulted in a more accepting attitude toward these manifestations of religiosity. Many multiculturalists are comfortable about granting exemptions to cultural minorities, such as allowing Muslim female applicants for drivers' licenses to be photographed wearing their head scarves. They would not oppose prioritizing ethnic identities, even among the offspring of immigrants. Some would view the construct of "just an American" as sociologically inaccurate and normatively unsound.[7]

American writers like Arthur Schlesinger Jr., Michael Barone, and Samuel Huntington share the French anxieties about the risks of institutionalizing diversity. They suggest that accepting a muscular version of preserving cultural differences, or what we have called hard multiculturalism, will cause the erosion of patriotism and feelings of national solidarity among ethnic minorities.[8] They fear that strong ethnic identifications and attachment to the nation will clash, resulting in conflict rather than consensus about national interests. Such views are contested, of course, and advocates of multiculturalism such as Kymlicka argue that affirming the value of minority cultures facilitates the development of national attachment among those not in the majority ethnic group.[9]

---

[6] Elaine Sciolino, "Tensions over French Identity Shape Voter Drives," *The New York Times*, May 30, 2007; Elaine Sciolino, "Ban on Head Scarves Takes Effect in France," *The New York Times*, September 3, 2004.

[7] See, e.g., Jacoby, "Rainbow's End."

[8] Schlesinger Jr., *The Disuniting of America*; Barone, *The New Americans*; Huntington, *Who Are We?*

[9] Kymlicka, *Politics in the Vernacular*, chapter 8.

A third possibility, however, is that most Americans, whatever their ethnic background, endorse the motto of *e pluribus unum* and the idea of sharing a common culture that evolves as newcomers add elements of their cultural heritage to the American way of life. Even if their own immigrant roots are in the distant past and attachment to their cultural heritage has faded away, Americans might still support the acceptance of growing diversity as consistent with America's identity as a nation of immigrants. In the pluralistic version of the melting pot that we described as soft multiculturalism in the preceding chapter, ethnic allegiances and patriotism might be complementary rather than competing identities.

We assess the empirical relationships between national and ethnic identities in Americans using three methodological approaches. We begin by looking at the cognitive dimension of social identity, the question of "who am I," or which identity respondents prefer. Then we examine the relationship between affective orientations toward the nation and one's ethnic group, each measured separately. If whites have appropriated the national identity as their own ethnic identity, white ethnic identity should be positively correlated with patriotism and other indicators of national attachment. If minority groups feel distant from the broader nation controlled by whites, as argued by some versions of the politicized group consciousness paradigm, then those two identities should be negatively related. Close identification with an ethnic minority group would come at the expense of patriotism.[10] Finally, we return to the question of whether national identity and multiculturalism are at odds by examining whether support for the norms described in the preceding chapter is associated with a weaker sense of strong national identity.

SELF-CATEGORIZATION: JUST AN AMERICAN OR MAINLY AN ETHNIC?

The cognitive dominance of a particular group identity was assessed in both the national 1994 General Social Survey (GSS) and several Los Angeles surveys using several different questions. The first directly offered the choice of either national or ethnic identity. In the GSS, the question read, "When you think of social and political issues, do you think of yourself mainly as a member of a particular ethnic, racial, or nationality group or do you think of yourself mainly as just an American?" The first and most important result is that 90 percent of

---

[10] Sidanius and Petrocik, "Communal and National Identity in a Multiethnic State"; Christian Staerklé, Jim Sidanius, Eva G. T. Green, and Ludwin Molina, "Ethnic Minority-Majority Asymmetry and Attitudes towards Immigrants across 11 Nations," *Psicologia Política* 30 (2005): 7–26. See Citrin, Wong, and Duff, "The Meaning of American National Identity: Patterns of Ethnic Conflict and Consensus"; and David O. Sears, "Experimental Social Psychology, Broader Contexts, and the Politics of Multiculturalism."

the sample responded, "Just an American." Only 7 percent responded with a particular ethnic, racial, or nationality group (and 0.2 percent with two or more groups). Although one might think people might resist this bald choice, only another 2 percent volunteered either "both" or "it depends." A follow-up question asked whether they thought of themselves that way on all issues, most issues, some issues, or just a few issues. Of the total sample, more than half (54 percent) stated they thought of themselves as just an American on all issues, and 28 percent on most issues. Less than 2 percent said they thought of themselves as being in some subgroup on all or most issues. For the population of the nation as a whole, American national identity seems to overpower any ethnic, racial, or nationality subgrouping as a source of political and social identity, at least when faced with a bald choice between those two alternatives.

In a national sample, of course, whites are by far the dominant group. And, not surprisingly, given the results just cited, they overwhelmingly (97 percent) preferred to think of themselves as just an American, as shown in Table 6.1. The Los Angeles data parallel the national results. In the 1994, 1995, and 1997 Los Angeles County Social Surveys (LACSSs), we repeated the same question. Again, whites almost unanimously (95 percent) say "just an American." Very few whites reported some hyphenated-American identity such as Armenian-American or Italian-American, much less an ethnic identity such as Armenian. This confirms findings in other studies about the gradual waning of nationality-based ethnic identities among white Americans. Similarly, in our extensive study of University of California, Los Angeles (UCLA) undergraduates alluded to earlier, only 6 percent of the whites gave a nationality-based ethnic response to the question of "what racial or ethnic groups do you most closely identify with?"[11] Among whites in America, ethnic subgroup identities no longer seem to compete successfully with national identity, at least nationally and in Los Angeles County.

But American national identity has this dominant power even for America's most disadvantaged racial minority group. Of the African Americans in the national GSS, 66 percent chose "just an American" (there were too few Hispanics and Asians to yield reliable estimates). Still, a significant number of blacks do not whole-heartedly embrace the nation, paralleling the results from a number of the indicators of attachment to the nation reviewed in Chapter 3; about a third said they felt their primary identity was racial. We have more extensive data on minorities' responses to this question from the LACSS. Even in Los Angeles, viewed by many outside observers as an ethnic cauldron in the wake of the Watts and Rodney King riots, a preference for "just an American" is dominant among all ethnic and racial minority groups, as shown in Table 6.1. Preference for an ethnic identity is limited to about 25 to 30 percent of each group. Given this stark dichotomous choice, then, even ethnic and racial

---

[11]   Richard Alba, *Ethnicity in America*; Sears, Fu, Henry, and Bui, "The Origins and Persistence of Ethnic Identity among the 'New Immigrant Groups.'"

TABLE 6.1. *American vs. Ethnic Self-Categorization, by Ethnicity*

	National			Los Angeles			Los Angeles			
	Just an American (%)	Ethnic Group (%)	N	Just an American (%)	Ethnic Group (%)	N	Just an American (%)	Both (%)	Ethnic Group (%)	N
White	97	3	1,120	95	5	791	73	22	5	446
Black	66	34	191	72[a]	28[a]	359	33	56[a]	12[a]	200
Latino	—	—	—	67[a]	33[a]	613	11[a]	57[a]	33	456
Asian	—	—	—	77[a]	23[a]	149	7[a]	79	15[a]	75

Question wording: Dichotomous indicator (panels 1 and 2): "When you think of social and political issues, do you think of yourself mainly as a member of a particular ethnic, racial, or nationality group, or do you think of yourself mainly as just an American?" Trichotomous indicator (panel 3): [1999, 2000] "How do you primarily think of yourself: just as an American, both as an American and (ethnicity), or only as (ethnicity) [in 2000: " and not as an American]?" Entries are % of each ethnic group choosing each response (missing data excluded from the base). The General Social Survey (GSS) contained too few Latinos and Asians (N ≤ 54) to provide reliable estimates.

Entries in any given column within a panel are significantly different ($p < .05$) unless they share the same superscript.

Source: Left panel: 1994 GSS; Middle panel: 1994, 1995, and 1997 Los Angeles County Social Survey (LACSS); Right panel: 1999 and 2000 LACSS.

minorities seem on average to define themselves mainly as "nationals" than as "ethnics."[12]

Hyphenated Americans

In our earliest surveys, respondents had to choose between American and ethnic identity; they were given no intermediate or mixed-identity alternative. In the later 1999 and 2000 Los Angeles surveys, however, respondents were explicitly given the further option of saying they thought of themselves as *both* an American *and* a member of their ethnic or racial group, opening the door to expressing a hyphenated identity. The question was, "How do you primarily think of yourself: just as an American, both as an American and (ethnicity), or only as (ethnicity)?" The great majority of whites (73 percent) continue to prefer to describe themselves as just an American, whereas 22 percent choose both, as shown in Table 6.1. Again, few (only 5 percent) preferred the pure ethnic designation. With the economic and cultural assimilation of the descendants of the massive wave of immigrants from Europe a century ago nearing completion, there are few visible markers to slow the dissolution of white Americans' ethnic identifications into a more diffuse attachment to America.

In contrast, the hyphenated ethnic-American identity dominates in all three ethnic and racial minority groups. The hyphenated ethnic-American designation was preferred by majorities of the black (56 percent), Latino (57 percent), and Asian (79 percent) respondents to either "just an American" or "just ethnic" in the Los Angeles County surveys, as also shown in Table 6.1. The greater importance of ethnicity in constituting the social identity of minority groups than of whites in America is manifest. But, at the same time, most blacks, Latinos, and Asians in America seem not to view their national and ethnic identities as irreconcilable.

However, beyond that similarity we again find an important divergence among the three minority groups. Among blacks, relatively few deny identification with America altogether. The majority feels themselves to be both American and black: 56 percent say both. But the "just American" response continues to be popular, attracting a rather large minority of blacks (33 percent), most of whose American lineage goes back centuries rather than merely years or decades. By contrast, Latinos and Asians are far less likely to select "just an American"; only 11 percent and 7 percent, respectively, did so.

---

[12] Here, we are assuming that these three measures of political identity – strength of ethnic identity, patriotism, and the tradeoff between American and national identity – are all measuring the intended concepts. To test this assumption, we correlated both strength of ethnic identity and patriotism with a dummy variable reflecting a choice between "just an American" and ethnic identity. The correlations were substantial among ethnic minorities, ranging from .39 to .46 for strength of ethnic identity, and from –.31 to –.55 for patriotism. This gives us additional confidence that the question asking for a choice between national and ethnic identities is in fact measuring genuine tradeoffs between the two underlying alternatives.

The predominance of hyphenated-ethnicity identities among Asians has also been observed in the Pilot National Asian American Political Survey, a multiethnic, multilingual, and multicity study of 1,218 adults eighteen years or older residing in five major population hubs.[13] Respondents were asked how they identified themselves, *in general*, and were given the selections of American, Asian American, Asian, ethnic (e.g., Chinese or Korean American), or their own national origin and allowed to select more than one option. About half chose some form of hyphenated identity, with 34 percent preferring a hyphenated national-origin American self-designation and another 15 percent the hyphenated pan-ethnic "Asian American." More Asians chose a purely ethnic identity (30 percent) and fewer (12 percent) chose the purely American identity than did African Americans, paralleling the results for Latinos, the other heavily immigrant group.

Very similar findings about ethnic minorities also emerged from the study of UCLA undergraduates cited earlier.[14] At college entry, they were asked what racial or ethnic group they identified with most closely. The great majority of blacks chose the hyphenated identities that combine both black and American (78 percent African- or Afro-American), and only 20 percent chose the purely racial "black." Of the Asians, 42 percent chose either pan-ethnic identities tailored specifically for America or hyphenated identities incorporating "American." So did 78 percent of the Latinos, with the remainder in each group identifying mainly with their national origins.

The Meaning of Hyphenated Identities

What is the meaning and significance of the choice of the hyphenated ethnic-American identity? Should it be taken at face value, as reflecting a dual identity, expressing both the continuing psychological resonance of their race and ethnicity as well as their Americanness? Or does it actually reflect the beginnings of diminishing identification with minorities' own ethnic groups?

In fact, among ethnic minorities, the choice of the hyphenated political identity does express at least in part the emotional significance of the ethnic connection. This can be seen by comparing the strength of ethnic identity among those selecting a hyphenated identity on the "just American" item in the LACSS with those who had selected a purely ethnic identity. Figure 6.1 shows the mean strength of ethnic identity for those giving each of the three responses to that choice, using the index measuring strength of ethnic identity introduced in Chapter 4. For example, 72 percent of the Latinos choosing a hyphenated ethnicity

---

[13] Pei-te Lien, M. Margaret Conway, and Janelle Wong, *The Politics of Asian Americans: Diversity and Community* (New York: Routledge, 2004).

[14] Sears, Fu, Henry, and Bui, "The Origins and Persistence of Ethnic Identity among the 'New Immigrant' Groups."

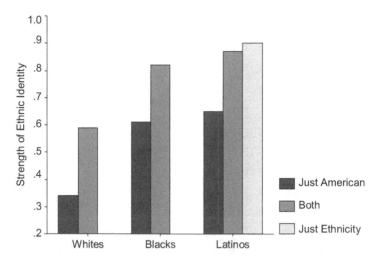

FIGURE 6.1. Strength of Ethnic Identity by American vs. Ethnic Self-Categorization, within Ethnicity
"Strength of Ethnic Identity" is an additive index of two items from the pooled 1999 and 2000 Los Angeles County Social Survey (LACSS): how often R sees self as a member of an ethnic group and how important R's ethnicity is to him or her. The index is scored from 0 = weakest ethnic identity to 1 = strongest ethnic identity. Data are not presented if $N < 45$.

regarded their ethnicity as very important to them, statistically equivalent to the 78 percent registered among those selecting a purely ethnic identity, whereas only 39 percent of those selecting "just American" thought their own ethnic identity comparably important. It is clear that ethnic identity is stronger for those giving either a pure ethnic response or a hyphenated-ethnicity identity than for Latinos giving a just American identity.

Many fewer blacks than Latinos selected the just ethnicity option, but the same finding holds for them. Blacks who choose the dual identity are far more likely than those who call themselves "just American" to express strong racial identities when asked about that alone, on all three pure racial identity items (see Table 4.3 for the exact wording). For example, 73 percent of black respondents choosing the dual mode of self-identification considered their race to be very important to them, compared to 43 percent of blacks who called themselves just Americans.

Finally, what about the American side of the hyphenated identity? Does that genuinely reflect a weakened ethnic identity? Here, the black exceptionalism hypothesis would lead us to expect a crucial difference between blacks and Latinos. If many blacks are walled behind a largely immovable color line, they may be quite patriotic but unable to escape their blackness by integrating into the broader society. Given that dilemma, a hyphenated identity would seem to be

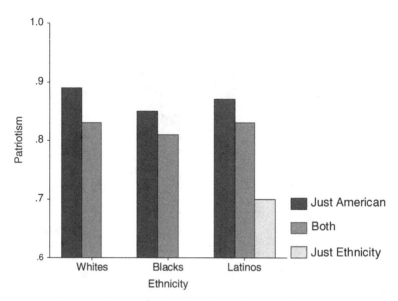

FIGURE 6.2. Patriotism by American vs. Ethnic Self-Categorization, within Ethnicity. "Patriotism" is an additive index of two items from the pooled 1998, 1999, 2000, and 2002 Los Angeles County Social Survey (LACSS): how proud R is to be American and R's level of agreement that seeing the U.S. flag is "moving," keyed such that high scores reflect more patriotism. Data are not presented if $N < 45$.

quite a realistic response. If, in contrast, Latino immigrants are in transition from foreign or alien status to a more fully assimilated status, a hyphenated-ethnic identity may be a kind of a halfway house between national and ethnic identity. To test this contrast, we examined the level of patriotism for each of our identity groups in Figure 6.2.

Consistent with the halfway house idea, hyphenated-ethnic Latinos were significantly more patriotic than the "just ethnic" Latinos, as if they were on their way to a more fully American identity like their European predecessors. Indeed, both the "just American" and "hyphenated-ethnic" Latinos had almost exactly the same level of patriotism as did their white counterparts. And the hyphenated-ethnicity whites' patriotism fell short of that of the "just American" whites, suggesting that the remaining hyphenated whites are also transitioning through an assimilation process themselves. So the hyphenated-ethnic identity gives every sign of being a transitional identity for assimilating Latinos rather than a separatist identity.

It seems to have different meaning for blacks. The label "African American" has become increasingly popular as an explicit statement by blacks that they, like almost all other Americans, stem from immigrant roots. African Americans, many more generations from their ancestral homes, are more likely to choose the hyphenated label than new immigrants, but less likely to do so than U.S.-born or naturalized Latinos. That would seem to be a mark of their stronger sense of common fate, presumably in response to a stronger color line and a more entrenched set of disadvantages. It also contrasts with whites, who much more rarely now choose the hyphenated identity, and who, as much other evidence cited earlier shows, are rapidly putting their immigrant backgrounds behind them.

To summarize, we have four main findings about how today's Americans respond to a choice between American and ethnic identity. First of all, a clear majority in all ethnic groups, whites and ethnic minorities alike, tend to choose "just an American" if forced to choose between that and a purely ethnic identity. Second, most of those in all three ethnic minority groups prefer the hyphenated identity that honors both of their identities. Third, such hyphenated identities reflect attachments to *both* ethnicity and nation. Among Latinos, for example, the hyphenated-ethnics have about as strong an ethnic identity as the just-ethnics and about as much patriotism as those with a purely American identity. In fact, ethnic minorities with hyphenated identities express nearly as much patriotism as do whites who feel just American. Hyphenated identities do not reflect a distancing from either the nation or their own ethnic group.

Finally, the new immigrant groups depart somewhat from blacks in two ways, consistent with the black exceptionalism hypothesis. Blacks' Americanness is highly salient to them, whether it takes the form of ignoring an exclusively racial identification or preferring the hyphenated American identity. Far more blacks select just an American, regardless of the other options, than do Latinos or Asians. Today's Latinos and Asians are, after all, predominantly immigrants, whereas blacks are not. So, for Latinos, a hyphenated identity seems to be something of a halfway house to assimilation into American society because it is accompanied by greater patriotism than is true for those who feel just ethnic.

ASSIMILATION OF IMMIGRANTS: FROM ETHNIC TO AMERICAN IDENTITY

Our assimilation hypothesis suggests that immigration status is also likely to be a key antecedent of the new immigrants' identity choices. They may often enter the United States with a strong sense of their origins and feel somewhat alien in American society. If they experience discrimination, this feeling may become even more intense. But as suggested in Chapter 4, the phase of feeling like a foreigner may be transitory. Students of ethnic politics and immigration assume that structural integration, defined in socioeconomic terms, reinforces cultural assimilation and fosters the political incorporation of minority groups and immigrants.[15] And, of course, learning English will speed that central dimension of cultural assimilation. Fluency in English is clearly related to nativity and a life

---

[15] Horowitz, *Ethnic Groups in Conflict*; Gordon, *Assimilation in American Life.*

removed from the sending country of immigrants, as seen in Chapter 2. It is reasonable to expect the effects of immigration to diminish with each succeeding generation of the new wave of immigrants, just as with their European predecessors, even though our society is still in the early stages of assimilating the current influx.[16]

The implication for identity choice is that immigrants should be more likely than the native-born to adopt either the "just ethnicity" or the hyphenated self-definition. Increasingly, however, their descendants will mostly adopt a hyphenated ethnic-American identity and show a stronger attachment to the United States. This could occur within a single lifetime, or it could occur over generations if the family continues to reside in the United States. In his classic *Assimilation in American Life*, Milton Gordon construes the psychological act of calling oneself an American as the final stage in the incorporation of immigrants. So, ultimately, this process might result in the abandonment of even a weak sense of hyphenated identity as the top of the family tree grows into a "just American" species, often due to multiple intermarriages that make it difficult to trace one's heritage back to a single foreign seed.

This discussion leaves us with three specific empirical expectations. First of all, among the descendants of immigrants, ethnic identity might be increasingly replaced by American identity as part of an assimilation process. That might involve, sequentially, naturalization, nativity, and then descent from a family with longer tenure in the United States. Second, identity as a hyphenated-American might be a "halfway house" in this assimilation process. Finally, in keeping with our black exceptionalism hypothesis, blacks' attitudes are likely to stand apart from these assimilative processes. Because they confront a more impermeable color line, they may retain a stronger racial identity than the Latinos and Asians who are native-born and/or from families with longer residencies in the United States, for whom the assimilation process may be well under way. The LACSS provides our best database for testing the political assimilation hypothesis because they provide sufficient immigrant cases, which most national surveys do not, plus information about the place of birth and citizenship of respondents. Because of our limited sample of Asians, we focus mainly on Latinos.

Assimilation in self-categorization does seem to occur as families gain longer tenure in the United States. Table 6.2 distinguishes among Latinos who are at different stages of the incorporation process. Given the dichotomous choice between a "just American" or a mainly ethnic identity, the native-born Latinos are considerably more likely to prefer the national identity (84 percent) than are either the foreign-born citizens (72 percent) or the noncitizens (56 percent). Even when offered the trichotomous choice, with its added option of a hyphenated identity, the U.S.-born continued to select "just an American" (25 percent)

---

[16] Alba and Nee, *Remaking the American Mainstream*; Barone, *The New Americans*; Brimelow, *Alien Nation*.

TABLE 6.2. *American vs. Ethnic Self-Categorization, by Ethnicity and Latino Immigration Status*

	Dichotomous			Trichotomous			
	Just an American (%)	Ethnic Group (%)	Total N	Just an American (%)	Both (%)	Ethnic Group (%)	Total N
Blacks	72[a]	28[a]	359	33[a]	54	12[a]	200
Latinos' immigration status							
Born in the United States	84	16	184	25[a]	69[a]	5	188
Naturalized	72[a]	28[a]	110	10	73[a]	16[a]	118
Noncitizen	56	44	318	3	41	55	322

Entries within any column in each panel are statistically different ($p < .05$) unless they share the same superscript.

more than naturalized citizens (10 percent), who in turn exceeded the noncitizens (3 percent).

By contrast, a purely ethnic choice was common only among foreign-born noncitizens, no matter which way the choice was posed. About half the noncitizens chose an ethnic identity with no reference to America, whereas very few of the native-born Latinos did so. Indeed, for noncitizens, a purely ethnic identity was far more common (55 percent) than was American identity (3 percent) when respondents were given the trichotomous choice. The choices of the naturalized citizens fell in between those of the native-born and the noncitizens. This suggests a surprisingly swift assimilation of Latino immigrants in their social identities. It is apparently well under way even in the relatively early stages of the massive post-1965 Latino immigration; a majority of our Latino respondents are true immigrants, and few of the native-born have American-born parents. Within just a few generations, the descendants of immigrants have increasingly shifted toward a purely American identity. Here, again, we find indications that the immigrant status of Latinos is considerably more important in contributing to their identity than is their ascribed niche in a supposedly rigid American racial and ethnic hierarchy.

Our second expectation was that a hyphenated ethnic-American identity would serve as a kind of halfway house between the purely ethnic identity of new immigrants and the assimilated purely American identity of those descended from earlier generations born in the United States. Table 6.2 shows that a large majority of either the native-born or the naturalized Latino respondents preferred the hyphenated identity. Even the foreign-born naturalized citizens far preferred the hyphenated-American identity to the purely ethnic mode of self-categorization – by a four-to-one margin. We infer that the emphasis must be on the American half of that identity because they overwhelmingly prefer just American to an ethnic identity when given only those two choices. The foreign-born noncitizens were the only group in which a majority chose a purely ethnic identity. So the hyphenated identity does seem to serve as a transitional identity, much as the hyphenated-American identities were in the early and mid-twentieth century for many European immigrant families. Given the very large proportion of immigrants in this Los Angeles sample of Latinos (70 percent), we suspect that we are detecting only the very early stages of an assimilation of these groups that will ultimately weaken the boundaries of their ethnic category.[17]

What happens if we look at indicators of incorporation into American society other than immigration status, such as language use? The language spoken at home turns out also to be a powerful correlate of identity choices. As shown in Table 6.3, those who speak only English at home are much more likely to choose just an American identity than are those who mostly (or only) speak some language other than English at home.[18] Those who are bilingual but mostly speak English prefer the hyphenated identity, as the halfway house hypothesis would expect. Almost none who mostly speak Spanish feels him- or herself to be just an American. In other words, the expectations of the assimilation model are supported using this alternate linguistic indicator of incorporation.

We should take a brief look at these same questions using our Asian subsample, although – as indicated earlier – we have less confidence in it. One would expect the same gap in the LACSS cumulative file between the many immigrant Asians (74 percent) and the relatively few native-born ones (26 percent).[19] Briefly, our assimilation hypothesis again works very well for Asians' cognitive self-categorization, although we do not present the data in Table 6.2. All of the U.S.-born Asians selected "just an American" in the dichotomous self-categorization, whereas only 53 percent of the recent immigrants did. None of the native-born Asians selected his or her ethnic group in the trichotomous self-categorization, whereas 41 percent of the recent immigrants did.

These findings resemble those from a larger study targeting only Asian Americans, the 2008 National Asian American Survey. U.S.-born Asians were more likely to select a pan-ethnic identity than their original nationality, and

---

[17] In analyses not shown, we also confirmed that these effects all hold up with controls for demographic variables. Ethnic minorities are more likely to describe themselves either as ethnic or as both American and ethnic than are whites, even with controls in the equation. Moreover immigrants are more likely to do so than are native-born minorities.

[18] These findings also hold up with other demographic variables controlled (not shown). Logit models of the tradeoff measure (trichotomous) for Hispanics yield strong predictive values. Either "just an American" or "both" is chosen far more by citizens than by noncitizens. Respondent educational level also contributes to this form of assimilation.

[19] Among Asians, the same pattern holds. On the dichotomous tradeoff item, the ethnic alternative is chosen by 26 percent of the foreign-born ($N = 104$), and 16 percent of the U.S.-born ($N = 45$). On the trichotomous tradeoff item, the ethnic alternative is chosen by 27 percent of the foreign-born ($N = 95$) and 8 percent of the U.S.-born ($N = 25$).

TABLE 6.3. *Latinos' National and Ethnic Identifications, by Language Spoken at Home*

| | American vs. Ethnic Self-Categorization | | | | | | | |
| | Dichotomous | | Trichotomous | | | Patriotism | | |
	Just an American (%)	Ethnic Group (%)	Just an American (%)	Both (%)	Ethnic Group (%)	High (%)	Low (%)	Minimum N
English only	92[a]	8	59	35	6	49[a]	51	104
Mostly English	92[a]	8	35	54[a]	11	46[a]	54	256
Mostly another language	56	44	8[a]	50[a]	42[a]	31[b]	69	430
No English	37	63	3[a]	54[a]	43[a]	25[b]	75	97

"Patriotism" is an additive index of two items from the pooled 1998, 1999, 2000, and 2002 Los Angeles County Social Survey (LACSS): how proud R is to be American and R's level of agreement that seeing the U.S. flag is "moving." The index is scored from 0 = weakest patriotism to 1 = strongest patriotism. Entries for patriotism are based on a median split on the two-item patriotism scale, whereby cases greater than the median score (.875) are assigned a value of "1" and cases less than or equal to the median score are assigned a "0." Entries within columns are significantly different ($p < .05$) unless they share the same superscript.

Source: "Dichotomous" panel from 1994, 1995, 1997 LACSS. "Trichotomous" panel from 1995, 1999, 2000 LACSS.

only 10 percent selected "Asian." In contrast, noncitizens were by far the most likely to select their original nationality (62 percent), and they did so significantly more than did naturalized citizens or the U.S.-born.[20] Similarly, in the earlier (2001) Pilot National Asian American Political Survey, respondents were asked how they identified themselves in general and were given several choices, including American. In keeping with the assimilation model, generations of Asians from earlier immigrating families were most likely to identify simply as American. Among third-generation Asian Americans, fully 43 percent chose a purely American national identity, as did 33 percent of the U.S.-born Asians. But respondents born in Asian countries were least likely to (5 percent). Beyond that, both structural and cultural integration fostered identification as an American. Respondents who had a longer family history in the United States, who were naturalized citizens, and who mainly spoke English at home and work were most likely to choose the American self-categorization. Also consistent with the assimilation model are the correlates of a purely ethnic self-identification: being educated outside the United States, participating in purely ethnic (rather than Asian-American) organizations and events, and experiencing racial discrimination. Our findings for Latinos and Asians therefore point to the importance of recent immigration as a determinant of ethnic, as opposed to national, identity.

Many whites are also recent immigrants, given the renewed immigration from Europe, Russia, and the Middle East in recent decades, especially in larger metropolitan areas. Cultural diversity today may be replicating the pattern of gradual assimilation of earlier European immigrants among them as well. Of the 2,029 whites interviewed in our pooled Los Angeles sample, just 7 percent were naturalized citizens, and 4 percent were noncitizens. Nevertheless, the findings are surprisingly powerful and replicate what we have seen earlier with Latinos and Asians. Only 11 percent of the recent white immigrants are above the median in patriotism versus 43 percent of the U.S.-born. Only 15 percent of the recent immigrants say they are "just-an-American," as against 31 percent of the long-term noncitizens and 79 percent of the U.S.-born. Indeed, 69 percent of the recent immigrants claim only an ethnic identity, against just 2 percent of the U.S.-born. This adds weight to our theoretical focus on the assimilation of non-African immigrants.

By way of summary, our third expectation returns us to the black exceptionalism hypothesis. We saw in Chapter 4 that blacks' racial and ethnic identities are similar in strength to those of recent immigrants. However, we suspect that the story is more complex and that blacks' strong racial identities do not reflect a psychological distance from the nation as a whole. Despite the obstacles posed by the historic racial color line, the just an American identity seems to be more common among ethnic minorities who have been in the United States the longest. It is more common among blacks, the great majority of whom have

---

[20] Janelle Wong, et al., *Asian American Political Participation*.

been Americans for many generations, than among native-born Latinos, and far less common among Latinos who are naturalized citizens or noncitizen immigrant Latinos.[21]

These, then, are among the most robust findings that we report in this volume. In every case, we see evidence of growing American national identity and diminishing salience of ethnic identity as Latinos and Asians work their way through the stages from recent immigration to being native-born Americans. This is also reflected in the dramatically reduced sense of ethnic identity and increased American national identity among those who speak English at home. The sense of ethnic identity, as opposed to a sense of national identity, is linked specifically to being a relatively recent immigrant.

THE ASSOCIATION OF NATIONAL AND ETHNIC IDENTITIES

Those worried about identity politics and its link to multiculturalism are concerned that minorities' attachments to the nation will be weakened if they strongly identify with their ethnic group. The politicized group consciousness paradigm assumes the American racial order to be quite stable, if not intractable in every individual case, with whites as the dominant group.[22] It therefore expects whites' identification with their own racial group to be positively associated with national identification, whereas among ethnic and racial minority groups strong ethnic identity should be associated with weak attachment to the nation. Nativists would perhaps not disagree, favoring conformity to the Anglo-Protestant tradition of the nation, as Huntington says. Cosmopolitan liberals, assuming anyone can become an American, would not see ethnic and national identity as incompatible, even among minorities.

Evaluating these alternative views requires assessing the empirical connection between ethnic identity and national attachment within each of the main ethnic groups. Our preference is, whenever possible, to measure the strength of ethnic identity directly. However, others have used more indirect measures instead, so we do both to ensure completeness. We start with the direct measures. The national surveys we are using, the GSS and American National Election Studies (ANES), are largely bereft of such measures of ethnic identification, although the 1996 GSS did include the question, "How close do you feel to your ethnic or racial group?" Rather, the best example in our datasets is the three-item Ethnic Identity Index in the LACSS, based on the items introduced in Chapter 4 (see Table 4.3). Measuring national attachment is largely uncontroversial. To measure

---

[21] To situate the progression of these groups, 95 percent of the blacks in the 2000 LACSS were U.S.-born, whereas 60 percent of the native-born Latinos in the LACSS cumulative file had immigrant parents.

[22] See, e.g., Jim Sidanius, Colette Van Laar, Shana Levin, and Stacey Sinclair, "Social Hierarchy Maintenance and Assortment into Social Roles: A Social Dominance Perspective," *Group Processes and Intergroup Relations* 6 (2003): 333–52.

patriotism, we created summary scales based on four indicators of attachment to the nation presented previously in Chapter 3: patriotism, chauvinism, national pride, and denial of criticism of the nation.[23]

Do we find the strong positive association among whites between strength of ethnic identity and attachment to the nation predicted by the politicized group consciousness approach? As can be seen in the top panel of Table 6.4, both of the correlations between strength of ethnic identity and patriotism among whites in the LACSS are nearly zero and not statistically significant. The closeness item in the 1996 GSS did have a consistent and significant, although not terribly strong, positive correlation with patriotism among whites (average $r = .14$), as shown in the second panel of Table 6.4. We also carried out regressions (not shown in tabular form to save space) testing the effects of perceived closeness to other whites on patriotism using demographic controls (age, education, income, and gender) and controls for political ideology to determine whether associations with other variables are suppressing true links between ethnic and national identity. Among whites there is a positive, statistically significant relationship between feeling close to other members of one's own racial group and all three measures of national attachment (average beta = .11). But these associations are relatively weak and merely hover around the margin of statistical significance.[24]

What about among ethnic and racial minorities? Is strong ethnic identity associated with greater alienation from the nation, as reflected in negative correlations between ethnic identity and the patriotism indices? Not among blacks or Latinos in the LACSS. None of the four correlations is negative, as shown in the top panel of Table 6.4. Among the small number of blacks in the

---

[23] Patriotism is a two-item index summing responses to the love of country and feelings about the U.S. flag items, rescaled to run from 0 to 1, where 1 is the highest level of patriotism. The National Pride index assigned responses to each of 10 items a 1 (no pride at all) to 4 (very proud) score, summed these, and then rescored the total, standardizing for the number of items to create a measure ranging from 0 (low pride) to 1 (high pride). For the specific pride items used in the construction of the scale, see Figure 3.1. The same procedure was used to create a Chauvinism index comprising five items: "I would rather be a citizen of the United States . . ."; "there are some things about the United States that make me ashamed . . ." (reverse scoring); "the world would be a better place if people from other countries were more like Americans"; "generally speaking the United States is a better country than most . . ."; and "people should support their country even if the country is in the wrong." Finally, Deny Criticism is a three-item index consisting of the extent of disagreement (rescaled so that maximum disagreement is coded 1 and minimum disagreement is 0) with three negatively worded national attachment items from the LACSS: America is not a particularly wonderful country, other places are better to live than the United States, and the flag should not be treated as a sacred object.

[24] In light of the discrepancy between the bivariate correlations and regression coefficients, we conducted a more rigorous statistical test that takes into account the full range of scores on both the emotional patriotism and ethnic identification measures. Following the lead of Sidanius and colleagues, we used the bivariate, unstandardized regression coefficients to estimate the degree to which patriotism is a function of ethnic identification in the LACSS. The array of results is strikingly consistent: in all three ethnic groups, including blacks, the relationship between ethnic identification and patriotism fails to attain even the weak $p < .10$ level of statistical significance.

TABLE 6.4. *Correlations of Ethnic and National Attachment*

Ethnic Identification	National Attachment	Whites	Blacks	Latinos	Survey
Ethnic identity	Patriotism	.03	.04	.00	LACSS
	Patriotism	.15***	.23***	.16***	ANES 2012
	Deny Criticism	.06	.14	.12	LACSS
Ethnic closeness	Patriotism	.14***	.24*	–	GSS 1996
	Chauvinism	.13***	.06	–	GSS 1996
	Pride	.16***	.08*	–	GSS 1996
Group affect					
In-group affect	Patriotism	.13***	-.05	.11***	LACSS
	Deny Criticism	.03	.00	.10	LACSS
	Patriotism	.22**	.11	–	ANES 2002
	Patriotism	.16**	.23**	.06	ANES 2004
	Patriotism	.16**	.30**	.03	ANES 2008
	Patriotism	.21***	.16***	.18***	ANES 2012
In-group	Patriotism	.11***	-.02	-.03	LACSS
favoritism	Deny Criticism	.07	.15	-.14	LACSS
	Patriotism	.12**	-.18	–	ANES 2002
	Patriotism	.19**	.11	-.24*	ANES 2004
	Patriotism	.14**	.23**	.04	ANES 2008
	Patriotism	.13***	.02	-.06	ANES 2012
Politicized ethnicity					
Common fate	Patriotism	-.06	-.15	.02	LACSS
Perceived discrimination	Patriotism	.10	-.19*	-.20**	LACSS

Entries are Pearson r's. LACSS entries based on cumulative file, but Deny Criticism measure available only in 1998.

*p < .05 **p < .01 ***p < .001

Patriotism is a two-item index summing responses to the love of country and feelings about the U.S. flag items, rescaled to run from 0 to 1, where 1 is the highest level of patriotism. The National Pride Index assigned responses to each of ten items a 1 (no pride at all) to 4 (very proud) score, summed these, and then rescored the total, standardizing for the number of items, to create a measure ranging from 0 (low pride) to 1 (high pride). (For specific pride items, see Figure 3.1.) The same procedure was used to create a Chauvinism Index comprising five items: "I would rather be a citizen of the United States ..."; "there are some things about the United States that make me ashamed ..." (reverse scoring); "the world would be a better place if people from other countries were more like Americans"; "generally speaking the United States is a better country than most ..."; and "people should support their country even if the country is in the wrong." Deny Criticism is a three-item index consisting of the extent of disagreement (rescaled so that maximum disagreement is coded 1 and minimum disagreement is 0) with three negatively worded national attachment items from the LACSS: America is not a particularly wonderful country, other places are better to live than the United States, and the flag should not be treated as a sacred object.

Source: American National Election Studies (ANES); General Social Survey (GSS); Los Angeles County Social Survey (LACSS).

1996 GSS sample, ethnic closeness was also positively associated with a strong sense of national identity, as assessed by the patriotism, chauvinism, and national pride indices. So, among ethnic minorities, none of the nine correlations are negative, contrary to the pattern predicted by the politicized group consciousness perspective. Four are actually significantly positive.

In other words, we do find some evidence of positive associations of the strength of white identity with patriotism in the national, but not Los Angeles, surveys. However, we find no evidence that ethnic identity, when measured directly, interferes with national identity for minorities. Instead, we find indications in both sets of surveys of positive associations among blacks and Latinos, just as among whites, although most are not significant. This casts doubt on the claim that ethnic pride among America's most disadvantaged minority groups systematically erodes attachment to the overarching national community.

Here, we have correlated patriotism with a direct measure of ethnic identity. We did so because we believe that approach most directly captures the core meaning of a strong, politicized ethnic identity – the belief that this group membership has great value and psychological significance. However, another approach has correlated patriotism with simple affect toward one's own ethnic group instead.[25] The affect measure used is the "feeling thermometer" developed for the ANES to measure diffuse emotional reactions to an array of political and social groups. The thermometer asks respondents to indicate the warmth of their feelings toward the group by assigning a number ranging from 0 to 100 degrees, with 50 degrees designated as a neutral state of neither warm nor cold.[26] In the present context, these feeling thermometers are used to assess affect toward the individual's own ethnic in-group. We want to reiterate our view that the global affective responses reflected by the feeling thermometer do not adequately capture the essence of one's social identity. But others disagree, so the approach deserves its day in court.[27]

With this caveat in mind, we look at the correlations of ethnic group affect and the two-item measure of patriotism in the 2002, 2004, 2008, and 2012 ANES and in the pooled LACSS samples.[28] As the politicized group consciousness view would suggest, whites tend to show a positive correlation between

[25] Jim Sidanius, Seymour Feshbach, Shana Levin, and Felicia Pratto "The Interface between Ethnic and National Attachment"; Sidanius and Petrocik, "Communal and National Identity in a Multiethnic State."

[26] Question wording: "I'd like to get your feelings toward some of our political leaders and other people who are in the news these days. I'll read the name of a person and I'd like you to rate that person using something we call the feeling thermometer. Ratings between 50 and 100 degrees mean that you feel favorably and warm toward the person; ratings between 0 and 50 degrees mean that you don't feel favorably toward the person and that you don't care too much for that person. You would rate the person at the 50 degree mark if you don't feel particularly warm or cold toward the person. If we come to a person whose name you don't recognize, you don't need to rate that person. Just tell me and we'll move on to the next one."

[27] Sidanius and Petrocik, "Communal and National Identity in a Multiethnic State."

[28] Ibid. See also Sidanius et al., "The Interface between Ethnic and National Attachment."

favorable affect toward whites as a group and patriotism (correlations range from $r = .13$ to $r = .22$, all significant; see the third panel of Table 6.4).[29]

However, such theories would also expect negative correlations between in-group affect and patriotism among minorities, with strong attachment to one's ethnic group fueling disaffection from the nation as a whole. However, the reverse holds, as with the measures of ethnic identity: only one of eleven correlations for blacks and Latinos is negative, and five are significantly positive. So, among minorities, liking one's own ethnic group does not interfere with affection for the nation. Data for the large black and Latino samples from the 2012 ANES are typical of these findings. Blacks' feelings about blacks are correlated at .16 with patriotism, and Latinos' warmth toward their own group is correlated at .18 with patriotism.

A second way to treat the thermometer data is to use an index of greater warmth toward one's in-group than toward ethnic out-groups: so-called in-group favoritism. For whites, we subtracted the average of the temperatures assigned the three minority groups from that assigned to whites; for minorities, we subtracted the temperature given to whites from that for one's own group. Consistent with much social psychological research, respondents in every ethnic group tended to express more warmth toward their own group than toward other ethnic groups. We should note, however, that this in-group favoritism usually does not reflect actual hostility toward members of other ethnic groups. In each survey, majorities in each ethnic group evaluated both their own ethnic group *and* the ethnic "other" warmly in absolute terms (more than 50 degrees on the feeling thermometer).[30]

But our primary concern here is with the association of ethnic in-group favoritism with attachment to the nation as a whole. Among whites in the six samples, in-group favoritism had a consistently positive association with patriotism, significant in all but one case but modest in size in all cases, as shown in the fourth panel of Table 6.4. Among blacks and Latinos there is again little evidence of a corrosive effect of in-group favoritism on patriotism. Only one of the eleven relationships is negative and significant (based on a small sample of Latino respondents in the 2004 ANES), whereas the association in the 2008 ANES among blacks is actually positive and significant. All the other correlations are small and statistically indistinguishable from zero. In short, most blacks and Latinos do express a preference for "their own" on these measures of global group affect, but they also revealed a high level of national attachment, as seen in Chapter 3. And there is no evidence that warmth toward their ethnic in-groups has eroded their attachment to the nation.

Perhaps a more realistic expectation is that the ethnic identifications of minority group members will make them less patriotic only if ethnicity gets

---

[29] Since consistent measures of chauvinism are not available in the National Election Studies, we present average correlations with patriotism.

[30] Sidanius et al., "The Interface between Ethnic and National Attachment."

politicized. In Chapter 4, we treated politicized ethnic group consciousness in terms of strong ethnic identity, a sense of common fate with fellow group members, and perceived discrimination against one's group. The requisite measures for testing this hypothesis were available only in the LACSS. Here, we finally find some link between ethnic attachments and weaker patriotism among minority group members, as shown in the bottom panel of Table 6.4. To be sure, sharing a sense of common fate with fellow ethnics is not correlated with the patriotism index. What does matter is the perception of discrimination against one's ethnic group. Among both black and Latino respondents, those who report higher levels of discrimination against their racial or ethnic groups feel significantly less patriotic than those who say their groups have been treated fairly.[31]

We attempted to estimate how many blacks and Latinos had the level of politicized ethnic consciousness sufficient to have lessened their attachment to the nation in this manner. Fewer than 3 percent of the blacks and Latinos in the 2002 LACSS sample fell into a potential "antinational" category, as defined by a high score on ethnic identity, a sense of linked fate with other members of their ethnic group, perceived discrimination, *and* a low score on the measure of patriotism. So, a relatively small number of our LACSS minority group respondents had sufficient ethnic group consciousness that their patriotism was compromised.

Finally, perhaps most immigrants arrive full of hope, but if their experience in their new country is one of persistent disadvantage, they might become increasingly disaffected from America. This is one implication of writings by scholars as disparate as Huntington, Sidanius and Pratto, Takaki, and Portes and Rumbaut.[32] If that is the case, we might find that the correlation between strong ethnic identity and national attachment among immigrant minorities should become increasingly negative with longer tenure in the nation. To be sure, we showed earlier that longer tenure in America is associated with *weaker* ethnic identity and with greater preference for "just an American" over an ethnic identity. But perhaps some immigrants with a longer time in the United States experience the opposite pattern; perhaps some feel locked into a fixed ethnic stratification system that blocks their advancement and, as a result, become cynical about supposed American ideals. To test this proposition, we repeated the correlations of Latinos' patriotism with the three dimensions of ethnic consciousness (see Table 4.3) within each of the three categories of immigration status we have been dealing with (see Table 6.2).

---

[31] Given these results, one possible interpretation of the null relationship between patriotism and ethnic identity among minorities is that it is simply overshadowed by the effects of perceived discrimination. But there is no evidence of this specification. There is no association between the scores of blacks and Hispanics on the patriotism and ethnic identity indices, regardless of whether they perceive much or little discrimination.

[32] Huntington, *Who Are We?*; Sidanius and Pratto, *Social Dominance*; Ronald Takaki, *A Different Mirror: A History of Multicultural America* (New York: Back Bay Books, 1993); Portes and Rumbaut, *Legacies*.

To make a long story short, the correlation between Latinos' ethnic identity and national attachment does not become more negative with longer tenure. Indeed, it is slightly negative for the noncitizens and is slightly more positive among naturalized citizens and the U.S.-born. None of the nine correlations, however, achieves statistical significance, so to save space we do not present them. The sense of ethnic identity, as opposed to a sense of national identity, is linked specifically to being a relatively recent immigrant – not to learning through long-term residence that the United States is a white-dominated society that oppresses its ethnic minorities.

In sum, here we tested the expectation of the politicized group consciousness approach that whites' ethnic identities will be positively associated with patriotism, presumably because dominant groups generally perceive little difference between their own group and the nation as a whole. Setting aside the correlations with politicized ethnicity, all eighteen such correlations were positive among whites, and the great majority achieved statistical significance. However, almost all were relatively weak, averaging just $r = .13$. This would not seem to warrant the conclusion that whites simply equate white and American identity.

Among blacks and Latinos, we found no evidence that ethnic identification is linked to diminished attachment to the nation. Pooling the two groups, about three-fourths of those thirty-one correlations were positive, too, and only one of the eleven significant associations was negative. The average correlations were +.10 for blacks and +.03 for Latinos. None of these findings changed when we used multivariate regressions rather than bivariate correlations or indices of group affect or the difference in affect between one's own ethnic group and out-groups. As in previous chapters, then, we consistently find that ethnic orientations do not compromise national attachment among even the two minority groups viewed in the politicized group consciousness theories as being at the bottom of the racial hierarchy, African Americans and Latinos.

Clearly, one could measure ethnic and national identities in ways that would encourage minority group members to treat these allegiances as antagonistic. For example, defining ethnic identity among blacks in terms of support for political separatism might well be negatively associated with extreme nationalistic chauvinism. However, much other research has shown little black support for racial separatism.[33] The indicators employed here, of course, lack that heavy ideological freight. They tap a diffuse sense of identification with others of one's own ethnic and racial group in a quite straightforward way. And although ethnic differences in outlook do emerge and the results vary slightly according to the population being surveyed, there seems to be no inherent clash between strong national and ethnic identities in the minds of the vast majority of the general public, either among the majority whites or the minority people of color.

---

[33] Dawson, *Black Visions*; P. Gurin, S. Hatchett, and J. S. Jackson, *Hope and Independence: Blacks' Response to Electoral and Party Politics* (New York: Russell Sage Foundation, 1989); Jennifer L. Hochschild, *Facing Up to the American Dream.*

NATIONAL ATTACHMENT AND MULTICULTURALIST NORMS

Ideological multiculturalism validates a strong sense of ethnic identity. It is ambiguous, we would argue, about how ethnic identity might relate to a sense of national attachment. One might argue that this would depend on the nature of the reigning ideologies about the nation's identity in a particular country. So, here we examine the relationship between support for multicultural norms and the strength of one's national identity. The critics of multiculturalism argue that the validation of cultural differences and support for a political outlook that places the interests and standing of one's ethnic group at the top of one's concerns will erode an overarching identification with the nation as a whole. Multiculturalism's defenders rebut this claim, arguing that officially recognizing minority cultures and assuring them access to political, economic, and cultural goods on a basis of equality with the majority whites actually will lead to social solidarity and a growing sense of patriotism among minorities experiencing tolerance and acceptance.

Incompatibility of National Identity with Multiculturalism?

To address this question, we look at the correlations between approval of multiculturalist norms and the most central indicators of national identity that we have used in the empirical chapters to this point: feelings of pride in the United States (Chapter 3), support for a general norm that people should think of themselves as Americans rather than ethnics (Chapter 5), and self-categorization as "just an American" rather than a member of an ethnic group (earlier in this chapter). Because we focus on the correlations *within* each group, we again rely only on the Los Angeles data because of the greater availability of minority respondents. The data are presented in Table 6.5. Negative coefficients in the table indicate clashes between support for multiculturalist norms and a positive sense of national identity.

These analyses present clear support for some tension, but not complete incompatibility, between support for multiculturalism and the strength of national identity among minorities. The correlations are negative in approximately three-fourths of the cases, regardless of which indicator of national attachment is used. By elevating the legitimacy of difference and prioritizing ethnic identifications, multiculturalist ideology seems to collide with national attachment. That said, these data suggest that any such incompatibility of multiculturalism with national identity is not very strong, consistent with the earlier analyses in this chapter. Slightly less than one-third of the coefficients achieve conventional levels of statistical significance, and the overall median is $r = -.08$.

Consistent with the black exceptionalism perspective, the negative associations between support for multiculturalism and national attachment are for the most part stronger among blacks than among Latinos. This is clearest when we

TABLE 6.5. *Correlations of Support for Multiculturalism Norms, by Attachment to Nation and Ethnicity*

	Pride in America			Norm of People Thinking of Selves as "American"			Identity as "Just an American"		
	Whites	Blacks	Latinos	Whites	Blacks	Latinos	Whites	Blacks	Latinos
Attention to ethnic history? (too little)	-.14*	.08	-.13*	-.11	-.17*	-.08	.01	-.21**	.02
Melting pot? (maintain distinct culture)	.02	-.04	-.11	-.17**	-.25**	-.11*	-.10	-.18	-.14
Better off if live and work with own (agree)	.02	.08	.06	-.03	-.02	-.08	.00	-.12	-.19**
People best represented by own (agree)	-.06	-.10	.02	-.16**	-.08	-.03	-.01	-.25**	-.16*
Representatives represent country in general or people like me? (like me)	.08	-.16	.01	NA	NA	NA	.02	-.08	.03
Ethnic organizations separatist (disagree)	-.09	-.06	-.16**	-.34**	-.15*	-.22**	-.06	-.11	-.19**
Minority experience taught by minorities (agree)	-.02	-.08	-.11	-.06	-.06	.01	-.02	-.22**	.06
Minimum Base N	245	216	241	246	216	241	239	70	171

Entries are Pearson correlations. A negative correlation indicates multiculturalism is associated with identity as an ethnic, not as an American, and with less pride in America. Identity as "just an American" is coded 0–1, with ethnic id as 0, both as .5, just American as 1; the norm of thinking of oneself as American (people should think of themselves as American rather than in ethnic terms) is a five category agree disagree item with strongly agree keyed high; pride in America is a single item with very proud keyed high. A negative correlation reflects an association between support for multiculturalism and weaker attachment to America.

* $p < .05$ ** $p < .01$ *** $p < .001$

Source: Los Angeles County Social Survey (LACSS) cumulative file. Based on 1994 and 1995 surveys except with superscript of "1" where based on 1998–99.

focus on self-categorization as just an American as opposed to either just ethnic (etc.) or both. Looking at the right-hand columns in Table 6.5, in all cases, the correlations for blacks are more negative than those for Latinos. We interpret this as further evidence that the color line in America sets blacks apart from other groups, making their own racial identity more salient to them and a stronger influence over their political thinking. Conversely, when one considers the question of pride in America, an index of attachment to the nation with no clear implication about race or ethnicity, the correlations for Latinos are mostly more negative than those for blacks. Support for multiculturalist norms seems not to be as implicated in the level of affect toward the nation as a whole as are attitudes relevant to race and ethnicity. The results for whites are in general consistent, in the sense that support for multiculturalism is negatively associated with identifying as just an American and a strong sense of pride in the United States, as show in the left-hand column of Table 6.5.

Finally, two caveats. As always, our conclusions are confined by the availability of the measures of multiculturalism. Moreover, there is doubtless a two-way flow of influence. Certainly, at the elite level it appears that nationalist theorists oppose multiculturalism as divisive, whereas those who preach the value of overriding loyalty to one's particular ethnic group often reject the primary claim of identification with the nation as a whole. It is possible that the same recursive relationship holds in the mass public, but our correlational data do not allow us to separate the two possibly divergent causal flows.

Civic versus Ethnic National Identity and the Assimilationist Norm

We conceived of national identity in terms of self-identification, emotional attachment, and beliefs about its normative content. With regard to the latter, we, along with other scholars such as Theiss-Morse and Schildkraut, distinguished between a civic (or cosmopolitan liberal) and an ethnic (or nativist) definition. Our expectation is that people who define American identity using ethnocultural criteria will be more opposed to multicultural norms that validate the equal worth of distinct cultures. This form of ethnocentrism, after all, was the hallmark of traditional nativism.

To test this, we use the 2004 GSS, with white respondents only because of insufficient minority cases. We examine the association of these contrasting definitions of national identity to beliefs about a central issue dividing multiculturalists and their critics – the belief that minorities should assimilate by blending into the mainstream culture "as in the idea of a melting pot." In the logistic regression analysis shown in Table 6.6, a "civic" conception of American nationhood was assessed by a respondent's propensity to say that respect for the country's laws and institutions was important for making one a true American, whereas the "ethnic conception" was measured by the choice of nativity and being a Christian as criteria of Americanism. The variable "Ethnic Conception

TABLE 6.6. *National Attachment and Ethnic Identity Effects on Support for Assimilation (National Data)*

	Dependent Variable: Blend In = 1, Maintain Distinctiveness = 0
Ethnic conception of American ID	.49*
National pride	.34
Ethnic closeness	.32
Female	−.24
Education	−.08
Age	.02**
Constant	−1.05
R^2	.07
N	813

*p < .05 **p < .01

Includes only white respondents. The dependent variable is coded 1 if the respondent said it was better for society if different racial or ethnic groups adapt and blend into the larger society and 0 if the respondent said it was better for them to maintain their distinct customs and traditions. Ethnic Conception of American ID is the level of support for an ethnic conception of American identity (as measured by the mean importance rating of being born in the United States and being Christian for making a person "truly American") minus the level of support for a civic conception of American identity (the importance rating of respecting American laws and institutions for making someone truly American). National pride is scored 1 if the respondent said she was very proud to be American, 0 otherwise. Ethnic closeness is a single-item in which respondents were asked how close they felt to their ethnic group. It is scaled to run from 0 = not at all close to 1 = very close.
Source: 2004 General Social Survey (GSS).

of American ID" subtracts the civic conception score from the ethnic conception score. We also included ethnic identity, measured by a question asking how close one felt to one's own ethnic group, and national identity, measured by feelings of pride in America. Finally, age, education, and gender were included as demographic controls.

These results support our expectations about the roles of national and ethnic identities in shaping preferences about assimilation versus the maintenance of cultural differences. Among whites, those who define American nationhood in exclusive, nativist terms tend to favor assimilation over the central multiculturalist principle that minorities should maintain their original cultural traditions. At the same time, the relatively muted level of in-group identification among whites does not have an independent effect. We also find that the young are less fervent about minorities blending into the mainstream, paralleling earlier support for the age-related piece of the vanguard hypothesis. Yes, national attachment does promote opposition to an important multicultural norm, but opposition is also stimulated, as one would expect, when people define Americanism in ethnocultural rather than inclusive terms.

CONCLUSION

Does ethnic identity compromise attachment to the nation? It is perhaps a truism that the most nationalistic whites will also show the greatest preference for their own white racial group. But a more trenchant question is whether the strong sense of group identification that the civil rights era catalyzed among blacks and other minorities threatens a common sense of national identity. The answer surely has implications for policies relating to mutual sacrifice and cooperation in both domestic and international politics.

It is true that whites overwhelmingly prefer to think of themselves as "just an American" rather than as a member of an ethnic group. But ethnic and racial minorities' dominant social identities are not as members of ethnic or racial groups, but are a hyphenated merger of their race or ethnicity with being American, such as African-American or Chinese-American. Thus being an American is an essential piece of most ethnic and racial minorities' social identities. Moreover, this hyphenated ethnic-American identity reflects the dual pulls of their ethnic identification and their tie to America, rather than the dominance of one or the other. We also found some evidence for black exceptionalism, that blacks' troubled history in America influences their social identity, but in a surprising way. Indeed, a substantial minority wants to be recognized as just Americans, and almost all the rest insist on a hyphenated identity that incorporates "American" as one of its pieces.

As the assimilation hypothesis predicted, Latinos and Asians are gradually transitioning from strong ethnic identities at immigration to identification with the American nation. The noncitizen immigrants were the most likely to select a purely ethnic identity, but naturalized immigrants were far less likely to. Naturalized and native-born Latinos were most likely to select a hyphenated identity, which seems to function as a stepping stone or halfway house for immigrants and their descendants who are undergoing the process of assimilation. Finally, native-born Latinos and Asians were much more likely to select "just an American" in preference to an ethnic identity. This same assimilating pattern held for patriotism as well, as seen in Chapter 3. Both findings held when assimilation was indexed with English language usage instead of immigration status.

The rapid development of strong American identities and patriotic feelings among immigrant populations, both after naturalization and in later generations, should assuage anxieties about ethnic balkanization and the demise of a common American identity. If our interpretation of the data is correct, the strong sense of national attachment among ethnic minorities should calm anxieties about America's increasing cultural diversity. Still, we need to learn more about how such dual identities are accommodated, both psychologically and politically.

In light of these assimilatory tendencies, the strong ethnic identifications seen among some Latinos and Asians earlier in Chapter 4 may perhaps reflect the society as a whole being in a transitional stage. Currently, a large proportion of those ethnic and racial minority groups are themselves immigrants. In retrospect, the period around World War I, with its great concern about Americanization of the large numbers of then quite recent Eastern and Southern European immigrants, seems to have been a similar transitional period. In the immediate aftermath of World War II, nearly half a century after the peak of European immigration, hyphenated European-American identities were still extremely common, if not dominant. The transition to pure American identities only came several decades later.[34] Unless we see another wave of draconian anti-immigrant legislation like that of the 1920s, both the numbers and proportions of native-born Latinos and Asians are bound to swell with time. If so, our data would seem to capture a relatively early phase of the transition being undergone by the large body of recent immigrants. Still, the extrapolation from our data to that later stage is based on trajectory and analogy, not as yet on observed fact. Huntington's dire prediction needs to be tested again as time passes.

We also tested the hypotheses from the politicized group consciousness paradigm that the strength of whites' ethnic identities would be highly positively correlated with patriotism, because they have appropriated the national identity for their own ethnic group, and negatively correlated among minorities, because a white-dominated nation feels more alien to them. We found mostly positive, albeit not terribly strong, correlations among whites. However, among minorities we found little trace of a negative correlation, other than a link to perceived discrimination against one's own group. In all these respects, then, both fears that there is a deep-seated alienation from the nation, even among American-born-and-bred ethnic minorities, and that their ethnic group ties cripple attachment to the United States as a whole, seem not be reflected in the general public's opinions.

But there is evidence of a link between a relatively weaker sense of American identity to support for multiculturalism among all three main ethnic groups. And in national data confined to white respondents, a nativist or ethnic conception of Americanness was associated with increased belief in cultural assimilation and, in that sense, reduced acceptance of soft multiculturalism. This should not be surprising given that support for maintaining diverse cultures and the claim that all are of equal worth conflicts with the belief in the superiority of America's dominant values and, in a less chauvinistic vein, on the utility of a common culture in assuring social solidarity in the face of ethnic change.

Finally, sometimes it is said that low levels of ethnic identification as "white" are due to whites' view that "American" is a synonym for "white." But we do not find much evidence of that outlook. The relatively weak sense of ethnic

---

[34] Ibid.; Alba, *Ethnicity in America*; Alba and Nee, *Remaking the American Mainstream*; Andrew Greeley, *Ethnicity in the United States* (New York: Wiley, 1974).

identity among whites seems instead to derive from two factors. One is the lack of a strong sense of common fate among whites, a large and diverse group who instead generally seem to adhere to the belief that their fate is an individual rather than a collective matter. The second is that relatively few in the white population are immigrants, compared to Latinos and Asian Americans. Few whites therefore have the strong sense of distinctiveness or even alikeness common in those new immigrant groups that share norms, traditions, and values through a common foreign ancestry.

7

Group-Conscious Policies: Ethnic Consensus and Cleavage

This chapter turns our attention away from opinions about general norms and principles to preferences regarding the major policy domains highest on the multicultural agenda in the United States. These policies have evoked heated legislative and electoral conflicts, often dividing the main political parties. Due to their visibility, they are more likely than abstract normative questions about descriptive representation or the maintenance of immigrant cultures to have penetrated mass consciousness.

To repeat our starting point, the two overriding purposes of multiculturalism are to redress entrenched political and economic inequalities between racial and ethnic groups and to assure that religious and cultural minorities can survive and flourish in the face of formal and informal pressures to blend in and conform to the mainstream. As articulated in Chapter 1, multiculturalists believe that solutions based on individual rights such as antidiscrimination laws and efforts to provide equality of opportunity are inadequate. Instead, multiculturalism endorses policies that are group-conscious, sometimes explicitly and sometimes only implicitly.

In the United States, the group-conscious policies advocated by the multicultural movement generally emanate from and are aimed at the minority groups embodied in the familiar ethnoracial pentagon of white, black, Hispanic, Asian, and Native American. Many of the concrete policies now described as multicultural in American politics first gained a following among black political activists in the late 1960s, a pivotal time when the civil rights movement successfully ended legal discrimination but failed to make as much progress as many desired in eroding entrenched social and economic inequalities between racial groups.

When immigration reform began to expand ethnic diversity in the United States, the constituencies for policies aimed at assisting and protecting minority groups expanded. New issues emerged, and political multiculturalism has developed by layering these demands, particularly on behalf of Latinos and Asians, on the older civil rights agenda aimed at achieving specifically *racial* equality for African Americans. Some issues were highly visible. Claims for multilingualism surfaced, intended to assist immigrant groups with little English fluency entering the United States from Latin America, Asia, and elsewhere. Language rights were defended on the grounds that immersion in the monolingual English-only environment hampered immigrants' ability to integrate into the larger society by making success in school and the navigation of public services more difficult. Insisting on English-only also threatened the maintenance of immigrants' original cultural traditions. Other issues connected to ethnic diversity were more subtle, often affecting many fewer people and more likely to be fought out in courtrooms than in the glare of public opinion. Often these centered on the demand for exclusions from dress codes and family law on religious grounds. Issues were raised by Muslims and Sikhs following in the wake of earlier cases involving Jews, the Amish, and others.

Because of data limitations and the desire to concentrate on issues that have aroused the most ongoing controversy in the public arena of American politics, this chapter confines itself to the systematic analysis of political attitudes in three policy domains: efforts to improve the position of blacks,[1] immigration,[2] and language policies.[3] It is, of course, true that these issues have historical antecedents that precede the emergence of multiculturalism as an ideological and political movement. Immigration and language issues were on the agenda in the nineteenth and early twentieth centuries. And affirmative action policy developed in the early 1960s as an effort to provide economic opportunity for African Americans. Nevertheless, these issues figure prominently in the list of policies proposed by theorists of multiculturalism. Moreover, this focus permits consideration of how the enduring debate over race meshes with issues created by the more varied cultural diversity produced primarily by heavy Latino and Asian immigration. Within each of these general policy domains, we focus on the concrete issues that have been the subject of most policy debate and that are addressed in both the national and Los Angeles surveys.

[1] For entrée into the relevant literature, see Sears, Sidanius, and Bobo, *Racialized Politics*; Kinder and Sanders, *Divided by Color*; Schuman et al., *Racial Attitudes in America*; Paul M. Sniderman and Thomas Piazza, *The Scar of Race* (Cambridge, MA: Harvard University Press, 1993).

[2] See Jack Citrin et al., "Testing Huntington"; Peter Schuck, *Diversity in America: Keeping Government at a Safe Distance* (Cambridge, MA: The Belknap Press of Harvard University Press, 2003), 40–72; Schuck, "Immigration"; John S. Lapinski, Pia Peltola, Greg Shaw, and Alan Yang, "Trends: Immigrants and Immigration," *Public Opinion Quarterly* 61 (1997): 356–83; Sears, Citrin, Cheleden, and van Laar, "Is Cultural Balkanization Psychologically Inevitable?"; Pew Research Center, "America's Immigration Quandary: No Consensus on Immigration Problem or Proposed Fixes" (2006), http://www.people-press.org/files/legacy-pdf/274.pdf.

[3] Citrin, Reingold, and Green, "American Identity and the Politics of Ethnic Change"; John Frendreis and Raymond Tatalovich, "Who Supports English-Only Language Laws? Evidence from the 1992 National Election Study," 78, no. 2 (1997): 354–68; Kathryn Pearson and Jack Citrin, "The Political Assimilation of the Fourth Wave," in *Transforming Politics, Transforming America: The Political and Civic Incorporation of Immigrants in the United States*, ed. Taeku Lee, Karthick Ramakrishnan, and Ricardo Ramirez (Charlottesville, VA.: University of Virginia Press, 2006); Deborah Schildkraut, *Press 'One' for English: Language Policy, Public Opinion, and American Identity* (Princeton, NJ: Princeton University Press, 2005).

This chapter assesses the degree of consensus and cleavage in these policy domains across the major ethnic and racial groups. Are Americans united across ethnic groups, as if the merits of alternative affirmative action, immigration, and language policies dominate ethnic differences in generating public responses to them? In the policy arena, do we find the same consensual repudiation of hard multiculturalism interwoven with acceptance of soft multiculturalism as we did with respect to more abstract multicultural norms? Or do opinions vary widely across diverse ethnic groups, in line with the claim that ethnic consciousness is so potent that people view government policies through the lens of identity politics, focusing primarily on how their own group is affected?

In exploring patterns of cleavage between ethnic groups, we contrast three general theoretical perspectives. One, growing out of the politicized group consciousness paradigm, suggests that public opinion might reflect the particular group interests of each ethnic group. This might well take into consideration the differences within heavily immigrant groups due to assimilation. A second, also consistent with some versions of that paradigm, is a "people of color" coalition in which all subordinate minorities differ from the dominant whites. A third is the black exceptionalism notion that conceives of African Americans as distinctively different from the new voluntary immigrants. In doing so, we speculate about whether the motives underlying observed ethnic differences vary across issues.

In this chapter, we review a wide variety of issues in these three policy domains. We present data on these specific issues in the tables, but obviously many other surveys contain other relevant items. In an effort to maintain our focus, we do not attempt a comprehensive presentation of all the data available in contemporary surveys, nor to provide a comprehensive review of the vast literature on public opinion about these multifaceted issues. Nevertheless, we would argue that the data we do present are representative of those that have emerged from other surveys.

CONSENSUS IN OPINION ON POLICIES REFLECTING THE MULTICULTURAL AGENDA

We begin by assessing areas of consensus across ethnic and racial groups about these three policy domains that bear on the interests of minority groups and that reflect the goals of multiculturalists, as well as of other actors. Perhaps the most important point to be made before we launch into the data is our criterion for "consensus." It is that a *majority* in *every* major ethnic group is on the *same* side of the issue. For the larger purpose signaled by the title of this volume, the major implication of consensus is that a common national outlook has superseded ethnic divisions. Here, we will make three general points, drawing in part on previous studies as well as our own.

First, the basic boundaries of public debate about the role of race and ethnicity in America appear to be set by consensus on the fundamentals in each domain: the national commitment that emerged from the civil rights era, to the equal treatment of all racial and ethnic groups; resistance to further increases in immigration after decades of sharply higher rates of legal and illegal immigration; and maintaining the nearly four-centuries-old reliance on English as the nation's common language. Second, we find a consensual rejection of hard multiculturalism because, we presume, it promotes the particularistic interests of specific ethnic groups at the expense of violating more universal traditional American values. And third, we find a broad acceptance of soft multiculturalism, a tolerant acceptance of pragmatic accommodations to cultural differences in a nation marked by sharply increased ethnic diversity.

We illustrate by examining each policy agenda in turn.[4] Table 7.1 presents trends over time in attitudes about multicultural policies on issues that have repeatedly appeared in the General Social Survey (GSS) and American National Election Studies (ANES). The data are presented separately for whites and blacks in the nation as a whole, with only the 2008 and 2012 surveys including a sufficient number of Latino respondents to allow for comparisons with that group. Table 7.2 uses the finer ethnic distinctions possible in the Los Angeles County Social Survey (LACSS) data, but pools across the years of the surveys to provide more reliable estimates within each ethnic group. All three issue domains are included. Table 7.3 presents items asked in the few national surveys that addressed a wider ranges of questions about policy, in the immigration and language domains only, thus providing valuable qualitative range across a variety of other issues in which over-time trends often were not assessed.

RACIALLY TARGETED POLICIES

At the most general level, racial issues in the United States have been through two phases. More than half a century ago, the civil rights struggle aimed to over-throw the legalized and formalized Jim Crow caste system in the South, along with many of its similar if sometimes less restrictive parallels elsewhere in the nation. The primary goal of this first phase was the elimination of legal segre-gation and discrimination, with the intention of giving African Americans the opportunity to participate and compete in the broader society. That agenda divided much of the white South from the rest of the nation. Public opinion research over the past several decades has assessed attitudes about this first racial agenda in terms of general principles of equal opportunity, equal treatment, and nondiscrimination. A large body of evidence has revealed a strong biracial

---

[4] Because of the paucity of Hispanic and Asian respondents in the national samples available to us, those survey data are used primarily to consider white and black attitudes.

TABLE 7.1. *Support for Group-Conscious Policies: Trends in National Data over Time, by Ethnicity*

	Whites						Blacks						Latinos	
	1994	1996	2000	2004	2008	2012	1994	1996	2000	2004	2008	2012	2008	2012
A. Race-Targeted Policies														
* Some people say that because of past discrimination, blacks should be given preference in hiring and promotion. Others say that such preference in hiring and promotion of blacks is wrong because it discriminates against whites (ANES: gives blacks advantages they haven't earned). What about your opinion – are you for or against preferential hiring and promotion of blacks?														
GSS (% for)	11	11	13	12	12	14	57	50	44	47	48	45	19	19
	(1,149)	(1,477)	(1,362)	(680)	(907)	(836)	(179)	(256)	(277)	(92)	(171)	(175)	(140)	(159)
ANES (% for)	9	17	13	14	10	11	50	64	41	58	53	55	26	20
	(1,519)	(1,292)	(840)	(765)	(981)	(802)	(194)	(166)	(131)	(149)	(464)	(430)	(400)	(398)
Should the government help improve blacks' living standards or should not be giving special treatment to blacks?														
GSS (mean; 5 = gov't. help, 1 = no special treatment)	2.2	2.2	2.3	2.2	2.2	2.1	3.7	3.5	3.7	3.4	3.6	3.3	2.8	2.5
	(1,621)	(1,519)	(1,432)	(652)	(931)	(851)	(243)	(244)	(258)	(92)	(175)	(194)	(156)	(171)
Should the government make every effort to improve the social and economic position of blacks or not make any special effort to help blacks?														
ANES (mean; 7 = gov't. help, 1 = blacks help selves)	3.1	3.1	3.1	3.2	2.8	2.8	4.4	4.1	4.0	4.7	4.6	4.4	3.8	3.6
	(1,411)	(1,341)	(804)	(782)	(1,022)	(785)	(174)	(176)	(117)	(163)	(474)	(438)	(372)	(384)
Are we spending too much money, too little money, or about the right amount on improving the conditions of blacks?														
GSS (% too little/ –% too much)	–1	0	11	8	17	13	77	84	74	76	82	69	25	19
	(1,082)	(996)	(930)	(952)	(627)	(573)	(184)	(195)	(193)	(164)	(130)	(143)	(92)	(113)
B. Immigration Policies														
Number of immigrants increased, left the same, or decreased?														
GSS 1994–04; ANES for 2008 and 2012														
% increase	5[a]	7	8[a]	9[b]	13[c]	14[d]	11	12	10[a]	12[b]	12[c]	16[d]	22	19
% decrease	67[a]	67	47	57	47	44	65[a]	60	39	53	50	29	27	27
	(1,160)	(951)	(1,047)	(1,578)	(1,055)	(818)	(182)	(134)	(175)	(228)	(506)	(462)	(443)	(424)

(continued)

TABLE 7.1 (continued)

	Whites						Blacks						Latinos	
	1994	1996	2000	2004	2008	2012	1994	1996	2000	2004	2008	2012	2008	2012

Increase federal spending on tightening border security and preventing illegal immigration, leave it the same, or decrease it? ANES 1996–2008

	Whites						Blacks						Latinos	
% increase		68	56[a]	68	62[b]			59	54[a]	58	60[b]		38	
% decrease		7[a]	9[b]	4	10[c]			6[a]	10[b]	8	9[c]		17	
		(1,433)	(1,347)	(772)	(1,144)			(198)	(202)	(156)	(543)		(485)	

On any given item, ethnic groups are significantly different ($p < .05$) unless they have the same superscript. Base N's are in parentheses.

* Indicates that exact wording is shown above. For other items, exact wording is given in Appendix 7.1

180

TABLE 7.2. *Support for Group-Conscious Policies: Los Angeles Surveys*

	Whites	Blacks	Latinos			Asians
			All	U.S.-Born	Foreign-Born	

A. Race-Targeted Policies
* Are you for or against preferential hiring and promotion of blacks?

	Whites	Blacks	All	U.S.-Born	Foreign-Born	Asians
(% for)	15	45	28[a]	35	24	28[a]
	(297)	(66)	(288)	(92)	(195)	(64)

Give blacks preference in hiring if a company has a history of discriminating

	Whites	Blacks	All	U.S.-Born	Foreign-Born	Asians
(% agree)	53[ab]	83	55[a]	61	51[b]	66
	(1,007)	(498)	(923)	(275)	(635)	(167)

Should spending for programs that assist blacks be increased, decreased, or kept about the same?

	Whites	Blacks	All	U.S.-Born	Foreign-Born	Asians
(+% increased/	+16[a]	+67	+16[a]	+26	+12	+19[a]
−% decreased)	(1,160)	(643)	(1,114)	(331)	(773)	(190)

* Do you feel that the government should help minorities, minorities should help themselves, or somewhere in between?

	Whites	Blacks	All	U.S.-Born	Foreign-Born	Asians
(% gov't. should help)	29	42[a]	51	49[b]	51[b]	40[a]
	(788)	(361)	(648)	(185)	(462)	(150)

Are you for or against preferential hiring and promotion of Hispanics?

	Whites	Blacks	All	U.S.-Born	Foreign-Born	Asians
(% for)	12	38	53	54[a]	52[a]	24
	(254)	(169)	(94)	(28)	(65)	(45)

B. Immigration Policies
* Do you think the number of immigrants from foreign countries who are permitted to come to the United States to live should be:

	Whites	Blacks	All	U.S.-Born	Foreign-Born	Asians
(% increased)	12[a]	13[a]	28	21[b]	30	22[b]
(% left the same as now)	41[a]	31	41[a]	37	42	46
(% decreased)	47	56	32[a]	42	28	32[a]
	(1,964)	(990)	(1,736)	(522)	(1,200)	(337)

* Do you think that immigrants who are here legally should be eligible for [government] services as soon as they come here?

	Whites	Blacks	All	U.S.-Born	Foreign-Born	Asians
(% eligible)	38[a]	38[a]	54	39[a]	60	56
	(526)	(295)	(457)	(125)	(132)	(93)

Should the government spend more money for deportation of illegal aliens?

	Whites	Blacks	All	U.S.-Born	Foreign-Born	Asians
(% no)	40	43	74	61	79	47
	(1,639)	(931)	(1,471)	(422)	(1,032)	(279)

Should undocumented aliens be entitled to have their children continue to qualify as American citizens if born in the United States?

	Whites	Blacks	All	U.S.-Born	Foreign-Born	Asians
(% yes)	47[a]	54	90	77	95	49[a]
	(804)	(354)	(679)	(195)	(482)	(140)

C. Language Policies
Make English the official language of the United States, meaning government business would be conducted in English only?

	Whites	Blacks	All	U.S.-Born	Foreign-Born	Asians
(% oppose)	26	29[a]	68	47	76	30[a]
	(1,991)	(1,005)	(1,791)	(516)	(1,258)	(344)

(*continued*)

TABLE 7.2 (*continued*)

	Whites	Blacks	Latinos			Asians
			All	U.S.-Born	Foreign-Born	
* How should children be taught who don't speak English when they enter our public schools?						
(% native language through high school)	3^a	12^b	14^b	7	16	5^a
(% 1–2 years in native language)	53^a	58^b	61^b	55^a	63	48
(% classes only in English)	44^a	30	26	38	21	47^a
	(798)	(363)	(669)	(189)	(477)	(152)
* How do you feel about bilingual education?						
(% favor)	48	65	84	73	88	59
	(1,063)	(580)	(1,003)	(283)	(710)	(183)

Groups are significantly different (p<.05) on any given item unless they have the same superscript. "All" Latinos were not compared to "U.S.-Born" or "Foreign-Born" Latinos. Base N's are in parentheses.

*Indicates that exact wording is shown above. For other items, exact wording is given in Appendix 7.1.

Source: Los Angeles County Social Survey (LACSS) cumulative file, 1994–2002. For item availability by year, see Appendix 7.1

contemporary consensus in support of abstract principles of racial equality and nondiscrimination.[5]

After the 1960s, a second phase focused on the use of race-conscious policies, such as busing to promote full school integration, affirmative action to ensure equal access to higher education and jobs, and offsets to achieve greater equality of results in government contracts. This second agenda was applied more nationwide and was more nationally controversial. Public opinion research over the past several decades has also distinguished political attitudes about what are sometimes called "implementing policies" – government policies aimed specifically at improving the status of specific categories of Americans, such as blacks and other minority groups – from other racial attitudes. These include some that single out blacks for preferential treatment and others that are targeted more for immigrants. Both sets spill over into the later multiculturalist perspective.[6]

When we turn to this post-civil rights racial policy agenda, we again see national consensus, but now in *opposition* to race-targeted policies that flow in part from the multiculturalist agenda of enhancing the position of minorities.

---

[5] Schuman, et al., *Racial Attitudes in America*.

[6] Schuman, et al., *Racial Attitudes in America*; Sears, van Laar, Carrillo, and Kosterman, "Is It Really Racism?"; Paul M. Sniderman, Gretchen C. Crosby, and William G. Howell, "The Politics of Race," in *Racialized Politics: The Debate about Racism in America*, ed. David O. Sears, Jim Sidanius, and Lawrence Bobo (Chicago: University of Chicago Press, 2000), 236–79.

TABLE 7.3. *Support for Group-Conscious Policies: Episodic National Data*

	Whites (%)	Blacks (%)	Latinos (%)
A. Immigration Policies vis-à-vis Legal Immigrants			
* Should immigrants who are here legally be eligible for public services as soon as they come, or should they not be eligible?			
GSS 1994 (% eligible)	34[a]	29[a]	
	(1,165)	(179)	
* Government spends too much money assisting immigrants.			
GSS 2004 (% disagree)	19[a]	21[a]	
	(938)	(158)	
* Children born in America of parents who are not citizens should have the right to become American citizens.			
GSS 2004 (% agree)	73[a]	79[a]	
	(932)	(164)	
* Legal immigrants to America who are not citizens should have the same rights as American citizens.			
GSS 2004 (% agree)	37[a]	40[a]	
	(958)	(157)	
B. Immigrant Policies vis-à-vis Illegal Immigrants			
* The United States should take stronger measures to exclude illegal immigrants.			
GSS 1996 (% disagree)	8	14	
	(1,094)	(183)	
GSS 2004 (% disagree)	11	16	
	(946)	(149)	
Children of illegal immigrants qualify as American citizens if born in the United States?			
GSS 1994 (% yes)	50[a]	56[a]	
	(1,126)	(179)	
Should "undocumented aliens" be entitled to work permits?			
GSS 1994 (% yes, entitled)	12[a]	18[a]	
	(1,164)	(180)	
* Should illegal immigrants be allowed to work in the United States for three years, after which they would have to go back to their home country?			
ANES 2008 (% favor)	22[a]	25[a]	43
	(580)	(262)	(276)
* Should the U.S. government make it possible for illegal immigrants to become U.S. citizens?			
ANES 2008 (% favor)	47	41	69
	(519)	(229)	(245)
* Should "undocumented aliens" be entitled to attend public universities at the same costs as other students?			
GSS 1994 (% yes, entitled)	68[a]	65[a]	
	(1,169)	(180)	

(continued)

TABLE 7.3 *(continued)*

	Whites (%)	Blacks (%)	Latinos (%)
C. Language Policies			
* Do you favor a law making English the official language of the United States, meaning government business would be conducted in English only?			
GSS 1994 (% oppose)	27	45	
	(1,069)	(160)	
GSS 2000 (% oppose)	21	25	
	(1,029)	(186)	
* Speaking English as the common national language is what unites all Americans.			
GSS 2000 (% disagree)	24[a]	21[a]	
	(1,102)	(204)	
* Do you believe that election ballots should be printed only in English, or in areas where lots of people don't speak English, should they also be printed in other languages?			
GSS 1994 (% other languages)	60	77	
	(1,174)	(188)	
GSS 2004 (% other languages)	64	74	
	(1,059)	(190)	
* English will be threatened if other languages are frequently used in large immigrant communities in the United States			
GSS 2004 (% disagree)	66[a]	68[a]	
	(1,104)	(204)	
How should children be taught if they don't speak English when they enter our public schools?			
GSS 1994			
% native language through high school	14	23	
% 1–2 years in native language	49[a]	48[a]	
% classes only in English	37	29	
	(1,176)	(186)	
* How do you feel about bilingual education?			
GSS 1994 (% favor)	64	85	
	(1,164)	(175)	
* Bilingual education programs should be eliminated in American public schools.			
GSS 2000 (% disagree)	76	84	
	(1,103)	(205)	
D. U.S. Government Policy Toward Illegal Immigrants			
ANES 2012 (% Deport)	19	7[a]	8[a]
(% Guest workers)	20	14[a]	11[a]
(% Pathway to Citizenship with penalty)	53	63[a]	67[a]
(% Pathway to Citizenship no penalty)	7	14[a]	14[a]
	(918)	(511)	(474)

Groups with the same superscript on a given item are not significantly different (*p* > .05).
Lack of matching superscripts indicates that the relevant group difference is significant at the .05 level or better. Base N's are in parentheses.
*Indicates that exact wording is shown above. For other items, exact wording is given in Appendix 7.1.

We classify explicitly black-targeted policies as going in the direction of harder multiculturalist solutions for racial inequality that institutionalize the group-conscious allocation of benefits. Of course, the survey items relating to group-conscious policies we analyze here do not tap the hardest multiculturalism policy proposals, such as specific quotas in political representation, which we found drew overwhelming and consensual opposition in Chapter 5 (see Table 5.2).

Majorities of Americans in almost all ethnic groups oppose preferential treatment of blacks in hiring and promotion, whether in national or Los Angeles surveys.[7] In the 2012 ANES, 80 percent of the Latinos opposed preferential treatment in employment for blacks. And in the LACSS, Latinos (72 percent) and Asians (72 percent) also registered opposition (see Table 7.2A). Even African Americans themselves were divided, with majorities in opposition to preferences as often as not. This broadly based opposition to explicitly race-based preferences parallels the main findings of other surveys about quotas, targets, and descriptive representation.[8] Indeed, income-targeted policies, race-neutral on the surface, generally receive much more support than does making race or ethnicity the criterion for receiving public benefits.[9]

Conversely, we also find consensual support for soft multiculturalism in the domain of race entailing some special assistance for African Americans. For example, even whites favor, on balance, the government's helping improve blacks' living standards and spending more money for programs that assist blacks (although this is more evident in Los Angeles than nationally; see Tables 7.1A, 7.2A). In contrast to the widespread opposition evoked by general racially targeted preferences in hiring and employment, preferences directly targeted to offset past injustices are widely supported across ethnic groups: most Los Angeles respondents in all groups supported affirmative action for blacks when it was explicitly targeted at companies with a history of past discrimination (Table 7.2A).[10] That is, we see consensus both in opposition to racial preferences based solely on a hard color line and in sympathetic support for softer proposals for assistance to blacks when discrimination in the past has

---

[7] Similar results hold for preferences in admissions to higher education, but are not shown here to save space.

[8] Le and Citrin, "Affirmative Action."

[9] Lawrence Bobo and Ryan A. Smith, "Antipoverty Policy, Affirmative Action, and Racial Attitudes," in *Confronting Poverty: Prescriptions for Change*, ed. Sheldon Danziger, Gary D. Sandefur, and Daniel H. Weinberg (Cambridge, MA: Harvard University Press, 1994), 365–95; Lawrence Bobo and James R. Kluegel, "Opposition to Race-Targeting: Self-Interest, Stratification Ideology, or Racial Attitudes?" *American Sociological Review* 58 (1993): 443–64.

[10] Similarly, soft efforts to provide special help to blacks in recruitment and training, to prepare them to compete better, usually are found to be much more acceptable to the American public than the idea of firm preferences in access to benefits, which dictate the results of competition, although we do not review such data here. See Charlotte Steeh and Maria Krysan, "Trends: Affirmative Action and the Public, 1970–1995" *Public Opinion Quarterly* 60 (1996): 128–58.

been shown, reflecting the post-civil rights consensus that outright discrimination against minorities is unfair.

LEGAL IMMIGRATION

Every wave of immigration to the United States has sparked some degree of a nativist reaction. In the late nineteenth century, industrialization generated a demand for cheap labor, and liberal immigration policies opened the door to many millions, especially from eastern and southern Europe. But nativist beliefs that these groups were unsuitable for Americanness led first to a program of coercive Americanization and then to restrictive legislation in the 1920s that shut new immigration to a trickle. The Immigration and Naturalization Act of 1965 sharply reversed the nation's course again by eliminating national quotas and basing visa preferences on family reunification, thereby enabling the ongoing influx of immigrants from Latin America and Asia.

Why do we treat liberal immigration policy as part of the multicultural political agenda? In most Western societies, immigration is the fuel that drives demands for group rights in language and cultural policies. In addition, even though immigrants come voluntarily and have not previously experienced discrimination in the United States, political decisions have led to their inclusion on the basis of ethnicity as beneficiaries of proposed multicultural policies such as affirmative action and bilingual education and ballots. Most black interest group leaders have now joined Latino and Asian activists in presenting a united front in favor of maintaining high levels of immigration and immigrant rights. Opinions about the level of immigration do not speak explicitly to the issue of group rights, but, at least at the elite level, advocacy of more immigration and special treatment for immigrants in schools and hiring tend to go together.

Our data show consensual opposition to multiculturalism in this domain as well, if this is defined in terms of support for increasing the level of immigration, even for minority groups who faced discrimination in the past. Only a small minority of Americans in national surveys since the early 1990s, regardless of race or ethnicity, have said that the level of immigration should be increased (Table 7.1B). The same held true in Los Angeles, although the numbers are not as overwhelmingly unfavorable (Table 7.2B). Nationally, the same finding held in the large-scale 2006 Pew Immigration Survey and persisted through the most recent Pew polling on the subject in 2013.[11] This reluctance to increase immigration has held for many years. In the most recent 2013 Gallup poll, a substantially higher percentage of the public favors decreasing immigration (35 percent) than increasing it.

---

[11] Pew Research Center for the People and the Press, "America's Immigration Quandary," March 30, 2006. Accessed online at http://www.people-press.org/2006/03/30/americas-immigration-quandary/ For wordings for all Pew questions cited, see Appendix 7.2.

Despite this steady history of resistance to large increases in immigration, however, there have been someother fluctuations over the years. Surveys conducted by Gallup every two years from 1965 to 2013 found that the modal answer has shifted back and forth over the past 15 years between keeping immigration at its present level and support for decreasing the amount of immigration.[12] The year 1994 was a high water mark in anti-immigrant sentiment, perhaps due to the impact of an economic recession and the politicization of the issue by Republicans during the congressional elections. By 2000, a changed economic and political climate had softened restrictionist sentiments, with the proportion of Americans nationally saying that immigration should be decreased declining by 20 percent in that period (Table 7.1B). Similarly, modest fluctuations occurred since 2001 in response to a Gallup question about whether "immigration is a good thing or a bad thing for this country today." The high point of "a bad thing" was slightly more than 40 percent (2002) and the low point around 25 percent in the most recent poll (2013) in which Gallup asked this question. The Gallup national surveys have found that the proportion supporting increased immigration has recently reached a high of 23 percent, up from a mere 10 percent in 1999, perhaps because of President Obama's support for a pathway to citizenship and softening opposition after his margin of victory among Latinos in the 2012 election.[13]

In both the GSS and the Gallup data, these trends also seem consensual, since they occur in parallel among whites and blacks.[14] Latinos in the 2008 and 2012 data do stand apart in being less in favor of restricting access than other ethnic groups. But even among Latinos only small minorities favored increasing immigration (25 percent in the most recent Gallup poll, nearly identical to the 27 percent of Latinos who supported increasing the level of immigration in the 2008 and 2012 ANES surveys).

There also is pervasive opposition to giving immigrants equal access to all government benefits (Tables 7.2B, 7.3A). Most white and black respondents, both nationally and in Los Angeles, favor a waiting period before legal immigrants could benefit from government health and welfare programs.[15] Similarly, most whites and blacks nationally believe that the government spends too much money assisting immigrants.

As with race-targeted policies, however, these negative attitudes toward increased immigration and immediate government benefits for them coexist with evidence of tolerance and pragmatism that we subsume under soft multiculturalism. Indeed, one should be cautious about reading too much into surveys

---

[12] Gallup: Americans More Pro-Immigration Than in Past: http://www.gallup.com/poll/163457/americans-pro-immigration-past.aspx; http://www.gallup.com/poll/1660/immigration.aspx.

[13] Ibid.

[14] They also occur in parallel among men and women, young and old, liberals and conservatives, although that is not shown here.

[15] Jack Citrin et al., "Public Opinion toward Immigration: The Role of Economic Motivations," *The Journal of Politics* 59, no. 3 (1997): 858–81.

that show that many more people want to decrease than to increase immigration. Most polls show that a large minority favors keeping the level of immigration the same. Those advocating the status quo can be viewed as generally sympathetic to immigration, given that existing levels of immigration since 1965 have admitted about one million legal newcomers a year and have increased the number of foreign-born residents in the United States to the highest point in a century.

Birthright citizenship is another central issue related to immigration. This principle is generally cited as a diagnostic indicator of the civic conception of nationality, and it is one on which multiculturalists and cosmopolitan liberals should agree.[16] Giving the children of noncitizen immigrants this soft, liberal option received overwhelming support in the 2004 GSS among both white and black Americans (Table 7.3A). Note that this item is not ideal, since it refers to noncitizen rather than illegal immigrants, a subset of noncitizens and a horse of a different political color. Nevertheless, the relatively high level of support for birthright citizenship for children of the larger group of non-citizens, despite the hostility toward that subset of illegal immigrants that we document in the next section, suggests that citizenship for the children of *legal* immigrants is broadly supported.

ILLEGAL IMMIGRATION

When we turn to the undocumented, often referred to as "illegal immigrants" or "illegal aliens," a strong consensus favors even more restrictive treatment. That has been true throughout the past two decades. Generally, in the late 1990s and early 2000s, majorities of whites and blacks nationally supported stronger barriers to illegal immigration, in terms of excluding illegal immigrants (in the 1996 and 2004 GSS, Table 7.3B) and, more specifically, tightening border security (1996–2008 ANES, Table 7.1B). In the Los Angeles surveys, the same racial consensus held on spending more money to deport illegal aliens (Table 7.2B).

More recently, this consensus on the toughness toward illegal immigrants emerged from the 2006 Pew Immigration Survey,[17] in which large majorities in all four major ethnic groups, ranging from 77 percent to 55 percent, favored requiring employers to check a government database establishing legal status before hiring anyone and mandating that potential employees carry a card verifying their legal status. Few Americans would allow illegal immigrants to stay for three years even with a firm mandate to return to their home countries afterward, according to the 2008 ANES (Table 7.3B). There has also been broad consensus on denying those illegally in the country some of the socioeconomic

---

[16] Rogers Brubaker, "Civic and Ethnic Nations in France and Germany," in *Ethnicity*, ed. John Hutchinson and Anthony Smith (Oxford: Oxford University Press, 1992).

[17] Pew Research Center for the People and the Press.

privileges that are normally available to those who play by the rules.[18] For example, in a 2010 Gallup poll, a plurality of Americans favored Arizona's recently passed law allowing state and local law enforcement agents to detain those they suspect of being in the country illegally (many others had not heard of the law).[19] Large minorities of whites (45 percent) and blacks (38 percent) meet the even more strenuous test of favoring a constitutional amendment that parents must be legal residents in the United States for their newborn child to be a citizen, according to the 2006 Pew Immigration Survey.

However, when it comes to the harsh option of deporting all undocumented immigrants, most support a more tolerant approach The 2006 Pew Immigration Survey found that, on average, members of all major ethnic groups rejected the idea that "illegal immigrants *all* [should] be required to leave the U.S." in favor of "some [should] be allowed to stay in a temporary work program provided they eventually leave" or "all [should] be allowed to stay on permanently" (emphases added).[20] Similarly, a 2011 Gallup poll asked whether all illegal immigrants should be deported (as opposed to remaining in the United States for a limited time to work or becoming citizens by meeting requirements that were unspecified in the item). Only about 20 percent favored deporting *all* of them over these more humane alternatives. Given that the majority of illegal immigrants are Latinos, primarily from Mexico, this reflects the weakness of nativism when it comes to such draconian, and probably unrealistic, options. Finally, a 2011 Pew Research Center poll assessed attitudes toward the idea of changing the Constitution in order to prevent the U.S.-born children of illegal immigrants from obtaining birthright citizenship. Latinos, for many of whom the issue carries a great deal of personal resonance, were quite strongly opposed (73 percent), whereas smaller majorities of whites (52 percent) and blacks (59 percent) also opposed removing birthright citizenship for children of illegal immigrants.[21]

And it should be noted that recognition of the political clout of Latinos after the 2012 election quickly produced a push for legalization of the estimated 11 million people living in the United States without permission, as well as for larger visa quotas for both high-tech and agricultural workers. As reflected in responses to a 2012 ANES question (Table 7.3D), most Americans in each major

---

[18] When we speak of consensus in these national surveys, we refer to agreement between whites and blacks. The limits of that consensus are shown in the sharp dissent from such restrictive treatment among Latinos in the Los Angeles surveys. We address those more complex ethnic cleavages in the next section of this chapter.

[19] Thirty-nine percent favored the law, and 30 percent opposed it. Gallup, 2010: More Americans Favor than Oppose Arizona Immigration Law, http://www.gallup.com/poll/127598/americans-favor-oppose-arizona-immigration-law.aspx.

[20] Pew Research Center for the People and the Press; see the results from Poll 1660, available at http://www.gallup.com/poll/1660/immigration.aspx/.

[21] Pew Research Center, 2011: http://www.people-press.org/2011/02/24/public-favors-tougher-bor der-controls-and-path-to-citizenship/.

ethnic group favored giving illegal immigrants a path to citizenship (as opposed to being offered temporary work permits or being made felons and deported), albeit with some penalties attached. Only a relatively small minority, even of whites (19 percent), favored deportation. Other national polling has tended to find majority support for a path to citizenship, although the extent of support varies with question wording and the alternatives offered.

Further evidence of consensual support for a soft position on policies toward the undocumented in some situations is that most Americans do not feel that the full burden of illegal immigration should be passed on to their children. This has been true for many years. In the 1994 GSS, about two-thirds of the whites and blacks alike felt that illegal immigrants who graduated from high schools in their state should be allowed to attend public universities for the same tuition as other students (Table 7.3B). The 2006 Pew Immigration Survey found that clear majorities in all major ethnic groups, ranging from 67 percent of whites to 93 percent of Latinos, agreed that "children of illegal immigrants [should be] allowed to attend public schools." The issue of what should be done about illegal immigrants brought to the United States as children came to the political fore when, in 2012, President Obama announced an executive order "deferring action for childhood arrivals," essentially banning the deportation of illegal immigrants who were brought to the United States before the age of sixteen years. His order applied to those who were under thirty years of age and had completed high school in the United States. It received the backing of 64 percent of Americans in a recent Bloomberg News national poll.[22] A Pew survey conducted around the same time similarly found 63 percent support for the deferred action order overall and overwhelming support (89 percent) among Latinos.[23]

So, although immigration is a complex issue or set of issues, we see the same widely consensual pattern as with race-targeted policies, one of opposition in all groups to policies smacking of hard multiculturalism, such as quota-driven increases in immigration or soft borders that would allow more illegal immigration. Yet there is consensus across ethnic groups in supporting soft multiculturalist adjustments to immigration policy, such as opposing wide-scale deportations, ultimately moving toward legalization (with penalties and conditions), and on making special allowances for those brought to this country as children by their parents.

LANGUAGE POLICIES

As a visible marker, language is an accessible basis for self-categorization and thus can be the foundation of a group's distinct political identity. Although the

---

[22] Bloomberg News Poll Report, November 2012, accessed online at http://media.bloomberg.com/bb/avfile/r27N5k5yzAsA

[23] Pew Research Center, 2012: http://www.pewhispanic.org/2012/10/11/latinos-and-immigration-policy/.

United States is ethnically one of the most heterogeneous nations in the world, linguistically it is one of the most homogeneous.[24] Nevertheless, a new round of conflict about language was sparked with the increased immigration after 1965, especially from non-English-speaking regions such as Latin America and Asia. The passage of the Bilingual Education Act in 1971 and subsequent demands for language rights by advocates of multiculturalism provoked opponents to claim that bilingualism threatened national unity. Many mobilized to pass state laws and referenda declaring English the official language of the United States.[25] The "Official English" movement represented a desire to assure assimilation and to oppose hard multiculturalism's goal of maintaining cultural differences.

These conflicts over language rights have had a particularly symbolic flavor, however, rather than very accurately reflecting life on the ground. The evidence from U.S. census data shows that most second-generation Latinos, like their European predecessors, have fluency in English. By the third generation, most are monolingual in English.[26] Indeed, the numerous states that have passed official English-language measures have seen little actual policy change. Nevertheless, conflicts over language policy have been numerous and contentious. Public opinion about language policy has consistently revealed broad support for English as the country's only national language. This consensus appears in both national and Los Angeles surveys, across time, and across items worded in various ways. Since the 1990s, a consistently strong national majority has supported legislation that would make English the official language of the United States. For example, the 2000 GSS showed that 79 percent of white Americans (and 75 percent of blacks) supported making English the official national language. Similar numbers agreed that speaking English as the common national language is what unites all Americans (all in Table 7.3C). A large majority of the public also believes that speaking English is an important criterion for making someone a true American.[27] In the Los Angeles data, the majority consensus on support for English as an official language goes beyond whites and blacks to encompass even U.S.-born Latinos (53 percent supportive) and Asians (70 percent supportive), both groups dominated by people with a relatively recent history of immigration (Table 7.2C). The ubiquitous dependence on the English language is consensually viewed as desirable, probably both as strong symbolic glue binding Americans to national unity and as

---

[24] Abigail Thernstrom, "Language: Issues and Legislation," in *Harvard Encyclopedia of American Ethnic Groups*, ed. Stephan Thernstrom (Cambridge, MA: Harvard University Press, 1980).

[25] Jack Citrin et al., "The 'Official English' Movement and the Symbolic Politics of Language in the United States," *The Western Political Quarterly* 43, no. 3 (1990): 535–59; Frendreis and Tatalovich, "Who Supports English-Only Language Laws?"

[26] Citrin, Lerman, Murakami, and Pearson, "Testing Huntington"; Alba and Nee, *Remaking the American Mainstream*.

[27] This is a consistent finding of the 1996 and 2004 GSS surveys, as well as of the national surveys of Theiss-Morse and Schildkraut.

a prerequisite for immigrants' economic and social mobility.[28] Perhaps because of the "give" in the majority's attitudes, as reflected in the acceptance of bilingualism on ballots and other official notices, there has not been a movement to make Spanish or any other language "official," as in other countries divided by language. There seems little doubt that a proposal to move in that direction would be widely unpopular.

Again, however, we also see evidence of consensual support for a softer version of language rights, given the practical realities of an increasingly culturally diverse nation. The broad insistence that America is an English-speaking country and must remain so is accompanied by equally wide support for various specific pragmatic policies allowing official recognition of multilingualism. For example, in both the 1996 and 2004 GSS, large national majorities of both whites and blacks supported the use of bilingual ballots "where lots of people don't speak English" and did *not* feel that the status of English was threatened by immigrants' use of other languages (see Table 7.3C).

Similar accommodations are shown to the practical necessities facing immigrant children who arrive without skills in English but who nevertheless need to be educated. Most surveys of whites and blacks nationally reveal ambivalence about the sink-or-swim method of conducting all classes in English for children who cannot speak English. Large majorities support bilingual education in the abstract, programs designed to meet the educational needs of children whose native language is not English (both in Table 7.3C). Los Angeles surveys show a consensus across all ethnic groups favoring a softer transitional approach to teaching non-English-speaking children in preference to a tough immersion regimen. Still, a strong consensus opposes the hard multiculturalism option of teaching immigrant children in their native languages throughout high school, sometimes advocated as a means to preserve the original cultures of those who have immigrated to the United States (Table 7.2C).[29]

Still, we have two caveats about this relatively accommodating stance toward bilingual education. First, there is a rare divergence between the national and Los Angeles data. Substantially less support for bilingual education shows up in Los Angeles than in national samples, among both white (from 48 percent to 64 percent) and black respondents (from 65 percent to 85 percent, as shown in Tables 7.2C and 7.3C, respectively), a contrast that still holds when only contemporaneously gathered Los Angeles and national data are compared.

Why this exception? First, national samples involve many respondents residing in areas with little direct experience with formal bilingual education programs. An early survey found that many if not most non-Hispanic Americans

[28] Citrin et al., "The 'Official English' Movement and the Symbolic Politics of Language in the United States."

[29] Citrin, Wong, and Duff, "The Meaning of American National Identity: Patterns of Ethnic Conflict and Consensus."; Citrin, Sears, Muste, and Wong, "Multiculturalism in American Public Opinion."

believed that bilingual education actually refers to foreign language instruction, such as French or German classes. The widespread support for bilingual education in national surveys may partly be a result of that misunderstanding.[30] Second, California has been the site of several contentious ballot propositions that have mobilized opposition to the multicultural policy agenda regarding language. Official English passed in 1986, and in 1998 Proposition 227 outlawed bilingual education in favor of an immersion approach, on the grounds that existing programs failed to make students fluent in English and kept them in transitional programs for too long. There is always the possibility that the results of a survey taken in a quiet political moment will differ from attitudes expressed in the midst of hard-fought political campaigns.

To summarize, in all three domains of multicultural policies analyzed here, there are similar patterns of consensus across ethnic groups, both in opposing policies that seem to codify racial and ethnic divisions and in accepting soft multicultural policies that recognize some need to assist racial minorities and smooth the path of integration for immigrants.

Ethnic and Racial Cleavages in Opinion

Within the parameters of the consensus described earlier, substantial ethnic and racial cleavages on multicultural policies also emerge. The psychological perspective we earlier called politicized group consciousness would expect policy choices to be motivated by particularistic group interests. But this could produce a variety of different patterns of group differences. It could involve interest-based competition among minority groups, with, for example, blacks opposing liberal immigration and language policies favored by Latinos and Asians, who might reciprocally reject racially targeted policies. It might also pit all people of color against whites if questions about group-conscious programs were framed as favoring the interests of all minority groups rather than singling out one specific group as beneficiaries. Finally, we might see a pattern mixing assimilation with black exceptionalism. Over time, Latino and Asian immigrants might gradually assimilate to the mainstream of society and adopt opinions similar to those of whites, with African Americans standing alone as the staunchest supporters of multiculturalist policies favoring minorities, a pattern we have seen in earlier chapters.

RACIALLY TARGETED POLICIES

The responses of blacks to racially targeted policies are consistent with a pattern of opinions motivated by their own group's interests. In all cases, they are far

---

[30] At least that was the clear finding of a national survey done in the 1980s. See Leonie Huddy and David O. Sears, "Qualified Public Support for Bilingual Education: Some Policy Implications," *The Annals of the American Academy of Political and Social Science* 508 (1990): 119–34.

more supportive of policies intended to help blacks than are the members of any other ethnic group. For example, in the national ANES surveys blacks are typically 40 percent more favorable than whites toward preferential treatment for blacks, plus or minus a little, and about 35 percent in the GSS (Table 7.1A). Similarly, 45 percent of the blacks, as against 15 percent of the whites, supported such preferential treatment in the LACSS (Table 7.2A). Blacks generally support, and whites generally oppose, giving special treatment to blacks or making every effort to improve the social and economic position of blacks (Table 7.1A). Both nationally and in Los Angeles, most surveys show similarly broad racial differences in attitudes toward government spending targeted to help blacks (Tables 7.1A and 7.2A). This sharp racial divide on every specific race-targeted policy item has remained virtually unchanged since the mid-1990s. This is consistent with the idea that blacks, like other racial and ethnic groups, are pursuing their own group's interests. However, more direct evidence than mere group differences would be needed to be confident of this motivational inference.

A second version of the politicized group consciousness perspective looks for a broad people-of-color coalition, allying Latinos and Asians with blacks against whites. However, racial policy issues do not show such a pattern, as reflected in data from the more ethnically rich Los Angeles surveys. Latinos' and Asians' levels of support for preferential treatment for blacks fell between the positions of whites and blacks. On the question of increasing government spending for programs that assist blacks, Asians and Latinos were actually more in agreement with whites than with African Americans. The only evidence of a people-of-color coalition emerges on the question of whether government should help minorities *in general* without pinpointing blacks in particular, which is not specific to helping further blacks' interests (all shown in Table 7.2A).

The dominance of the particularistic group interests of each minority group is perhaps shown most clearly by contrasting an item on preferential hiring and promotion for blacks with a parallel item targeting Hispanics. Blacks were considerably more likely to support preferences for *their* own group (45 percent) than were Latinos (28 percent), whereas Latinos supported preferences targeted for Hispanics, *their* ethnic group (53 percent) far more than did blacks (38 percent). Both groups showed less support for the other group's interests, although this self-interested pattern was stronger among Latinos (Table 7.2A).[31] The ethnic and racial cleavages displayed on the racially targeted policy issues fit a clear pattern of group-interested preferences, then, in which blacks support policies benefiting their own in-group more than does any other ethnic group, even fellow people of color.

---

[31] In Chapter 4 we saw that immigrant Latinos shared the unusually strong group-conscious perspectives of African Americans more than did U.S.-born Latinos. Here, however, that difference generally does not hold. Indeed, U.S.-born Latinos are significantly more favorable toward blacks' interests than are foreign-born Latinos on three of the five race-targeted items. Perhaps the former have a better understanding of historic discrimination against blacks.

IMMIGRATION POLICIES

Latinos and Asians of course, comprise the large majority of newcomers to America following the 1965 immigration reforms that prioritized family reunification. Group interest might therefore motivate recent immigrants and their brethren to be the strongest supporters of maintaining or increasing access to the United States for their co-ethnics rather than pulling up the drawbridge once they themselves have crossed it. In contrast, competition with immigrants for jobs and political influence might lead blacks to a more group-interested opposition to immigrants, rather than following the lead of minority elites into a multicultural people-of-color coalition.

The most extensive data come from surveys of Latinos. Consistent with the group interest hypothesis, they are distinctively more pro-immigration than are whites or blacks. The national 2008 and 2012 ANES surveys for the first time included a sufficient number of Latino respondents to compare with whites and blacks. Latinos were far more in favor of either increasing or keeping immigration at its current level (Table 7.1B) and more supportive of a path to citizenship for illegal immigrants (Table 7.3B). Similarly, the 2011 Pew Hispanic Center poll found much higher support among Latinos (84 percent) for illegal immigrant eligibility for in-state tuition than among non-Latinos (48 percent) and greater support for prioritizing a path to citizenship over border security (42 percent of Latinos and 24 percent of non-Latinos).[32] Similarly, in the Los Angeles data, Latinos were always significantly more favorable to immigration and immigrant rights than were either whites or blacks. Latinos' margin of support for their group's interests was extremely large on all items (Table 7.2B).[33]

Also consistent with the group interest hypothesis, Latinos and Asians seem to share much the same views on immigration and predictably are distinctly more supportive of it than whites or blacks. The 2006 Pew Immigration Survey found that both were far more likely than whites and blacks to believe that immigration "strengthens American society" and to feel that immigrants "strengthen our country because of their hard work and talents" and did not differ much from each other. Similarly, the 2013 Pew Hispanic Poll found that 74 percent of Latinos thought immigration a benefit, as did 72 percent in Pew's 2012 survey of Asian Americans, both far higher than the 52 percent of blacks and 41 percent of whites who felt immigrants strengthen the country.[34]

---

[32] Pew Hispanic Center 2011: http://www.pewhispanic.org/2011/12/28/iv-views-of-immigration-policy-2/.

[33] Earlier, the Gallup Minority Rights and Relations Polls had found gaps between Latinos, on the one hand, and whites and blacks, on the other, in every year from 2001 to 2007 in support for current levels of immigration and in believing that immigration is a good thing for the nation.

[34] Pew Research Center 2012 survey of Asian Americans, http://www.people-press.org/2013/03/28/most-say-illegal-immigrants-should-be-allowed-to-stay-but-citizenship-is-more-divisive/; Pew Research Center, 2013, http://www.people-press.org/2013/03/28/most-say-illegal-immigrants-should-be-allowed-to-stay-but-citizenship-is-more-divisive/

The issue of citizenship for illegal immigrants is especially fraught with controversy, as indicated earlier. Americans jealously guard the rights conferred by citizenship. A consensus favoring it seems only to emerge when the question alludes to unspecified conditions being met over an unspecified period of time, as in the Gallup question referenced earlier: "allow[ing] illegal immigrants to remain in the United States and become U.S. citizens, but only if they meet certain requirements over a period of time." We do see the usual split on the equally vague 2008 ANES question asking whether "the U.S. government [should] make it possible for illegal immigrants to become U.S. citizens": Latinos are highly supportive, whereas whites and blacks are slightly opposed (Table 7.3B). And the fate of the American-born children of undocumented immigrants deeply divides the public (Table 7.3B). In Los Angeles, Latinos strongly (90 percent) supported letting such children continue to qualify as American citizens, but whites and blacks were evenly divided (Table 7.2B).

At first glance, the conclusion that narrow group interests motivate intergroup cleavages is tempered somewhat by differences between Asians and Latinos, the two largest heavily immigrant groups. True, in Los Angeles, they both strongly support liberal policies about *legal* immigration, as shown by questions about the optimal level of legal immigration and legal immigrants' access to public services. For example, almost 70 percent of either Latino or Asian respondents said that immigration should be kept at least at current levels, considerably greater than the 53 percent of whites and 44 percent of blacks. Latino (54 percent) and Asian (56 percent) respondents also were equally likely, and both were more likely than whites or blacks (both 38 percent), to agree that legal immigrants should be eligible for government services as soon as they arrive in the United States (Table 7.2B).

But when it comes to *illegal* immigrants, Asians part with Latinos, instead sharing whites' and blacks' less sympathetic attitudes. Only 30 percent of Asian Americans in the 2008 National Asian American Survey agreed that the United States should provide a path to citizenship for people in this country illegally, whereas nearly three-quarters of Latinos (74 percent) in the 2006 Latino National Survey selected either immediate legalization or a guest worker program eventually leading to legalization as the preferred policy on illegal immigration. In a similar vein, the 2006 Pew Immigration Survey found that 62 percent of the Asians but only 35 percent of the Latinos thought illegal immigration was a bigger problem for the United States than legal immigration. Asians were also significantly more likely to favor requiring illegal immigrants to leave the nation than were Latinos. Indeed, Asians' views, in the aggregate, were almost identical to whites' and blacks'.[35] In the Los Angeles data, half of the Asians opposed the government's allocating more money for the deportation of illegal aliens, whereas three-fourths of the Latinos did so. Asians were about evenly divided over the current policy of giving citizenship to the children of

---

[35] Pew Center for the People and the Press.

illegal aliens, whereas Latinos were overwhelmingly (90 percent) supportive (Table 7.2B). In fact, though, illegal immigration is much more common among Latinos than among Asian Americans, given the proximity of the Mexican border to and the distance of East Asia from the United States. Latinos' more supportive stance toward illegal immigrants is therefore fairly easily understood as another manifestation of group interest and solidarity.

In the realm of immigration policies, again contrary to the notion of a people-of-color coalition, we often see blacks more in agreement with whites than with Latinos and Asians. Earlier we noted blacks' and whites' similarity in response to whether legal immigration should be increased or decreased: over five national surveys between 1994 and 2008, blacks averaged only 4 percent more support for the same or greater immigration (Table 7.1B). The difference in the LACSS is larger, but actually reversed: blacks were significantly more supportive of *decreased* immigration in a region that has seen heavy Latino in-migration to previously black neighborhoods (Table 7.2B). Similarly, blacks supported pro-immigration policies by an average of only 4 percent more than whites over the fourteen items from national surveys that we have analyzed, significantly half the time (Tables 7.1B, 7.3A, and 7.3B). Overall, then, there is little evidence that blacks evaluate the level and value of immigration more favorably than do whites or have large differences from them on other immigration policies, despite most immigrants being fellow people of color.[36]

The assimilation prototype is broadly consistent with the patterns of opinion within the Latino population. In Los Angeles, U.S.-born Latinos resembled whites in being significantly less favorable to immigration and immigrants than were foreign-born Latinos in terms of the rate of legal immigration and immigrant eligibility for government services. Similarly, the lesser sympathy of the U.S.-born than foreign-born Latinos for illegal immigrants emerges quite clearly regarding both spending on their deportation and support for birthright citizenship. For example, 77 percent of the U.S.-born Latino respondents, against an overwhelming 95 percent of the foreign-born, said that the American-born children of illegal immigrants should continue to qualify as citizens. Overall, the U.S.-born averaged about 18 percent less sympathy for immigrants across the four items included in the LACSS than did foreign-born Latinos, and all the differences were significant (all shown in Table 7.2B).

LANGUAGE POLICIES

We assess ethnic cleavages about language policies using only the Los Angeles data, given the paucity of such items in national surveys and especially the paucity of Latino and Asian respondents. Again, particularistic group interests

[36] Tatishe Nteta, "The Impact of Differentiation on African American Attitudes toward Immigration," paper presented at the 2006 annual meeting of the Midwest Political Science Association.

seem to dominate policy opinions. Latinos were far more opposed than either whites or blacks to declaring English as the official language of the country and far more favorable to bilingual education, especially preferring it or a gradual transition to English rather than English immersion for immigrant children (see Table 7.2C). Latino distinctiveness shows up in actual voting behavior about language issues, as well as in surveys. Latinos were the only major ethnic group in which a majority voted against the official English and antibilingual education referenda in California.[37]

However, the equally heavily immigrant Asians do not show this apparently group-interested set of language policy attitudes. They did not differ materially from whites, with only 30 percent (compared to 26 percent of whites) opposing official English and 53 percent (compared to 56 percent of whites) favoring maintenance of non-English schooling or transitional movement to English for non-English-speaking children. Significantly more favored bilingual education, however, although we have reservations about what they believed it meant. Among possible explanations for Asians' lesser support than Latinos' for multilingualism include the greater educational level of Asian immigrants and the lesser likelihood that they frequently move back and forth between the United States and their home country. Partly for that reason, Huntington would add his suspicion that many Latinos are less committed than Asian Americans to fully assimilating as Americans.[38] And, as mentioned earlier, our Asian subsamples are more biased toward the English-fluent than are our Latino subsamples.

The people-of-color hypothesis fares poorly on the core value of English as the primary national language, as it had on race-targeted and immigration issues. Blacks and whites are similar on such language issues, differing by an average of only 5 percent on five such items, with just one difference greater than 4 percent. Yet when fundamental rights are at stake, blacks once again show more sympathy for immigrants. Blacks were on average 14 percent more supportive of bilingual ballots and of bilingual education (or at least gradual transitions to English) than were whites, and all seven such comparisons were statistically significant (all shown in Tables 7.2C and 7.3C).

Consistent with the assimilation hypothesis, multiculturalist positions on language again find far less support among the U.S.-born than among first-generation immigrants. Of the U.S.-born Latinos in the LACSS, 47 percent oppose official English compared to fully 76 percent of the foreign-born. Similarly, the U.S.-born, most fluent in English themselves, were significantly more favorable to English immersion programs than the foreign-born Latinos.

---

[37] Jack Citrin, et al., "The 'Official English' Movement and the Symbolic Politics of Language"; Jack Citrin, Jocelyn Kiley, and Kathryn Pearson, "Direct Democracy Takes on Bilingual Education: Framing the Influences of Ethnicity and Identity in Four State Initiatives," paper presented at the 2003 annual meeting of the American Political Science Association, Philadelphia, PA.

[38] Huntington, *Who Are We?*

On language issues, then, U.S.-born Latinos are much closer to the opinions of whites and blacks than are the foreign-born.

But the positions of even first-generation immigrants on bilingual education seem rooted more in pragmatism than in an ideological commitment to multiculturalism. Although only 21 percent of first-generation Latinos in the LACSS polls preferred the English immersion variant of bilingual education, even fewer (16 percent) favored the multiculturalist choice of taking classes in Spanish throughout high school. Transitional programs in which some classes are taught in Spanish until students have learned English are the modal choices of all ethnic groups and even of first-generation Latino immigrants.

Coherence of Public Thinking about Multiculturalist Policies

Among political elites, attitudes toward multiculturalism often seem to reflect a considered and coherent ideology. A normative stance about the moral significance of group identities and the responsibility to protect and assist minorities guides opinion formation across a range of specific issues. As a result, among political and academic elites, the intellectual proponents and critics of multiculturalism usually line up on opposite sides of issues in all three policy domains examined here.

The conventional wisdom among political psychologists is that the level of coherence among elites is not usually matched in the general public. Indeed, in Chapter 5 we found little evidence of strong coherence in public views about abstract multicultural norms. In this chapter, we have described a complex pattern of aggregate differences across items even within the same issue domain. Still, it is worth exploring the degree of coherence in individuals' opinions more directly. The familiarity of the widely debated issues we are considering and the visibility of such unifying cues as benefits for racial and ethnic minorities might promote more widespread use of organizing principles that tie opinions across the three domains together than is normally seen across policy areas. To test this, we examine the constraint among policy opinions by calculating the correlations among responses to all the race-targeted, immigration, and language questions in the GSS and LACSS data.[39]

The national data, limited to whites again because of insufficient cases in the other groups, are shown in Table 7.4. The nine intradomain correlations for respondents in the four GSS range from .37 (immigration policy in 1996) to .24 (language policy in 2000). They average $r = .30$. The Los Angeles data, broken

[39] The standard for such tests was set by Converse, "The Nature of Belief Systems in Mass Publics." We follow his model. This might be described as *horizontal* links across issues. Later, we turn to the *vertical* links between the more abstract multicultural norms and indicators of ethnic and national identity on the one hand and policy positions on racial issues, immigration, and language policies on the other. Due to the small number of black and Latino respondents in the GSS, analysis of the national data is limited to the white subsamples.

TABLE 7.4. *Issue Constraint: Whites in National Surveys*

	1994	1996	2000	2004
Within Issue Domains				
Race-targeted	.33	.32	.33	.27
Immigration	.24	.37	–	.26
Language	.30	–	.24	–
Mean	.29	.34	.28	.26
Between Issue Domains				
Race-targeted × Immigration	.21	.24	–	.26
Race-targeted × Language	.24	–	.22	–
Immigration × Language	.19	–	–	–
Mean	.21	.24	.22	.26

Cell entries represent the mean bivariate correlation coefficients when all relevant items are measured. The items within each domain and for each year are listed in Appendix 7.1. All items are coded with the conservative position as positive. The top panel shows correlations of issue attitudes within each issue domain. The bottom panel shows correlations of attitudes in one domain by attitudes in another domain. *Source*: General Social Surveys (GSS) in the years specified.

down by ethnic group, are shown in Table 7.5. The intradomain correlations range a little more broadly than the national data, from $r = .47$ to $r = .21$, but the average is very similar, at $r = .34$. There were few ethnic differences.

If an overarching multiculturalist ideology were widely present in the mass public, the between-domain correlations might approach the level of within-domain correlations. But the correlations between issue positions are generally higher among items dealing with the same topic than when they range widely across issue domains. The GSS data show that, among whites, the .31 within-domain average correlation on race-targeted issues declines to an average between-domain correlation of .24. The average within-domain correlations for immigration ($r = .29$) and language policy ($r = .27$) decline in the between-domain correlations involving either immigration or language policies to an average of .22, as shown in Table 7.4. We again use the Los Angeles data when we turn to the ethnic minority groups, which have a clearer group interest in multicultural issues. The average within-domain correlation of $r = .34$ declines to a between-domain correlation of $r = .22$, as shown in Table 7.5. Again, there are no obviously important ethnic differences.

That issue constraint within a domain is higher than between-domain constraint is not surprising. Both the underlying concept and the manifest symbols contained in the question are more similar in the within-domain cases, thus cuing consistency of responses. However, the weak level of between-domain constraint again suggests that most ordinary people do not possess what might be

TABLE 7.5. *Issue Constraint by Ethnicity: Los Angeles Surveys*

	Whites	Blacks	Latinos
Within Issue Domains			
Race-Targeted	.29	.35	.21
Immigration	.33	.32	.34
Language	.39	.38	.47
Mean	.34	.35	.34
Between Issue Domains			
Race-Targeted × Immigration	.17	.15	.13
Race-Targeted × Language	.22	.20	.18
Immigration × Language	.30	.27	.35
Mean	.23	.21	.22

Cell entries represent the mean bivariate correlation coefficients when all relevant items are measured. The items within each domain and for each year are listed in Appendix 7.1. All items are coded with the conservative position as positive. The top panel shows correlations of issue attitudes within each issue domain. The bottom panel shows correlations of attitudes in one domain by attitudes in another domain.
Source: Los Angeles County Social Surveys (LACSS).

termed a multiculturalist ideology that generates consistent beliefs across multiple policy questions. There is somewhat more constraint when people respond to concrete policies rather than to more abstract norms, and somewhat stronger connections occur between preferences on immigration and language issues than between these and beliefs on race-targeted issues. But the dominant finding here is that the seeming coherence of elite thinking about multiculturalism is not replicated among the general public. The public's opinions lack an obvious unifying thread, a result foreshadowed perhaps by the pattern of ethnic cleavages described earlier. A practical implication of these findings for the remaining empirical chapters is that we ought to continue to analyze the three issue domains separately rather than attempting to combine them in a single composite multiculturalism policy scale.

Conclusion

We have seen fairly clear consensus on multicultural issues across ethnic groups on two points. There is consensus on opposition to hard multiculturalist positions that privilege race and ethnicity as categories for resource allocation. Most members of all ethnic groups are opposed to ethnic preferences in jobs and college admission, most do not favor expanded immigration, and most favor maintaining English as the only national language. At the same time, we find consensus on a number of softer adaptations to the realities of a diversifying society, such as in government aid to minorities, access to public universities, and bilingual ballots. Yet this aggregate-level pattern of consensus lies on top of the relative lack of coherence among individuals' beliefs about concrete issues, as is often true in studies of public opinion, as Converse long ago warned us.[40]

We also repeatedly found ethnic differences that seem to parallel the distinctive interests of each ethnic group. Without digging further into the psychological origins of these group cleavages about multiculturalist policies, we can only hint at how they fit the alternative prototypes of American ethnic relations. Four summary observations are worthwhile, however.

Consistent with both multiculturalist ideology and the psychological theories mentioned in earlier chapters that emphasize a tendency of dominant groups to protect their advantages, whites generally are more opposed than other ethnic groups to race-targeted government assistance and to freer immigration, citizenship, and multilingual language policies. Such theories would also lead us to expect that racial minorities will support policies that provide narrowly targeted benefits to their own group. The data reported earlier are consistent with this idea: blacks were the only strong supporters of race-targeted policies, and Latino immigrants in particular seem to support immigration and language policies that parallel their own particular interests.

But it also is true that each ethnic group departed from a crude definition of its own group interests in several ways. Although whites consistently repudiated the harder variant of group-conscious multicultural policies, a stance that can be readily interpreted as a defense of group advantages, they accepted bilingual ballots and transitional bilingual education programs, perhaps because these policies promote assimilation rather than the enduring preservation of cultural differences. Differences of opinion among Latinos reflect the persistent impact of assimilation, with second- and third-generation immigrants adopting policy positions closer to those of whites. Finally, confidently attributing these policy preferences to the self-conscious calculation of ethnic group interests will require more direct evidence concerning the strength of in-group loyalties and feelings about out-groups.

Some in the multicultural movement may wish for the emergence of a coalition of minorities uniting all people of color against the dominant whites. But this seems to be a chimerical hope out of step with mass opinion. For example, in the issues we examine, the black–white divide is substantial only in matters of race – issues with a long and historically distinct progeny from the multicultural agenda focused on cultural pluralism. When it comes to immigration and language policies, black and white opinion is largely the same and tilts against hard multicultural positions. The heavily immigrant Latinos and Asians show similar responses to legal immigrants, but diverge with respect to the undocumented, toward whom the Latino population, drawn overwhelmingly from nearby Mexico with its permeable boundaries, is considerably more sympathetic.

[40] Converse, "The Nature of Belief Systems in Mass Publics."

Finally, at the other extreme, there is little evidence of ethnic balkanization, if this provocative phrase is taken to mean large, consistent, and hardened differences of opinion between groups across a range of issues. What we find instead, even in Los Angeles, an area often described as an ethnic cauldron in the aftermath of the Watts and Rodney King riots, are patterns of consensus and cleavage that vary in nuanced fashion from one issue domain to another. Support for soft multiculturalist policies that acknowledge other groups' practical needs and evidence of the gradual assimilation of immigrants over generations are two clear cases in point.

8

The Dynamics of Group-Conscious Policy Preferences

In the preceding chapter, we described the pattern of ethnic differences on a range of race-targeted, immigration, and language issues, focusing on the level of support for group-conscious policies endorsed by multiculturalism. Here, we pursue the psychological underpinnings of those policy preferences in two ways. We start with the associations of policy preferences with the affective dimensions of national identity and ethnic group identity and with how these identities are prioritized. Second, we test hypotheses about the roots of preferences in the three issue domains we focus on, using the psychological perspectives introduced in Chapter 2.

Throughout this chapter, we again concentrate on race-targeted, immigration, and language policies. But we should provide two caveats at the outset. Liberal policies in each domain generally are supported by multicultural elites. But those elites are by no means their only supporters. We identify them here with multiculturalism simply as an effort to explore fully its group-conscious agenda. Analyzing the full range of issues that have been politically debated within each domain or even the more limited set described in the preceding chapter would lead us to lose sight of the theoretical forest for the trees. Accordingly, in the race-targeted domain, we focus just on affirmative action in terms of special preferences for minorities and government assistance to blacks and other minorities. In the immigration domain, we focus on the preferred level of legal immigration. Finally, the main language policies examined are support for "official English" laws and bilingual education.[1]

---

[1] There is a large literature on the origins of these policy preferences, of course. To mention just a few sources, on race-targeted issues, see Sears, Sidanius, and Bobo, *Racialized Politics*; Kinder and Sanders, *Divided by Color*; and Paul M. Sniderman and Edward G. Carmines, *Reaching Beyond Race*. On immigration, Kinder and Kam (2009), Schildkraut (2011), and Jens Hainmuller and David Hopkins's review essay "Public Attitudes toward Immigration," *Annual Review of Political Science* 17 (forthcoming 2014). On language, see Citrin, Green, Reingold, and Walters, "The

THE ROLES OF ETHNIC IDENTITY AND NATIONAL ATTACHMENT IN POLICY PREFERENCES

A central question for this study involves the competing tugs of ethnic and national identities in the public's responses to both demographic and political multiculturalism. What are the roles of these underlying attachments in explaining support for or opposition to policies that propose benefits for minority groups? Do patriotism and more ethnic conceptions of national identity accentuate opposition to group-conscious positions favored by multiculturalists in the domains of race, immigration, and language, especially among whites?[2] Among minorities, does a strong ethnic identity promote a group-interested mentality about such policies?

We begin with the relationship of policy preferences to national attachment, using the patriotism index as the indicator of this attitude.[3] Next, we consider the role of ethnic group identity. When we looked at ethnic groups in the aggregate in the last chapter, their policy preferences seemed parallel to their presumed ethnic group interests. But those parallels do not necessarily stem from individuals' self-conscious motives to further their own group's interests. More direct evidence of group-interested motivations would come from associations of support for group-conscious multiculturalist positions with stronger ethnic identification, as measured with the items introduced in Chapter 4. Finally, we test the effects of the identity choice, using the questions about whether people

---

'Official English Movement' and the Symbolic Politics of Language in the United States"; Schildkraut, *Press One for English*. For research focusing on the links between policy preferences and both national and ethnic identifications, see Citrin et al., "Testing Huntington"; and Sears and Savalei, "The Political Color Line in America."

[2] In the analysis to follow, we create multi-item racial policy and language policy indices. The question dealing with legal immigration is the single item asking about the preferred level of immigration into the United States. This question is asked on all the GSS and LACSS surveys we are dealing with and is the indicator used most commonly in studies of both American and European attitudes (Citrin et al., "Public Opinion toward Immigration"; John Sides and Jack Citrin, "European Attitudes toward Immigration: The Role of Interests, Identities, and Information," *British Journal of Political Science* 37, no. 3 (2007): 477–504; Lapinski, Peltola, Shaw, and Yang, "Trends: Immigrants and Immigration"; Lincoln Quillian, "Prejudice as a Response to Perceived Group Threat: Population Composition and Anti-Immigrant and Racial Prejudice in Europe," *American Sociological Review* 60 (1995): 586–611. One reason for constructing the racial and language policy indices is that an exploratory factor analysis with an oblimin rotation based on the intercorrelations summarized earlier yielded single dimensions for both sets of items. The outcome for the immigration items was more complex. For white respondents (in both the LACSS and GSS), a single factor comprising both the legal and illegal immigration items emerged. However, the analysis for the black and Latino LACSS respondents yielded two distinct, although correlated factors – one defined by the legal immigration questions, the other by the items dealing with undocumented aliens. This outcome is one reason for analyzing the legal and illegal immigration issues separately.

[3] The patriotism index comprises items about pride in America and feeling positive about the flag.

thought of themselves as just an American or as a member of an ethnic group that we introduced in Chapter 6.[4] We begin with the Los Angeles County Social Surveys (LACSS), which provide better data on minority groups than most national surveys, and we supplement these results using the 2012 American National Election Studies (ANES) black and Latino oversamples. In this section, we present the bivariate relationships (shown in Table 8.1) and later in the chapter move on to multivariate regression analyses.

Whites

Patriotism is consistently associated with whites' opposition to the positions congenial to multiculturalism – support for hiring preferences and more spending for blacks and other minorities, increasing immigration rather than the nativist position of a more restrictive policy, and support for bilingualism rather than the English-only stance historically pushed by nativists. The average correlation between patriotism and these group-conscious positions in the LACSS data was $r = -.24$ across domains (all three associations are statistically significant).

Ethnic group identities among whites were shown earlier to be relatively weak. However, ethnic consciousness among whites does have at least a weak connection positions on group-conscious policies, yielding an average correlation of $r = -.14$ in the LACSS, attaining statistical significance in the cases of opposition to expanded immigration and to greater multilingualism.[5] The item asking whether one thought of oneself as just an American or as a member of an ethnic group was not significantly related to any of the policy attitudes, although, as seen earlier, this choice is heavily skewed in the direction of national identity among whites. Overall, then, we would conclude that whites' patriotism is significantly, if not very strongly, associated with their opposition to group-conscious policy preferences. Their ethnic identification is not as closely linked, perhaps surprisingly, given the centrality of group consciousness in multiculturalist ideology. Furnishing evidence that these earlier findings from the LACSS generalize to the U.S. white population as a whole and have persisted over the past decade, these conclusions are both closely replicated in the 2012 ANES results shown in the bottom panel of the table.

This array of results also does not map closely onto the hypothesized role of whites in some politicized group consciousness theories that emphasize their desire to dominate a racial hierarchy. On the other hand, the significant

---

[4] The specific policy items used in these analyses are described in Appendix 7.1.

[5] This quite limited effect of white ethnic identity on racial policy attitudes parallels other findings elsewhere (e.g., David O. Sears and Tom Jessor, "Whites' Racial Policy Attitudes: The Role of White Racism," *Social Science Quarterly* 77 (1996): 751–59; Sears and Henry, "Over Thirty Years Later." For contrary results in quite a different domain, dealing with white hostility toward Native Americans over hunting and fishing rights, see Bobo and Tuan, *Prejudice in Politics*.

TABLE 8.1. *Ethnic Identification, National Identity, and Support for Group-Conscious Policies: Los Angeles Surveys and 2012 American National Election Studies (ANES)*

		Race-Targeted			Immigration			Language		
		White	Black	Latino	White	Black	Latino	White	Black	Latino
LACSS										
Ethnic identity	Ethnic identity	-.09 (503)	.13* (124)	.08 (452)	-.18** (763)	.01 (180)	.17** (650)	-.14* (218)	-.02 (52)	.29** (173)
	Ethnic vs. American self-identification	.02 (283)	.36** (65)	-.01 (261)	.06 (764)	.04 (350)	.13** (597)	.11 (255)	-.02 (217)	.15* (244)
National identity	Patriotism	-.19** (750)	-.04 (498)	.03 (633)	-.21** (940)	.04 (409)	-.12** (820)	-.32** (230)	-.28* (53)	-.27 (171)
ANES 2012										
Ethnic identity	Importance of ethnic identity	-.07** (3243)	.03 (946)	.18** (915)	-.15** (3191)	-.14** (928)	.16** (899)			
National identity	Patriotism	-.17** (3252)	.07* (948)	-.05 (914)	-.10** (3203)	.02 (930)	-.12** (899)			

Entries are Pearson correlation coefficients. Positive correlations indicate that strong ethnic identities or weak national identities are associated with support for group-conscious policies. The race-targeted policy scale is based on two items, on affirmative action for companies with a history of discrimination and spending for blacks; immigration policy, the desired level of legal immigration; and language policy, a two-item scale on support for bilingual education and English as an official language. Policy variables are coded from 0 = oppose group-conscious policies 1 = support group-conscious policies; the identity items are coded from 0 = weak/American to 1 = ethnic; the patriotism item is coded from 0 = low to 1 = high. For question wordings, please see Appendix 7.1.

*$p < .05$ **$p < .01$

Source: Los Angeles County Social Survey (LACSS) cumulative file 1994–2002 and American National Election Studies (ANES) 2012; year of coverage for specific LACSS entries depends on the items used.

relationships that did emerge involved policy issues related to America's changed demography. They therefore hint at a tension, at least among whites, between support for multiculturalism and a strong sense of American identity.

Blacks and Latinos

In Chapter 4, we showed that ethnic identification plays a stronger and more consistent political role for members of minority groups than for whites. In the preceding chapter, we saw that minorities generally gave their strongest support to policies favoring their own group's interests. As a result, we expected that ethnic identification among blacks and Latinos would be most strongly engaged by and promote support for the policies most relevant to their interests.

The LACSS results in the top panel of Table 8.1 show that the strength of racial identification among blacks was significantly related to increased support for such racially targeted policies as affirmative action or increased government spending for blacks. The correlation in the 2012 ANES between the importance of racial identity and support for race-targeted policies is small and nonsignificant, however. Similarly, ethnic identification among Latinos was significantly associated with support for policies presumptively targeting *their* interests, such as maintaining current levels of immigration, rejecting English-only laws, and supporting bilingual education programs. This finding is mirrored in the 2012 ANES, although only immigration policy, not language policy, was tested. In the LACSS, then, all six correlations of minorities' ethnic identity and group-interested policy preferences are significant, although only one of the two in the ANES is.

However, we see some differences between the Los Angeles surveys and the national ANES, which we have not encountered to the same extent elsewhere in this study. The correlations for minorities between ethnic identity and support for group-interested policies are stronger in the LACSS, and for whites, weaker. These differences may stem from any number of sources, of course, including how strength of ethnic identity was measured, the use of national versus local samples, the fact that noncitizen Latinos were included in the LACSS and not in the ANES, and the different periods in which the studies were done.

A central question throughout this volume is whether or not national cohesion is threatened by multiculturalism and sharp divisions between solidary ethnic groups. As just noted, whites' emotional attachment to the symbols of American nationhood is fairly consistently related to opposition to the group-conscious positions favored by multiculturalists on the three issues under scrutiny. By contrast, patriotism has a weaker and less consistent impact among ethnic minorities. Patriotism was scarcely associated at all with attitudes about race-targeted policies among blacks and Latinos, as shown in Table 8.1. Among blacks, there was no relationship between patriotism and support for expanded immigration in either the LACSS or 2012 ANES data, although there was a weak statistically significant negative association among Latinos in both surveys. The one exception is that among both minority groups, as among whites, patriotism is strongly and significantly associated with support for English-only policies. We regard this link between patriotism and opposition to official multilingualism, consistent across ethnic groups, as an important indicator of how widespread the idea is that a common language – English – is a crucial marker of American nationhood.

What role did minorities' ethnic group identification play in their attitudes about policies central to the interests of *other* groups? The people-of-color hypothesis would suggest that it would promote support for policies serving other minorities' interests, whereas a group-conflict hypothesis would suggest that it might promote competitive repudiation of other groups' interests. The LACSS data in Table 8.1 shows no support for either idea. Stronger feelings of group identity among blacks were not associated with opposition to higher levels of immigration or to multilingualism, policies that presumably serve the interests of Latinos and Asians more. Similarly, ethnic identification among Latinos is unrelated to support for assistance aimed at helping blacks. In other words, ethnic minorities' group consciousness and a preference for ethnic over American identity did not spill over into either more general support for assistance to all people of color or rejection of policies favored by a potentially rival ethnic group. Again, the 2012 ANES provides contradictory data, with blacks appearing to respond competitively and Latinos supportively. Relevant to the differences between the LACSS and ANES findings here perhaps is the more limited measures of ethnic identity and the absence of noncitizen Latinos in the 2012 national sample.

In replicating these analyses on the national General Social Survey (GSS) samples, we are as usual limited by the small number of minority group respondents and by the paucity of measures of ethnic group consciousness. In Table 8.2, we therefore report results for white respondents only and use a wider range of measures of patriotism. These include single-item questions about pride in and closeness to America, as well as the National Pride index (ten items) and Chauvinism index (five items) described in Chapter 3, and the Ethnic National Identity index built from the "true American" questions relating to nativity and religion.

Among whites, attachment to the nation is associated in all fifteen cases with greater opposition to the group-conscious positions, as shown in Table 8.2. Most of the correlations are significant.[6] On average, the correlations are quite similar across issue domains: $r = .13$ for immigration issues, $r = .12$ for language issues, and $r = .12$ for racial issues. But they are not as large as we saw for patriotism in the Los Angeles data in Table 8.1, which averaged $r = .24$ across

---

[6] The 1996 and 2004 GSS also had a single item on perceived closeness to one's own ethnic group. Among whites, that had a modest correlation with opposition to group-conscious policy ($r = .14$ with race-targeted policy in 1996; $r = .14$ and .04 with opposition to immigration in the two years, respectively).

TABLE 8.2. *Correlations of National Attachment and National Identity with Support for Group-Conscious Policies: National Surveys (Whites Only)*

| | | Policy Domain | | |
	Year	Race-Targeted	Immigration	Language
Patriotism				
Pride in being American (1 item)	1994	−.11*	−.10**	−.12**
		(362)	(1149)	(1085)
Closeness to America (1 item)	1996	−.04	−.05	NA
		(152)	(924)	
	2004	NA	−.09**	NA
			(875)	
National Pride (10-item index)	1996	−.13	−.02	NA
		(126)	(795)	
	2004	NA	−.06	NA
			(746)	
Chauvinism (5-item index)	1996	−.20*	−.16**	NA
		(144)	(903)	
	2004	NA	−.25**	NA
			(858)	
Conceptions of American Identity				
Ethnic conception (2-item index)	1996	−.13	−.23**	NA
		(151)	(910)	
	2004	NA	−.22**	NA
			(863)	

Cell entries represent Pearson correlation coefficients. N's in parentheses. The two-item race-targeted policy scale is based on preferences in hiring for blacks and government assistance to blacks; the immigration item, on the desired level of legal immigration; and the two-item language scale, on English as an official language and preferred mode of language teaching for English as second language (ESL) students. All items are keyed such that higher levels of national attachment, ethnic nationalism, and support for group-conscious policies receive higher scores. For question wordings, please see Appendix 7.1.

*$p < .05$ **$p < .01$

Source: General Social Survey (GSS) for the years specified.

domains. Taken together, though, we would conclude that stronger national identity is rather consistently associated with whites' opposition to the multi-culturalist policy agenda in each issue domain.

There is in addition some interesting texture across different indicators of national attachment. Table 8.2 shows that opposition to that agenda is more closely associated with the more belligerent emotions of chauvinism (involving the perceived superiority of America to other nations) and ethnic conceptions of national identity (defining Americanism in terms of nativity and religion) than with the more emotionally neutral patriotism indices reflecting pride in being an

American or in the country's political, economic, and cultural achievements. These findings are consistent with prior research showing the connection between beliefs in the superiority of one's own in-group, whether nation or ethnic group, and prejudice against racial and religious minorities.[7] Ethnocentrism, which encompasses chauvinism, seems to be more closely linked to whites' opposition to multiculturalism than is simple love of country, the core element of patriotism.

Two main conclusions emerge from this array of associations. First, stronger ethnic identification does seem to promote group-interested preferences more clearly among ethnic minority groups than among whites. This is consistent with the views of multiculturalism's critics who fear that identity politics sows divisiveness. But we also find that the effects of ethnic consciousness are bounded, limited to the issues most directly relevant to each minority group's own interests rather than stimulating either a unified coalition of all minorities against whites or opposition to other groups' desires.

Second, national attachment does sometimes conflict with policies advocated by multiculturalism, particularly among whites. Many whites may be reluctant to openly define the boundaries of nationhood in racial or ethnic terms, but it is clear that they are particularly sensitive to threats to the hegemony of the English language. Among ethnic minorities, however, support for group-interested positions mostly does not consistently conflict with national attachment, contrary to the fears of critics of multiculturalism such as Huntington or Schlesinger. The exception is over language rights, underlining the broadly sensed centrality of the English language to national unity, even among the most recent, often primarily Spanish-speaking Latino immigrants.

Psychological Origins of Attitudes toward Multicultural Positions

In the preceding analyses, we limited ourselves to describing the roles of ethnic and national identities at the bivariate level. In exploring the psychological origins of attitudes toward policies favored in multiculturalist ideology, as well as by others, of course, we now turn to more comprehensive multiple regression equations that consider simultaneously the influences of a wider set of predispositions and social background variables. As in previous chapters, we focus on five specific hypotheses.

1. Group consciousness theories propose that stronger senses of ethnic identity should help bring policy preferences into line with the individual's own group interests, both promoting white opposition to group-conscious policies in general as well as minorities' support for policies that provide tangible or symbolic benefits to their own groups.

[7] Theodore W. Adorno et al., *The Authoritarian Personality* (New York: Harper & Row, 1950); Donald Kinder and Cindy D. Kam, *Us against Them: Ethnocentric Foundations of American Opinion* (Chicago: University of Chicago Press, 2009).

2. Symbolic politics theory suggests that prejudice against the ethnic groups that would benefit from group-conscious policies may trigger opposition to those policies. It also suggests that prejudice may well operate independently of in-group identification, although some group consciousness theories (e.g., sense of group position theory) see them as closely linked.[8]

3. A strong sense of national identity generally should be related to concerns about the potential impact of group-targeted policies on cultural unity and social cohesion. Accordingly, a common hypothesis is that patriotism and other manifestations of a strong national attachment should be associated with greater opposition to group-conscious policies that emphasize the preservation of cultural differences.[9]

4. The vanguard hypothesis argues that the socializing experiences of younger and college-educated respondents in the contemporary zeitgeist foster sympathy for policies linked to multiculturalist ideology, although in earlier tests the generational rather than the education half of the hypothesis seemed most consistent with the data. To some extent, of course, any greater support for group-conscious policies in these vanguard groups may be mediated by stronger ethnic identifications, weaker racial prejudice, and/or weaker patriotism.

5. The assimilation hypothesis suggests that U.S.-born Latinos should show less support than would foreign-born Latinos (whether naturalized citizens or not) for policies benefitting immigrant Latinos, such as liberal immigration and language policies.

The predictors included in these regression equations are, therefore, patriotism, ethnic identity, antagonism toward out-groups, and the two vanguard variables, age and education.[10] In the case of the Latino subsample, we also use immigration status to assess evidence of assimilation, presenting two separate regression analyses. The first uses the same predictors as for whites and blacks, and so the coefficients for the three groups are directly comparable. The second adds dummy variables for nativity and naturalization, with noncitizens serving as the reference group. It tests whether assimilation is occurring among Latinos within the first generation (if so, naturalization should diminish support for

---

[8] See Bobo and Tuan, *Prejudice in Politics*.

[9] It could be argued that the causal direction flows in the opposite direction, with support for multiculturalism's image of the nation as a confederation of ethnic groups to which members owe their primary loyalty eroding love for and pride in the nation as a whole. Our preference is to rely on symbolic politics theory and the evidence that feelings of positive national identity are established early in childhood and so to interpret the correlations as assessing whether a strong sense of national identity functions to diminish support for multicultural policies.

[10] We have introduced all these measures before except for anti—out-group affect, which is indexed by the familiar feeling thermometer ratings that ask people how warmly they feel about specific groups (a high score relects cold feelings toward the out-group).

group-conscious policies) or in the second generation (if so, nativity should have the same effect). In addition, the standard demographic factors of gender and income are treated simply as controls but are not shown in the tables to simplify the presentation. To facilitate interpretation of the coefficients, the policy-attitude dependent variables are keyed in the pro-group-conscious direction, as in earlier tables in this chapter. We begin with the Los Angeles data because, again, they provide adequate numbers of each ethnic group to allow for separate equations for each, as well as containing the best measure of the strength of ethnic identity. We present the results for race-targeted policies, immigration, and language policies in that order.

Race-Targeted Policies

Among whites, the bivariate associations seen earlier between patriotism and opposition to race-targeted policies remain intact and highly significant in the multivariate analysis, as shown in Table 8.3. However, ethnic identity continues

TABLE 8.3. *Origins of Support for Group-Conscious Positions on Race-Targeted Policies: Los Angeles Surveys*

	Whites	Blacks	Latinos (1)	Latinos (2)
Ethnic identity	−.00	.07	.11*	.14**
Patriotism	−.21***	−.06	.01	−.00
Out-Group Antagonism				
Whites	−	.04	.07	.07
Blacks	−.24***	−	−.22***	−.19***
Latinos	.01	.02	−	−
Vanguard Demographics				
Age	−.00	−.00	.00	.00
Education	.01	−.02	.01	.00
Immigration Status				
U.S.-born	−	−	−	.08**
Naturalized	−	−	−	.01
R²	.07	.02	.04	.05
N	776	357	719	715

Entries are unstandardized ordinary least squares (OLS) regression coefficients predicting policy attitudes. The race-targeted policy scale is based on two items, on affirmative action for companies with a history of discrimination, and spending for blacks, keyed from 1 = most supportive of race-targeted policies to 0 = least supportive. Predictors keyed so that high = stronger ethnic identity, higher patriotism, higher prejudice (out-group antagonism), older, and more education. In the case of Latinos, a second regression equation is added to include immigration status, based on dummy variables for being U.S.-born or a naturalized citizen, in which the reference category is foreign-born noncitizens. The equations also include controls for gender and income. For further descriptions of how these variables are constructed, please see Appendix 7.1.

*$p < .05$ **$p < .01$ ***$p < .001$

Source: Los Angeles County Social Surveys (LACSS) in 1998, 1999, and 2002.

to have no effect on preferences on race-targeted policies (the unstandardized regression coefficient is .oo). As might be expected, the role of out-group antagonism is highly specific: that aimed at blacks is significantly associated with opposition to race-targeted policies, but whites' feelings toward Latinos are not engaged. Again we see that in-group identity and out-group antagonism are not two sides of the same coin. The vanguard hypothesis fails in the sense that there are no direct effects of age and education. However, given that the elderly and better-educated tend to be somewhat less patriotic and less antagonistic to out-groups, at least among whites the vanguard effect may be mediated by the role of patriotism and out-group antagonism.

We find no significant predictors of support for race-targeted policies among blacks, perhaps not surprisingly because most blacks support them, so there is little variance to be explained. Perhaps most important, neither patriotism nor racial identity has any association with support for race-targeted policies; here, there is no collision between identification with the in-group and national attachment. Among blacks, antagonism toward out-groups plays no part either.

Among Latinos, too, patriotism is unrelated to support for race-targeted policies. As among whites, though, antagonism toward blacks does boost opposition to race-targeted policies. Controlling for such feelings, ethnic identification among Latinos actually enhances support for programs that primarily help blacks. In addition, U.S.-born Latinos are significantly more favorable than the foreign-born, and adding that variable does not materially diminish the role of ethnic identification. Here, then is perhaps a glimmer of a people-of-color coalition. Ethnic consciousness and/or feeling warmly toward blacks are associated with more Latino willingness to support policies that benefit another minority group. However, we find no collision between multiculturalism and national attachment with respect to race-targeted policies in either of the two largest minority groups.

Immigration

Explanations for white attitudes about immigration are quite similar to those for race-targeted policies. Again, patriotism and a quite specific out-group antagonism, this time aimed at Latinos rather than blacks, stand out as the main predictors of opposition to liberal immigration policy, as can be seen in Table 8.4. However, in this case, ethnic identification among whites does have a significant, albeit modest, effect on preferences for reducing immigration, a finding that may reflect some sense that the changing ethnic composition of America wrought by immigration is a threat to the dominant role of whites in defining national norms. There are no direct effects of age or education on immigration preferences. The links of patriotism, white racial identity, and anti-Latino affect to anti-immigration opinions give some support to the nativist hypothesis in the case of immigration.

TABLE 8.4. *Origins of Support for Group-Conscious Positions on Immigration Policy: Los Angeles Surveys*

	Whites	Blacks	Latinos (1)	Latinos (2)
Ethnic identity	−.09**	−.02	.12**	.09*
Patriotism	−.22***	.07	−.03	−.02
Out-Group Antagonism				
Whites	–	−.03	.08	.09*
Blacks	.10	–	−.09*	−.11**
Latinos	−.22***	−.12	–	–
Vanguard Demographics				
Age	−.00	.00	.00	−.00
Education	.02	−.02	−.02**	−.02*
Immigration Status				
U.S.-born	–	–	–	−.10***
Naturalized	–	–	–	−.04
R^2	.06	.02	.04	.05
N	1,097	407	872	869

Entries are unstandardized ordinary least squares (OLS) regression coefficients predicting policy attitudes. Immigration policy is measured as the desired level of legal immigration, keyed from 1 = most supportive to 0 = least supportive. Predictors keyed so that high = stronger ethnic identity, higher patriotism, more prejudice (out-group antagonism), older, and more education. In the case of Latinos, a second regression equation is added to include immigration status, based on dummy variables for being U.S.-born or a naturalized citizen, with the reference category being foreign-born noncitizens. The equations also include controls for gender and income. For further descriptions of how these variables are constructed, please see Appendix 7.1.

$^*p < .05$ $^{**}p < .01$ $^{***}p < .001$
Source: Los Angeles County Social Survey (LACSS) in 1998, 1999, 2000, and 2002.

As with race-targeted policies, this model fails to predict black opinion about immigration very well: the only variable whose effect approaches statistical significance is affect toward Latinos. Again, we see no association between a lack of patriotism and support for the multicultural agenda, contrary to the expectation of incompatibility between national identity and racial identity in the American minority group with arguably the most difficult history.

Among Latinos, the pattern is more complex. As with blacks, patriotism plays no part. However, ethnic identity increases support for immigration, as one would expect in the group with the largest number of recent immigrants, as does antagonism toward blacks, suggesting an unsurprising element of conflict between the two groups over immigration. Noteworthy is the greater opposition to immigration among the U.S.-born, perhaps a hint of an assimilatory pulling-up-the-drawbridge once over it sometimes suspected of Latinos in generations further removed from immigration. Here, ethnic identification and being foreign-born both independently contribute to greater support for group-conscious immigration policy. The negative coefficient for education in Table 8.4 indicates that

Latinos who are better educated are more agreeable to limiting immigration. These results support the idea of assimilation: native-born, educated Latinos are distancing themselves from the immigration policy that is generally thought to be tied to their heavily immigrant ethnic group's particular interest. However, the link of anti-white sentiment to support for immigration is difficult to reconcile with the assimilation story.

Language Policy

In large part, multilingual policies follow the same pattern as the other two policy domains. Patriotism again is a strong predictor of whites' opposition to such policies, and indeed is far stronger than in the other two domains, as can be seen in Table 8.5. Again, the specific out-group antagonism of anti-Latino affect is a significant predictor, paralleling the effects of whites' prejudices against the most interested group in the other domains of group-targeted policies. Here, however, we also find some support for the vanguard hypothesis, in that younger

TABLE 8.5. *Origins of Support for Group-Conscious Positions on Language Policy: Los Angeles Surveys*

	Whites	Blacks	Latinos (1)	Latinos (2)
Ethnic identity	.03	.00	.34***	.29***
Patriotism	-.43***	-.16*	-.16**	-.14***
Out-Group Antagonism				
Whites	–	.07	.02	-.02
Blacks	-.02	–	.13**	.09
Latinos	-.23*	-.02	–	–
Vanguard Demographics				
Age	-.00***	-.00	-.00	-.00
Education	.01	.00	-.06***	-.05***
Immigration Status				
U.S.-born	–	–	–	-.14***
Naturalized	–	–	–	.03
R^2	.10	.01	.15	.16
N	997	414	890	886

Entries are unstandardized ordinary least squares (OLS) regression coefficients predicting policy attitudes. Language policy is measured as a two-item scale on support for bilingual education and for English as an official language (reverse-keyed), keyed from 1 = most supportive of multilingualism to 0 = least supportive. Predictors keyed so that high = stronger ethnic identity, higher patriotism, more prejudice (out-group antagonism), older, and more education. In the case of Latinos, a second regression equation is added to include immigration status, based on dummy variables for being U.S.-born or a naturalized citizen, with the reference category being foreign-born noncitizens. The equations also include controls for gender and income. For further descriptions of how these variables are constructed, please see Appendix 7.1.

*$p < .05$ **$p < .01$ ***$p < .001$

Source: Los Angeles County Social Surveys (LACSS) in 1998 and 1999.

whites are more supportive of liberal language policies, which had not been the case for the other two policy domains.

Among minorities, language policy draws a different pattern of support from the other domains in one important respect. In this instance, patriotism is a strong predictor of opposition to group-targeted policy and support for an English-only stance among blacks and Latinos as well, although the strength of the effect is greatest among whites. Among Latinos, ethnic identity also plays a strong explanatory role. The concerns of the critics of multiculturalism bear fruit regarding Latinos' attitudes about language policies, then. The greatest support for liberal policies comes from those with the strongest sense of group identification and those who are least attached to America as a nation. The assimilation hypothesis again gains support among Latinos: the better-educated and/or U.S.-born are significantly more likely than their less-educated and foreign-born counterparts to favor the English-only policies in the public sphere and schools, as whites do. As with immigration policy, both ethnic identification and being foreign-born contribute independently to greater support for group-conscious policy preferences.

National Data

We replicate the multivariate analysis of group-targeted policy issues with national data, using the relevant ANES and GSS studies. The analyses reported in Table 8.6 include white respondents only and employ similar although not identical measures of patriotism and out-group antagonism. Table 8.7 uses 2012 ANES black and Latino (citizen) oversamples to corroborate the LACSS results on national minority samples. Unfortunately, the measure of ethnic identity is available only in the 2004 GSS, but this is not a serious issue given the substantial evidence we have reported earlier about the limited impact of this attitude among whites. The predictors, then, are patriotism; out-group antagonism; ethnic identity, where available; the measure of Ethnic National Identity, which is a composite index summing responses to the importance of nativity and religion in making one a true American (only in the 2004 GSS); age; and education, with gender and income used as controls but not shown in the table.

The strong and consistent association of patriotism with white opposition to all three group-conscious policies remains intact in surveys conducted between 1992 and 2012. The stronger white Americans' emotional attachments to the nation and its leading symbols, the more they oppose race-targeted assistance, higher levels of immigration, and multilingual programs. And, as predicted, the more whites defined Americanism in terms of nativity and religion, the more they opposed multiculturalism, at least in the case of immigration policy.

Antagonism toward blacks does influence opposition to race-targeted policies, as was the case in the Los Angeles data. And antagonism toward Latinos did emerge as a significant factor in opposition to more immigration in the national data, as well as in the LACSS. Finally, the vanguard hypothesis receives

TABLE 8.6. *Predictors of Whites' Support for Group-Conscious Policies: National Surveys*

	Race-Targeted				Immigration		Language	
	2004 ANES	2008–09 ANES	2012 ANES	2004 GSS	2004 ANES	2012 ANES	1992 ANES	1994 GSS
Patriotism	-.17*	-.04*	-.22***	-.24**	-.21***	-.11***	-.28***	-.08**
Out-Group Antagonism								
Blacks	-.21	-.05**	.24***	–	-.08	.02	.01	-.17***
Latinos	.01	.00	.04	–	-.16**	-.27***	.00	–
Ethnic Identity								
Closeness to own ethnic group	–	–	–	.09	–	–	–	–
Ethnic conception of Americanness	–	–	–	-.49***	–	–	–	–
Importance of ethnic group identity	–	–	-.02	–	–	-.09***	–	–
Vanguard Demographics								
Age	.00	.00	.01	-.01*	.00	-.01	-.00*	-.00***
Education	.01	.01	.02*	.17***	.06***	.09***	.01*	-.02
R^2	.06	.08	.07	.11	.15	.11	.10	.06
N	404	920	3,166	746	746	3,119	748	1,018

Entries are unstandardized ordinary least squares (OLS) regression coefficients predicting policy attitudes, where 1 = support for group-conscious policies and 0 = opposition to them. The two-item race-targeted policy scales are based on preferences in hiring for blacks and government assistance to blacks (in 2008, race-targeted policy includes only an affirmative action in hiring item); immigration, the desired level of legal immigration; and the two-item language scale, English as an official language and preferred mode of language teaching for English as second language (ESL) students. Predictors keyed so that high = stronger ethnic identity, higher patriotism, more prejudice (out-group antagonism), more closeness to own ethnic group, older, and more education. Note that in the 1994 General Social Survey (GSS), affect toward blacks is captured by an index of questions asking how frequently respondents have felt sympathy and admiration for blacks rather than using the feeling thermometer questions employed in the other surveys. The 2004 GSS included no comparable questions. The equations also include controls for gender and income. For further descriptions of how these variables are constructed, please see Appendix 7.1.

*$p < .05$ **$p < .01$ ***$p < .001$

Source: American National Election Studies (ANES) 1992, 2004, 2008–09, and 2012; GSS 2004.

TABLE 8.7. *Predictors of Minorities' Support for Group-Conscious Policies: 2012 ANES*

	Race-Targeted Policy		Immigration Policy	
	Blacks	Latinos	Blacks	Latinos
Ethnic Identity Importance	.01	.13***	.13***	.16***
Patriotism	.07	−.08	.05	−.15***
Out-Group Antagonism				
Whites	.06	.20***	.08	−.15***
Blacks	–	−.25***	–	−.17***
Latinos	.02	–	.18***	–
Vanguard Demographics				
Age	.04**	.00	−.03**	−.02
Education	.04*	−.00	.08***	.09***
R^2	.03	.08	.07	.11
N	922	881	907	867

Entries are unstandardized ordinary least squares (OLS) regression coefficients predicting policy attitudes, where 1 = support for group-targeted policy and 0 = opposition to it. The two-item race-targeted policy scale is based on preferences in hiring for blacks and government assistance to blacks (in 2008, race-targeted policy includes only an affirmative action in hiring item); immigration, the desired level of legal immigration. Predictors keyed so that high = stronger ethnic identity, higher patriotism, more prejudice, more closeness to own ethnic group, older, and more education.

  $*p < .05$ $**p < .01$ $***p < .001$

Source: American National Election Studies (ANES).

substantial support when it comes to immigration and language policies, but not in the case of race-targeted programs. Especially notable is the strong tendency for higher levels of formal education to enhance support for immigration.

The multivariate results for the minority respondents in the 2012 ANES largely corroborate the correlational analysis shown in Table 8.1. Self-reported importance of ethnic identity predicts support for liberal immigration policy among Latinos but does not predict support among blacks for policies intended to help their own race. The question of whether a strong ethnic identity among minorities predicts support for policies benefiting other minority groups, as in the people-of-color paradigm, receives a sharply split decision. Latino citizens' strength of ethnic identity is positively associated with their support for policies benefiting blacks, but blacks' strength of racial identity is significantly negatively associated with support for liberal immigration policy. Latino citizens with a strong sense of ethnic identity may be cueing off co-ethnic leaders in politics, who, with the notable exceptions of those of Cuban origin, were by 2012 mostly well ensconced in the civil rights wing of the Democratic Party. Blacks who feel their race is an important part of their identity may, by contrast, be more likely to view liberal immigration policy as a threat to their group's economic well-being.

Conclusion

This chapter considered the psychological origins of preferences about the three domains of policy closely linked to multiculturalism's political project first examined in the preceding chapter. Among whites, we find that national attachment is consistently significantly linked to opposition to group-targeted policies. These findings hold in both the bivariate and regression analyses. Put another way, the less patriotic feelings about America, the more support for race-targeted policies, more immigration, and bilingualism. Opposition to a policy agenda linked to multiculturalism was especially strong among those who defined the boundaries of American nationhood in ethnic or ascriptive terms. Given the strong, reflexive patriotism among most white Americans, this finding confirms that ethnic tensions are more likely to emerge when policies benefitting minorities are framed in ways that challenge traditional American norms regarding individualism and the role of English as the country's common language. It also implies that a sense of cultural threat is a potent factor in opposition to the changing ethnic composition of the United States, largely due to immigration.

A second consistent finding was that prejudice toward the specific group targeted by the policy is a consistent predictor of whites' policy opposition. Anti-black antagonism predicts opposition to race-targeted policies, and anti-Latino antagonism predicts opposition to liberal immigration and language policies.

These results largely parallel other recent studies with similar concerns about how ethnic identifications and national attachment influence whites' opinions about race, immigration, and language. Kinder and Kam show that out-group hostility is a significant predictor of opposition to race-targeted policies and increased immigration and boosts support for English-only education and official English laws, even after the imposition of multiple controls for demographic and attitudinal variables.[11] One difference between their findings and ours is that they also find that in-group pride leads whites to oppose such group-conscious policies, whereas we find that white ethnic identity plays a muted role. One possible reason is that our measures of ethnic identity are somewhat more direct than the feeling thermometers they use to assess ethnocentrism.

Schildkraut uses a version of the "true" Americanism items to distinguish between ethnocultural and civic republican conceptions of national identity. In a multivariate analysis with multiple controls she finds that an ethnocultural conception of Americanism predicts support for restrictive language and immigration policies. The civic conception of American identity, by contrast, supports bilingual language programs.[12]

But what about possible conflicts between ethnic and national identities among minorities ? We do find evidence that strong ethnic identity contributes

---

[11] Kinder and Kam, *Us against Them.*
[12] Schildkraut, *Americanism in the Twenty-First Century.*

to Latinos' preferences about all three group-targeted policies. Surprisingly, support for such policies is *not* associated with either the strength of blacks' racial identification or with the level of their disaffection from the nation as a whole, even though they are the most victimized minority group in American society and arguably the original source of the multicultural movement in the United States. So, by and large, among these groups we find little evidence of a collision between ethnic and national identity insofar as support for the group-conscious policy positions in these domains is concerned.

The exception is in the domain of language policy. Patriotism was associated with more support for English-only among both blacks and Latinos, conforming to the pattern of white attitudes. Among Latinos, this held even with immigration status controlled, indicating that patriotism played a role for the new immigrants, as well as among those in generations further removed from immigration. Yet the U.S.-born were significantly more supportive of English-only than were the foreign-born, another sign of assimilation to the dominant cultural norm regarding the status of speaking English as a marker for belonging to America and presumably a requirement for social acceptance and economic success. Although language is not a sufficient condition for a common national identity, it is a fundamental element in the creation of the imagined community that is the psychological DNA of nationhood. The consensus among all ethnic groups on the role of English, even among new immigrants, is an important barrier against the ethnic balkanization so often attributed to multiethnic and/or immigrant-heavy societies.

Here, we might note that American opinion is replicated in cross-national surveys. Modern publics in advanced industrial societies believe that it is better for a country to have a common language and that this is a critical criterion of belonging to the national community.[13] In this they echo the positions of theorists of nationalism ranging from John Stuart Mill in the nineteenth to Ernest Gellner in the twentieth century.[14]

More generally, the assimilation hypothesis did receive consistent support among Latinos. The U.S.-born and better educated, presumably more integrated into the broader society and more likely to be fluent in English, more closely resembled whites in their opinions about the policies that most directly affect Latinos, both immigration and language. Finally, in this multivariate analysis there was little evidence for the vanguard hypothesis in any ethnic group.

How does the structure of opinions among Latinos bear on Huntington's gloomy view of the consequences of massive immigration from Latin America, especially from Mexico? He was concerned about southwestern states being overwhelmed with floods of poorly assimilated Latinos who would live in ethnic enclaves and fail to learn English, ultimately providing a solid base of continuing

---

[13] John Stuart Mill, "Of Nationality," chapter 16, in his *Considerations on Representative Government*, 1861; Gellner, *Nations and Nationalism*, 1984.
[14] Gellner, *Nations and Nationalism*.

political support for immigration and language policies that would further impede assimilation and work against the development of attachment to broader American society.

His concern does seem consistent with our data in two respects. In our tests of the vanguard hypothesis, low levels of education among Latinos are significantly associated with support for both more immigration and continued multilingualism. In general, ethnic identification is a stronger contributor to support for group-conscious policies among Latinos than among either whites or blacks, even when their immigration status is held constant. The strong and consistent effects of ethnic identification on support for such policies among Latinos also would be consistent with the pattern of narrow group interest and ethnic balkanization Huntington feared.

However, as argued in earlier chapters, Huntington's concerns fail to appreciate the very recent immigration of much of the contemporary Latino population. Nor do they adequately recognize the fast-paced changes within the Latino community; many in successive generations after immigration have already begun to assimilate. It will be recalled that in the preceding chapter we found that U.S.-born Latinos were substantially less group-interested in their attitudes about immigration and language than were the foreign-born noncitizens. U.S.-born Latinos were particularly supportive of English-only language usage. They also were more sympathetic to race-targeted policies. Compared to foreign-born Latinos, then, U.S.-born Latinos move significantly away from ethnic balkanization in their attitudes toward both the policies benefiting their own group and policies benefiting other minorities.

Rather than the continued social separation of the Latino population, bolstered by group-interested politics, what we may be seeing are the beginnings of a lengthy, gradual, and sometimes uneven process of assimilation of Latinos, one that occurs in fits and starts and likely to take place more across generations than within individual lifetimes. The aggregate impact of this, if our projection is correct, could be increasingly felt as an increasingly larger share of the Latino population becomes U.S.-born.

If so, Huntington may have been portraying more a transitional stage in Latino assimilation than a permanent feature of American society. In other words, the bleak portrait painted by Huntington of widespread Latino political support for a permanent Latino enclave, sustained by continued high levels of immigration and continued reliance on Spanish as a language, holds only if we ignore the continuing transition of the Latino population from heavily immigrant to one that ultimately will be dominated by the U.S.-born and bred. The U.S.-born Latinos resemble the later generations of earlier waves of European immigrants to America. We believe our findings on this point deserve special credibility given that our data come from Los Angeles, arguably ground zero of Latino immigration.

9

Multiculturalism and Party Politics

The multicultural moment in American politics begins in the turbulent 1960s.[1] Cultural nationalism and cries for black power among African-American activists; the embrace of affirmative action by the Johnson administration and then, more briefly, by Richard Nixon; immigration reform and its consequences for language policy; and the emergence of feminist and gay rights movements together made claims based on group identity a prominent feature of political debate. The multicultural movement argued that representation and recognition of disadvantaged groups – defined variously by race, ethnicity, language, gender, or sexual orientation – is paramount to attaining equal access to desired resources in society, whether money, power, or status. And these historically disadvantaged groups and demographic minorities merited special assistance from the government to overcome the obstacles they confront in the crucible of majoritarian politics.

The gradual adumbration of these ideas in elections, government policy, and academic debates proceeded apace through the 1970s and beyond. As multiculturalism and diversity became political catchwords, the social and ideological underpinnings of party politics underwent radical change. The civil rights movement precipitated the collapse of the New Deal coalition that had undergirded the dominance of the Democrats in national politics between 1932 and 1968. Civil unrest, the war in Vietnam, and the issues of "acid, amnesty, and abortion" further prodded a realignment that ended the South's exceptional status as a one-party Democratic region. This nationalization of electoral politics culminated in the Republican takeover of Congress in 1994. But well before that the two major parties began to polarize, with potential implications for conflict over policies related to the balance of national and ethnic identities.

---

[1] Bass, "The Multicultural Moment."

Until now, we have not considered how the politics of multiculturalism dovetails with the broader partisan and ideological fault lines in American politics. The chapter therefore addresses five main questions. We start by assessing the extent of partisan and ideological differences in (1) national attachment, (2) ethnic identity and beliefs about multiculturalist norms, and (3) attitudes about group-conscious policy issues. Then we ask (4) whether national and ethnic identifications shape responses to multiculturalist positions independent of the impact of partisan divisions and conclude by (5) examining how group-conscious policy issues resonant with the multiculturalist agenda about immigration and language fit in the public opinion space occupied by other domains such as economic and social issues, including older racial issues such as affirmative action.

THE SCOPE OF GROWING PARTISAN POLARIZATION

Political observers today often comment on the intense partisan polarization of today's politics; for example, "American politics is now marked by sharper divisions and more intense conflicts than has been the case in earlier times."[2] Of course, the violent events of the 1960s and early 1970s – Watts and other ghetto riots, bombings on campus, kidnappings and assassinations, mass marches on Washington, armed confrontations between the National Guard and antiwar protestors – led to similar observations in that era. Still, the primary focus of today's heralds of polarization is not the politics of the barricades and the streets, but rather the militarization of congressional and electoral politics.

In an earlier era, party coalitions were ideologically and regionally diverse at the elite level. Even divisive issues like the war in Vietnam, civil rights, and Medicare did not break down along purely party lines. By contrast, today's congressional parties resemble cohesive armed camps, with forward units probing enemy lines to exploit the slightest opening and ruthlessly punishing defectors (such as Joseph Lieberman). Civility, comity, and adherence to informal norms of cooperation have given way to invective and heavy-handed tactics.[3] The Republican takeover of Congress in 1994 may have initiated the new rules of engagement that greatly empowered the leaders of the majority caucus. But when the Democrats regained the majority in 2006, they proved quick to adapt and follow the new battle plan. Reversion of the House to GOP control in 2010 yielded more of the same under the watchful eyes of Tea Party zealots.

---

[2] Marc J. Hetherington, "Putting Polarization in Perspective," *British Journal of Political Science* 39 (2009): 413.

[3] Eric Uslaner, *The Decline of Comity in Congress* (Ann Arbor: University of Michigan Press, 1994).

Elite versus Mass Partisan Polarization

There is broad consensus today about party polarization among political elites – members of Congress, party activists, interest groups, and media outlets. A number of well-known studies have shown that even before our launch of public opinion data regarding multiculturalism in the mid-1990s, members of Congress had moved to the ideological poles, with Democrats clustered on the liberal end of the continuum and Republicans at the conservative end.[4] The most common measure of ideology in congressional voting is Poole and Rosenthal's DW Nominate scores, which are based on all votes cast on nonunanimous roll-calls in each session. The first dimension gives a member's score on traditional left-right issues. DW Nominate scores are bounded at −1 and +1, and the distribution generates two modes clustering around −0.5 and 0.5, respectively.[5]

Average party differences on this dimension are stark and have steadily increased from .51 in the 92nd Congress of 1971–1972 to .91 in the 109th Congress of 2005–2006.[6] In addition, the internal cohesion of both parties' members grew during this period, as indicated by the standard deviations of their Nominate scores. Perhaps the most compelling sign of party polarization in Congress is that in the House today there no longer is any Republican to the left of any Democratic member. Liberal Republicans and conservative Democrats, if not quite extinct, certainly are highly endangered species.

The range of polarization across issues is a slightly different question from its extent on average. One can, for example, imagine large partisan differences on economic issues but more mixed views when it comes to social and cultural issues. And even if there is evidence of cross-domain ideological coherence among elites, it is not clear that this extends to matters of patriotism, historically a consensual value, or multiculturalism, a relatively new idea with ambiguous connections to traditional American values.

Moreover, evidence of polarization at the elite level, by now conventional wisdom in both the political and academic classes, does not mean that ordinary citizens have followed in their wake. Indeed, there is substantially less agreement about whether the increased distance between the two main parties, and the internal cohesion of each, extends to the mass public.

That the public, too, has polarized is certainly plausible enough. Dating as far back as the 1970s, among the hypothesized sources of polarization are the role of race in spurring the Republican revival in the South, the emergence of moral issues such as abortion rights and gay marriage that evoke passionate feelings,

---

[4] Joseph A. Schlesinger, "The New American Political Party," *American Political Science Review* 79 (1985): 1152–69; David W. Rohde, *Parties and Leaders in the Post-Reform House* (Chicago: University of Chicago Press, 1991); Keith T. Poole and Howard Rosenthal, "The Polarization of American Politics," *Journal of Politics* 46 (1984): 1061–79.

[5] Hetherington, "Putting Polarization in Perspective," 417.

[6] Ibid., 413.

and the concomitant resurgence of religion as a potent political force in the 1980s, creating new cleavages between the progressive and the orthodox factions in all denominations.[7] In the 1990s, Hunter popularized the term "culture wars," stressing that issues such as race, abortion, and the death penalty are easily understood at an emotional level. When these issues were placed on the national agenda, he argues, enduring and intense policy preferences in the mass public developed, and voters could more easily gravitate to the party whose elites shared their point of view.[8] Add to this the fact that the last two presidents before Obama were, to quote Gary Jacobson, "dividers not uniters."[9] Clinton was an object of hatred and contempt for the political right, Bush for the political left. Jacobson argues that the unprecedented partisan differences in evaluations of George W. Bush fostered a huge gap between Democrats and Republicans on policies that went far beyond the war in Iraq. Finally, growing income inequality and the resurgence of class-based voting is another putative cause of a polarized public in recent years.[10]

On the other hand, Morris Fiorina and his co-authors argue in *Culture War?* that the modal voter is a moderate even on hot button issues like abortion and gay rights, that in the aggregate ordinary citizens haven't moved farther apart over time, and that, if anything, they are increasingly tolerant of cultural differences.[11] Most self-identified Democrats and Republicans do not place themselves at the extremes of the liberal–conservatism continuum but clump toward the middle.[12] Fiorina argues that the image of a country divided into homogeneous blue and red blocs is overstated, pointing out that most aggregate differences on issues between red and blue state voters and between self-identified Democrats and Republicans range between 10 and 15 percent.

Against this, Fiorina's critics point to the increasing consistency of issue beliefs among ordinary voters and to the tendency of Democratic and Republican identifiers to differ on issues in ways that parallel the divergences among party elites.[13] And as to the size of issue differences between party

---

[7] James Q. Wilson, "How Divided Are We?" *Commentary* (February 2009).

[8] James Davison Hunter, *Culture Wars* (New York: Basic Books, 1991).

[9] Gary Jacobson, *A Divider, Not a Uniter: George W. Bush and the American People* (New York: Pearson, 2007).

[10] Nolan McCarty, Keith T. Poole, and Howard Rosenthal, *Polarized America: The Dance of Ideology and Unequal Riches* (Cambridge, MA: MIT Press, 2006); Larry Bartels, *Unequal Democracy: The Political Economy of the New Gilded Age* (Princeton, NJ: Princeton University Press, 2009).

[11] Morris P. Fiorina, Samuel J. Abrams, and J. C. Pope, *Culture War? The Myth of a Polarized America* (New York: Pearson Longman, 2004); Morris P. Fiorina and Samuel J. Abrams. "Where's the Polarization?" in *Controversies in Voting Behavior*, 5th edition, ed. Richard G. Niemi and Herbert F. Weisberg (Washington, DC: CQ Press, 2011).

[12] Hetherington, "Putting Polarization in Perspective," 432.

[13] Alan I. Abramowitz, "Disconnected or Joined at the Hip?" in *Red and Blue Nation?: Characteristics and Causes of America's Polarized Politics*, vol. 1, ed. Pietro S. Nivola and David W. Brady (Washington, DC: Brookings, 2006); Alan I. Abramowitz, *The Disappearing*

identifiers, how big is *big* always is a matter of context. Hetherington shows that even the differences between southern and nonsouthern voters on civil rights issues in 1964, thought to be a high point of domestic conflict, were only 20 percent or less. This is greater than partisan differences in 2004 on some issues (abortion, death penalty) but not as great as the current partisan divide on gay marriage.[14] And measuring the extent of polarization is complicated by differences in the salience of particular issues and by the emergence of new issues, such as global warming or terrorism. A relatively modest partisan difference may nonetheless be significant in deciding electoral outcomes if the issue becomes salient in a campaign.

Even without more polarization in the sense of large numbers of partisan voters clustering at their respective ideological poles, a gap between partisans can grow as people sort themselves out into more ideologically congenial groups. Pro-life Democrats might exit and join a more congenial Republican home; pro-choice Republicans might move in the opposite direction. And it is clear from the survey evidence that that has happened over the years since the peak of the civil rights movement. Multiply this process over a number of issues, and the observable outcome is greater issue constraint within each set of partisans. In addition, among the more active and politically knowledgeable respondents, the evidence of this sorting is even clearer.[15]

The implication of party sorting is that the strongest Democrats and Republicans in the mass public are increasingly divided from each other not just on economic issues, but on social and cultural issues, racial resentment, and beliefs about traditional values.[16] The so-called party base may not be the majority in either party, but they are more likely to be politically active and act as a centrifugal force on candidates. Whether more people now choose a party on the basis of issue positions[17] or form their preferences on the issues to reconcile them with a prior party affiliation[18] is unclear, but both processes suggest that elite polarization has had a trickle-down effect with consequences for how voters filter information about new issues, changing conditions, and political events.

Center: Engaged Citizens, Polarization, and American Democracy (New Haven, CT: Yale University Press, 2010.

[14] Hetherington, "Putting Polarization in Perspective," 434–35.

[15] Ibid., 438.

[16] Marc J. Hetherington, "Partisanship and Polarization," in *New Directions in Public Opinion*, ed. Adam Berkinsky (New York: Routledge Press, 2011).

[17] Donald P. Green, Bradley Palmquist, and Eric Schickler, *Partisan Hearts and Minds: Political Parties and the Social Identities of Voters* (New Haven, CT: Yale University Press, 2002); Alan Abramowitz and Kyle L. Saunders, "Is Polarization a Myth?" *Journal of Politics* 70 (2006): 542–55.

[18] Thomas M. Carsey and Geoffrey Layman, "Changing Sides or Changing Minds?: Party Identification and Policy Preferences in the American Electorate," *American Journal of Political Science* 50 (2006): 464–77.

What does party polarization have to do with conceptions of American national identity and the multicultural agenda? The so-called culture wars did touch on questions of group identity, focusing primarily on the rights of women and homosexuals, with Democrats generally lining up on the side of group rights and Republicans either opposed or studiously silent. Still, the main protagonists in the academic debate over mass polarization have rarely if ever spoken of patriotism, language policy, immigration, or cultural rights. The protracted philosophical debate about the compatibility of multiculturalism and liberalism, and the curriculum wars centering on teaching history and the Western canon, waxed and waned in academia for three decades without seeming to penetrate deeply into the consciousness of mass publics.

Partisan Polarization over Patriotism in National Politics

Politics has never really stopped at the water's edge. In the lead-up to World War II, the parties were polarized over the question of American involvement. As the Cold War took hold, vehemently anticommunist Republicans such as Senator Joseph McCarthy appropriated symbols of patriotism and charged liberals and Democrats with being "un-American." In the aftermath of the Vietnam War, Republicans seized the mantle of nationalism again and queried the patriotic credentials of Democratic leaders. Ronald Reagan's "Morning in America" slogan was a paean to national pride, and his foreign policy contrasted a stronger and more virtuous United States with an evil Soviet empire. The Reagan Administration confidently invoked the image of a city on a hill, with the iconic flag planted firmly at the top.

In the 1988 presidential campaign, George H. W. Bush subtly impugned his Democratic opponent Michael Dukakis's patriotism by attacking his veto of a Massachusetts bill that would have made it compulsory for public school teachers to lead students in the Pledge of Allegiance. In office, Bush led the effort to overturn the Supreme Court's 1989 decision that laws against flag burning were unconstitutional. In the congressional maneuvering on a proposed constitutional amendment to that effect, Bush and the Republicans led the charge while the majority Democratic leadership worked successfully to finesse the effort. In 1992, Clinton's earlier participation in antiwar rallies and his slipperiness regarding his status in the military draft was contrasted with Bush's stellar World War II record. Democrats counterattacked after the 2000 election by deriding Republican leaders such as George W. Bush and Dick Cheney as "chicken hawks" who themselves had avoided service in the Vietnam War. In 2004, John Kerry accepted the Democratic nomination for president by saluting the convention and announcing that he was reporting for duty, an obvious response to Republican taunts that his party was insufficiently muscular on defense and terrorism issues. In return, his military record was "swift-boated," with the quality of his combat service in Vietnam challenged. In 2008, Barack Obama, competing against John McCain, a war hero, felt compelled in the midst of his presidential campaign to start wearing an American flag in his lapel.

The ubiquity of the flag on bumper stickers, team uniforms, fire engines, and gas stations; the playing of the national anthem at most sporting events; and recitation of the Pledge of Allegiance all suggest that open expressions of patriotism are common throughout American society. In Chapter 3, we documented the high level of patriotism expressed in public opinion surveys of Americans, including in attitudes about the flag.[19] Flag burning became an occasional vehicle for protesting American policy during the Vietnam War and thereafter. As a result, the treatment of those who burn the flag became a hot political issue. It provides an excellent example for exploring partisan differences on an issue that reeks with patriotic overtones and to contrast the positions of elites and ordinary citizens, respectively.

The year 1989 was a watershed. Before that, the Supreme Court had dealt several times with laws that banned various forms of disrespect to the flag. It had ruled that barring disrespectful words about the flag violated the First Amendment and found another flag protection law to be unconstitutionally vague. In the 1989 *Texas v. Johnson* decision, by a vote of 5–4, the court ruled that burning the flag was a form of symbolic speech protected by the constitution and, therefore, that laws criminalizing desecration of the flag could not stand. Both the majority and minority included surprising bedfellows. The strongly conservative Justice Scalia joined liberal justices Brennan and Marshall in holding flag burning to be constitutionally protected; the dissenters brought conservative Chief Justice Rehnquist and liberal Justice Stevens together.

The public's immediate response to the decision was highly disapproving. The decision was announced in mid-June; between June 23 and August 21, 1989, national surveys found disagreement with the decision ranging from 65 percent to 78 percent.[20] Five times between 1989 and 2006, Gallup asked, "Do you favor or oppose a constitutional amendment that would allow Congress and the state governments to make it illegal to burn the American flag?" A consistent majority (65 percent in 1989 and 62 percent in 2006) supported amending the Constitution to forbid flag burning.

Well aware of the public's outrage, Congress quickly reacted. An immediate response was to pass resolutions expressing symbolic support for the flag. These resolutions passed virtually unanimously. When partisan disagreement emerged and sharpened, it centered on the idea of a constitutional amendment banning the physical desecration of the flag. The Bush White House and Republican leaders in the Senate strongly favored this approach.

---

[19] See also Smith and Jarkko, "National Pride."

[20] Peter Hanson, "Flag Burning," in *Public Opinion and Constitutional Controversy*, ed. Nathaniel Persily, Jack Citrin, and Patrick J. Egan (New York: Oxford University Press, 2008), 187.

The Democrats in Congress faced a more complicated political situation. Congress seemed to have been united in its anger against the Court, and even the Democratic Speaker Tom Foley stated that the flag was "a unique symbol of national consciousness," a view that resonated so strongly that it led to the many resolutions honoring the flag. However, although Speaker Foley and the Democrats recognized the political imperative to be seen to stand by the flag and feared that the Republicans would once again monopolize the label of "patriot," they were wary of amending the Constitution. The solution the Democrats embraced, therefore, was a statute.

The partisan battle lines were thus drawn: statute or constitutional amendment? The Democrats proposed and passed the Flag Protection Act; indeed, the bill won overwhelming bipartisan support. However, the Supreme Court duly declared it unconstitutional. The Bush Administration, if not Republican legislators, had opposed the statutory solution, correctly anticipating that it would not pass constitutional muster. Instead, the administration introduced a constitutional amendment. When this was finally put to a vote in the Senate, it secured just the bare and inadequate majority of 51 votes. The Senate later foundered from 1990–2007 on several new constitutional amendments to ban flag burning. All failed to win the requisite two-thirds majority.

We examined the votes (summarized in online Appendix 9.1)[21] taken on resolutions expressing opposition to *Texas v. Johnson* and on proposals to amend the constitution to forbid flag burning that were introduced between 1989 and 2005. Symbolic defense of the flag was virtually unanimous; for example, more than 87 percent of Republicans *and* Democrats in both the House and the Senate voted for the 1989 Flag Protection Act, which directly contravened the Supreme Court's ruling in *Texas v. Johnson*.

But when it came to voting on a constitutional amendment to prevent desecration of the flag, Republicans were overwhelmingly in favor, usually by 90 percent or more, whereas Democrats were divided. Although a majority of Democrats usually voted against the constitutional amendment, significant numbers, ranging from a high of 48 percent in the House in 1997 to a low of 27 percent in the Senate in 2000, voted in favor. The Democrats favoring the constitutional amendment predictably come from more conservative districts, often in the South, where Republican candidates for president had run well. In fact, the votes of members in either House showed that when Democrats were split, Democratic votes against flag burning were always correlated with their conservatism on other roll-call votes, as reflected in the first dimension (liberalism-conservatism) of DW Nominate scores.

---

[21] In an online appendix (http://www.igs.berkeley.edu/files/citrin_ch9_online_appendix-1.pdf) to this chapter, we detail how representatives and senators voted on the flag-burning legislation and also on a series of bills and amendments relating to immigration and language policy. Those debates are discussed in later sections.

Partisan Polarization over Patriotism in Mass Attitudes

What about partisan differences about patriotism and flag burning in the mass public? Peter Hanson's summary of public opinion does record partisan and ideological differences, but smaller in magnitude than the party polarization in Congress. Democrats have generally been more opposed to a flag-burning amendment than Republicans, but this is largely a function of the opinions of college-educated Democrats. The views of non–college-educated Democrats resemble those of Republicans. And in a multivariate logit analysis based on the 1990–1992 American National Election Studies (ANES) Panel data, Hanson found that although political ideology and a measure of patriotism strongly predicted support for the flag-burning amendment, party identification did not have a statistically significant additional independent effect.[22]

The flag-burning case suggests that in the contemporary era there is reason to expect that Republicans and conservatives bring a stronger sense of American identity to deciding on specific issues than do Democrats and liberals,[23] either because they are responding to cues from political leaders and interest group spokesmen or because they have selected a political identification congenial to their underlying values and emotional commitments.

Turning to our own review of national data, Table 9.1 compares the attitudes of Republicans and Democrats and self-identified liberals and conservatives on a number of indicators of patriotism in national surveys from 1992 to 2012.[24] The ANES Patriotism Index is composed of questions about how much one loves America and positive feelings about the American flag. On this measure of emotional attachment (scored from 0 to 1), Table 9.1 shows that feelings of patriotism were pervasive in all partisan and ideological groups in all three years presented. Nevertheless, Republicans were, by conventional tests of statistical significance, more patriotic than Democrats or Independents, and conservatives were more patriotic than self-identified liberals. In addition, Republicans and conservatives were more likely to have shifted in the direction of more intense patriotism between 1992 and 2008, a period that notably overlapped with the events of September 11, 2001.

Do the relationships between political outlook and American identity persist after controlling for differences in the social background of respondents? We conducted multiple regression analyses with the ANES measures of national attachment as the dependent variables. These estimations included age, education, gender, and region (South, non-South), as well as party affiliation and

[22] Hanson, "Flag Burning," 190.
[23] Citrin, Wong, and Duff, "The Meaning of American National Identity"; Theiss-Morse, *Who Counts as an American?*
[24] In classifying partisan and ideological groupings from the familiar seven-point scales, we code "leaners" as partisans, so the Independents are those who locate themselves at "4" in the center of the scale. The same categorization was used for political ideology, so moderates are just those who place themselves in the exact center of the continuum.

TABLE 9.1. *Mean Affective Attachment to the Nation among Whites, by Party Identification and Ideology*

		1992	1996	2004	2009	2012
ANES feeling when seeing U.S. flag	Democrat	.69[a]	–	.70[a]	.78[a]	.72[a]
	Independent	.70[a]	–	.73[a]	.76[a]	.72[a]
	Republican	.81	–	.90	.92	.82
	Liberal	.62	–	.65	.76[a]	.67
	Moderate	.76[a]	–	.78	.78[a]	.76
	Conservative	.78[a]	–	.85	.91	.81
ANES love for country	Democrat	.77[a]	–	.81[a]	.82[a]	.87[ab]
	Independent	.76[a]	–	.80[a]	.79[a]	.83[a]
	Republican	.86	–	.91	.92	.92[b]
	Liberal	.74	–	.78	.81[a]	.85[a]
	Moderate	.81[a]	–	.85[a]	.80[a]	.87[ab]
	Conservative	.84[a]	–	.88[a]	.92	.90[b]
GSS closeness to America	Democrat	–	.70[a]	.76[a]	–	–
	Independent	–	.68[a]	.77[a]	–	–
	Republican	–	.73[a]	.85	–	–
	Liberal	–	.68[a]	–	–	–
	Moderate	–	.71[a]	–	–	–
	Conservative	–	.74[a]	–	–	–
GSS 10-item pride index	Democrat	–	.70[a]	.71[a]	–	–
	Independent	–	.68[a]	.73[a]	–	–
	Republican	–	.72[a]	.80	–	–
	Liberal	–	.67[a]	–	–	–
	Moderate	–	.71[a]	–	–	–
	Conservative	–	.73[a]	–	–	–
GSS 5-item chauvinism index	Democrat	–	.76[a]	.73[a]	–	–
	Independent	–	.77[a]	.79[ab]	–	–
	Republican	–	.79[a]	.86[b]	–	–
	Liberal	–	.71	–	–	–
	Moderate	–	.78[a]	–	–	–
	Conservative	–	.80[a]	–	–	–
Minimum N	Democrat	845	495	192	1,098	2,874
	Independent	210	136	177	256	717
	Republican	787	420	186	956	1,855
	Liberal	588	265	115	749	1,370
	Moderate	210	385	146	373	1,688
	Conservative	1,016	334	191	1,066	1,855

Group differences within years are significant ($p < .05$ level) unless marked with the same superscript. All dependent measures are scored from 0 = least close/patriotic to 1= most close/patriotic. The table reports mean values of these measures in each specified subgroup.

ideological self-identification as predictors. We do not show these analyses to save space but will provide them on request.

Two main findings emerge. First, conservative ideology tends to have a stronger relationship to patriotism than does partisanship; when both variables are included in the regression equation, the coefficient for party identification is diminished and sometimes does not achieve conventional levels of statistical significance. Second, confirming the results of the bivariate analyses in Table 9.1, partisanship became a more important predictor of patriotism between 1996 and 2004. A possible reason for this polarization is the role of the war in Iraq and the resultant cognitive linkage of President Bush and his party with ardent American nationalism.[25] However, this heightened partisan polarization did not persist through the 2008–09 and 2012 ANES surveys.

Table 9.2 turns from emotional attachment to America to the normative content of national identity as assessed by beliefs about what makes someone a true American. Here, partisan and ideological differences are even more pronounced. Conservatives and to a slightly lesser extent Republicans were more likely to identify a range of traits as very important for making someone a true American. Republicans were significantly more likely to say this about both "ethnic" traits such as religious affiliation and language but also, less intuitively, for more inclusive attributes such as citizenship, respect for the law, and simply feeling American. Perhaps Republicans and conservatives simply are more accepting of nationalism's assumption that there is something like a true American with a distinctive identity.

During the period spanning 9/11, national identity appeared to become more salient in the country as a whole. Specifically, these partisan differences were more pronounced in 1996 than in the 2004 General Social Survey (GSS). Democrats, Independents, and Republicans all moved in the direction of emphasizing a range of attributes as important for defining American nationhood. In addition, more ethnic and exclusionary beliefs about what it means to be an American also became more widespread, an unsurprising response to a sense of national threat from a culturally dissimilar "other."

Finally, we should emphasize that the partisan differences in national attachment are quite modest and hardly reflect bitter polarization. Overwhelmingly, a strong sense of patriotism is the consensus, despite the noticeable partisan differences in how people interpret what it means to be an American.

To compare possible partisan and ideological polarization in national identity across ethnic and racial groups, we turn to the Los Angeles data and national data from the 2012 ANES. Because of the heavy predominance of Democrats among blacks and Latinos, we do not consider party differences and confine the analysis to a comparison of self-identified liberals, moderates, and conservatives in levels of patriotism. Table 9.3 shows that, in the Los Angeles data, among both white and black respondents, conservatives are consistently significantly

---

[25] Jacobson, *A Divider, Not a Uniter*.

TABLE 9.2. Cross-Tabulations of Whites' Conception of a "True American," by Party Identification and Ideology

	Born in America		Christian		Lived in the United States for Most of Life		Able to Speak English		American Citizenship		Respect for Institutions and Laws		Feel American		# of "Very Important" Responses	
	1996	2004	1996	2004	1996	2004	1996	2004	1996	2004	1996	2004	1996	2004	1996	2004
Democrat	40[a]	51[a]	34[a]	39[a]	44[a]	53[a]	69[a]	78[a]	72[a]	79[a]	62[a]	69[a]	63[a]	64[a]	4.0[a]	4.5[a]
Independent	32[a]	58[ab]	32[a]	45[ab]	40[a]	62[b]	73[a]	83[ab]	70[a]	79[a]	63[a]	58	60[a]	70[ab]	3.8[a]	4.6[a]
Republican	36[a]	59[b]	38[a]	54[b]	42[a]	59[ab]	74[a]	85[b]	80	88	68[a]	82	64[a]	76[b]	4.0[a]	5.0
Liberal	29	–	20	–	30	–	58	–	63	–	56	–	54	–	3.4	–
Moderate	42[a]	–	36	–	49	–	73	–	77[a]	–	64	–	64[a]	–	4.1[a]	–
Conservative	40[a]	–	45	–	43	–	80	–	81[a]	–	74	–	66[a]	–	4.3[a]	–
Total	38	56	36	47	43	58	72	82	75	83	65	73	63	71	4.0	4.7
Minimum N	159	151	155	149	156	153	160	153	162	151	160	151	158	150	184	190

Cell entries for individual traits represent the percentage of respondents claiming that the trait is "very important." For "# of very important" column, the number of times the respondent answered "very important" was summed, ranging from 0 = none to 7 = all. Group differences within years are significant ($p < .05$) unless marked with a common superscript.

Source: General Social Survey (GSS) 1996 and 2004.

TABLE 9.3. Cross-Tabulations of Ideology by National and Ethnic Identity, by Ethnicity

	Whites			Blacks			Latinos (Citizen)			Latinos (Noncitizen)		
	Lib.	Mod.	Cons.	Lib.	Mod.	Cons.	Lib.	Mod.	Cons.	Lib.	Mod.	Cons.
NATIONAL DATA												
Patriotism												
How does R feel about this country? (% love it) (ANES 2012)	59% (782)	67% (944)	76% (1,363)	56%[a] (270)	52%[a] (320)	69% (158)	54%[a] (239)	58%[a] (309)	58%[a] (218)	—	—	—
When R sees the American flag, R feels? (% extremely good) (ANES 2012)	29 (779)	44 (939)	52 (1,361)	33[a] (268)	25 (320)	38[a] (156)	34[a] (237)	48 (308)	37[a] (218)	—	—	—
LOS ANGELES DATA												
Patriotism												
How proud is R to be American? (% extremely proud) (LACSS 1994, 1997)	39%[a] (140)	44%[ab] (257)	52%[b] (148)	32%[a] (75)	34%[a] (146)	45%[a] (56)	38%[a] (65)	37%[a] (90)	33%[a] (160)	15%[a] (46)	10%[a] (114)	17%[a] (69)
"I am proud to be American" (% strongly agree) (LACSS 1998, 1999, 2000, 2002)	67 (283)	81 (477)	91 (213)	69[a] (130)	76[a] (214)	93 (88)	66 (134)	75[a] (212)	78[a] (112)	52[a] (98)	31 (183)	44[a] (131)
R has great love for country (% strongly agree) (LACSS 1997, 1998, 1999)	59 (242)	75 (402)	82 (201)	45[a] (53)	61[a] (102)	86 (42)	54 (99)	62[ab] (157)	73[b] (93)	64[a] (80)	47[ab] (159)	50[ab] (103)
R finds flag moving (% strongly agree) (LACSS 1997–2000, 2002)	40 (357)	54 (599)	68 (293)	40[a] (145)	40[a] (246)	54 (100)	46[a] (162)	50[a] (246)	61 (148)	44[a] (115)	41[a] (245)	49[a] (159)
National vs. Ethnic Identity												
American vs. ethnic identity (dichotomous measure) (% just American) (LACSS 1994, 1995, 1997)	93[a] (211)	96[a] (356)	96[a] (219)	60 (89)	75[a] (190)	78[a] (68)	84[a] (83)	72 (129)	87[a] (74)	56[a] (59)	54[a] (149)	58[a] (92)

TABLE 9.3 (continued)

	Whites			Blacks			Latinos (Citizen)			Latinos (Noncitizen)		
	Lib.	Mod.	Cons.	Lib.	Mod.	Cons.	Lib.	Mod.	Cons.	Lib.	Mod.	Cons.
American vs. ethnic identity (trichotomous measure) (% just American) (LACSS 1995, 1999, 2000)	73[a] (207)	76[a] (319)	77[a] (173)	25[a] (75)	31[a] (138)	26[a] (55)	12 (96)	22[a] (143)	22[a] (64)	3[a] (71)	3[a] (147)	2[a] (97)

Base N for each racial group and ideological category in parentheses. Ideological differences within ethnic group differ significantly ($p < .05$) unless they carry the same superscript. The ethnic identity scale includes the degree to which R identifies with his or her ethnic group, its importance to him or her, and how often R thinks of him- or herself as an ethnic group member.

Source: American National Election Studies (ANES); Los Angeles County Social Survey (LACSS).

the most likely to express pride in being American, to feel great love for the country, and to say they find the flag a moving symbol. With the exception of the item relating to the flag, racial differences are minor; blacks as a group are less emotional about the flag than whites. This is another example of what we had seen earlier in Chapter 3: racial differences between whites and blacks about national attachment are discernible but generally minor. Still black conservatives, too, feel more positive about America than do black liberals. In the national data, ideological differences among whites are large, whereas those among blacks are present but smaller and less consistent.

Among Latino respondents, the now-familiar assimilation pattern emerges. Rather than making the U.S.-born versus foreign-born distinction used in previous chapters, here we distinguish citizens versus noncitizens because we are focusing on partisan dispositions that are primarily relevant to voting, a behavior limited to citizens. Because the ANES surveys only citizens, we are unable to observe assimilation within the national data. Among citizens in the Los Angeles results, the tendency of conservatives to express more intense patriotism recurs; they are conforming to the national norm. Among noncitizens, however, there is no consistent ideological pattern. One possible explanation is that the meaning of these terms and how they fit in American political discourse is less clear to immigrants who are not yet citizens,[26] whereas even naturalized citizens have been socialized into the standard understanding of the liberal and conservative categories in American political culture. But our point is that assimilation is occurring here as well as elsewhere, as Latinos pass from noncitizen into citizen status.[27]

We also conducted multiple regression analyses to determine if the results reported in Table 9.3 generally hold up with controls for social background factors. They do, although again we do not present the analyses to save space. Among whites, both party identification and ideology are associated with higher levels of patriotism, even after controls. Among blacks also, a conservative self-identification boosts an emotional attachment to the nation. Among Latinos, evidence of the assimilation prototype reappears. First-generation immigrants, both citizens and noncitizens, regardless of their political ideology, are less patriotic than their native-born counterparts and more likely to have a strong sense of ethnic rather than American identification. More generally, the high overall level of patriotism in American culture among followers of both major

---

[26] Zoltan Hajnal and Taeku Lee, *Why Americans Don't Join the Party: Race, Immigration, and the Failure (of Political Parties) to Engage the Electorate* (Princeton, NJ: Princeton University Press, 2010).

[27] Some caution is in order because the relationship between ideology and patriotism does not show up in the purely citizen Latino sample in the 2012 ANES. There are well-known differences among Latinos from different nationality groups in ideology and partisanship, and a national sample of Latinos is more heterogeneous than the heavily Mexican-American population of Los Angeles and the Southwest more generally. For an analysis of the development of party identification among immigrants, see Hajnal and Lee, *Why Americans Don't Join the Party*.

parties has strategic relevance for how to advantageously frame the policy debate on a range of foreign and domestic policy issues. Specifically, when trade, immigration, or language issues are perceived as challenging traditional conceptions of America's virtues, they are unlikely to gain widespread popular legitimacy.

When it comes to emotional attachment to the nation, to patriotism and feelings of Americanism, therefore, party identification and ideology do play a part among politically incorporated minority groups, as well as among whites. Republicans and conservatives are more favorable toward patriotic and nationalistic symbols and express a stronger belief in the meaningfulness and significance of a unique American identity.

PARTISAN POLARIZATION OVER MULTICULTURAL NORMS

What about the parties' responses to multiculturalism's defense of official representation and recognition on the basis of group identity? Democratic and liberal elites have been more receptive to claims for group representation and recognition that go beyond nondiscrimination, whereas Republicans and conservatives are quick to condemn the identity politics of hyphenation as divisive and inegalitarian. These partisan and ideological fault lines are evident in the judicial responses to affirmative action, the legislative actions relating to official English, and the controversies regarding diversifying the curriculum in schools and colleges.

Similarly, in intellectual circles the claims of multiculturalism resonated much more strongly on the left than the right. Occasionally, an Old or New Left scholar such as Arthur Schlesinger Jr.[28] or Todd Gitlin[29] would warn that identity politics and demands for group rights based on ethnicity would undermine a sense of common identity and individual rights. But conservatives of both traditional and neo varieties were united in opposition to official recognition of minority cultures, bilingual education, and affirmative action. Elected officials of both parties tended to be circumspect when state referenda on official English and affirmative action appeared, with many Republicans reluctant to publicly oppose minority group activists and voters. Clearly, though, over time Democratic politicians became more favorable to the identity claims of both ethnic and sexual minorities.

Multiculturalism accepts prioritizing ethnic identity, especially among minorities. To start with, then, we examine partisan polarization over the strength of ethnic identification. There is a surprising similarity in the degree to which liberals, moderates, and conservatives in every minority ethnic group express a strong sense of ethnic consciousness. We assessed what the proportion of each

---

[28] Schlesinger, Jr., *The Disuniting of America*.
[29] Gitlin, *The Twilight of Common Dreams*.

ethnic group scoring above the mean on a three-item ethnic identity index.[30] When it comes to one's strength of ethnic identity, group membership matters and ideological orientation has almost no impact. Blacks and Latinos, whatever their ideological self-identification, have a stronger sense of ethnic consciousness than whites. But in no group does ideological self-identification have a statistically significant association with one's strength of ethnic identification.

Earlier, we examined responses to the choice between American and ethnic identity, a central focus of our study. We have seen considerable ideological polarization over patriotism but not over ethnic identity. Interestingly, Table 9.3 shows very little association between political ideology and identity choice, as assessed by the item asking respondents whether they see themselves primarily as just Americans, mainly a member of their ethnic group, or both. The data are broken down by ethnicity. The one exception is when black respondents are posed the dichotomous choice between national and ethnic identity. Conservatives (78 percent) and moderates (75 percent) are more likely than liberals (60 percent) to opt for the overarching American identity, which we regard as a reflection of the stronger resonance of national symbols, including the symbolic reference to "America," on the political right. What these data suggest is that the politics of *ethnic* identity are more fundamentally related to group membership and group-based norms than they are to cleavages along partisan and ideological lines. Minority groups – here we examine just blacks and Latinos – are more likely to espouse a strong sense of ethnic identity, and this tendency generally cuts across ideological lines.

Next we examine the link to multiculturalist norms. Ethnic differences were bounded so here again we limit ourselves to those attitude measures that seemed best to capture divisions in public opinion about group identity, cultural recognition, and group representation for minorities. Our purpose here is to assess whether there are important partisan and ideological underpinnings for acceptance of multicultural norms. The data are shown in Table 9.4.

There were no significant partisan or ideological differences in the perceived distinctiveness of ethnic groups, the essentialist idea about ethnicity. For example, 52 percent of Democrats and 49 percent of Republicans in the 2002 GSS agreed that whites were a distinct group; 62 percent of self-identified liberals and 61 percent of self-identified conservatives agreed that ethnic minority groups in the United States are very distinct from each other.

Partisan and ideological differences do emerge when respondents are asked about the value of recognizing and preserving ethnic and racial cultures, as shown in Table 9.4A. Democrats and liberals are twice as likely to believe that

[30] Inconsistencies in the number of items across chapters are attributable to the differential availability of these ethnic identity items in different surveys. We use the maximum available for any given analysis. In this case, the questions concerned the importance of one's ethnicity, strength of identification with one's ethnic group, and how often one thinks of oneself in terms of membership in one's ethnic group. See Table 4.3 for frequencies and exact wordings.

too little attention is being paid to minority groups in high schools and colleges. But even among Republicans and conservatives, the notion that teaching about the history of ethnic groups is being emphasized too much is a minority point of view, more evidence of consensual acceptance of soft multiculturalism.

Partisan differences also emerge about whether minorities should assimilate or maintain distinctive cultures. When asked whether minority groups in the United States should maintain their distinct customs or blend into the larger society, as in the idea of the melting pot, Republicans and conservatives are significantly more likely than Democrats and liberals to endorse the assimilationist blend-in option in most of the national surveys shown in Table 9.4A. Concern about maintaining a common culture seems to have grown over time along with a growing ideological divergence on the issue; choices of the blend-in alternative rose from 32 percent to 47 percent from 1994 to 2004. Given the added element of large partisan differences about the proper scope of government, it comes as no surprise that Democrats and liberals are more favorable to such government assistance than are Republicans and conservatives. However, majorities in all partisan and ideological groups are opposed to a policy of active government assistance, presumably in the form of funding programs for the preservation of minority customs, the prevailing official policy in Canada and elsewhere.

As we have seen in Chapter 5, public support for multiculturalism drops radically when we ask about guarantees for group representation rather than tolerance for cultural diversity. Table 9.4B shows that virtually without exception, Democrats and Republicans, and liberals and conservatives alike overwhelmingly oppose guaranteed group representation. This blanket disapproval occurs regardless of whether respondents are asked if people are best represented by leaders from their own ethnic background, if organizations based on race or ethnicity are divisive, and if congressmen and teachers should reflect the background of their constituents or be chosen purely on the basis of ability. The differences are statistically significant in some cases, but of trivial magnitude. Admittedly, these questions do not ask how one would choose among people of different background but equal ability. Still, the overriding evidence is that although Americans of all political colorations accept the reality of ethnic differences and accept the private expression of diverse cultural practices (at least at an abstract, symbolic level), there is pervasive opposition to institutionalizing ethnic differences through government policy such as quotas for minority groups in the legislature or teaching profession.

Multivariate analysis with controls for age, education, gender, and southern residence does not alter the results just presented, so, for the sake of space, we do not report the equations in full. Party and ideology remain statistically significant predictors of beliefs about whether too much attention is being paid to minority groups in history classes, about whether the government should assist the preservation of minority cultures, and whether minority groups should blend into the mainstream culture. On these questions, Republicans and conservatives

TABLE 9.4A. *Whites' Beliefs about Social Multiculturalism, by Party Identification and Ideology*

	Ethnic minority groups are distinct. (% Agree)	Whites are distinct from minorities. (% Agree)	Attention to the experiences of ethnic minority groups in high school and college history? (% too little)	Gov't assistance to preserve customs? (% Agree)		Maintain distinct customs or blend into broader society? (% Maintain)				
	2002 GSS	2002 GSS	1994 GSS	1996 GSS	2004 GSS	1992 ANES	1994 GSS	1996 GSS	2000 GSS	2004 GSS
Democrat	62%[a]	52%[a]	32%	22%[a]	32%	37[b]	35[a]	47%[a]	34[a]	50[a]
Independent	60[a]	50[a]	18[a]	21[a]	19[a]	28[a]	27[a]	49[a]	33[a]	51[a]
Republican	62[a]	49[a]	15[a]	9	15[a]	32[ab]	28[a]	32	29[a]	42
Liberal	62[a]	48[a]	37	22[a]	–	38	40	54	34[a]	–
Moderate	61[a]	52[a]	20[a]	17[ab]	–	31[a]	28[a]	36[a]	30[a]	–
Conservative	61[a]	52[a]	18[a]	12[b]	–	31[a]	28[a]	39[a]	30[a]	–
Total	61	50	32	17	23	34	32	42	31	47
Minimum N	514	516	168	178	150	260	181	129	267	194

(continued)

TABLE 9.4B. *Whites' Beliefs about Political Multiculturalism, by Party Identification and Ideology*

	Are people best represented in politics by leaders from their own racial or ethnic background, or doesn't the leader's background make much difference? (% ethnic background)	Political organizations based on race or ethnicity promote separatism and make it hard for all of us to live together. (% disagree)	Should congressmen have the same racial or ethnic background as their constituents or be considered purely on the basis of ability? (% background)	Should teachers in public schools and universities reflect students' ethnicity or be considered purely on the basis of ability? (% background)
	1994 GSS	1994 GSS	1994 GSS	1994 GSS
Democrat	37[a]	19%[a]	12%[a]	10%[a]
Independent	32[a]	15[ab]	7[a]	8[a]
Republican	33[a]	12[b]	6[a]	5[a]
Liberal	37[a]	19[a]	14[a]	12[a]
Moderate	35[a]	17[a]	8[a]	6[a]
Conservative	35[a]	13[a]	7[a]	6[a]
Total	36	16	9	8
Minimum N	177	181	176	182

All respondents included. Between-party and between-ideology differences within each survey are significant ($p < .05$), **unless** they carry the same superscript. For the maintain/blend item, the number of response options vary by survey. The 1992 American National Election Studies (ANES) allows respondents to choose maintain, blend, or "neither/both"; the 1994 General Social Survey (GSS) employs a ten-point scale, the 2000 GSS employs a seven-point scale, and the 1996/2004 GSS forces a dichotomy. In the former three cases, any response on the side of "maintain" was included.

are more likely to oppose multiculturalist principles. On the matter of group representation, multivariate analysis introduces only minor nuances, and the substantive significance of these small differences is quite limited.

To explore ethnic differences in the political foundations of beliefs about multiculturalism, we rely on the Los Angeles surveys, which included most of the items used in the national surveys, as indicated in Chapter 5. However, they were included only in the 1994 and 1995 Los Angeles County Social Survey (LACSS), which limit the number of available cases. The data for whites reveal much the same pattern as the national surveys, so we do not present them in detail to save space. There are clear partisan differences (in the range of 10–15 percent) in support for recognition of ethnic minorities in terms of teaching ethnic history over maintaining distinct cultures and over ethnically based political organizations, although given the limited numbers of cases not all the differences are significant. In most cases, partisan and ideological differences within each ethnic minority group are small. At the level of abstract norms and symbolic identifications, ethnic and political differences on these questions are minor, and the consensus clearly opposes the tenets of hard multiculturalism.

Overall, then, we generally find considerable partisan and ideological cleavage over multiculturalist norms in the white mass public. That parallels the consistent association of partisanship with patriotism, with the Republicans and conservatives having captured the issue of patriotism to some extent. To return to our starting point, there does seem to be some cost to national unity of multiculturalists' emphasis on ethnic identity, but one that is carried primarily through partisan and ideological cleavages among whites.

PARTISAN AND IDEOLOGICAL POLARIZATION OVER GROUP-CONSCIOUS POLICIES

Political elites probably provide more information and clearer cues on policies that bear directly on the interests of groups making up party coalitions than on the rather abstract and rarely debated multicultural norms. If so, we should see stronger effects of partisanship and ideology on public opinion about the multicultural positions on salient group-conscious policies than about more abstract multicultural norms.

Elite Cleavages

Affirmative action, immigration policy, and bilingualism have been on the national agenda since the mid-1960s. The tug of war over affirmative action's limits has mainly taken place in the federal courts, with liberals lining up on the side of an expansive policy to overcome the persisting effects of past discrimination, and conservatives restricting the application of group preferences, arguing that it violates rights guaranteed to individuals under the Fourteenth Amendment.

By contrast, immigration reform has presented a more complex political battlefield for American policy makers, inspiring deep divisions within both major party coalitions. More than many other policies, immigration is a potent cross-cutting issue in American politics, one that often defies the standard partisan and ideological divides among elites. Party coalitions split on immigration because the ideological principles that divide left and right (cultural pluralism and economic security versus market efficiency and national sovereignty) often clash when it comes to concrete policy choices.

Legal immigration has spurred some debates, particularly in times of economic stress, although not as much as illegal immigration. Since 1965, a liberal, expansive approach to legal immigration has attracted bipartisan support as major interest groups allied with both the Republicans and Democrats have been able to perceive distributive benefits in accepting it.[31] Policy debates about it center on three main issues: the numbers to be let in, the type of newcomer to be let in, and the scope of the rights to be enjoyed by noncitizens living in the United States. On the left, economic protectionists concerned about the jobs of native workers may oppose postnationalists who lean toward virtually open borders; on the right, pro-business expansionists find themselves in tension with cultural protectionists demanding tight border control. Business and labor groups are not unified; nor are organizations representing different ethnic groups. Although the major black civil rights organizations have come around to supporting liberal immigration policies, that was not always so.

This is not the place for a detailed analysis of the complicated efforts to find a legislative solution for the problems posed by immigration, legal and illegal. We will, however, briefly summarize how members of Congress lined up on major pieces of legislation since the historic 1965 Hart-Celler Act that amended the existing Immigration and Nationality Act to abolish national origins quotas and initiated a system of visa preferences based on family reunification and, secondarily, employment needs. Although this landmark reform won large majorities from both parties, Republicans were somewhat more favorable in both the House and the Senate because of the strong opposition of conservative southerners, then overwhelmingly Democrats. It should be said, of course, that neither party anticipated that the consequence of this legislation would be the ethnic transformation of the immigrant population and the subsequent massive growth in the Hispanic and Asian-origin segments of American society.

Illegal immigration has presented a much more contentious problem, with multiple, overlapping lines of controversy. The crafting of majority coalitions has often required finding incongruous common ground among the left and the right. For a start, the term "illegal" has negative connotations; defenders of individuals who admittedly have broken laws that are at the heart of national sovereignty face an uphill battle. Border "hawks" see the immigration problem

---

[31] Daniel Tichenor, "Strange Bedfellows: The Politics and Pathologies of Immigration Reform," *Labor Studies in Working Class History* 5 (2008); Schuck, "Immigration."

as a breakdown of the federal government's capacity to enforce its own laws.[32] When every effort at tightening implementation of border controls or employer sanctions seems to fail, anger and mistrust grow.

The political right claims that the country's fundamental interest in law enforcement has given way to the power of immigrant rights lobbies and the quest for Hispanic votes. Legalization of the status of illegal immigrants – what the right disdains as amnesty – evokes intense emotions on both sides. On the economic front, the pro-immigration conservatives devoted to economic growth have insisted on the need for immigrant labor both in high-tech industries and in low-skill jobs, especially in agriculture, restaurants, and construction. Economic protectionists in both parties have claimed that illegal immigration helps the corporate rich while taking jobs away from working-class Americans. And some labor leaders, including Cesar Chavez, have opposed guest worker programs as undercutting efforts to unionize local workers and as a way of denying workers fundamental benefits. Employer sanctions have been viewed by business as burdensome and by immigrant activist groups as a cruel means of tracking down and deporting illegal immigrants. Finally, liberals and Latino leaders often have supported a path to citizenship for undocumented immigrants on humanitarian grounds, arguing that law-abiding, hard-working people who have spent many years living in fear of discovery deserve acceptance into mainstream society.

This brief foray into the politics of immigration makes it clear why compromise has been so difficult in the face of intense, cross-cutting disagreements. So, after five years of effort, Republican Senator Alan Simpson and Democratic Representative Romano Mazzoli produced omnibus legislation in 1986 on both legal and illegal immigration. As the bill labeled the Immigration Reform and Control Act (IRCA) was formed and reformed, it encountered strong resistance from both left and right: a broad coalition of business interests joined with ethnic and civil rights groups, the American Civil Liberties Union (ACLU), and the National Immigration Forum to oppose employer sanctions and a national identity card. Finally, gridlock was overcome by a bargain that included watered-down sanctions, a guest worker program, and legalization for illegal immigrants living in the country since 1982. However, fewer Republicans than Democrats supported this legislation in both the House and the Senate.

In 1990, despite rising concern about illegal immigration, pro-immigration Democrats and Republicans united behind a 40 percent increase in annual visa allocations benefiting both employment-based admissions and family reunification programs for legal immigrants.[33] By then Republican support for expansive immigration had eroded a little: 53 percent of House Republicans compared to 67 percent of House Democrats voted for the 1990 act; in the Senate, the equivalent figures were 84 percent and 93 percent.

---

[32] Tichenor, *Dividing Lines*.
[33] Ibid.

However, a decade later, clearly neither Simpson-Mazzoli nor the 1990 legislation had stopped the tide of illegal immigration. A new legislative effort was made in 1996 when the Republicans controlled Congress. The Illegal Immigration and Immigrant Responsibility Act increased border enforcement, restricted immigrant entitlements to public benefits, and tightened asylum procedures. An amendment to deny access of illegal immigrants to virtually all public services was defeated, as were proposed cuts in legal immigration (a similar proposition had appeared on the California ballot in 1994 and passed). The final compromise won overwhelming bipartisan support in the Senate. More revealing is the partisan division in the House on a version much tougher on illegal immigrants; this version was successful, receiving support from 97 percent of the Republicans but only 38 percent of the Democrats.

Finally, as a harbinger of what may come in the future, a quick look at the second President Bush's failed effort to craft a compromise of strict border control and a guest worker program in the early 2000s may be instructive. Unanimous support did not come even from Democrats. On previous votes, restrictionist votes among Democrats were associated with more conservative roll-call voting in general (as reflected in positions on the first dimension DW Nominate scores). Conversely, Republican divisions on immigration also were connected to differences in political ideology, with the more conservative legislators less likely to support even compromise proposals if they included the conservative bogeyman of amnesty for illegal immigrants.

Since 1996, Latino voter registration has grown rapidly, and this electoral demographic, along with Asian voters, has become a key target for both parties. Democrat Bill Clinton succeeded mightily with these groups of voters. But Republican George W. Bush, a candidate with a record of opposition to English-only proposals and a sympathetic outlook toward Latinos in Texas, made a major effort to appeal to Latino voters. Bush increased his party's share of the Latino vote to 34 percent in 2000 from 21 percent in 1996.[34]

In 2004, Bush went further, proposing a new guest worker program and renewable permits that would ultimately be a path toward citizenship. This plan included a promise to tighten border controls. But Bush also defended the overall project with praise for Mexican immigrants as adding to America the traditional values of hard work, faith in God, and love of family. In the 2004 election, Bush won a record (for Republicans) 40 percent of the Latino vote. However, critics on both the left and the right did not embrace his immigration reform proposal. Conservatives attacked the amnesty proposal, although business groups welcomed the guest worker program. Democrats, by contrast, opposed these

---

[34] For results for the Latino vote from exit polls from the last several presidential elections, see National Council of La Raza, "Latino Voters and the 2010 Election: Numbers, Parties, and Issues," 4. Accessed online at http://www.nclr.org/images/uploads/publications/REPORT_-_NCLR_Latino_Vote_in_2010_JK.pdf.

programs as opening up the door to abuse and exploitation while also reducing wages.[35]

Intense conflict was generated in 2005 and 2006 over H.R. 4437, a bill that made illegal presence in the United States a felony. It immediately sparked massive pro-immigrant demonstrations. In the end, Bush's effort at reform died in the Senate with Republican opposition defeating the cloture votes required to bring the legislation to the floor. In the 2008 and 2012 presidential elections, Obama won overwhelmingly among Latino voters. The expectation among Latino activists has been that he would deliver immigration reform that would include a path to citizenship for illegal immigrants. After 2012, Republican strategists became nervous about their prospects among the growing number of Latino voters. That changed the calculus in Washington to a significant extent and has revealed some fault lines within the Republican coalition. But Democrats remain, and are likely to remain, far more supportive of liberal immigration policy than are Republicans, whose divisions remain at this writing the main obstacle to President Obama's new effort at immigration reform.

Language policy presents a more straightforward account of partisan division in congressional voting than the immigration case. There is overwhelming evidence that most Americans regard speaking English as an important criterion for belonging to the country, as well as for getting ahead economically.[36] Controversy over the role of English has ancient echoes in the late nineteenth- and early twentieth-century attacks on teaching German in the schools. In the mid-1980s, language politics erupted again. In 1971, Congress passed the Federal Bilingual Education Act that authorized teaching in a language other than English if a certain percentage (5 percent) of the children in a school district had a native language other than English. But opposition mounted on the grounds both that bilingual education was undermining the place of English as the country's unifying language and that students were being encouraged to retain their native customs rather than assimilate.[37] In 1986, four Western states with large Latino populations amended their state constitutions to designate English as the official language.

The official English measures have proved largely symbolic because implementation was fragmentary, in that courts prevented them from actually restricting the use of non-English languages. They were, however, often accompanied by legislative conflicts over whether to extend provisions for multilingualism in elections and other public services. In roll-call voting in Congress on language policy, partisan differences have been large and consistent. Republicans have always been much more opposed to diverse language rights than Democrats and

---

[35] Tichenor, "Strange Bedfellows."

[36] As described in Chapter 3 of this volume, in 2004 more than 80 percent of both blacks and whites in the General Social Survey (GSS) said that speaking English was very important to making someone "truly American."

[37] Citrin, Reingold, and Green, "American Identity and the Politics of Ethnic Change."

much more fervent in asserting the unique status of English in American life. The major conflicts have revolved around declarations of English as the official language of the United States, proposals to make English fluency a category in evaluating visa applications of immigrants, and the long series of revisions to voting rights that influenced the scope of multilingual balloting. (The roll-call voting data on the flag-burning, immigration, and language votes are provided in online Appendix 9.1.)

One example was the House vote on HR 123, a 1996 resolution declaring English the official language of the United States: 95 percent of Republicans in favor, compared to only 18 percent of the Democrats. In 2007, the Salazar amendment came up for a vote, acknowledging English was the common and unifying language of the land but insisting on no change in existing rights to use non-English languages. It was quickly interpreted by Republicans as a Trojan horse. Only 22 percent of Republican senators supported it, compared to fully 92 percent of the Democratic senators. Similar partisan differences appeared over proposals to eliminate bilingual election materials, to raise (or lower) the numerical criteria for passing tests taken by language minority students, and for requiring federal funding to offset the cost of compliance with bilingual voting requirements.

These partisan differences have been widely recognized, among other things in how interest groups evaluate representatives. The website www.votesmart. org provides both roll-call votes and grades for members of Congress. The anti-immigration group Federation for American Immigration Reform (FAIR) consistently rates Republican votes more favorably; the pro-immigration American Immigration Lawyers Association rates the Democrats more highly. And when it comes to language policy, the group U.S. English, the main proponent of official English laws, gives Republicans a grade of A to A minus and Democrats an F.

Partisan Divisions in the Mass Public

How closely does public opinion conform to this pattern of elite conflict? Table 9.5 uses the two major ongoing national surveys, the ANES and GSS, to report party and ideological differences in the opinions of white Americans on three issues favored by the multicultural movement, as well as on a range of liberal and minority interest groups: affirmative action in hiring, the level of immigration, and English as the country's official language. The table dichotomizes the dependent variables, presenting the proportion opting for the group-conscious response option and using a chi-square test to test for significance.

The table shows consistent partisan and ideological differences in white support for group-targeted policies on all three issues, with Democrats and liberals more favorable than are Republicans or conservatives to affirmative action, increasing immigration, and opposing the designation of English as an official language. Clearly, though, these partisan and ideological differences are weakest and least consistent when it comes to the issue of immigration, a finding that parallels the preceding account of splits on this issue at the elite level.

TABLE 9.5. *Attitudes toward Group-Conscious Policies, by Party Identification and Ideology: National Surveys*

	Preferential Hiring For Blacks (% In Favor)				Desired Immigration Level (% Increased)						English as Official Language (% Opposed)		
	1992 ANES	2004 ANES	2008 ANES	2012 ANES	1992 ANES	1996 GSS	2000 GSS	2004 ANES	2008 ANES	2012 ANES	1992 ANES	1994 GSS	2000 GSS
Democrat	30%	32%	36%	25%	10%[a]	10%[a]	12%[a]	14%[a]	15%[a]	18%	32%[a]	31%[a]	25%[a]
Independent	17	19	21	12	8[ab]	11[a]	9[ab]	10[ab]	14[a]	12[a]	31[a]	30[a]	27[a]
Republican	11	6	5	6	6[b]	7[a]	6[b]	7[b]	14[a]	10[a]	22	21	16
Liberal	27	31	31	27	13	11	15	17	22	23	37	39	28
Moderate	17	17	22	13	8[a]	7[a]	7[a]	8[a]	13[a]	10[a]	26[a]	23[a]	22[a]
Conservative	11	9	13	9	7[a]	8[a]	9[a]	10[a]	16[a]	11[a]	23[a]	24[a]	18[a]
Total	20	17	21	16	9	9	10	11	17	14	28	27	22
Minimum N	560	198	383	792	509	160	263	209	395	792	567	185	259

All respondents included. Between-party and between-ideology differences within each survey are significant ($p < .05$) unless they carry the same superscript.
Source: American National Election Studies (ANES); General Social Survey (GSS).

The Los Angeles data afford us the opportunity to examine partisan polarization broken down by race and ethnicity. The evident polarization at the national level could conceivably mainly reflect divisions between whites and minorities, rather than partisan conflict among whites, for example. Table 9.6 repeats the analysis within ethnic groups in Los Angeles. It is quite evident that multiculturalism sharply polarizes whites. White Democrats and liberals are much more supportive of group-conscious policy positions than are white Republicans and conservatives, regardless of whether the issue is affirmative action, immigration, or language policy. Still, there is more disagreement within partisan groups about immigration than about the other two issues. For example, white Democrats are 21 percent more favorable to affirmative action and 19 percent more favorable to liberal language policies than are white Republicans but only 8 percent more favorable to expanded immigration.

We turn for corroboration to the 2012 ANES as shown in Table 9.5. Responses to the affirmative action in hiring and level of immigration questions there record the levels of strong support for affirmative action and a desire to increase the number of immigrants "a lot." White Democrats are roughly twice as supportive of affirmative action as are white Republicans. Republicans, and white Democrats expressed somewhat more pro-immigrant sentiment than white Republicans. This is consistent with our other findings that show partisanship producing sharper cleavages on affirmative action than immigration. Not surprisingly, there is little partisan polarization about these issues among blacks, who overwhelmingly are Democrats, in either the LA County or national data.

Reinforcing another of our themes throughout the book, we see support for the assimilation hypothesis among Latinos in the Los Angeles data. Among Latinos who are citizens, party identification is closely related to support for immigration and language – just as it is among whites. Indeed, on those issues, so relevant to Latinos in general, Latino citizens are polarized by party just as much as whites are. The same cannot be said for noncitizen Latinos, who are considerably more favorable to benign treatment of the newest immigrants, as we saw in the last chapter. Among ethnic minorities, ideology does not play the same role as party identification in predicting positions on group-conscious issues. Party seems to be a simpler and more powerful political cue for them. Perhaps ideological splits among minorities are linked more closely to lifestyle issues, such as those associated with religious cleavages, than the purely political issues of the sort we focus on in this chapter.

Finally, has partisan polarization about issues targeted to favor minorities increased over the past two decades? Returning to the national data displayed in Table 9.5, we see that polarization certainly did increase concerning affirmative action. The partisan difference increased from 19 percent in 1992 to 31 percent in 2008. However, partisan polarization appeared to diminish again between 2008 and 2012. There is also no clear 1992–2012 trend in the association between affirmative action policy and liberal–conservative self-identification. Changes in the relationships between political outlook and either

TABLE 9.6. *Cross-Tabulations of Support for Group-Conscious Policies by Party Identification and Ideology within Ethnic Groups: Los Angeles Surveys*

	Affirmative Action Index (0 = most opposed to 1 = most in favor)				Desired Immigration Level (0 = decreased a lot to 1 = increased a lot)				Language Policy Index (0 = most nativist to 1 = least nativist)			
	W	B	L-C	L-NC	W	B	L-C	L-NC	W	B	L-C	L-NC
Democrat	.63	.81ᵃ	.57ᵃ	.56ᵃ	.40ᵃ	.31ᵃ	.49ᵃ	.53ᵃ	.44ᵃ	.41	.66ᵃ	.81ᵃ
Independent	.53	.76ᵃ	.56ᵃ	.51ᵃ	.37ᵃᵇ	.36ᵃ	.45ᵃᵇ	.53ᵃ	.39ᵃ	.53ᵃ	.68ᵃ	.84ᵃ
Republican	.42	.80ᵃ	.51ᵃ	.52ᵃ	.32ᵇ	.35ᵃ	.36ᵇ	.49ᵃ	.25	.53ᵃ	.48	.80ᵃ
Liberal	.65	.84ᵃ	.58ᵃ	.58	.43	.33ᵃ	.44ᵃ	.54ᵃ	.51	.47ᵃ	.63ᵃ	.84ᵃ
Moderate	.52	.78ᵃ	.56ᵃ	.51ᵃ	.36	.32ᵃ	.47ᵃ	.52ᵃ	.34	.45ᵃ	.64ᵃ	.82ᵃ
Conservative	.42	.76ᵃ	.52ᵃ	.49ᵃ	.30	.34ᵃ	.44ᵃ	.53ᵃ	.26	.43ᵃ	.66ᵃ	.82ᵃ
Total	.53	.80	.56	.53	.36	.33	.45	.53	.37	.45	.63	.83
Minimum N	224	29	73	28	480	54	139	74	257	27	77	36

W = Whites, B = Blacks, L-C = Latino Citizens, L-NC = Latino Noncitizens. Differences among party or ideological groups within each column are significant ($p < .05$) unless they carry the same superscript.

Affirmative Action index includes preferences for jobs when history of discrimination in company and desired level of government spending on blacks – it includes data from the 1994 and 1995 Los Angeles County Social Surveys (LACSS). Desired immigration level is a single item, available in years 1994–2002 inclusive. Language policy index includes preference for English as an official language and desire for bilingual education in schools, available in 1994, 1998, 2000, and 2001.

immigration or language policy in the general public are much smaller and inconsistent. Overall, the changes in attitudes toward group-conscious policies are small and occur in parallel across those with different political loyalties. With the exception of affirmative action, therefore, the increased partisan divide evident at the elite level does not appear in the general public on these policies. Presumably this is due in part to the internal divisions within parties concerning immigration. It may also reflect the increased racialization of partisanship among whites during the Obama era, which would spill over onto affirmative action more than onto immigration.[38]

MULTICULTURALISM IN THE BROADER ISSUE SPACE

Party polarization in the electorate implies more than increased disagreement between Republicans and Democrats on one or two salient issues, such as abortion rights or tax cuts. Rather, the implication is that ordinary voters are following in the wake of members of Congress and ending up on opposite sides of the liberal–conservative continuum on virtually every issue. In Philip Converse's terms, polarization and party sorting entail high levels of issue constraint *across* issue domains.[39] Fiscal liberals will be social liberals, social conservatives will be fiscal conservatives, and cross-cutting categories like the Reagan Democrats will shrink and soon become things of the past.

But even if this were the case, where in the broader space of national issues would preferences about issues consonant with the multiculturalism agenda fit? The cultural dimension of liberal–conservatism refers to moral issues involving individual choice and the sanction of traditional authorities; the fiscal dimension refers to economic redistribution and the role of the state in regulating the market. As an ideology, multiculturalism has egalitarian and redistributive themes – affirmative action and immigration affect jobs and public benefits, and language policies influence educational and professional opportunities. So one might expect support for multicultural issue positions to be linked to economic liberalism. Yet multiculturalism often focuses on official recognition of the *cultural* equality of minority groups through accommodating language differences and other traditions among new immigrants. Accordingly, one might also anticipate support for multicultural policy to be linked to social or cultural conservatism. So how the multiculturalist policy agenda of group consciousness fits in with the broader panoply of economic and social issues is not self-evident. It could be linked to cultural issues, economic issues, or both. The question is even more indeterminate when we consider the mass public, which is less polarized than party elites and does not show high levels of constraint about the principles of multiculturalism. We therefore examine how positions on group-conscious policies dovetail with issue preferences on matters in other

---

[38] Tesler and Sears, *Obama's Race.*
[39] Converse, "The Nature of Belief Systems in Mass Publics."

policy domains. Here, we use the shorthand of equating "group-conscious" with "multiculturalist" policies to simplify the text.

To address this question, we began by trying to replicate the two-dimensional cultural versus economic solution to political issue space that others have obtained.[40] We performed a principal components factor analysis of eight policy questions that appeared on both the 1992 and 2004 ANES surveys, the national studies we have been relying on for the group-conscious policy issues considered in this chapter. Although not all items were available in the 2012 ANES panel study and the 2012 ANES time series study, we replicated the findings reasonably closely using similar items.[41]

White respondents alone were included in the analysis. To start with, a principal components analysis with an oblimin rotation consistently identified two distinct latent dimensions. One is a cultural policy dimension comprising the abortion, school prayer, and gay rights issues. The other is an economic policy factor comprising questions about whether there should be a government health care plan with universal coverage, whether the government should guarantee everyone a job, whether the government should provide more services or reduce taxes, whether spending on Social Security should be increased or not, whether there should be more spending on health and education services, and whether a large role for government was required rather than trusting the free market to handle society's problems.[42] Analyzed in this way, we did succeed in replicating the two-factor solution separating the economic and cultural dimensions that others have obtained.

The next step was to add the group-conscious policy items in a new principal components analysis.[43] This new analysis extracted a third, multiculturalism component on which the affirmative action, immigration, and language items all loaded .50 or higher in an oblimin rotation. Only the affirmative action item had a relatively high loading on one of the other two dimensions (.43 on the economic policy dimension in 2004 and .53 in 2012). This finding further suggests that the multiculturalism policy dimension related only modestly to other standard issue clusters around which domestic politics has revolved in recent decades. (These factor analyses are shown in online Appendix 9.1.)[44]

---

[40] See D. Sunshine Hillygus and Todd G. Shields, *The Persuadable Voter: Wedge Issues in Presidential Campaigns* (Princeton, NJ: Princeton University Press, 2008).

[41] The details of the differences in the availability and selection of the items for subsequent analysis are spelled out in footnotes 43, 44, 45.

[42] The 1992 study did not ask about gay rights, and the 2004 study did not ask about prayer in the schools so, in each case, there were two items defining the social conservatism–liberalism dimension. For reasons of space, the results of this analysis are provided in an appendix along with the wording of the issue questions.

[43] In the case of the 1992 study, the items referred to affirmative action in hiring, whether immigration should be increased or decreased, and whether English should be named the country's official language. The 2004 study was the same except that the language policy item was not available.

[44] In the 2012 ANES, we were forced to use a slightly different set of available measures. Economic issues included preferred level of spending on health, education, unemployment, and Social

To address the question of cross-domain constraint further, we constructed cultural and economic indices by summing responses to the items making up the two distinct dimensions identified in the first factor analysis. These indices were rescored from 0 to 1, with high scores in the direction of conservatism. Then we correlated those two indices with the specific group-conscious policy items (two, other than three in 1992), keyed such that a high score reflected opposition to multiculturalism. The eighteen resulting correlations are rather low in general; they average $r = .13$, and only one exceeds $r = .15$, as can be seen in Table 9.7. However, most are statistically significant.

Although the three group-conscious items do cluster with each other, as seen in the preceding chapter, their relationships to cultural and economic issues differ somewhat. Affirmative action links strongly to the economic policy domain but is less related to the social issues of abortion, school prayer, and gay rights. This is a hint that policies promoting racial equality and issues relating to cultural recognition may not have the same adherents. However, immigration and language policy attitudes are not closely linked to other issue positions, averaging just $r = .10$.[45]

The only consistent changes in these linkages of multiculturalist issues with other political attitudes between 1992 and 2004 involve affirmative action. Its correlation with the economic policy factor rose from $r = .15$ to $.36$, a correlation that remained high through 2012, and affirmative action became more closely related to partisanship and ideology. As we have seen earlier, partisan polarization over affirmative action among whites has grown over time. Table 9.7 also shows the pattern of correlations of the three issue clusters with patriotism. It has as strong a statistical relationship to group-conscious policies as to social or economic issue positions. Patriotism, like affirmative action, became increasingly linked to both issue factors, as well as to partisanship and ideology.

Security; support for government-guaranteed jobs; preference for spending or services; and support for the Obama healthcare law. Social issues questions included an index of support for gay rights, composed of questions about gay marriage, protection for gays from job discrimination, service of gays in the military, and views on adoption by gays, as well as the standard four-point question soliciting views on abortion (substituting an index created from scales measuring support for abortion under a variety of conditions did not materially change the results). The two multicultural issues questions were affirmative action in hiring and the level of immigration. Again, clear economic and social issues dimensions were evident in the factor analysis, and, again, the immigration level item loaded weakly onto these, although there was also again some evidence of shared variance between affirmative action views and the economic issues. We should note, however, that the results of these analyses are sensitive to specification (principal components analysis versus exploratory factor analysis) and the number and wording of items included, and that the composition of samples varies from study to study. This indicates the need for some caution about the robustness of the finding regarding a distinct multiculturalist issue dimension, which is the dominant outcome in these analyses.

[45] As shown in the third panel of Table 9.7, the correlations are somewhat higher using the 2008–2009 and 2012 items but continue to manifest weak interrelationships.

TABLE 9.7. *Whites' Issue Constraint: National Data (ANES)*

1992	Party Identification	Ideology	Patriotism	Economic Issue Index	Cultural Issue Index	Affirmative Action	Desired Immigration Level	English Official Language
Party ID	1.00	–	–	–	–	–	–	–
Ideology	.39**	1.00	–	–	–	–	–	–
Patriotism	.18**	.21**	1.00	–	–	–	–	–
Economics	.45**	.34**	.15**	1.00	–	–	–	–
Culture	.10	.23**	.07	-.02	1.00	–	–	–
Affirmative action	.21**	.14**	.21**	.15**	.06	1.00	–	–
Immigration level	.07**	.08*	.07*	.03	.07	.11**	1.00	–
English official language	.11**	.13**	.16**	.03	.09*	.16**	.11**	1.00

2004	Party Identification	Ideology	Patriotism	Economic Issue Index	Cultural Issue Index	Affirmative Action	Desired Immigration Level
Party ID	1.00	–	–	–	–	–	–
Ideology	.60**	1.00	–	–	–	–	–
Patriotism	.30**	.28**	1.00	–	–	–	–
Economics	.49**	.50**	.26**	1.00	–	–	–
Culture	.22**	.34**	.13**	.12**	1.00	–	–
Affirmative action	.31**	.29**	.22**	.36**	.02	1.00	–
Immigration level	.07	.14**	.13**	.00	.14**	.10**	1.00

2008–09	Party Identification	Ideology	Patriotism	Economic Issue Index	Cultural Issue Index	Affirmative Action	Illegal Immigration Index
Party ID	1.00	–	–	–	–	–	–
Ideology	.66**	1.00	–	–	–	–	–
Patriotism	.20**	.27**	1.00	–	–	–	–

(continued)

TABLE 9.7 (continued)

2008-09	Party Identification	Ideology	Patriotism	Economic Issue Index	Cultural Issue Index	Affirmative Action	Illegal Immigration Index
Economics	.45**	.44**	.19**	1.00	–	–	–
Culture	.49**	.66**	.25**	.31**	1.00	–	–
Affirmative action	.25**	.24**	.11**	.28**	.18**	1.00	–
Illegal immigration Index	.21**	.28**	.09**	.11*	.22**	.24**	1.00

2012	Party Identification	Ideology	Patriotism	Economic Issue Index	Cultural Issue Index	Affirmative Action	Desired Level of Immigration
Party ID	1.00						
Ideology	.68**	1.00					
Patriotism	.17**	.25**	1.00				
Economics	.59**	.61**	.15**	1.00			
Culture	.43**	.49**	.11**	.37**	1.00		
Affirmative action	.31**	.33**	.15**	.38**	.14**	1.00	
Desired level of immigration	.15**	.19**	.09**	.11**	.19**	.17**	1.00

**$p < .01$ *$p < .05$. Entries are Pearson correlation coefficients. Sample is whites only. Due to item availability differences, 2008–09 items are substantially different from those in 1992 and 2004. The 1992 and 2004 Economic Issue Index includes government health insurance, government guarantee of jobs/standard of living, federal spending and services, and government versus free market economy. Cultural Issue Index includes school prayer and abortion for 1992, and gays in the military and abortion for 2004. For specific items used in the 2008–09 and 2012 American National Election Studies (ANES) surveys, please consult footnote 40. Affirmative action and illegal immigration items are keyed so that higher values represent more opposition to the proposed policies. Other variables coded so that higher values represent greater conservatism. High values on patriotism indicate more patriotic attitudes.

This is some indication that both patriotism and affirmative action are participants in the "great sort" that is dividing the more partisan segments of the electorate into increasingly cohesive camps. And, to the extent that minority groups at the lower end of the economic ladder continue to disproportionately favor the Democrats, that party's leadership will be pushed toward supporting multiculturalist positions that have limited support among its white identifiers.

DOES PARTISANSHIP EXPLAIN THE CLASH OF MULTICULTURALISM WITH PATRIOTISM?

One of our central questions throughout this study is whether multiculturalism is associated with a diminished sense of national identity, so reducing national unity. We began in Chapter 5 with norms of multiculturalism. In Chapters 7 and 8, we turned to policy issues intended to benefit specific racial and ethnic groups. There we found that, indeed, the two foci of identity clash among whites, but not among minorities. That is, support for group-conscious positions was indeed correlated with weak patriotism and other forms of attachment to the nation among whites, but that correlation was not present among minorities. This finding was somewhat contrary to the fears expressed by Huntington and others who have worried that declining national attachment might be harmed by demographic multiculturalism rather than by increased divisions among the majority whites.

But do the lower levels of patriotism found among the stronger white supporters of multiculturalist positions on group-conscious issues reflect instead merely collateral damage from the rising partisan polarization that seems to be infecting all major political issues? To test that possibility requires that we reassess those associations with controls for partisanship. Hence, we conducted multivariate regression analyses in the 1992 ANES (all three issues), the 1994 (language) and 1996 GSS (immigration), and the 2012 ANES (affirmative action and immigration). Party identification and patriotism were treated as predictors of policy preferences, after controlling for the background variables of age, education, gender, and region (South/not-South).[46] Again, we do not show these analyses to save space but make them available on request.

What is striking is that weaker patriotism continues to be significantly related to greater white support for multicultural positions on the group-conscious policies examined, even with party identification controlled. This is true both for affirmative action and language policy from 1992 on ($p < .01$ in each of the five models tested). Clearly, affirmative action and language policy are issues that allocate tangible and symbolic costs and benefits differently across ethnic groups. Therefore, it is particularly noteworthy that feelings of patriotism, which arguably reflect a distinctive conception of the American national

---

[46] We did not include ideology in these analyses because of its high correlation with party identification.

community, promote opposition to positions that benefit racial minorities and immigrants. On the other hand, patriotism survived as a significant predictor of whites' anti-immigration policy preferences, with party identification controlled in only the 2012 ANES, another indication of the fractured partisan status of immigration as an issue.

We repeated these analyses with the Los Angeles data, where we could look separately at all three main ethnic groups. Again, our regression equations used patriotism as a predictor of policy preferences, with party identification and demographic variables included as controls. In this case, we also included the ethnic identity index as a control to test once again the possible competition between national and ethnic identities. Among whites in Los Angeles, patriotism has an even stronger and more consistent association with opposition to group-conscious preferences (including anti-immigration sentiments) than it had in the national samples, even with party identification controlled. Among whites, too, a sense of ethnic consciousness had a significant but lesser effect, appearing only on the desire to reduce immigration. So the tension between patriotism and multiculturalism persists even when the partisan cleavages with which both are correlated are taken into account.

The data are again contrary to those fearful that multiculturalism will be associated with divisions over national unity among black respondents. We continue to find no link between weak patriotism and support for group-conscious policies among blacks, even after adding controls for partisanship. Among Latinos, too, we continue to find little association between weak patriotism and such policy preferences, even controlling for partisanship. Patriotism does not have a significant relationship to any of the three policy attitudes, among either citizen or noncitizen Latinos.[47] However, here, stronger ethnic identification is significantly connected to support for multiculturalism on all three policies, at least among citizens. Perhaps they are the ones most engaged by such issues. For noncitizens, stronger ethnic identities are strongly linked to support for liberal language policies but not to the other issue preferences. Language is, of the three policy areas, arguably the one that presumably affects noncitizens the most tangibly. In short, once again, the divisive effects of multiculturalism occur primarily among whites, rather than among ethnic minorities.

CONCLUSION

In this chapter, we raise the question of how partisan politics fits into our story. We begin with the consensus among political observers, including political scientists, that political elites have become increasingly polarized along partisan

---

[47] Again, we use the citizen versus noncitizen comparison because we are examining the role of partisanship, which is primarily relevant for those eligible to vote. The exception again is the 2012 ANES citizen-only sample.

and ideological lines. There is less agreement about whether the mass public, too, has become more polarized.

Here, we present data on partisan and ideological polarization of the two components of public opinion we have focused on, patriotism and multiculturalism. We show that in national surveys patriotism is very much a focal point of partisan and ideological division. Republicans and conservatives seemed to have captured the flag and other symbols of attachment to the nation. That is true in the Los Angeles surveys as well, and it is true within each major ethnic and racial group. Among Latinos, however, such partisan polarization over patriotism occurs only among citizens. We take that as another sign of the gradual political assimilation of that population over time that we have seen in other ways earlier in this volume.

Partisan and ideological polarization seems to affect support for multicultural norms unevenly. In national surveys, it does not affect perceptions of the strength of ethnic differences nor ethnic group consciousness. However, Democrats and liberals are more supportive of the recognition of minority groups and less insistent on their assimilation than are Republicans and conservatives. Descriptive representation is not popular in any partisan or ideological camp. When we turned to the Los Angeles data and examined difference between ethnic groups, we find patterns very similar to the national data among whites but little involvement of partisanship among minorities.

When we look at policy issues, we find that support for multiculturalism is likewise quite closely associated with both partisanship and ideology in national surveys. The Los Angeles data again tell us this reflects divisions among whites alone. This is but one indication that multiculturalism does indeed divide Americans, but not where its critics usually look for conflict. As an ideology, multiculturalism is a component of the partisan divisions among the majority whites more than it is a cleavage between whites and minorities.

A central theme of this volume is the possible tension between patriotism and national identity, on the one hand, and multiculturalism and ethnic identity, on the other. In the preceding chapter, we found that positions on three prominent group-conscious policies sympathetic to multiculturalism were indeed linked to weaker expressions of patriotism, at least among whites. Minorities were more supportive of these policies, but that did not interfere with their patriotism. In this chapter, we find considerable partisan polarization about multiculturalism and about patriotism among whites, but partisanship is not responsible for the link between the two. Multiculturalism has little to do with minorities' national identities, contrary to the fears of its leading critics.

Although national attachment is the modal position among all partisan and ideological groups, the intensity of such feelings is greater among Republicans and conservatives than among Democrats and liberals. Moreover, the normative content of American identity has somewhat divergent meanings among these political camps, and they also diverge on group-conscious issues. This raises the issue of whether the common emotional attachment to America will fray as minority groups supporting aspects of the multicultural agenda increasingly align with the Democratic party, and competing notions of what it means to be an American and how to cope with ethnic diversity dovetail with party lines and with other issues polarizing the nation. Rather than the fact of diversity, it is the way in which parties perceive the incentives of particular appeals that may either reinforce or shatter the traditional consensus on American identity and attachment to the nation.

10

Conclusion

The catalyst for this book was the confluence of increased ethnic diversity and the rise of identity politics in the United States beginning in the mid-1960s due to the civil rights movement and immigration reform. These developments raised anew questions about the solidity of a shared American identity and the capacity to sustain a sense of social solidarity in a multiethnic polity. After years in which the racial divide defined intergroup relations in the United States, a massive and ongoing influx of Hispanic and Asian immigrants complicated the dynamics of ethnic relations in the United States by adding new modes of perception, interaction, and conflict. That the new Americans were neither white nor of European origin raised doubts about whether the historical patterns of assimilation – as promoted by the idea of the melting pot – would recur.

Our book addressed the enduring problem of *e pluribus unum* in this context of demographic and political change. Demography may become destiny, but only as shaped by politics and culture. In the contemporary world, the choice confronting elites was how to accommodate claims for recognition and representation by minority groups. These claims we and others group under the rubric of multiculturalism, which when viewed as an ideology represents a new approach for governing a multiethnic polity.

Historically, two competing narratives have shaped American thinking about the relationship of ethnicity to politics and culture. Philip Gleason summarizes the liberal cosmopolitan approach, writing that "to be or to become an American, a person did not have to have any particular national, linguistic, religious, or ethnic background. All he had to do was to commit himself to the political ideology centered on the abstract ideals of liberty, equality, and republicanism."[1] In other words, American nationality was universalistic in character. Of course, American history revealed the failure to implement the inclusive

[1] Gleason, "American Identity and Americanization."

stance in practice. The treatment of blacks and Native Americans stands out, but, in addition, every subsequent wave of immigration engendered resistance in the form of nativism (or ethnocentrism). Immigrants were opposed in part because they did not fit a conception of American identity defined in racial, ethnic, and religious terms. White, Anglo-Saxon Protestants were the national prototype; in the ethnocultural version of American identity, belonging meant not just belief in democratic ideals but assimilation to a particular culture. Immigrants, who were needed for economic purposes, nevertheless had to past this test, whose content varied over time but that always included learning English as a key marker of national identity.

Recent scholarship has come to emphasize that all nations have a cultural core that goes beyond mere acceptance of democratic political principles.[2] For Samuel Huntington, this meant that American identity encompassed not just the democratic creed but religious belief, adhering to Anglo-Protestant values, speaking English, and maintaining a European cultural heritage.[3] From this vantage point, it is easy to suppose that massive immigration from widely divergent cultures would threaten national unity, a threat perhaps best addressed either by altering the rules governing visa preferences – a tall order in a political system hostile to change – or by strengthening programs to accelerate linguistic and cultural assimilation. These ideas are congenial to the nativist narrative of American nationhood, a perspective that holds that only people of certain background have the moral and cultural perquisites for democratic citizenship.

Both the liberal conception of American identity – in either its pure civic or more culturalist incarnation – and its nativist counterpart agree on the need to prioritize nationality over ethnicity to achieve collective goals. Multiculturalism, which arose in the 1970s as a different approach for managing cultural diversity, sometimes has taken a radically different tack, arguing that preserving differences in values and cultural traditions rather than pursuing assimilation to dominant norms was both morally valid and ultimately compatible with social solidarity.

Writing recently, Sarah Song comments that some of today's leading multiculturalists advocate *deeper* diversity that goes beyond Horace Kallen's earlier version of cultural pluralism that accepted assimilation in matters *political*.[4] The idea of deeper diversity seems to imply that minority groups, both immigrants and others, have distinctive modes of belonging to America because of their particular experiences of exclusion and different ways of being "political." These modes should be recognized and given a rightful share of the nation's self-definition. This precept seems to challenge the legitimacy of the dominant

[2] Anthony D. Smith, *The Ethnic Origins of Nations* (Oxford: Blackwell, 1986), 216.
[3] Huntington, *Who Are We?*, 20, cited in Sarah Song, "What It Means to Be an American?" *Daedalus* (Spring 2009): 31–39.
[4] Song, "What It Means to Be an American?," 37.

conception of a nation's identity and throws it open to political renegotiation, an enterprise that seems bound to spark a backlash.

Our book skirted the philosophical fray about which identities should be validated. Nor did we engage in policy analysis about the consequences of adopting group-conscious policies or other multiculturalist principles. Instead, we measured public opinion and described how ordinary citizens balance their national and ethnic identifications and how these multiple identities shape responses to the guiding principles of the multiculturalist solution for *e pluribus unum*. A signal feature of our approach was to take repeated looks not just at global opinion or that of the majority whites, but to probe the differences and similarities across America's majority and minority groups.

We began our research in the mid-1990s, when elite debates about multiculturalism centered on its centrifugal potential. Would identity politics, with its elevation of the ethnic part over the national whole, break America apart? Writing some fifteen years later, we would question assertions that the nation has moved beyond multiculturalism into some "postethnic" or "postracial" era today.[5] True, the historic election of Barack Obama and progress in growing a black middle class, along with evidence of the ongoing assimilation of immigrants, provide some evidence of the declining salience of ethnicity in some domains. Yet the sobering statistics on black unemployment and incarceration, the continuing racial gap in income, the ethnic differences in policy attitudes when group interests are engaged, and compelling evidence of the racialization of the Obama candidacies and his administration lead us to conclude that the tensions emanating from ethnic diversity are as relevant as ever.[6]

In exploring ethnic differences in opinion, we have considered the fit between our results and alternative theoretical paradigms drawn from the study of group consciousness in psychology. One paradigm is labeled "politicized group consciousness," a perspective that maintains that members of all ethnic groups, including whites, feel a strong sense of group identity that can undermine a common attachment to the nation and that they are motivated in the political realm by distinctive group interests. The second perspective is "black exceptionalism," which holds that because of their unique experience of discrimination and exclusion in the United States, blacks stand apart in the intensity of their ethnic identities and in their cohesive pursuit of political goals. Finally, the assimilation paradigm, in some ways the close cousin of black exceptionalism, holds that today's largest other minority groups – Hispanics and Asian immigrants – are,

---

[5] David A. Hollinger, "Authority, Solidarity, and the Political Economy of Identity: The Case of the United States," *Diacritics* 29, no. 4 (1999): 116–27.

[6] Donald R. Kinder, and Allison Dale-Riddle, *The End of Race?: Obama, 2008, and Racial Politics in America* (New Haven, CT: Yale University Press, 2012); Michael Tesler and David O. Sears, *Obama's Race: The 2008 Election and the Dream of a Post-Racial America* (Chicago, IL: University of Chicago Press, 2010); Michael Tesler, "The Spillover of Racialization into Health Care: How President Obama Polarized Public Opinion by Racial Attitudes and Race," *American Journal of Political Science*, 56 (2012): 690–705.

over time, likely to acculturate to the positions of the dominant white majority, as did their European predecessors; although, as usually written, it does not say as much about African Americans. By now, the reader must realize that we regard the politicized group consciousness model as having limited applicability but that black exceptionalism and assimilation together capture many of our findings.

NATIONAL ATTACHMENT

Our first question was whether American national identity is waning. Anyone writing an obituary for American patriotism, in joy or in sorrow, should wait a while. Americans of all ethnicities feel positive about their national identity by most measures of national attachment in studies conducted from 1992 to 2012. Expressions of pride in and love of country are pervasive and more widespread than in almost every other advanced democracy. And although chauvinistic expressions of America's superiority to other countries also are plentiful, they are far less common than what has been termed "constructive" patriotism, an outlook that combines a strong emotional attachment to one's country with recognition that it is not perfect. The enduring strength of American national identity is confirmed by numerous other studies cited earlier.

More important for our purposes was the finding that ethnic differences in patriotic feelings were modest at best, belying the claims of social psychological theories emphasizing the intractability of intergroup conflict and the idea that people regard American as "white." In our data, drawn from a number of national and local surveys, blacks are somewhat less positive about the country than are whites, particularly when asked about their feelings for the American flag. They were also understandably less likely to express pride about America's history or its treatment of all social groups. So there is a racial divide in the strength of American identity, but it is manifesting itself at the high end of the continuum of national attachment. The majority outlook among blacks is one of strong commitment to their country and no desire to move elsewhere.

Our analyses also should assuage fears that immigration, especially from Latin America, is eroding national attachment. It seems implausible to expect recent immigrants to be as likely to think of themselves as American or to feel as positively about the country as the as native-born. More important is that native-born Latinos are just as patriotic as whites. This finding is consistent in both the national and Los Angeles data, and it holds with relevant background factors controlled. Over time, assimilation to the patriotic norm clearly is occurring among Hispanic immigrants and, although there is no direct evidence available to us, there is no reason to doubt that a similar trajectory of growing patriotism as more time is spent in the United States is occurring among Asian Americans.

We also examined the content of American national identity, including beliefs about the prototypical "true American," delineating the subjective boundaries of membership in the so-called American "circle of we." A politicized group consciousness approach might suggest that each ethnic group would define the prototypical American in self-promoting terms: the dominant whites in terms of ancestry, nativity, language, and religion; blacks in terms of nativity and language, along with egalitarian values; whereas Latinos and Asians might shy away from these ethnocultural attitudes and emphasize factors such as citizenship, respect for the laws, and economic self-reliance.

However, our national data find consensus across ethnic groups in this respect as well. All give the greatest importance to commitment to the civic American creed, stressing equal treatment of all people, working hard to get ahead, and respecting American laws and institutions as the primary components of being a true American. In addition, all ethnic groups stress the importance of speaking English, which we interpret not as an exclusionary statement but rather recognition that full participation in American economic and political life requires knowing English. The Pew surveys of Hispanic and Asian Americans consistently confirm that these streams of immigrants endorse the importance of linguistic assimilation, as do Deborah Schildkraut's and Theiss-Morse's surveys using items on the qualities of a true American that are similar to ours. Their surveys also confirm the numerical predominance of civic over ethnic conceptions of American identity. Only 7 percent in Theiss-Morse's national survey said that being white was important for being a true American.[7] Similarly, in a 2008 national internet survey, Matthew Wright, Jack Citrin, and Jonathan Wand found that 55 percent of the respondents were "pure civics," only 5 percent pure "ethnics," and 18 percent partial "ethnics."[8]

Partisan cleavages over patriotism are in fact more glaring than ethnic differences. American politicians of virtually every stripe salute the flag, proclaim the nation's greatness, and, perhaps now more than ever, say glowingly that we are a nation of immigrants. This consensual patriotism notwithstanding, for most of the period since World War II, at the elite level Republicans have sought to seize the mantle of patriotism, sometimes putting the Democrats on the defensive. We earlier used the flag-burning disputes in Congress as an example. In the mass public, we find consistent and substantial partisan differences in patriotism that mirror elite cleavages, especially among whites. Conservative opponents of multiculturalism worry about the country being divided along ethnic lines, damaging consensual attachment to the nation. But equally noteworthy, if not more so, is the partisan polarization among whites about the symbols of patriotism.

ETHNIC IDENTITY AND CONSCIOUSNESS

In complex modern societies, the social self has multiple identities. These group memberships are often nested, with, for example, ethnic or regional identities clustered within the larger national unit. The presence of multiple identities

---

[7] Theiss-Morse, *Who Counts As an American?*, 45.
[8] Matthew Wright, Jack Citrin, and Jonathan Wand, "Alternative Measures of American National Identity: Implications for the Civic-Ethnic Distinction," *Political Psychology* 33 (2012): 469–82.

raises the questions of prioritization and compatibility, as between national attachment and loyalty to one's ethnic group. One would have to be blind to deny the salience of ethnic affinity in American politics. Indeed, partisan divides linked to religion and ethnicity were a feature of American history from the beginning, and the strength of ethnic ties among successive waves of immigrants is often cited as one reason for the absence of socialism in the United States.[9] Clearly, ethnicity is fairly salient for the identities of ethnic minorities in contemporary America. For example, in our Los Angeles data, 55 percent of blacks and 75 percent of foreign-born Latinos thought of themselves as an [ethnic] person "very often." It is considerably less pervasive among whites, only 11 percent of whom gave the same response. But we need to be clear about terminology. The salience of ethnicity for one's self-concept does not guarantee the kind of politicized ethnic group consciousness posited by multiculturalism.

Our general finding is that politicized group consciousness is not very common in American ethnic groups, even among minorities sometimes described as subordinated groups in the American racial hierarchy. Evidence for this comes from our typology of aggrieved ethnic consciousness, which incorporates strength of ethnic identity, a sense of common fate with other group members, and the respondent's perception of being discriminated against due to his or her group membership. In Los Angeles, only 25 percent of blacks, 14 percent of Latinos, and 5 percent of Asians scored above the overall sample median on all three dimensions, and a miniscule 1 percent of whites met that standard. The psychological foundation for multiculturalism, then – large numbers of minorities who have a strong sense of ethnic consciousness combined with a feeling of one's ethnic group being victimized – seems to be present only for blacks, even in the Los Angeles metropolitan area, which is sometimes described as America's premier third-world region.

A second key psychological foundation for multiculturalism should be perceptions of endemic interethnic conflict. Here, our evidence was mixed. In the Los Angeles surveys, clear majorities in all ethnic groups perceived themselves as "in conflict" rather than "getting along." However, only a minority felt that ethnic diversity had hurt the quality of life; a majority seemed confident that group relations would improve in the future and perceived that conflict has diminished over time.

Ethnic cleavages on group-conscious policies in the domains of race, immigration, and language are present, of course. Those cleavages seem to parallel each group's interests. Whites are consistent in being most opposed to allocating benefits to minorities in all three domains. The positions of the three main minority groups varied according to how each issue engages their particular group's interests. Blacks were most favorable to race-targeted policies. Latinos and Asians most approved of increased immigration. Latinos had the greatest sympathy for undocumented immigrants and support for bilingual education.

---

[9] Lipset and Marks, *It Didn't Happen Here*.

None of these ethnic cleavages is surprising. However, they speak to the absence of a unified people-of-color coalition of minorities allied against whites.

Moreover, this apparently group-interested response to group-conscious policies among ethnic minorities should not be interpreted as necessarily propelled by their ethnic group consciousness. Blacks' ethnic identities were not significantly related to greater support for group-conscious policies in any domain, once appropriate controls for other factors are introduced. On the other hand, stronger ethnic identities among Latinos were linked to greater policy support in all three domains, especially for liberal language policies. Whites' more muted ethnic identifications were significantly related only to restricting immigration. All in all, minorities' ethnic identities are sometimes contributors to group-interested policy attitudes, but not consistently and rarely centrally. In this sense, growing ethnic diversity seems not to be producing enough group consciousness to trigger strong centrifugal pressures in the broader society.

COLLISION OF AMERICAN AND ETHNIC IDENTITY?

We earlier used a nesting metaphor to describe the possible interrelationship of national and ethnic identities, with the latter nested within the former. That peaceful image should not lead one to overlook the possibilities for tension in the psychological and political relations between nationality and ethnicity, especially among racial and ethnic minorities. Indeed, an enduring controversy is whether national and ethnic identities are compatible or collide. In other words, does a stronger sense of ethnic consciousness among minority groups weaken their patriotic attachment to the nation, as critics of multiculturalism often claim?

Our public opinion data provide little support for this anxiety because we find no evidence that minorities with a strong sense of ethnic consciousness frequently are alienated from the nation as a whole. To begin, we remind readers that only a minority of blacks and Latinos chose to define themselves in purely ethnic terms, preferring either the "just American" or hyphenated ethnic-American self-categorization. More to the point, we examined a larger number of general population surveys and a broader array of measures than have previous studies, but failed in this comprehensive search to find any trace of a negative association between ethnic identification and national attachment among blacks and Latinos.

A collision of the national attachment and ethnic identification appeared only among the small group of minority respondents who combined a strong sense of ethnic consciousness with feelings of grievance founded on perceived discrimination against their group. Such politicization of ethnic consciousness among minorities has, in other nations, channeled hostility against common national symbols and institutions. In the American context, however, this conflict of minorities' ethnic pride with patriotic feelings has been quite limited.

Patriotism as it is usually measured is an emotional construct; it refers to love and admiration of one's country and its dominant symbols such as the flag, anthem, monuments, and historical triumphs. This diffuse feeling can plausibly be attached to quite different policies – for example, both support for or opposition to drilling for oil on public lands. Here, we considered the association of patriotism to group-conscious policies favored by multiculturalists and other advocates for the interests of minority groups. Is support for these policies, generally opposed by whites, linked to weaker patriotism among minority group members? Not consistently. Patriotism was not negatively associated with greater support for either race-targeted or liberal immigration policies among blacks and Latinos. In the case of language policy, however, patriotism boosted support for official English, albeit only modestly, and represented a case of national attachment opposing the multiculturalist defense of bilingualism.

Among whites, however, there is a clearer clash between patriotism and support for multiculturalist positions of these group-conscious policies. These results emerge in both the Los Angeles data and in national surveys conducted between 1992 and 2012. Among whites, Republican Party affiliation is both positively associated with patriotism and negatively related to policy positions consistent with multiculturalism. Does partisanship therefore explain the link of patriotism to opposition to group-conscious policies among whites? No. Patriotism, as measured by emotional attachment to the country and its leading symbols, has a significant and consistent association with opposition to such policies even after controls for party and ideology are included.[10] Moreover, nativist views about the boundaries of the national community intensify this relationship. This is a troubling intrusion of patriotism into domestic political concerns bearing on minorities' well-being. From a normative perspective, this apparent conflict among white Americans between national attachment and acceptance of policies designed to benefit racial minorities and immigrants has potential hazards, including the persistence of deadlock over immigration policy, as well as increased disaffection among minorities.

To summarize, we find America's new ethnic diversity to be quite compatible with maintaining a pervasive sense of national attachment. Despite some differences by race and nativity, patriotism is the norm among all the main ethnic groups. What remains a consistent fault line is the lesser patriotism among younger Americans. They are more reluctant than older generations to endorse the idea of a unique national identity worthy of enthusiastic support. This more detached outlook among the vanguard, along with disaffection among a bloc of blacks, seem together to be a greater challenge to national solidarity than immigration. Although we have repeatedly argued that the image of America as a balkanized society, with ethnic groups at each other's throats, is quite misleading, the collision among whites between patriotism and group-conscious policies aimed at helping minorities is sobering because it may signal growing polarization on ethnic lines tied to partisan conflict. The pervasive love of

---

[10] See Chapter 9; Citrin and Wright, "Defining the Circle of We"; Schildkraut, *Americanization in the Twenty-First Century*; Theiss-Morse, *Who Counts As an American?*

country does not preclude the mobilization of emotions in ways that heighten ethnic tensions.

MULTICULTURALISM IN AMERICAN PUBLIC OPINION

The United States, unlike Canada and Australia, has not declared itself a multi-cultural country. It has nevertheless adopted many policies consistent with multiculturalist goals. These include, among many other things, affirmative action programs that include immigrants as beneficiaries, bilingual education and ballots, the official designation of ethnic history months, and a Voting Rights Act intended to assure the representation of minority legislators. Beyond the political sphere, diversity is a word on almost everyone's lips and a driving force behind policies in a range of institutions. In higher education, many colleges promote recruitment of students and faculty from underrepresented minority groups, build ethnic studies programs, provide advising and support services that target minority students, and monitor behavior to assure sensitivity to and sympathy for cultural differences. Multiculturalism centers are a staple of University of California campuses and doubtless elsewhere as well. In the private sector, similar efforts at recruitment and attentiveness to cultural differences among employees have spread. Demographic change creates market opportunities, such as in ethnic food sections in supermarkets or the development of niche products aimed at specific ethnic groups. As more ethnic minorities move into the middle class, car dealers and other merchants increasingly employ more racially and ethnically diverse sales forces to appeal to broader customer bases.

Following Kymlicka and other theorists, we have portrayed multiculturalism, in its ideological incarnation, as a formula for justice and solidarity in a multi-ethnic society. This is to be achieved by redistributing power and privilege to provide minority groups greater equality in the realms of politics, economics, and culture. We have contrasted a maximalist hard with a minimalist soft variant of multiculturalism. The core of hard multiculturalism is that race or ethnicity should be a key basis on which a variety of important benefits are allocated, ranging from legislative seats to places in college, jobs, awards, and time on public radio, among other things.[11] Communal representation on the basis of proportionality is the ultimate weapon of hard multiculturalism. The effort to institutionalize group-conscious allocation of benefits is something of a departure from America's historical prioritization of individualism and merit-based competition and to some degree reflects the familiar distinction between equality of opportunity and equality of results.

The softer version of multiculturalism shares the desire for greater equality for minority groups and for the preservation of minority cultures. Although eschewing communal representation based on a quota system or political vetoes for

---

[11] Gender is often also a basis for such equitable allocations in multiculturalist ideology, but as already noted we do not address that in this volume.

minority groups, as in the idea of a confederation, soft multiculturalism also calls for governments to give official recognition and tangible support for the maintenance of minority cultures. Soft multiculturalism emphasizes treating minorities with greater respect; frowning on explicit antiminority prejudice; paying more attention to minority cultures and history in the school curriculum; implementing bilingual education, balloting, and public services; and recognizing the achievements of minority groups through public holidays and other displays. Both variants of multiculturalism accept the idea of some exemptions from general rules on religious or cultural grounds, deviating in this way from the liberal principle of nondiscrimination, but this is an issue on which our surveys were silent.

Just as with multiculturalism, one can distinguish between a hard version exemplified by the Americanization program of the early twentieth century and a soft version of assimilation that conforms more closely to current attitudes. Indeed, acceptance of facets of soft multiculturalism, which favors the integration of immigrants into mainstream society on pluralistic terms, dovetails rather than conflicts with the milder version of the assimilationist ethos. Yes, there is an insistence on learning English and patriotism, but little objection to bilingual ballots, bilingual signage in urban areas with large immigrant communities, ticket-balancing, holidays that now include Cinco de Mayo as well as St. Patrick's Day, and the incorporation of new words, foods, music, dances, and modes of entertainment into American popular culture. The preservation of most ethnic traditions through voluntary associations also seems unproblematic to the public, although Americans generally object to the idea of government funding for preserving cultural differences.

Given the realities of demographic change and the intensity of the debate about multiculturalism among political and academic elites, it is surprising that prior studies have given so little attention to public opinion about multiculturalism's guiding principles. Our own surveys did ask a number of questions specifically about multiculturalist norms and found strong resistance to the harder variant. All ethnic groups were strongly opposed to such hard multiculturalist proposals for institutionalizing descriptive representation for legislative and professional positions as apportioning legislative seats according to an ethnic group's size in the population. Majorities of all groups also are suspicious of organizations based on ethnicity alone, viewing them as contributing to separatism. There was more support for multicultural norms among the minority groups targeted as its beneficiaries than among whites, but the divergence was generally modest. The more important conclusion is that hard multiculturalism fails to resonate strongly in American public opinion, and so it falls short as a theory of how to accomplish a unified national identity in an increasingly diverse society.

At the same time, a close reading of the data suggests substantial support for softer versions of multiculturalism. Most notably, many Americans view cultural pluralism as compatible with widespread cultural assimilation. For example, both whites and blacks were divided about whether immigrants and minority groups should blend into the mainstream or maintain their distinctive cultures. There was also wide tolerance for persisting ethnic differences and support for the voluntary efforts of ethnic and racial groups to maintain their traditions and for giving more attention to ethnic and racial history in schools. Most Americans in a 2002 General Social Survey (GSS) agreed that ethnic minority groups are different from each other and from whites. But respondents did not accept the essentialist view that these differences were unshakeable. Less than one-fifth of whites, blacks, and Latinos agreed that ethnic minority groups will never really fit in with mainstream American culture.

Preferences about group-conscious policies in part parallel ethnic group interests, as just noted. Beyond that, the balance of opinion is again a combination of opposition to positions consistent with hard multiculturalism and acceptance of pragmatic soft policies that recognize ethnic diversity and aid minority mobility without challenging dominant American values. Accordingly, majorities in all ethnic groups oppose explicit race-targeted preferences or quotas in hiring, promotion, and college admissions. At the same time, there is support in all ethnic groups for government efforts to assist blacks, particularly in a context of discriminatory conduct. Similarly, for the past forty years, more Americans in all ethnic groups have favored reducing than have favored increasing immigration, and majorities of blacks and whites support tighter border security and more deportation. However, in a softer vein, a large bloc of opinion says the current high level of immigration should stay the same, and birthright citizenship for the children of legal immigrants is widely endorsed.

Public opinion on language policy reveals broad opposition to the official recognition of bilingualism, at least among blacks and whites who generally instead support English as an official language. Large segments of Latinos and Asians feel differently, however, and only a minority of Latinos voted in favor of state initiatives proposing "official English" or limiting bilingual education.[12] Interestingly, though, even Latinos and Asians do not support the lasting use of bilingualism in the schools, the vast majority insisting that all children learn English. At the same time, however, practical programs that allow some language flexibility for the non-English-proficient win approval. There is support in all ethnic groups for bilingual ballots and for bilingual education, if it is framed as a path toward learning English rather than for maintaining cultural differences. Even those who want less immigration advocate giving visa preferences to those who conform to the cultural norms of speaking English and working hard, according to another study.[13]

---

[12] Jack Citrin, Beth Reingold, and Donald P. Green, "American Identity and the Politics of Ethnic Change"; Campbell, Wong, and Citrin, "Racial Threat, Partisan Climate, and Direct Democracy: Contextual Effects in Three California Initiatives."

[13] Jens Hainmuller and Daniel Hopkins, "The Hidden American Immigration Consensus: A Conjoint Analysis of Attitudes toward Immigrants," *SSRN Working Paper Number 2106116* (2012).

What are the prospects for increased support for the more fundamental principles of hard multiculturalism? Here, one obstacle may be the lack of coherence in public thinking. The normative principles animating multiculturalism may constitute coherent belief systems for many political and academic elites, but they have not been at the forefront of elite political debate. In the mass public, party and ideology are not closely associated with opinions on hard multicultural norms, such as guarantees for descriptive representation. The rare exceptions are those debated in the political arena, such as the amount of attention that should be paid to minority groups in history classes, where Republicans and conservatives are more likely to oppose multiculturalist principles. Perhaps as a result, these ideas have not penetrated the mass public in ways that produce broad recognition of a coherent multiculturalist ideology. That is, empirically, we fail to find any real connections among the various normative ideas, values, and beliefs that support a politics of difference.

Preferences about group-conscious policies, however, do have considerably greater resonance in partisan politics. Democratic elites are considerably more favorable than Republicans to affirmative action for blacks and other minorities, of course. But elites in both parties are internally divided on immigration issues. Republican free-market ideologues, high-tech industries, and agribusiness favor an expansive policy, whereas more populist organizations highlight the costs of immigration, and nativists resist the infusion of still more foreigners into a nation still dominated by those of European ancestry. On the Democratic side, opposition to liberal immigration policies, such as a pathway to citizenship for the undocumented, has eroded, although some environmentalists, labor unions, and black leaders retain restrictionist sentiments. Over time, congressional voting on immigration issues has become more sharply divided along partisan lines, with Republicans more opposed to liberalization of access and immigrant rights than are Democrats.[14] Partisan polarization is even more evident on language issues, where Republicans almost unanimously line up in favor of English-only proposals whereas Democrats unite in opposition.

This greater partisan cleavage over group-conscious policies than over more abstract multicultural norms perhaps reflects the fact that the latter are vaguer and less crystallized in the mass public than are the more widely debated policy issues. This by no means guarantees a continuing lack of partisan polarization over multicultural norms. Cues from party elites with highly constrained belief systems may over time trickle down and produce responses in the mass public. In addition, the greater allegiance of most Latinos and Asians to Democrats rather than Republicans may enhance the polarization of the parties along ethnic as well as ideological lines.

---

[14] Peter H. Schuck, "The Disconnect between Public Attitudes and Policy Outcomes in Immigration," in *The Politics of Immigration Reform*, ed. Carol Swain (Cambridge: Cambridge University Press, 2007), 223.

Given the trajectory of demographic change, this may, over time, increase the prospects of the Democrats reemerging as a dominant party. At the same time, diminished ethnic overlap in party coalitions would be yet another nail in the coffin of bipartisan cooperation. As an example, despite the fact that a more tolerant attitude toward illegal immigrants has become a litmus test for the rapidly growing body of Latino voters, resolving this issue in a polarized Congress in which one party has little support from Latinos poses an increasingly difficult political problem.

LATINO ASSIMILATION

One of our most dramatic and pervasive findings is of the assimilation of Latinos, in a variety of respects. Our main data come from our surveys in Los Angeles, a metropolitan area that has received millions of immigrants from Mexico and Central America. Our primary standard for assessing the assimilation of immigrant groups is their trajectory across generations since immigration, on those criterion variables that show differences between whites and either Latinos or Asians. We interpret assimilation as occurring if the U.S.-born native Latinos are closer to whites than are the foreign-born, and especially if the U.S.-born natives do not differ significantly from whites. As was the case with the wave of European immigrants a century ago, assimilation is occurring more across generations than within generations. Perhaps most compelling is how quickly after immigration English has become Latinos' dominant language, even in a region like Los Angeles, with its proximity to Mexico and the frequency of travel back and forth across the border. Among noncitizens who have been in the United States for at least ten years, only 25 percent at least "mostly" speak English at home; in the second generation, 60 percent do; whereas in the third generation (U.S.-born of U.S.-born parents), 95 percent do.

This pattern of assimilation spills over into almost all the core perceptions and attitudes of our study. Foreign-born Latinos are, not surprisingly, less patriotic than whites or blacks, the vast majority of whom are U.S.-born. However, both national and Los Angeles data show that native-born Latinos, with relevant background factors controlled, are just as patriotic as whites.[15] Over time, assimilation to the patriotic norm clearly is occurring among Latino immigrants.

The assimilation paradigm also fits how Latinos prefer to identify themselves. When asked whether they thought of themselves mainly as just American or mainly as a member of a racial or ethnic group, a significant minority of Latinos chose the ethnic option. But immigration status made a large difference. Almost half of the noncitizen immigrant Latinos chose "ethnic," whereas 84 percent of the U.S.-born felt "just American." When language spoken at home was

---

[15] See the 2008 American National Election Studies (ANES) and the Los Angeles County Social Survey (LACSS) data cited in Chapter 3, as well as Theiss-Morse, *Who Counts As an American?*, 50, 56.

substituted for immigration status as a predictor of identity choice, English-speakers showed similar major increases in "just American" identities compared to other-language speakers, underlining the importance of linguistic assimilation over generations in the United States.

When the question wording allowed respondents the option of identifying themselves as *both* American *and* as a member of an ethnic group, the hyphenated "both" identity became the modal choice for native-born and naturalized Latinos. We therefore regard the preference for a hyphenated self-definition as a kind of halfway house for immigrants. For example, 41 percent of noncitizen Latinos selected the hyphenated identity, but among the naturalized foreign-born, 73 percent did, as did 69 percent of the U.S.-born Latinos. But native-born Latinos are moving on from the halfway house: 10 percent of the naturalized and 25 percent of the U.S.-born, self-identified as "just American."

The recent Pew study of Latinos cited earlier found a similar trajectory of identity choice. Respondents were asked which term they used to describe themselves most often. Overall, 75 percent named either their country of origin or a pan-ethnic Latino label, and just 21 percent said "an American." But these choices differed widely across immigrant generations in the predictable manner. In addition, the choice of an American identity was related to standard indicators of assimilation such as education and using English rather than Spanish as one's dominant language.[16] Similar evidence of assimilation is also reported in a Pew survey of Asian Americans: 30 percent of the foreign-born Asian Americans, compared to 65 percent of the native-born, say they think of themselves as typical Americans.[17]

Another aspect of Latino assimilation is the diminished intensity of their group consciousness over generations. For example, 65 percent of the foreign-born Latinos show either mild or severe aggrieved ethnic group consciousness, whereas only 36 percent of the U.S.-born Latinos did, a sharp move toward the microscopic 5 percent of whites who did. The big drops in the central ingredients of group consciousness –perceived discrimination and the strength of ethnic identity – occur in the second and third generations of immigrant offspring. Latinos as a whole diverge from blacks and whites as being more likely to agree to the value of people of the same ethnic background living and working with people like themselves. But again, U.S.-born Latinos are different, twice as likely as noncitizens to oppose the idea of living in an ethnic enclave. New immigrants are, of course, largely unfamiliar with the historic, bitter debates about the integration of racial minorities. In addition, their relative tolerance for ethnic isolation may simply reflect the reality of beginning life in America in an enclave of fellow-Latinos rather than a genuine preference for a segregated existence for the longer term.

---

[16] Pew Hispanic Center, "When Labels Don't Fit: Hispanics and Their Views of Identity," April Report (2012): 12–13.

[17] Pew Research Center, "The Rise of Asian Americans," 79, 80.

Over the generations after immigration, Latino support for group-conscious policies also drops, sometimes approaching whites' tilt toward opposition and sometimes not. The changes are most dramatic, as might be expected, for immigration and language policy. In both cases, foreign-born Latinos are much more likely to favor policies benefiting Latinos than are the U.S.-born, even with appropriate controls for demographic and political factors. But our data had some interesting nuances. U.S.-born Latinos had similar attitudes as whites about legal immigration, but retained markedly more sympathetic views about illegal immigrants.

Taken as a whole, these findings point to a process of political and cultural assimilation among the current wave of immigrants that resembles the experience of earlier waves of newcomers. Still, a cautionary note is in order. Our data capture a relative early phase of the societal transformation instigated by the post-1965 influx. Immigration today is ongoing, whereas the restrictive reforms of 1921 and 1924 effectively ended the inflow from Europe. Presumably that facilitated cultural and linguistic assimilation by interrupting the numerous interactions with the "Old Country" that we see in many of today's immigrants. As this implies, politics and public policies can shape the pace of assimilation in either direction.

BLACK EXCEPTIONALISM

The weight of current evidence continues to point to the dominance of assimilative forces for immigrants, then, reinforcing the continuing exceptionalism of the circumstances of blacks. We argue that the enduring significance of the color line, specific to those of discernible African ancestry, impedes the full integration of blacks into the broader society. As a result, multiculturalism's pressure for group-conscious programs may be most closely connected to the unique experience of African Americans.

In our analysis, the key test of black exceptionalism compares blacks with U.S.-born Latinos. That holds overall socioeconomic status largely constant and examines the extent to which the latter are assimilating and the former are not. To start with, black exceptionalism is quite evident in the strength of the ethnic identification. For example, when respondents were asked whether they felt more like just an American or a member of an ethnic group, blacks (like naturalized Latinos or noncitizens) were considerably more likely to say ethnic than were U.S.-born Latinos. Similarly, blacks almost without exception scored significantly higher than U.S.-born Latinos or Asians on our surveys' measures of the strength of racial identity, sense of common fate, and perceived discrimination. Therefore, as noted earlier, blacks were much more likely to score at the highest level of our aggrieved group consciousness (25 percent) than was true among U.S.-born Latinos (7 percent).

Perceptions of intergroup conflict in Los Angeles varied across groups in ways that seem not to reflect contemporary realities. Whites and Asians would seem objectively to be in more competition with each other than with other ethnic groups, in terms of access to higher education, upper status jobs, affluent neighborhoods, and so on. Yet both whites and Asians saw blacks as the group with whom they experienced the most conflict, perhaps a somewhat outdated, or at least narrow, vision of interethnic conflict. On the other hand, blacks and Latinos did see each other as their own group's main adversaries, a perception consistent with objective changes in residential and school composition, employment, and crime that have occurred as Latinos become more numerous in previously black neighborhoods, a phenomenon not confined to Los Angeles. Perhaps as a result, blacks' normative conceptions of American identity stressed the distinctive history and experience of their race, nativity, and length of time living in America, elevating their status above that of recent immigrants.

IS A STRONG NATIONAL IDENTITY VALUABLE?

Within the field of political theory, there is deep disagreement about the value of strong national identities. Theorists of liberal nationalism such as David Miller and Yael Tamir[18] argue that an overarching national identity supersedes the many other affiliations people may have and so functions as a kind of public good, providing the ideological cement that holds diverse societies together and the sense of solidarity that sustains mutual support and cooperation. Among other things, if the nation is a team, in Miller's formulation, then those strongly identifying with it should support helping other members of the national in-group. One way to help might include redressing the lot of the disadvantaged through support of the welfare state.[19] Opposing this argument are theorists who stress that a strong national identity is a two-edged sword. The impetus for helping "us" goes along with indifference to or even hostility to "them," some of whom may even share one's official nationality.

Our own study and those of many others have demonstrated the pervasiveness of Americans' national attachment. A crucial empirical question, then, is whether people strongly attached to the national group feel a distinctive obligation to help their fellow nationals, especially the disadvantaged, and in what way?[20] In this regard, the evidence in the research literature is mixed. Theiss-Morse reports that the more strongly Americans feel a sense of common identity with the American people, "the more likely they are to help in a crisis or disaster,

[18] Miller, On Nationality; Yael Tamir, Liberal Nationalism (Princeton, NJ: Princeton University Press), 1993.
[19] Ibid.; Markus Crepaz, Trust beyond Borders: Immigration, the Welfare State, and Identity in Modern Societies (Ann Arbor: University of Michigan Press, 2008).
[20] Theiss-Morse (Who Counts As an American?) has an excellent discussion of this in chapter 4 of her book.

give to charity, volunteer in their community, fight in wars and pay taxes."[21] According to this result, national attachment makes for good citizenship.

An important question, however, concerns the boundaries of solidary behavior, both in terms of who is helped and in what ways. The concern of multiculturalists, of course, is that those boundaries may not extend beyond the majority ethnic group. Indeed, our own data indicated that patriotism and nativism were consistently associated with whites' opposition to policies targeted to help minorities. Other research has shown that patriotism and a nativist conception of Americanism made people less willing to give even *legal* immigrants access to government benefits, at least without a waiting period.[22] Thiess-Morse also reports that those with a strong American identity are less likely to favor more government spending for welfare, blacks, or urban areas.

Some argue that this link between whites' patriotism and opposition to redistributive programs reflects animus toward minority groups. Others argue that it reflects an individualistic opposition to government action on the grounds that Americans should conform to the norm of self-reliance. That remains a question that attracts much political and some scholarly debate.[23] But what is clear is that opposition to government programs benefiting minorities, immigrants, and the poor increases with the combination of both a strong sense of national identity and the belief that ascribed traits such as nativity, religion, or race define the meaning of being an American.[24] We are more prepared to help our fellow nationals if they are deemed to be deserving, and deservingness seems related to fitting the national prototype and conforming to the dominant cultural norms, as well as to the more obvious factor of belonging to the white majority group.

For those defending the importance of a strong American identity in a multiethnic society, the onus is to define the "circle of we" in inclusive terms that encompass the country's ethnic diversity. One recent review of psychological research on the consequences of experimentally creating a common in-group identity among diverse ethnic groups concludes that "the power of a sense of

---

[21] Theiss-Morse, *Who Counts As an American?*, 105.

[22] Jack Citrin, Donald P. Green, C. Muste, and Cara Wong, "Public Opinion and Immigration Reform: The Role of Economic Motivations."

[23] The question is piece of a larger argument about the relative roles of racial animus or ethnocentrism, on the one hand, and race-neutral ideology or values, on the other, in determining whites' opposition to racially redistributive policies or minority political candidates. See, in particular, David O. Sears and P. J. Henry, "The Origins of Symbolic Racism," *Journal of Personality and Social Psychology* 85, no. 2 (2003): 259–74. Sears, Sidanius, and Bobo, *Racialized Politics*; Sniderman and Carmines, *Reaching Beyond Race*; Kinder and Kam, *Us against Them*; Tesler and Sears, *Obama's Race*. Little effort has been made to examine where this link to patriotism fits in that argument, and trying to parse out its pieces goes beyond the scope of this book.

[24] Matthew Wright, "Policy Regimes and Normative Conceptions of National Identity in Mass Public Opinion," *Comparative Political Studies* 44 (2011): 23; Theiss-Morse, *Who Counts As an American?*, 111.

We" is impressive.[25] Categorizing people as members of one's own group makes us feel closer to them, more trusting of them, helpful to them, and more willing to forgive them.[26] In-group identification maintains positive orientations toward fellow members that generate intragroup harmony and cohesion, but also create a psychological foundation for bias against members of out-groups. Accordingly, John Dovidio, Samuel Gaertner, and Tamar Saguy propose that a dual identity that combines common affiliation to the nation and identification with an ethnic or religious subgroup also can be a foundation of self-esteem, as well as a way of improving attitudes toward those in the subgroup with strong ethnic identifications.[27] This is support for the hyphenated identity that we found to be congenial to American minorities.

That view remains controversial. Others argue that majority group members, such as whites in America, favor a common one-group identity as a means of defusing opposition to their dominant position in society.[28] Much social psychological theorizing about intergroup relations proceeds from a starting point like that of multiculturalist ideology, sharing an image of American society as constructed in part around a racial hierarchy composed of ethnic groups living apart from each other as if in silos, and a hierarchy in need of change. In this view, minority group members who give up their previous group identity in favor of a superordinate national identity are less likely to challenge existing inequalities or participate in collective action to reduce intergroup disparities. In other words, identity politics in a context of discrimination and inequality is often argued to be a force for equality and social justice.[29] Any attempt to resolve this dispute, the heavily normative subtext of which seems to have compromised the value of empirical analysis, goes beyond the scope of this study.

AMERICAN IDENTITY IN THE NEW AMERICA

Two narratives of American peoplehood have competed for primacy throughout the nation's history. What we labeled as cosmopolitan liberalism is inclusive in spirit and readily accommodates the new wave of Latino and Asian immigrants. The core of this version of American identity is patriotism and commitment to the civic religion of constitutionalism, self-reliance, and equality before the law, albeit spoken in English. In contrast to this civic version of nationality is

---

[25] Jack Dovidio, Samuel L. Gaertner, and Tamar Saguy, "Commonality and the Complexity of 'We': Social Attitudes and Social Change," *Personality and Social Psychology Review* 13, no. 1 (2009): 1–30.

[26] Ibid., 14.

[27] Ibid., 7

[28] See Conover, "The Politics of Recognition."

[29] For an overview of these, see "Experimental Social Psychology, Broader Contexts, and the Politics of Multiculturalism" by David O. Sears in *The Political Psychology of Democratic Citizenship*, edited by Eugene Borgida, Christopher M. Federico, and John L. Sullivan (New York: Oxford University Press, 2009), pp. 325–43.

nativism, which holds that only people of a certain background are fit to become true Americans. If immigration somehow has allowed the entry of those whose values are alien, then nativists believe that a rigorous program of Americanization that requires shedding one's original culture and produces conformity to Anglo-Protestant values is warranted. In our study, the nativist conception of American identity was upheld by just such a minority. The nativist outlook was even less likely to be advocated by the vanguard of educated and younger respondents, as is true for other aspects of public opinion that reflect racial or ethnic prejudice. So we feel safe in saying that the liberal version of American identity is in the ascendancy; politicians of virtually all stripes refer to the United States as a nation of immigrants, and few openly challenge the virtue of diversity. Indeed, the use of ethnic stereotypes almost always calls forth at least a public apology and sometimes a swift resignation.

In different ways, cosmopolitan liberalism and nativism proclaim the existence and value of a common national identity. Hard multiculturalism deviates from this position, emphasizing the stability and importance of subnational identities. Its concept of a national community is difficult to grasp, for it conceives of the states as a confederation of nations with equal rights rather than as a community of individuals with a sense of common identity. This hard multiculturalist perspective does not resonate among most Americans for whom *e pluribus unum* remains a worthwhile ideal. Soft multiculturalism, which is widely supported, as we have seen, differs in providing a mixed model. Both minorities and the society at large do some adjusting, so that all remain under the general umbrella of a common national identity, redefined in civic terms. As we have argued, aspects of soft multiculturalism resemble the thin version of assimilation that seems to predominate in modern America.

In considering the psychology of ethnic differences in opinion throughout this book, we contrasted three main paradigms: (1) a politicized group consciousness perspective maintaining that a highly stable racial hierarchy exists in America, that every racial and ethnic group has a strong sense of in-group identity that governs its preferences, and that whites are at the top of the hierarchy, differentiated from all groups of "people of color," who fall at the bottom; (2) an assimilation perspective that assumes that much of any such hierarchy is transitional as new immigrant groups assimilate over time to the mainly white mainstream; and (3) a black exceptionalism perspective that contrasts the continuingly distinctive treatment of blacks, and their heightened sense of group consciousness, with the gradual integration over generations of new immigrants.

Without again reviewing the evidence in detail, we simply state that it conformed most often to the black exceptionalism model. Whites expressed a strong sense of racial identity far less often than did the other ethnic groups, and a people-of-color coalition emerged only rarely. Confirming previous research,[30]

---

[30] Dawson, *Behind the Mule.*

we find that blacks are more likely than other Americans to express a strong sense of group consciousness and more likely to be guided by this sense of in-group identity in forming preferences on issues that engage their interests. Among Latinos, by contrast, the strength of ethnic identity weakened among the native-born and immigrants who had lived in the United States a long time. This suggests that, in psychological terms as well as on the sociological and economic dimensions documented elsewhere,[31] the greater diversity of American society may have complicated the analysis of ethnic relations in the United States, but it has not changed the fact that the racial divide between African Americans and others remains the central American dilemma.

Can black exceptionalism diminish? The main impetus for this, of course, would be greater economic and social equality. And in the longer run, changing patterns of social contact may erode the ethnic identities that census categories and government policies reinforce. We know that the extent and character of cross-group marriage, cohabitation, and reproduction is blurring the lines between the standardized census groups.[32] Since 2000, the U.S. census has permitted the option to categorize oneself within more than one ethnic or racial group. Despite his mixed racial ancestry, President Obama chose not to make this multiracial choice and identified himself as black only. Interestingly, by a margin of nearly three to one, respondents in a 2010 Internet national survey said he should have identified himself as both black and white, an indication that people may be weaning themselves from the "one drop of blood" rule of hypodescent.[33] Of course, an individual's responses to the census are a matter of personal preference, not popular vote. But this result indicates broad awareness that Obama's social categorization as black masks a biologically mixed heritage.

Intermarriage rates are growing among all ethnic groups, although here, too, there is evidence of black exceptionalism, with black–white marriages far less frequent than those between Hispanics and whites or Asians and whites. Indeed, 29 percent of Asians newlyweds between 2008 and 2010 married outside of their ethnic group, and this proportion was higher among those born in the United States. Children of mixed marriages or religions either add a new array of diversities for multiculturalism to defend or, more plausibly,

---

[31] See, e.g., David Card, "Is the New Immigration Really So Bad?" *Economic Journal* 115 (2005): 300–23; for an alternative view, see George Borjas, *Heaven's Door: Immigration Policy and the American Economy* (Princeton, NJ: Princeton University Press, 1999).

[32] David Hollinger, "From Identity to Solidarity," *Daedalus* 135, no. 4 (2006); Jennifer Hochschild, Vesla Weaver, and Traci Burch, *Creating a New Racial Order: How Immigration, Multiracialism, Genomics, and the Young Can Remake Race in America* (Princeton, NJ: Princeton University Press, 2012).

[33] Morris Levy, Jack Citrin, and Robert Van Houweling, "Americans Fill Out President Obama's Census Form: What Is His Race?" Unpublished paper presented at the 2012 Midwest Political Science Association Conference in Chicago, IL.

grow a generation of people who conceive of American society in nonethnic or postethnic terms.[34]

Hochschild, Weaver, and Burch have recently developed the provocative idea that the traditional "American racial order," as they describe it, is becoming destabilized for a number of reasons. The heavy flow of new immigration over the past half century has radically upended the traditional black–white binary, as we have repeatedly noted earlier. As mentioned, the census has recognized multiracial and multiethnic identities, presumably reflecting changes in the population as a whole. Genomic science increasingly allows individuals to determine their own genetic roots, which frequently turn out to be surprisingly mixed. America turns out to be not only a nation of immigrants but also a nation of "mutts." And, for all these reasons, the notion of a fixed and immutable "race" or races has faced increased skepticism among scientists and perhaps in the public at large.

In the long run, the only viable American identity for the country's increasingly diverse society is the universalistic, civic variant espoused long ago by de Crevecoeur, Tocqueville, and Emerson. Recent developments suggest the same lesson is resonating abroad, particularly in Europe. Immigration has punctured cultural homogeneity in most Western countries, unsettling ideas about the foundations of nationhood and forcing elites to cope with a new demographic reality. The problem is in some ways more complicated in Europe because immigration is not part of the national narrative and because a large proportion of immigrants after 1980 have come from culturally dissimilar Muslim countries.

Comparisons of public opinion in Europe and the United States show that Americans are more willing to accept religious heterogeneity and less insistent that it is better for a country if everyone shares the same customs.[35] In Europe as in the United States, strong feelings of national pride boost opposition to immigration,[36] and definitions of nationhood based on ancestry, nativity, and religion consistently are linked to opposition to multiculturalism and anti-immigrant sentiment.[37] In Europe, too, the individual characteristics associated with stronger patriotism, ethnic conceptions of nationality, and opposition to multiculturalism are being older, having less formal education, and having right-wing political identifications.[38]

---

[34] David Hollinger, "From Identity to Solidarity," 4. See also Hochschild, Weaver, and Burch, *Creating a New Racial Order.*

[35] Jack Citrin and John Sides, "Immigration and the Imagined Community in Europe and the United States" *Political Studies* 56 (2008): 33–56.

[36] This emerges from analyses of World Value and European Value Surveys as well as the International Society of Political Psychology (ISPP) data.

[37] See Matthew Wright, "Policy Regimes and Normative Conceptions of National Identity in Mass Public Opinion."

[38] John Sides and Jack Citrin, "European Opinion about Immigration: The Role of Identities, Interests, and Information."

In responding to this demographic change, in the 1980s, European governments adopted the rhetoric and many policy prescriptions of the politics of difference. Yet a series of reports documenting the failure of immigrant integration and then the specter of terrorism has swung the policy pendulum from multiculturalism to assimilation.[39] In 1999, no European country had civic integration policies emphasizing linguistic and cultural assimilation. By now, most countries do, as governments are partly motivated by the mobilization of anti-immigrant sentiment by radical right parties.[40] In the American political system, similar nativistic political reactions to liberal immigration policies have emerged at the state level, such as in Arizona and Alabama. The Tea Party movement is hostile to immigration and sympathetic to nativist ideas, and it has become a powerful faction in national Republican Party politics.[41]

ROSE-COLORED GLASSES?

Our analysis has portrayed a rosier future for American unity than the worrisome scenario envisaged by Huntington, Schlesinger, and others. This is not to say that dark clouds do not exist. What to do about illegal immigration obviously looms large, with the polarizing effects of the status quo on Latinos versus other ethnic groups. On this and other issues relating to national identity, competing visions of America seem to be increasingly tied to party identification, in our view an undesirable prospect. The presence of cross-cutting cleavages within a consensus on fundamental values leavens national unity and democratic stability. So if the Republicans increasingly become an all-white party and the meanings of Americanism become tightly linked to party affiliation, the foundations of national unity surely become shakier. But the threat comes more from the political and economic inequality of African Americans and other minority groups and party polarization than from the increasing diversity of the population. The evidence is accumulating that today's immigrants are acculturating much as in the past.

National unity often is spurred by war and tragedy. World War II accelerated the assimilation of foreign-born Americans, helped reunite the North and South, and helped push the country toward desegregation. The terrorist attacks of September 11, 2001, similarly sparked demonstrations of loyalty and solidarity that overrode customary social and political divisions. On the first anniversary

---

[39] Roger Brubaker, "The Return of Assimilation?" in *Ethnicity without Group*, ed. Roger Brubaker (Cambridge, MA: Harvard University Press, 2004), 116–31.

[40] Sara Goodman and Marc Howard, "Evaluating and Explaining the Restrictive Backlash in Citizenship Policy in Europe," unpublished paper presented at the March 5, 2011 Conference on the Political Incorporation of Immigrants, Berkeley, CA. Paper available at www.igs.berkeley.edu.

[41] Theda Skocpol and Vanessa Williamson, *The Tea Party and the Remaking of Republican Conservatism* (Cambridge, MA: Harvard University Press, 2012); Christopher S. Parker and Matt A. Barreto, *Change They Can't Believe In: The Tea Party and Reactionary Politics in America* (Princeton, NJ: Princeton University Press), 2013.

of September 11, television devoted much of the day to memorial ceremonies, reprises of heroism, and vignettes about the families of victims. Quite often, the commercial break in the collective process of national remembering was this pictorial statement from the Advertising Council of America: The Statue of Liberty fills the screen before fading into a montage of faces representing every ethnic strain. There is a recognizable Sikh, Latino, orthodox Jew, Asian, Caucasian, African American, and Arab. One at a time they proclaim, "I am an American." As the verbal mantra fades, the words *e pluribus unum* appear alone on the now-blank screen.

So, are we all multiculturalists, all assimilationists, both, or neither? If multiculturalism means the need to recognize a new social reality and eliminating discrimination against minority groups, most Americans are multiculturalists. If assimilation means the desirability of immigrant groups learning English and America's civic values, most are assimilationists. Defined in this way, it is easy to be both. And it is easy to be neither if multiculturalism means the permanent hardening of ethnic differences and assimilation means stamping out the voluntary practice of cultural pluralism.

As we look forward, then, it seems that American identity is not so much waning as changing in tone. The views of the young vanguard point to a less strident, less chauvinistic patriotism. The changed ethnic composition of society puts nativist and white-supremacist views increasingly on the defensive. And the assimilation of immigrants suggests that the distinctively high level of patriotism in America will endure and the specter of balkanization is a chimera. Don't give away your flag just yet.

Appendices

APPENDIX 2.1 ETHNIC COMPOSITION IN LOS ANGELES COUNTY SOCIAL SURVEYS (LACSS), BY YEAR AND LEVEL OF EDUCATION

	LA County								
	1994	1995	1997	1998	1999	2000	2001	2002	2000
White									
No high school	0%	0%	3%	0%	2%	3%	4%	2%	3%
Some high school	6	3	0	2	3	22	4	4	7
High school degree/GED	10	9	15	20	21	22	13	36	19
Some college/ two-year degree	40	39	52	50	47	11	34	18	25
College degree +	43	49	30	28	28	42	46	40	45
N	279	259	275	282	289	165	226	237	
White % of total	34	45	46	45	43	32	31	37	31
Latino									
No high school	27	17	26	23	23	45	20	21	36
Some high school	9	12	3	10	11	11	17	14	21
High school degree/GED	28	29	36	33	34	28	35	43	18
Some college/ two-year degree	28	32	26	26	24	8	20	12	14
College degree +	8	10	8	8	7	8	8	11	10
N	264	202	205	225	264	194	251	209	
Latino % of total	32	35	34	36	40	37	34	33	45
Black									
No high school	3	3	3	1	2	13	2	3	5
Some high school	9	3	3	4	5	25	5	7	16
High school degree/GED	17	6	16	26	30	24	23	44	24

(continued)

	LA County								
	1994	1995	1997	1998	1999	2000	2001	2002	2000
Some college/ two-year degree	49	56	54	43	43	15	40	13	29
College degree +	22	32	24	25	20	23	29	33	26
N	231	71	63	76	56	146	219	151	
Black % of total	28	12	10	12	8	28	30	24	11
Asian									
No high school	2	0	0	0	3	6	0	0	10
Some high school	0	2	2	2	7	28	5	0	7
High school degree/GED	26	4	5	21	7	17	3	28	15
Some college/ two-year degree	28	30	58	50	46	17	27	15	24
College degree +	45	64	36	26	37	33	65	56	43
N	47	47	59	42	59	18	37	39	
Asian % of total	6	8	10	7	9	3	5	6	13
Total									
No high school	9	6	10	8	10	20	8	7	16
Some high school	7	6	2	5	6	19	8	7	14
High school degree/GED	19	15	22	25	25	24	22	40	19
Some college/ two-year degree	38	38	45	42	39	11	32	16	26
College degree +	26	34	22	20	20	26	30	31	25
N	821	579	602	625	668	523	733	636	

Source: LACSS 1994–95, 1997–2002, and U.S. Census 2000, FactFinder.

APPENDIX 3.1 QUESTION WORDING FOR SURVEY ITEMS

I. National Data

A. *General Social Survey (GSS)*
I would rather be a citizen of America than of any other country in the world. (agree strongly, agree, neither agree nor disagree, disagree, disagree strongly)

How close to you feel to America? (very close, close, not very close, not close at all)

Generally speaking, America is a better country than most other countries. (agree strongly, agree, neither agree nor disagree, disagree, disagree strongly)

The world would be a better place if people from other countries were more like Americans. (agree strongly, agree, neither agree nor disagree, disagree, disagree strongly)

America should follow its own interests even if this leads to conflicts with other nations. (agree strongly, agree, neither agree nor disagree, disagree, disagree strongly)

People should support their country even if it is in the wrong. (agree strongly, agree, neither agree nor disagree, disagree, disagree strongly)

There are some things about America today that make me feel angry. (agree, neither agree nor disagree, disagree)

There are some things about America today that make me feel ashamed of America. (GSS: agree strongly, agree, neither agree nor disagree, disagree, disagree strongly; American National Election Survey [ANES]: agree, neither agree nor disagree, disagree)

B. American National Election Studies (ANES)

How strong is your love for your country? (extremely strong, very strong, somewhat strong, or not very strong); ANES time-series studies

Do you love the United States, hate it, or neither love nor hate it? ... How much do you (love/hate) the United States? (a great deal, a moderate amount, a little); ANES time-series studies

When you see the American flag flying does it make you feel (extremely good, very good, somewhat good, or not very good)?; ANES time-series studies

When you see the American flag flying does it make you feel good, feel bad, or neither feel good nor bad? ... Extremely (good/bad), moderately (good/bad), or slightly (good/bad)? 2008–09 ANES panel study

How strongly do you feel you must support the country, regardless of whether what it does is right or wrong? (extremely strongly, very strongly, moderately strongly, slightly strongly, or not at all); 2008–09 ANES panel study

Do you think there should be more criticism of the United States, less criticism of the United States, or about the same amount of criticism of the United States as there is now? ... A great deal (more/less), a moderate amount (more/less), or a little (more/less)?; 2008–09 ANES panel study

II. Los Angeles County Social Surveys (LACSS)

I have great love for America. (strongly agree, somewhat agree, neither agree nor disagree, somewhat disagree, strongly disagree); 1997, 1998, 1999

I am proud to be an American. (strongly agree, somewhat agree, neither agree nor disagree, somewhat disagree, strongly disagree); 1998, 1999, 2000, 2002

How proud are you to be an American? (extremely proud, very proud, somewhat proud, not at all proud); 1994, 1997

I find the sight of the American flag very moving. (strongly agree, somewhat agree, neither agree nor disagree, somewhat disagree, strongly disagree); 1997, 1998, 1999, 2000, 2002

America is not a particularly wonderful place to live. (strongly agree, somewhat agree, neither agree nor disagree, somewhat disagree, strongly disagree); 1998

Other countries are better places to live than the United States (strongly agree, somewhat agree, neither agree nor disagree, somewhat disagree, strongly disagree); 1998

The American flag should not be treated as a sacred object. (strongly agree, somewhat agree, neither agree nor disagree, somewhat disagree, strongly disagree); 1998

APPENDIX 7.1 PRECISE QUESTION WORDINGS IN NATIONAL DATA

I. Precise wordings for paraphrased items in 1992–2012 studies used in Table 7.1

    a. Some people think that blacks have been discriminated against for so long that the government has a special obligation to help improve their living standards. Others believe that the government should not be giving special treatment to blacks. Where would you place yourself on this scale, or haven't you made up your mind on this?

    b. Some people feel that the government in Washington should make every effort to improve the social and economic position of blacks. Others feel that the government should not make any special effort to help blacks because they should help themselves.

    c. We are faced with many problems in this country, none of which can be solved easily or inexpensively. I'm going to name some of these problems, and for each one I'd like you to tell me whether you think we're spending too much money on it, too little money, or about the right amount.... Improving the conditions of blacks.

    d. Do you think the number of immigrants from foreign countries who are permitted to come to the United States to live should be increased a lot, increase a little, left the same as it is now, decreased a little, or decreased a lot? (in 2004, the question refers to "the number of immigrants to American nowadays")

    e. Now I'm going to read you a list of federal programs. For each one, I would like you to tell me whether you would like to see spending increased, decreased or kept about the same...tightening border security to prevent illegal immigration.

II. Los Angeles County Social Survey (LACSS) Data (items in Table 7.2 by Years of Availability, 1994–2002)

    a. Some people say that because of past discrimination, blacks should be given preference in hiring and promotion. Others say that such preference is wrong because it discriminates against others. What about your opinion – are you for or against preferential hiring and promotion of blacks? Are you (strongly for – strongly against) giving preference in hiring and promotion strongly or not strongly? 1994, 1995

b. Some people feel that the government in Washington should make every effort to improve the social and economic position of blacks and other minority groups. Others feel that the government should not make any special effort to help minorities because they should help themselves. Do you feel that the government should help improve the position of minorities, that minorities should help themselves, or is your position somewhere in between (and if not in between, to a great extent or only to some extent)? 1994, 1995

c. Some people say that because of past discrimination, Hispanics should be given preference in hiring and promotion. Others say that such preference is wrong because it discriminates against others. What about your opinion – are you for or against preferential hiring and promotion of Hispanics? Are you (for/against) giving preference in hiring and promotion strongly or not strongly? 1994, 1995

d. Do you think the number of immigrants from foreign countries who are permitted to come to the United States to live should be increased a lot, increased a little, left the same as it is now, decreased a little, or decreased a lot? All Years

e. What about undocumented aliens: that is, those who have immigrated to this country illegally? Should they be entitled to have their children continue to qualify as American citizens if born in the United States, or not? 1997, 1998

f. Do you favor a law making English the official language of the United States, meaning government business would be conducted in English only, or do you oppose such a law? All Years, "Neither favor nor oppose" option included only in 1994, 1995

g. There are several different ideas about how to teach children who don't speak English when they enter our public schools. Please tell me which of the following statements best describes how you feel: all classes should be conducted only in English, have classes in their native language just for a year or two until they learn English, or many classes should be in Spanish or other languages all the way through high school? (All classes only in English, Classes in native language just for a year or two, Many classes in other languages through high school) 1994, 1995, 1997 (All classes should be conducted only in English so that students have to learn English right from the start, Children who don't know English could have classes in their native language for up to a year, They should take classes in their native language for as long as it takes to learn English, or Students who want to keep up their native languages and cultures should be able to take many of their classes in their native languages all the way through high school) 2000, 2001, 2002 ("as long as it takes" option not included in 2002)

III. Episodic National Data (precise wordings for paraphrased items in Table 7.3)

a. What about undocumented aliens, that is, those who have immigrated to this country illegally? Should they be entitled to have their children continue to qualify as American citizens if born in the United States, or not?

b. What about "undocumented aliens," that is, those who have immigrated to this country illegally? Should illegal immigrants be entitled to work permits, or not?

c. There are several different ideas about how to teach children who don't speak English when they enter our public schools. Please look at the card and tell me which statement best describes how you feel (card options: all classes should be taught in English so that children have to learn English right from the start, Children who don't know English should have classes in their native language for just a year or two until they learn English, Students who want to keep up with their native languages and cultures should be able to take many classes in Spanish or other languages all the way through school).

APPENDIX 7.2 PRECISE WORDINGS OF PEW RESEARCH CENTER QUESTIONS

1. Should legal immigration into the United States be kept at its present level, increased, or decreased?

2. Would you favor or oppose a new government database of everyone eligible to work – both American citizens and legal immigrants, and requiring employers to check that database before hiring someone for any kind of work?

3. Would you favor or oppose requiring everyone seeking a new job to have a new kind of driver's license or Social Security card that proves they are U.S. citizens or are in the country legally?

4. I'd like to get your reaction to proposals for dealing with the issue of immigration in the United States. First, thinking about immigrants who are now living in the U.S. ILLEGALLY. Should illegal immigrants be required to go home, or should they be granted some kind of legal status that allows them to stay here?

IF REQUIRED TO GO HOME: Should it be possible for some illegal immigrants to remain in the U.S. under a temporary worker program under the condition that they would eventually go home, or don't you think so?

IF ALLOWED TO STAY: Should they be allowed to stay only as temporary workers who must eventually return to their home countries, or should it be possible for them to stay in the U.S. permanently? Should the children of illegal immigrants who are in the U.S. be permitted to attend public schools, or don't you think so?

5. I'm going to read you some pairs of statements that will help us understand how you feel about a number of things. As I read each pair, tell me whether the FIRST statement or the SECOND statement comes closer to your own views – even if neither is exactly right:

   Immigrants today strengthen our country because of their hard work and talents versus immigrants today are a burden on our country because they take our jobs, housing, and health care.

6. Would you favor changing the Constitution so that the parents must be legal residents of the United States in order for their newborn child to be a citizen, or should the Constitution be left as it is?

7. Now thinking about our country, which of these is a bigger problem for the United States right now... legal immigration, illegal immigration, both equally, or neither?

APPENDIX 9.1 ROLL-CALL VOTES ON GROUP-CONSCIOUS POLICIES AND FACTOR ANALYSIS OF ISSUE CONSTRAINT

Available online at www.igs.berkeley.edu/files/citrin_ch9_online_appendix-1.pdf

Bibliography

Abbott, Philip. "Still Louis Hartz after All These Years: A Defense of the Liberal Society Thesis." *Perspectives on Politics* 3, no. 1 (2005): 93–109.

Abramowitz, Alan I. *The Disappearing Center: Engaged Citizens, Polarization, and American Democracy.* New Haven, CT: Yale University Press, 2010.

"Disconnected or Joined at the Hip?" In *Red and Blue Nation?: Characteristics and Causes of America's Polarized Politics, vol. 1,* ed. Pietro S. Nivola and David W. Brady. Washington, DC: Brookings, 2006.

Abramowitz, Alan I., and Kyle L. Saunders. "Is Polarization a Myth?" *Journal of Politics* 70 (2006): 542–55.

Abramson, Harold J. "Assimilation and Pluralism." In *Harvard Encyclopedia of American Ethnic Groups,* ed. Stephan Thernstrom. Cambridge, MA: Belknap Press of Harvard University Press, 1980.

"The 2008 Election: Polarization Continues," in *Controversies in Voting Behavior,* 5th edition, ed. Richard G. Niemi, Herbert F. Weisberg, and David C. Kimball. Washington, DC: Congressional Quarterly Press, 2010.

Adorno, Theodore W., Else Frenkel-Brunswik, Daniel J. Levinson, and Nevitt R. Sanford. *The Authoritarian Personality.* New York: Harper & Row, 1950.

Alba, Richard. *Ethnicity in America: The Transformation of White Ethnicity.* New Haven, CT: Yale University Press, 1990.

Alba, Richard, and Victor Nee. *Remaking the American Mainstream.* Cambridge, MA: Harvard University Press, 2003.

Allen, James P., and Eugene Turner. *The Ethnic Quilt: Population Diversity in Southern California.* Northridge: Center for Geographical Studies, California State University, Northridge, 1997.

Anderson, Benedict R. O'Gorman. *Imagined Communities: Reflections on the Origin and Spread of Nationalism.* New York: Verso, 1983.

Appiah, K. Anthony, and Amy Guttmann. *Color Conscious: The Political Morality of Race.* Princeton, NJ: Princeton University Press, 1996.

Baldassare, Mark. *The Los Angeles Riots: Lessons for the Urban Future.* Boulder, CO: Westview Press, 1994.

Banaji, Mahzarin R., and Thierry Devos. "American = White?" *Journal of Personality and Social Psychology* 88, no. 3 (2005): 447–66.

Banting, Keith, and Will Kymlicka. "Introduction Multiculturalism and the Welfare State: Setting the Context." In *Multiculturalism and the Welfare State: Recognition and Redistribution in Contemporary Democracies,* ed. Keith Banting and Will Kymlicka. New York: Oxford University Press, 2010.

Barnes, Jessica S., and Claudette E. Bennett. "The Asian Population: Census 2000 Brief." U.S. Census Bureau: C2KBR/01–16 (2002). Available online at: www.census.gov/prod/2002pubs/c2kbr01-16.pdf.

Barone, Michael. *The New Americans: How the Melting Pot Can Work Again.* Washington, DC: Regnery Publishing, 2001.

Barry, Brian. *Culture and Equality.* Cambridge, MA: Harvard University Press, 2002.
Justice as Impartiality. Oxford: Clarendon Press, 1995.

Bartels, Larry. *Unequal Democracy: The Political Economy of the New Gilded Age.* Princeton, NJ: Princeton University Press, 2009.

Bass, Shana B. "The Multicultural Moment: The Politics of the Multiculturalism Movement in the United States." Unpublished PhD dissertation, UCLA Department of Political Science, 2005.

Billig, Michael. *Banal Nationalism.* London: Sage Publications, 1995.

Black, Earl, and Merle Black. *The Rise of Southern Republicans.* Cambridge, MA: Harvard University Press, 2002.

Black-Branch, Jonathan L. Making Sense of the Canadian Charter of Rights and Freedoms: A Handbook for Administrators and Teachers. Toronto, Ontario: Canadian Education Association, 1995.

Blalock, Hubert M. *Toward a Theory of Minority-Group Relations.* New York: John Wiley and Sons, 1967.

Bloomberg News Poll Report. November 2012, accessed online at http://media.bloomberg.com/bb/avfile/r27N5k5yzAsA.

Blumer, Herbert. "Prejudice as a Sense of Group Position." *The Pacific Sociological Review* 1, no. 1 (1958): 3–7.

Bobo, Lawrence. "Prejudice as Group Position: Micro-Foundations of a Sociological Approach to Racism and Race Relations." *Journal of Social Issues* 55 (1999): 445–72.
"Race, Public Opinion and the Social Sphere." *Public Opinion Quarterly* 61 (1997): 1–15.
"Whites' Opposition to Busing: Symbolic Racism or Realistic Group Conflict?" *Journal of Personality and Social Psychology* 45 (1983): 1196–1210.

Bobo, Lawrence, and Vincent Hutchings. "Perceptions of Racial Group Competition: Extending Blumer's Theory of Group Position to a Multiracial Social Context." *American Sociological Review* 61 (1996): 951–72.

Bobo, Lawrence, and Devon Johnson. "A Taste for Punishment: Black and White Americans' Views on the Death Penalty and the War on Drugs." *Du Bois Review: Social Science Research on Race* 1, no. 1 (2004): 151–80.
"Racial Attitudes in a Prismatic Metropolis: Mapping Identity, Stereotypes, Competition, and Views on Affirmative Action." In *Prismatic Metropolis: Analyzing Inequality in Los Angeles*, ed. Lawrence Bobo, Melvin Oliver, James Johnson, and Abel Valenzuela. New York: Russell Sage Foundation, 2000.

Bobo, Lawrence, and James R. Kluegel. "Opposition to Race-Targeting: Self-Interest, Stratification Ideology, or Racial Attitudes?" *American Sociological Review* 58 (1993): 443–64.

Bobo, Lawrence, and Ryan A. Smith. "Antipoverty Policy, Affirmative Action, and Racial Attitudes." In *Confronting Poverty: Prescriptions for Change*, ed. Sheldon Danziger, Gary. D. Sandefur, and Daniel H. Weinberg. Cambridge, MA: Harvard University Press, 1994.

Bobo, Lawrence, and Mia Tuan. *Prejudice in Politics: Group Position, Public Opinion and the Wisconsin Treaty Rights Dispute.* Cambridge, MA: Harvard University Press, 2006.

Bonilla-Silva, Eduardo. *Racism without Racists: Colorblind Racism and the Persistence of Racial Inequality in the United States*, 2nd ed. Lanham, MD: Rowman & Littlefield Publishers, 2006.

Bonilla-Silva, Eduardo, and Karen S. Glover. "We Are All Americans: The Latin Americanization of Race Relations in the United States." In *The Changing Terrain of Race and Ethnicity*, ed. Maria Krysan and Amanda E. Lewis. New York: Russell Sage Foundation, 2004.

Borjas, George. *Heaven's Door: Immigration Policy and the American Economy.* Princeton, NJ: Princeton University Press, 1999.

Bosniak, Linda. "Citizenship Denationalized." *Indiana Journal of Global Legal Studies* 7 (2000): 447–509.

Brewer, Marilynn B. "Identity and Conflict." In *Intergroup Conflicts and Their Resolution: Social Psychological Perspectives*, ed. Daniel Bar-Tal. New York: Psychology Press, 2011.

  "The Importance of Being We: Human Nature and Intergroup Relations." *American Psychologist* 62, no. 8 (2007): 728–38.

  "The Many Faces of Social Identity: Implications for Political Psychology." *Political Psychology* 22, no. 1 (2001): 115–25.

  "Social Identity and Citizenship in a Pluralistic Society." In *The Political Psychology of Democratic Citizenship*, ed. Eugene Borgida, Christopher M. Federico, and John L. Sullivan. New York: Oxford University Press, 2009.

Brewer, Marilynn B., and Sonia Roccas. "Individual Values, Social Identity, and Optimal Distinctiveness." In *Individual Self, Relational Self, Collective Self*, ed. Constantine Sedikides and Marilynn B. Brewer. Philadelphia: Psychology Press, 2001.

Brimelow, Peter. *Alien Nation: Common Sense about America's Immigration Disaster.* New York: Random House, 1995.

Brown v. Board of Education of Topeka, 347 U.S. 483 (1954).

Brown, Robert A., and Todd C. Shaw. "Separate Nations: Two Attitudinal Dimensions of Black Nationalism." *The Journal of Politics* 64, no. 1 (2000): 22–44.

Brubaker, Rogers. *Citizenship and Nationhood in France and Germany.* Cambridge, MA: Harvard University Press, 2002.

  "Civic and Ethnic Nations in France and Germany." In *Ethnicity*, edited John Hutchinson and Anthony Smith. Oxford: Oxford University Press, 1992.

  "The Manichean Myth: Rethinking the Distinction between 'Civic' and 'Ethnic' Nationalism." In *Nation and National Identity: The European Experience in Perspective*, ed. Kriesi Hanspeter, et al. Zurich: Ruegger, 1999.

  "The Return of Assimilation?" In *Ethnicity without Group*, ed. Rogers Brubaker. Cambridge, MA: Harvard University Press, 2004.

Campbell, Andrea Louise, Cara Wong, and Jack Citrin. "'Racial Threat,' Partisan Climate, and Direct Democracy: Contextual Effects in Three California Initiatives." *Political Behavior* 28, no. 2 (2006): 129–50.

Campbell, Angus, Philip E. Converse, Warren E. Miller, and Donald E. Stokes. *The American Voter.* New York: Wiley, 1960.

Card, David. "Is the New Immigration Really So Bad?" *The Economic Journal* 115 (2005): 300–23.

Carsey, Thomas M., and Geoffrey Layman. "Changing Sides or Changing Minds? Party Identification and Policy Preferences in the American Electorate." *American Journal of Political Science* 50 (2006): 464–77.

Cheney, Lynne. "The End of History." *Wall Street Journal,* October 20, 1994.

Chong, Dennis. "Free Speech and Multiculturalism In and Out of the Academy." *Political Psychology* 27, no. 1 (2006): 29–54.

Citrin, Jack, Donald P. Green, Christopher Muste, and Cara Wong. "Public Opinion toward Immigration: The Role of Economic Motivations." *Journal of Politics* 59 (1997): 858–81.

Citrin, Jack, Donald P. Green, Beth Reingold, and Evelyn Walters. "The 'Official English' Movement and the Symbolic Politics of Language in the United States." *The Western Political Quarterly* 43, no. 3 (1990): 535–59.

Citrin, Jack, Ernst B. Haas, Beth Reingold, and Christopher Muste. "Is American Nationalism Waning?" *International Politics Quarterly* 38:1 (1994): 1–31.

Citrin, Jack, Jocelyn Kiley, and Kathryn Pearson. "Direct Democracy Takes on Bilingual Education: Framing the Influences of Ethnicity and Identity in Four State Initiatives." Paper presented at the 2003 annual meeting of the American Political Science Association, Philadelphia, PA.

Citrin, Jack, Amy Lerman, Michael Murakami, and Kathryn Pearson. "Testing Huntington: Is Hispanic Immigration a Threat to American Identity?" *Perspectives on Politics* 1 (March 2007): 31–48.

Citrin, Jack, Beth Reingold, and Donald P. Green. "American Identity and the Politics of Ethnic Change." *Journal of Politics* 52 (1990): 1124–54.

Citrin, Jack, David O. Sears, Christopher Muste, and Cara Wong. "Multiculturalism in American Public Opinion." *British Journal of Political Science* 31, no. 2 (2001).

Citrin, Jack, and John Sides. "Immigration and the Imagined Community in Europe and the United States." *Political Studies* 56 (2008): 33–56.

Citrin, Jack, Cara Wong, and Brian Duff. "The Meaning of American National Identity: Patterns of Ethnic Conflict and Consensus." In *Social Identity, Intergroup Conflict, and Conflict Reduction,* ed. Richard D. Ashmore, Lee Jussim, and David Wilder. Oxford: Oxford University Press, 2001.

Citrin, Jack, and Matthew Wright. "Defining the Circle of We: American Identity and Immigration Policy." *The Forum* 7, no. 3 (2009). Available online at www.bepress .com/forum/vol7/iss3/art6.

"The Politics of Immigration in a Nation of Immigrants." In *New Directions in American Politics,* ed. Ray La Raja. New York: Routledge, 2013.

City of Richmond v. J. A. Croson and Co. 488 U.S. 469 (1989).

Conover, Pamela Johnston. "The Politics of Recognition: A Social Psychological Perspective." In *The Political Psychology of Democratic Citizenship,* ed. Eugene Borgida, Christopher M. Federico, and John L. Sullivan. New York: Oxford University Press, 2009.

Conover, Pamela Johnston, Donald D. Searing, and Ivor M. Crewe. "The Deliberative Potential of Political Discussion." *British Journal of Political Science* 32, no. 1 (2002): 21–62.

Converse, Philip E. "The Nature of Belief Systems in Mass Publics." In *Ideology and Discontent*, ed. David E. Apter. London: Free Press of Glencoe, 1964.

Converse, Philip E., and Angus Campbell. "Political Standards in Secondary Groups." *In Group Dynamics*, ed. Dorwin Cartwright and Alvin Zander. New York: Harper Row, 1968.

Crepaz, Markus. *Trust beyond Borders: Immigration, the Welfare State, and Identity in Modern Societies*. Ann Arbor: University of Michigan Press, 2008.

Crocker, Jennifer, and Riia Luhtanen. "Collective Self-Esteem and Ingroup Bias." *Journal of Personality and Social Psychology* 58 (1990): 60–67.

Dawson, Michael C. *Behind the Mule: Race and Class in African-American Politics*. Princeton, NJ: Princeton University Press, 1994.

   Black Visions: The Roots of Contemporary African-American Political Ideologies. Chicago: University of Chicago Press, 2003.

De Figuereido, Rui J. P., and Zachary Elkins. "Are Patriots Bigots? An Inquiry into the Vices of In-Group Pride." *American Journal of Political Science* 47, no. 1 (2003): 171–88.

de la Garza, Rodolfo O., Angelo Falcon, Chris F. Garcia, and John A. Garcia. "Latino National Political Survey, 1989–1990" (ICPSR 6841). Available online at www .icpsr.umich.edu/icpsrweb/ICPSR/studies/6841

de la Garza, Rodolfo O., Angelo Falcon, and Chris F. Garcia. "Will the Real Americans Please Stand Up: Anglo and Mexican-American Support of Core American Political Values." *American Journal of Political Science* 40, no. 2 (1996): 335–51.

de Tocqueville, Alexis. *Democracy in America*, translated by Harvey C. Mansfield and Delba Winthrop. London: Penguin Books, 2002 [1835].

Doane, Ashley W. "Dominant Group Ethnic Identity in the United States." *Sociological Quarterly* 38, no. 3 (1997): 375–97.

Dovidio, Jack, Samuel L. Gaertner, and Tamar Saguy, "Commonality and the Complexity of 'We': Social Attitudes and Social Change." *Personality and Social Psychology Review* 13, no. 1 (2009): 1–30.

DuBois, W. E. B. *The Souls of Black Folk*. New York: Cosimo, 2007 [1903].

Eberhardt, Jennifer L., and Jennifer L. Randall. "The Essential Notion of Race." *Psychological Science* 8 (1997): 198–203.

Emerson, Rupert. *From Empire to Nation: The Rise to Self-Assertion of Asian and African Peoples*. Boston: Beacon Press, 1960.

Erikson, Erik H. *Childhood and Society*. New York: W. W. Norton & Company, 1993 [1950].

Fiorina, Morris P., and Samuel J. Abrams. "Where's the Polarization." In *Controversies in Voting Behavior*, 5th edition, ed. Richard G. Niemi and Herbert F. Weisberg. Washington, DC: CQ Press, 2011.

Fiorina, Morris P., Samuel J. Abrams, and J. C. Pope. *Culture War? The Myth of a Polarized America*. New York: Pearson Longman, 2004.

Fiske, Susan T., and Steven L. Neuberg. "A Continuum of Impression Formation, from Category-Based to Individuating Processes: Influences of Information and Motivation on Attention and Interpretation." In *Advances in Experimental Social Psychology*, ed. Mark P. Zanna. New York: Academic Press, 1990.

Frederickson, George M. "Models of American Ethnic Relations: A Historical Perspective." In *Cultural Divides*, ed. Deborah Miller and Dale Prentice. New York: Russell Sage Foundation, 1999.

Frendreis, John, and Raymond Tatalovich. "Who Supports English-Only Language Laws? Evidence from the 1992 National Election Study." *Social Science Quarterly* 78, no. 2 (1997): 354–68.

Gaertner, Samuel L., John F. Dovidio, et al. "Across Cultural Divides: The Value of a Superordinate Identity." In *Cultural Divides: Understanding and Overcoming Group Conflict*, ed. Deborah A. Prentice and Dale T. Miller. New York: Russell Sage Foundation, 1999.

Gallup: Americans More Pro-Immigration Than in Past. Available online at www.gallup .com/poll/163457/americans-pro-immigration-past.aspx; www.gallup.com/poll/1660/ immigration.aspx;

Gallup, 2010: More Americans Favor than Oppose Arizona Immigration Law. Available online at www.gallup.com/poll/127598/americans-favor-oppose-arizona-immigra tion-law.aspx.

Gans, Herbert. "Symbolic Ethnicity: The Future of Ethnic Groups and Cultures in America." *Ethnic and Racial Studies* 2, no. 1 (1979): 1–20.

Geertz, Clifford. "Ideology as a Cultural System." In *Ideology and Its Discontents*, ed. David Apter. New York: Free Press, 1964.

Gellner, Ernest. *Nations and Nationalism.* London: Oxford University Press, 1983.

Giles, Michael W., and Kaenan Hertz. "Racial Threat and Partisan Identification." *American Political Science Review* 88, no. 2 (1994): 317–26.

Gitlin, Todd. *The Twilight of Common Dreams: Why America Is Wracked by Culture Wars.* New York: Metropolitan Books, Henry Holt and Company, 1996.

Glazer, Nathan. "Black and White after Thirty Years." *National Affairs* 121 (Fall 1995). "Is Assimilation Dead?" *The Annals of the American Academy of Political and Social Science* 530, no. 122 (1993): 122–36.

We Are All Multiculturalists Now. Cambridge, MA: Harvard University Press, 1997.

Gleason, Philip. "American Identity and Americanization." In *Harvard Encyclopedia of American Ethnic Groups*, ed. Stephan Thernstrom. Cambridge, MA: Harvard University Press, 1980.

Goodman, Sara, and Marc Howard. "Evaluating and Explaining the Restrictive Backlash in Citizenship Policy in Europe." Unpublished paper presented at the March 5, 2011 Conference on the Political Incorporation of Immigrants, Berkeley, CA. Available online at www.igs.berkeley.edu.

Gordon, Milton M. *Assimilation in American Life: The Role of Race, Religion, and National Origins.* New York: Oxford University Press, 1964.

Greeley, Andrew. *Ethnicity in the United States.* New York: Wiley, 1974.

Green, Donald P., Bradley Palmquist, and Eric Schickler. *Partisan Hearts and Minds: Political Parties and the Social Identities of Voters.* New Haven, CT: Yale University Press, 2002.

Gryn, Thomas A., and Luke J. Larsen. "Nativity Status and Citizenship in the United States: 2009." *American Community Survey Briefs.* October 2009. Available online at www.census.gov/prod/2010pubs/acsbr09-16.pdf.

Guinier, Lani. *The Tyranny of the Majority: Fundamental Fairness in Representative Democracy.* New York: Simon & Schuster, 1995.

Gurin, Patricia, Shirley Hatchett, and James S. Jackson. *Hope and Independence: Blacks' Response to Electoral and Party Politics.* New York: Russell Sage Foundation, 1989.

Haas, Ernst B. *Beyond the Nation-State: Functionalism and International Organization.* Stanford, CA: Stanford University Press, 1964.

Hacker, Andrew. *Two Nations: Black and White, Separate, Hostile, Unequal.* New York: Charles Scribner's Sons, 1992.

Hainmueller, Jens, and Daniel Hopkins. "The Hidden American Immigration Consensus: A Conjoint Analysis of Attitudes toward Immigrants." *SSRN Working Paper Number 2106116* (2012).

"Public Attitudes toward Immigration." *Annual Review of Political Science* 17 (forthcoming 2014).

Hajnal, Zoltan. *Changing White Attitudes toward Black Political Leadership.* New York: Cambridge University Press, 2006.

Hajnal, Zoltan, and Taeku Lee. *Why Americans Don't Join the Party: Race, Immigration, and the Failure (of Political Parties) to Engage the Electorate.* Princeton, NJ: Princeton University Press, 2010.

Hartz, Louis. *The Liberal Tradition in America: An Interpretation of American Political Thought since the Revolution.* New York: Harcourt Brace, 1955.

Hanson, Peter. "Flag Burning." In *Public Opinion and Constitutional Controversy*, ed. Nathaniel Persily, Jack Citrin, and Patrick J. Egan. New York: Oxford University Press, 2008.

Hanson, Victor Davis. *Between War and Peace: Lessons from Afghanistan to Iraq.* New York: Random House, 2004.

Hetherington, Marc J. "Partisanship and Polarization." In *New Directions in Public Opinion*, ed. Adam Berkinsky. New York: Routledge Press, 2011.

"Putting Polarization in Perspective." *British Journal of Political Science* 39 (2009): 413–48.

Higham, John. "Multiculturalism and Universalism: A History and Critique." *American Quarterly* 45, no. 2 (1993): 195–219.

Strangers in the Land: Patterns of American Nativism, 1860–1925. Brunswick, NJ: Rutgers University Press, 1955.

Hillygus, D. Sunshine, and Todd G. Shields. *The Persuadable Voter: Wedge Issues in Presidential Campaigns.* Princeton, NJ: Princeton University Press, 2008.

Himmelfarb, Gertrude. *One Nation, Two Cultures.* New York: Alfred A. Knopf, 1999.

Hirschfield, Lawrence A. *Race in the Making: Cognition, Culture, and the Child's Construction of Human Kinds.* Cambridge, MA: MIT Press, 1996.

Hochschild, Jennifer. *Facing Up to the American Dream: Race, Class, and the Soul of the Nation.* Princeton, NJ: Princeton University Press, 1995.

Hochschild, Jennifer, Vesla Weaver, and Traci Burch. *Creating a New Racial Order: How Immigration, Multiracialism, Genomics, and the Young Can Remake Race in America.* Princeton, NJ: Princeton University Press, 2012.

Hollinger, David A. "Authority, Solidarity, and the Political Economy of Identity: The Case of the United States." *Diacritics* 29, no. 4 (1999): 116–27.

"From Identity to Solidarity." *Daedalus* 135, no. 4 (2006).

Postethnic America: Beyond Multiculturalism. New York: Basic Books, 2006.

Horowitz, Donald L. *Ethnic Groups in Conflict.* Berkeley: University of California Press, 1985.

Huddy, Leonie, and Nadia Khatib. "American Patriotism, National Identity, and Political Involvement." *American Journal of Political Science* 51, no. 1 (2007): 63–77.

Huddy, Leonie, and David O. Sears. "Qualified Public Support for Bilingual Education: Some Policy Implications." *Annals of the American Academy of Political and Social Science* 508 (1990): 119–34.

Hunter, James Davison. *Culture Wars*. New York: Basic Books, 1991.

Huntington, Samuel P. "The Hispanic Challenge." *Foreign Policy* (March/April 2004): 32.
Who Are We? The Challenges to America's National Identity. New York: Simon & Schuster, 2004.

Hurtado, Aida, Patricia Gurin, and Timothy Peng. "Social Identities – A Framework for Studying the Adaptations of Immigrants and Ethnics: Mexicans in the United States." *Social Problems* 41, no. 1 (1994): 129–51.

Hyman, Herbert. "Problems in the Collection of Opinion-Research Data." *American Journal of Sociology* 55, no. 4 (1950): 362–70.

Hyman, Herbert, and Paul B. Sheatsley. "Attitudes toward Desegregation." *Scientific American* 211 (1966): 16–23.

"The Authoritarian Personality: A Methodological Critique." In *Studies in the Scope and Method of the Authoritarian Personality*, ed. Richard Christie and Marie Jahoda. Glencoe, IL: Free Press, 1954.

Jacobson, Gary. *A Divider, Not a Uniter: George W. Bush and the American People*. New York: Pearson, 2007.

Jacoby, Tamar. "Rainbow's End." *The Washington Post*, May 16, 2004, p. BW03. Available online at www.washingtonpost.com/wp-dyn/articles/A25699-2004May13.html.

Joppke, Christian, and Steven Lukes. "Introduction: Multicultural Questions." In *Multicultural Questions*, ed. Christian Joppke and Steven Lukes. Oxford: Oxford University Press, 1999.

Jost, John T., Mahzarin R. Banaji, and Brian S. Nosek. "A Decade of System Justification Theory: Accumulated Evidence of Conscious and Unconscious Bolstering of the Status Quo." *Political Psychology* 25 (2004).

Jost, John T., Christopher M. Federico, and Jaime L. Napier. "Political Ideology: Its Structure, Function, and Electoral Affinities." *Annual Review of Psychology* 60 (2009): 307–37.

Kallen, Horace. *Cultural Pluralism and the American Idea: An Essay in Social Philosophy*. Philadelphia: University of Pennsylvania Press, 1956.

Karsten, Peter. *Patriot-Heroes in England and America*. Madison: University of Wisconsin Press, 1978.

Kateb, George. *Patriotism and Other Mistakes*. New Haven, CT: Yale University Press, 2006.

Kelley, Harold H. "Two Functions of Reference Groups." In *Society for the Psychological Study of Social Issues, Readings in Social Psychology*, ed. Guy Swanson, Theodore Newcomb, and Eugene Hartley. New York: Holt, 1952.

Kelly, Paul. "Introduction: Between Culture and Equality." In *Multiculturalism Reconsidered*, ed. Paul Kelly. Malden, MA: Polity Press, 2002.

Kennedy, Randall. *The Persistence of the Color Line: Racial Politics and the Obama Presidency*. New York: Pantheon, 2011.

Key, V. O., Jr. *Southern Politics in State and Nation*. New York: Alfred A. Knopf, 1949.

Kibria, Nazil. "The Concept of 'Bicultural Families' and Its Implications for Research on Immigrant and Ethnic Families." In *Immigration and the Family. Research and Policy on U.S. Immigrants*, ed. Alan Booth, Ann C. Crouter, and Nancy Landale. Mahwah, NJ: Lawrence Erlbaum Associates, 1997.

Kincheloe, Joe, and Shirley Steinberg. *Changing Multiculturalism*. London: Open University Press, 1997.

Kinder, Donald R. "Attitude and Action in the Realm of Politics." In *Handbook of Social Psychology*, ed. Daniel Gilbert, Susan Fiske, and Gardner Lindzey. Boston: McGraw-Hill, 1998.

"Belief Systems after Converse." In *Electoral Democracy*, ed. Michael McKuen and George Rabinowitz. Ann Arbor: University of Michigan Press, 2000.

Kinder, Donald, and Allison Dale-Riddle. *The End of Race? Obama, 2008, and Racial Politics in America*. New Haven, CT: Yale University Press, 2012.

Kinder, Donald, and Cindy D. Kam. *Us against Them: Ethnocentric Foundations of American Opinion*. Chicago: University of Chicago Press, 2009.

Kinder, Donald R., and Lynn M. Sanders. *Divided by Color: Racial Politics and Democratic Ideals*. Chicago: University of Chicago Press, 1996.

Kinder, Donald R., and David O. Sears. "Prejudice and Politics: Symbolic Racism versus Racial Threats to the Good Life." *Journal of Personality and Political Psychology* 40 (1981): 414–31.

King, Desmond. *Making Americans: Immigration, Race, and the Origins of the Diverse Democracy*. Cambridge, MA: Harvard University Press, 2000.

Kukathas, Chandran. "The Life of Brian, or Now for Something Completely Difference-Blind." In *Multiculturalism Reconsidered*, ed. Paul Kelly. Malden, MA: Polity Press, 2002.

Kymlicka, Will. *Multicultural Citizenship: A Liberal Theory of Minority Rights*. Oxford: Oxford University, 1995.

Politics in the Vernacular: Nationalism, Multiculturalism, and Citizenship. Oxford: Oxford University Press, 2001.

Lapinski, John S., Pia Peltola, Greg Shaw, and Alan Yang. "Trends: Immigrants and Immigration." *Public Opinion Quarterly* 61 (1997): 356–83.

Le, Loan, and Jack Citrin. "Affirmative Action." In *Public Opinion and Constitutional Controversy*, ed. Nathaniel Persily, Jack Citrin, and Patrick J. Egan. New York: Oxford University Press, 2008.

Lee, Jennifer, and Frank D. Bean. "America's Changing Color Lines: Immigration, Race/Ethnicity, and Multiracial Identification." *Annual Review of Sociology* 30 (2004): 221–42.

The Diversity Paradox: Immigration and the Color Line in Twenty-First Century America. New York: Russell Sage Foundation, 2010.

Levine, Robert, and Donald T. Campbell. *Ethnocentricism: Theories of Conflict, Ethnic Attitudes and Group Behavior*. New York: Wiley, 1972.

Levy, Jacob T. *The Multiculturalism of Fear*. Oxford: Oxford University Press, 2000.

Levy, Morris, Jack Citrin, and Robert Van Houweling. "Americans Fill Out President Obama's Census Form: What Is His Race?" Unpublished paper presented at the 2012 Midwest Political Science Association Conference, Chicago, IL.

Lewis-Beck, Michael S., William G. Jacoby, Helmut Norpoth, and Herbert F. Weisberg. *The American Voter Revisited*. Ann Arbor: University of Michigan Press, 2009.

Lien, Pei-te, M. Margaret Conway, and Janelle Wong. "The Contours and Sources of Ethnic Identity Choices among Asian Americans." *Social Science Quarterly* 84, no. 2 (2003): 461–81.

The Politics of Asian Americans: Diversity and Community. New York: Routledge, 2004.

Lind, Michael. *The Next American Nation: The New Nationalism and the Fourth American Revolution*. New York: Free Press, 1995.

Lipset, Seymour Martin, and Gary Marks. *It Didn't Happen Here: Why Socialism Failed in the United States*. New York: W. W. Norton & Company, 2000.

McCarty, Nolan, Keith T. Poole, and Howard Rosenthal. *Polarized America: The Dance of Ideology and Unequal Riches*. Cambridge, MA: MIT Press, 2006.

Mannheim, Karl. "The Problem of Generations." In *Essays on the Sociology of Knowledge*, by Karl Mannheim, ed. Paul Kecskemeti. Orlando, FL: Mariner Books, 1955.

Massey, Douglas S., and Nancy A. Denton. *American Apartheid: Segregation and the Making of the Underclass*. Cambridge, MA: Harvard University Press, 1993.

Medin, Douglas L., and Andrew Ortnoy. "Psychological Essentialism." In *Similarity and Analogical Reading*, ed. Stella Vosniadou and Andrew Ortony. New York: Cambridge University Press, 1989.

Migration Policy Institute Data Hub. Available online at www.migrationinformation.org/DataHub/charts/final.fb.shtml (accessed June 25, 2013).

Migration Policy Institute Data Hub. Available online at www.migrationinformation.org/datahub/acscensus.cfm# (accessed June 25, 2013).

Mill, John Stuart. *Considerations on Representative Government*. London, England: Parker, Son, and Bourn, 1861, chapter 16.

Miller, Arthur H., Patricia Gurin, Gerald Gurin, and Olga Malanchuk. "Group Consciousness and Political Participation." *American Journal of Political Science* 25 (1981): 494–511.

Miller, David. *Citizenship and National Identity*. Cambridge, UK: Polity Press, 2000.

Market, State, and Community: Theoretical Foundations of Market Socialism. Oxford, UK: Clarendon Press, 1989.

On Nationality. New York: Oxford University Press, 1995.

Miller, Warren E., and J. Merrill Shanks. *The New American Voter*. Cambridge, MA: Harvard University Press, 1996.

Moller Okin, Susan, Joshua Cohen, Matthew Howard, and Martha C. Nussbaum. *Is Multiculturalism Bad for Women?* Princeton, NJ: Princeton University Press, 1999.

Myrdal, Gunnar. *An American Dilemma: The Negro Problem and Modern Democracy*. New York: Harper & Row, 1942.

Nash, Gary B., Charlotte Crabtree, and Ross E. Dunn. *History on Trial: Culture Wars and the Teaching of the Past*. New York: Alfred A. Knopf, 1997.

National Council of La Raza. "Latino Voters and the 2010 Election: Numbers, Parties, and Issues." Available online at www.nclr.org/images/uploads/publications/REPORT_-_NCLR_Latino_Vote_in_2010_JK.pdf.

Nielsen, Kai. "Cultural Nationalism, Neither Ethnic nor Civic." In *Theorizing Nationalism*, ed. Ronald Beiner. Albany: State University of New York Press, 1999.

Norman, Wayne. "Theorizing Nationalism (Normatively): The First Steps." In *Theorizing Nationalism*, ed. Ronald Beiner. Albany: State University of Press of New York, 1999.

Nteta, Tatishe. "The Impact of Differentiation on African American Attitudes toward Immigration." Paper presented at the 2006 annual meeting of the Midwest Political Science Association. Chicago, IL.

Oakes, Penelope. "Psychological Groups and Political Psychology: A Response to Huddy's 'Critical Examination of Social Identity Theory.'" *Political Psychology* 23, no. 4 (2002): 809–24.

Omi, Michael. "Shifting the Blame: Racial Ideology and Politics in the Post-Civil Rights Era." *Critical Sociology* 18, no. 3 (1999): 77–98.

Parekh, Bhikhu. "Barry and the Dangers of Liberalism." In *Multiculturalism Reconsidered*, ed. Paul Kelly. Malden, MA: Polity Press, 2002.

Rethinking Multiculturalism. Cambridge, MA: Harvard University Press, 2000.

Parker, Christopher S., and Matt A. Barreto. *Change They Can't Believe In: The Tea Party and Reactionary Politics in America*. Princeton, NJ: Princeton University Press, 2013.

Parrillo, Vincent N. *Diversity in America*. Thousand Oaks, CA: Pine Forge Press, 1996.

Passel, Jeffrey. "Mexican Immigration to the U.S.: The Latest Estimates" (2011). Available online at http://migrationin.ucdavis.edu/cf/files/2011-may/passel-new-patterns-in-usimmigration.pdf.

Pearson, Kathryn, and Jack Citrin. "The Political Assimilation of the Fourth Wave." In *Transforming Politics, Transforming America: The Political and Civic Incorporation of Immigrants in the United States*, ed. Taeku Lee, Karthick Ramakrishnan, and Ricardo Ramirez. Charlottesville: University of Virginia Press, 2006.

Pew Hispanic Center. "When Labels Don't Fit: Hispanics and Their Views of Identity." April Report (2012): 12–13.

"2002 National Survey of Latinos: Summary of Findings." Washington, DC, December. Available online at www.pewhispanic.org/files/reports/15.pdf.

"2011 Views of Immigration Policy." Available online at www.pewhispanic.org/2011/12/28/iv-views-of-immigration-policy-2/.

Pew Research Center. "America's Immigration Quandary: No Consensus on Immigration Problem or Proposed Fixes" (2006). Available online at www.people-press.org/files/legacy-pdf/274.pdf.

"The Rise of Asian Americans," Washington, DC, July 2012. Available online at www.pewsocialtrends.org/files/2012/06/SDT-The-Rise-of-Asian-Americans-Full-Report.pdf.

"2011 Public Favors Tougher Border Controls and Path to Citizenship." Available online at www.people-press.org/2011/02/24/public-favors-tougher-border-controls-and-path-to-citizenship/.

"2012 Latinos and Immigration Policy." Available online at www.pewhispanic.org/2012/10/11/latinos-and-immigration-policy/.

2012 Survey of Asian-Americans. Available online at www.people-press.org/2013/03/28/most-say-illegal-immigrants-should-be-allowed-to-stay-but-citizenship-is-more-divisive/.

Pew Research Center for the People and the Press. "In Gay Marriage Debate, Both Supporters and Opponents See Legal Recognition as 'Inevitable.'" June 6, 2013.

Portes, Alejandro, and Ruben G. Rumbaut. *Legacies: The Story of the Immigrant Second Generation*. Berkeley: University of California Press, 2001.

Prentice, Deborah, and Dale Miller. "Some Consequences of a Belief in a Group Essence: The Category Divide Hypothesis." In *Cultural Divides: Understanding and Overcoming Group Conflict*, ed. Deborah Prentice and Dale Miller. New York: Russell Sage Foundation, 1999.

Phinney, Jean S. "Ethnic Identity in Adolescents and Adults: Review of Research." *Psychological Bulletin* 108, no. 3 (1990): 499–514.

Pickus, Noah. *True Faith and Allegiance: Immigration and American Civic Nationalism*. Princeton, NJ: Princeton University Press, 2005.

Pitkin, Hanna. *The Concept of Representation*. Berkeley: University of California Press, 1972.

Poole, Keith T., and Howard Rosenthal. "The Polarization of American Politics." *Journal of Politics* 46 (1984): 1061–79.

Portes, Alejandro, and Dag MacLeod. "What Shall I Call Myself? Hispanic Identity Formation in the Second Generation." *Ethnic and Racial Studies* 19, no. 3 (1996): 523–47.

Portes, Alejandro, and Rubén Rumbaut. *Immigrant America: A Portrait*. Berkeley: University of California Press, 1996.

Legacies: The Story of the Immigrant Second Generation. Berkeley: University of California Press, 2001.

Portes, Alejandro, and Min Zhou. "The New Second Generation: Segmented Assimilation and Its Variants." *Annals of the American Academy of Political and Social Science* 530 (1993): 74–96.

Prentice, Deborah A., and Dale T. Miller, eds. *Cultural Divides: Understanding and Overcoming Group Conflict*. New York: Russell Sage Foundation, 1999, pp. 23–24.

Prewitt, Kenneth. "Demography, Diversity, and Democracy: The 2000 Census Story." The Brookings Institution (2002). Available online at www.brookings.edu/articles/2002/winter_demographics_prewitt.aspx.

Quillian, Lincoln. "Prejudice as a Response to Perceived Group Threat: Population Composition and Anti-Immigrant and Racial Prejudice in Europe." *American Sociological Review* 60 (1995): 586–611.

Reich, Robert B. *The Work of Nations: Preparing Ourselves for 21st Century Capitalism*. New York: Simon & Schuster, 1993.

Rhea, Joseph Tilden. *Race Pride and the American Identity*. Cambridge, MA: Harvard University Press, 1997.

Rodriguez, Richard. *Hunger of Memory: The Education of Richard Rodriguez*. New York: The Dial Press, 1982.

Rohde, David W. *Parties and Leaders in the Post-Reform House*. Chicago: University of Chicago Press, 1991.

Sabagh, Georges, and Mehdi Bozorgmehr. "Population Change: Immigration and Ethnic Transformation." In *Ethnic Los Angeles*, ed. Roger Waldinger and Mehdi Bozorgmehr. New York: Russell Sage Foundation, 1996.

Salins, Peter D. *Assimilation, American Style*. New York: Basic Books, 1997.

Sassen, Saskia. *Losing Control? Sovereignty in an Age of Globalization*. New York: Columbia University Press, 1996.

Schatz, Robert T., Ervin Staub, and Howard Lavine. "On the Varieties of National Attachment: Blind vs. Constructive Patriotism," *Political Psychology* 20, no. 1 (1999): 151–74.

Schildkraut, Deborah J. *Americanization in the Twenty-First Century: Public Opinion in the Age of Immigration*. New York: Cambridge University Press, 2011.

"The More Things Change ... American Identity and Mass and Elite Responses to 9/11." *Political Psychology* 23, no. 3 (2009): 511–35.

Press 'One' for English: Language Policy, Public Opinion, and American Identity. Princeton, NJ: Princeton University Press, 2005.

Schlesinger, Arthur M., Jr. *The Disuniting of America: Reflections on a Multicultural Society*. New York: W. W. Norton & Company, 1998.

Schlesinger, Joseph A. "The New American Political Party." *American Political Science Review* 79 (1985): 1152–69.

Schrag, Peter. *Paradise Lost: California's Experience, America's Future*. New York: New Press, 1998.

Schuck, Peter H. "The Disconnect between Public Attitudes and Policy Outcomes in Immigration." In *Debating Immigration*, ed. Carol Swain. New York: Cambridge University Press, 2007.

Diversity in America: Keeping Government at a Safe Distance. Cambridge, MA: The Belknap Press of Harvard University Press, 2003.

"Immigration." In *Understanding America: The Anatomy of an Exceptional Nation*, ed. Peter H. Schuck and James Q. Wilson. New York: Public Affairs, 2008.

Schuman, Howard, and Stanley Presser. *Questions and Answers in Attitude Surveys*. San Diego: Academic Press, 1981.

Schuman, Howard, Charlotte Steeh, Lawrence D. Bobo, and Maria Krysan. *Racial Attitudes in America: Trends and Interpretations*, Revised Edition. Cambridge, MA: Harvard University Press, 1997.

Sciolino, Elaine. "Ban on Head Scarves Takes Effect in France." *The New York Times*, September 3, 2004.

"Tensions over French Identity Shape Voter Drives." *The New York Times*, May 30, 2007.

Sears, David O. "Black-White Conflict: A Model for the Future of Ethnic Politics in Los Angeles." In *New York and Los Angeles: Politics, Society, and Culture: A Comparative View*, ed. David Halle. Chicago: University of Chicago Press, 2003.

"Experimental Social Psychology, Broader Contexts, and the Politics of Multiculturalism." In *The Political Psychology of Democratic Citizenship*, ed. Eugene Borgida, Christopher M. Federico, and John L. Sullivan. New York: Oxford University Press, 2009, pp. 325–43.

Sears, David O., Jack Citrin, Sharmaine Cheleden, and Colette van Laar. "Is Cultural Balkanization Psychologically Inevitable?" In *Cultural Divides: Understanding and Overcoming Group Conflict*, ed. Deborah Prentice and Dale Miller. New York: Russell Sage Foundation, 2000.

Sears, David O., Mingying Fu, P. J. Henry, and Kerra Bui. "The Origins and Persistence of Ethnic Identity among the 'New Immigrant' Groups." *Social Psychology Quarterly* 66, no. 4 (2008): 419–37.

Sears, David O., and P. J. Henry. "The Origins of Symbolic Racism." *Journal of Personality and Social Psychology* 85, no. 2 (2003): 259–74.

"Over Thirty Years Later: A Contemporary Look at Symbolic Racism." In *Advances in Experimental Social Psychology*, vol. 37, ed. Mark P. Zanna. New York: Academic Press, 2005, 95–150.

Sears, David O., Carl. P. Hensler, and Leslie K. Speer. "Whites' Opposition to 'Busing': Self-Interest or Symbolic Politics?" *American Political Science Review* 73 (1979): 369–84.

Sears, David O., John J. Hetts, Jim Sidanius, and Lawrence Bobo. "Race in American Politics: Framing the Debates." In *Racialized Politics: The Debate about Racism in America*, ed. David O. Sears, Jim Sidanius, and Lawrence Bobo. Chicago: University of Chicago Press, 2000.

Sears, David O., and Tom Jessor. "Whites' Racial Policy Attitudes: The Role of White Racism." *Social Science Quarterly* 77 (1996): 751–59.

Sears, David O., and Donald Kinder. "Whites' Opposition to Busing: On Conceptualizing and Operationalizing Group Conflict." *Journal of Personality and Social Psychology* 48 (1985): 1141–47.

Sears, David O., and John B. McConahay. *The Politics of Violence: The New Urban Blacks and the Watts Riot*. Boston: Houghton Mifflin, 1973.

Sears, David O., and Victoria Savalei. "The Political Color Line in America: Many 'Peoples of Color' or Black Exceptionalism?" *Political Psychology* 27, no. 6 (2006): 895–924.

Sears, David O., Jim Sidanius, and Lawrence Bobo, eds. *Racialized Politics: The Debate About Racism in America*. Chicago: University of Chicago Press, 2000.

Sears, David O., Colette van Laar, Mary Carrillo, and Rick Kosterman. "Is It Really Racism?: The Origins of White American Opposition to Race-Targeted Policies." *Public Opinion Quarterly* 61 (1997): 16–53.

Sen, Amartya. "Beyond Identity: Other People." *The New Republic* (December 18, 2000): 23–30.

Shamir, Michal, and Asher Arian. "Collective Identity and Electoral Competition in Israel." *American Political Science Review* 93 (1999): 265–77.

Shelby County, Alabama v. Holder, Attorney General, et al. 570 U.S. (2013).

Sidanius, Jim, Colette van Laar, Shana Levin, and Stacey Sinclair. "Social Hierarchy Maintenance and Assortment into Social Roles: A Social Dominance Perspective." *Group Processes and Intergroup Relations* 6 (2003): 333–52.

Sidanius, Jim, Seymour Feshbach, Shana Levin, and Felicia Pratto. "The Interface between Ethnic and National Attachment: Ethnic Pluralism or Ethnic Dominance?" *Public Opinion Quarterly* 61 (1997): 102–33.

Sidanius, Jim, and John Petrocik. "Communal and National Identity in a Multiethnic State: A Comparison of Three Perspectives." In *Social Identity, Intergroup Conflict, and Conflict Reduction*, ed. Richard D. Ashmore, Lee Jussim, and David Wilder. New York: Oxford University Press, 2001.

Sidanius, Jim, and Felicia Pratto. *Social Dominance: An Intergroup Theory of Social Hierarchy and Oppression*. New York: Cambridge University Press, 1999.

Sides, John, and Jack Citrin. "European Opinion about Immigration: The Role of Identities, Interests, and Information." *British Journal of Political Science* 37 no. 3 (2007): 477–504.

Simon, Bernd, and Bert Klandermans. "Politicized Collective Identity: A Social Psychological Analysis." *American Psychologist* 56, no. 4 (2001): 319.

Singer, Audrey. "The Rise of New Immigrant Gateways." *The Living Cities Census Series*. Washington, DC: The Brookings Institution, 2004.

Skocpol, Theda, and Vanessa Williamson. *The Tea Party and the Remaking of Republican Conservatism*. Cambridge, MA: Harvard University Press, 2012.

Smith, Anthony D. *The Ethnic Origins of Nations*. Oxford: Blackwell, 1986.

National Identity. Reno: University of Nevada Press, 1991.

Smith, Rogers M. "Beyond Tocqueville, Myrdal, and Hartz: The Multiple Traditions in America." *The American Political Science Review* 87, no. 3 (1993): 549–66.

Civic Ideals: Conflicting Visions of Citizenship in U.S. Public Law. Chelsea, MI: Yale University Press, 1997.

"Living in a Promise Land?: Mexican Immigration and American Obligation." *Perspectives in Politics* 9, no. 3 (September 2011): 545–557.

Smith, Tom W., and Lars Jarkko. *National Pride: A Cross-National Analysis*. GSS Cross-National Report No. 19. Chicago: NORC, 1998.

Smith, Tom W., and Seokho Kim. "National Pride in Comparative Perspective: 1995/96 and 2003/04." *International Journal of Public Opinion Research* 18 (2006), 127–36.

Sniderman, Paul M., and Edward G. Carmines. *Reaching Beyond Race*. Cambridge, MA: Harvard University Press, 1997.

Sniderman, Paul M., Gretchen C. Crosby, and William G. Howell. "The Politics of Race." In *Racialized Politics: The Debate about Racism in America*, ed. David O. Sears, Jim Sidanius, and Lawrence Bobo. Chicago: University of Chicago Press, 2000.

Sniderman Paul M., and Thomas Piazza. *The Scar of Race*. Cambridge, MA: Harvard University Press, 1993.

Sonenshein, Raphael J. *Politics in Black and White: Race and Power in Los Angeles*. Princeton, NJ: Princeton University Press, 1994.

Song, Sarah. "Multiculturalism." *Encyclopedia of Political Theory*, ed. Mark Bevir. Thousand Oaks, CA: Sage, 2010.

"What It Means to Be an American?" *Daedalus* (Spring 2009): 31–39.

Spinner, Jeffrey. *The Boundaries of Citizenship*. Baltimore: Johns Hopkins Press, 1994.

Spiro, Peter J. *Beyond Citizenship: American Identity after Globalization*. New York: Oxford University Press, 2007.

Staerklé, Christian, Jim Sidanius, Eva G. T. Green, and Ludwin Molina. "Ethnic Minority-Majority Asymmetry and Attitudes towards Immigrants across 11 Nations." *Psicologia Política* 30 (2005): 7–26.

Staub, Ervin. "Blind versus Constructive Patriotism: Moving from Embeddedness in the Group to Critical Loyalty and Action." In *Patriotism in the Lives of Individuals and Nations*, ed. Dani Bar-Tal and Ervin Staub. Chicago: Nelson-Hall and Schatz, 1997.

Steehm, Charlotte, and Maria Krysan. "Trends: Affirmative Action and the Public, 1970–1995." *Public Opinion Quarterly* 60 (1996): 128–58.

Stoll, Michael A. "African Americans and the Color Line." In *The American People: Census 2000*, ed. Reynolds Farley and John Haaga. New York: Russell Sage Foundation, 2005.

"Job Sprawl and the Spatial Mismatch between Blacks and Jobs." Washington, DC: The Brookings Institution, February 2005.

Tafoya, Sonya M., Hans Johnson, and Laura E. Hill. "Who Chooses to Choose Two?" In *The American People: Census 2000*, ed. Reynolds Farley and John Haaga. New York: Russell Sage Foundation, 2005.

Tajfel, Henri. "Social Categorization, Social Identity, and Social Comparison." In *Differentiation between Social Groups: Studies in the Social Psychology of Intergroup Relations*, ed. Henri Tajfel. London: Academic Press, 1978.

Tajfel, Henri, and John C. Turner. "The Social Identity Theory of Inter-Group Behavior." In *Psychology of Intergroup Relations*, ed. William Austin and Stephen Worchel. Chicago: Nelson-Hall, 1986.

Takaki, Ronald. *A Different Mirror: A History of Multicultural America*. New York: Back Bay Books, 1993.

Tamir, Yael. *Liberal Nationalism*. Princeton, NJ: Princeton University Press, 1993.

Taylor, Charles. "The Politics of Recognition." In *Multiculturalism: Examining the Politics of Recognition*, ed. Amy Gutmann. Princeton, NJ: Princeton University Press, 1994.

Tesler, Michael. "The Spillover of Racialization into Health Care: How President Obama Polarized Public Opinion by Racial Attitudes and Race." *American Journal of Political Science*, 56 (2012): 690–705.

Tesler, Michael, and David O. Sears. *Obama's Race: The 2008 Election and the Dream of a Post-Racial America*. Chicago: University of Chicago Press, 2010.

Theiss-Morse, Elizabeth. *Who Counts As an American? The Boundaries of National Identity*. New York: Cambridge University Press, 2009.

Thernstrom, Abigail. "Language: Issues and Legislation." In *Harvard Encyclopedia of American Ethnic Groups*, ed. Stephan Thernstrom. Cambridge, MA: Harvard University Press, 1980.

Thernstrom, Stephan, and Abigail Thernstrom. *America in Black and White: One Nation, Indivisible*. New York: Simon & Schuster, 1997.

Thibaut, John W., and Harold H. Kelley. *The Social Psychology of Groups*. New York: John Wiley & Sons, 1959.

Tichenor, Daniel. *Dividing Lines: The Politics of Immigration Control in America*. Princeton, NJ: Princeton University Press, 2002.

"Strange Bedfellows: The Politics and Pathologies of Immigration Reform." *Labor Studies in Working Class History* 5 (2008).

United States. *Kerner Commission, Report of the National Advisory Commission on Civil Disorders*. Washington, DC: U.S. Government Printing Office, 1968.

U.S. Census Bureau, 2011. "An Overview: Race and Hispanic Origin and the 2010 Census." Available online at www.census.gov/prod/cen2010/briefs/c2010br-02.pdf (accessed August 20, 2013).

U.S. Census Bureau. State & County QuickFacts. Available online at http://quickfacts .census.gov/qfd/states/06/0644000.html (accessed August 20, 2013).

Uslaner, Eric. *The Decline of Comity in Congress*. Ann Arbor: University of Michigan Press, 1994.

Vaca, Nicholas. *Presumed Alliance*. New York: Harper Collins, 2004.

Valentino, Nicholas A., and David O. Sears. "Old Times There Are Not Forgotten: Race and Partisan Realignment in the Contemporary South." *American Journal of Political Science* 49, no. 3 (2005): 672–88.

Valls, Andrew. "A Liberal Defense of Black Nationalism." *American Political Science Review* 104, no. 3 (August 2010): 467–81.

Waldinger, Roger, and Mehdi Bozorgmehr, eds. *Ethnic Los Angeles*. New York: Russell Sage Foundation, 1996.

Walzer, Michael. *What It Means to Be an American*. New York: Marsilio Publishers, 1992.

Waters, Mary. *Black Identities: West Indian Dreams and American Realities*. Cambridge, MA: Harvard University Press, 2001.

Ethnic Options: Choosing Identities in America. Berkeley: University of California Press, 1990.

Wilson, James Q. "How Divided Are We?" *Commentary* (February 2009).

Wong, Cara J. *Boundaries of Obligation in American Politics: Geographic, National, and Racial Communities*. New York: Cambridge University Press, 2010.

Wong, Janelle, S. Karthick Ramakrishnan, Taeku Lee, and Jane Junn. *Asian American Political Participation: Emerging Constituents and Their Political Identities*. New York: Russell Sage Foundation, 2011, 162.

Wright, Matthew. "Policy Regimes and Normative Conceptions of National Identity in Mass Public Opinion." *Comparative Political Studies* 44 (2011): 598–624.

Wright, Matthew, Jack Citrin, and Jonathan Wand. "Alternative Measures of American National Identity: Implications for the Civic-Ethnic Distinction." *Political Psychology* 33 (2012): 469–82.

Yack, Bernard. "The Myth of the Civic Nation." In *Theorizing Nationalism*, ed. Ronald Beiner. Albany: State University of New York Press, 1999.

Young, Iris Marion. *Justice and the Politics of Difference*. Princeton, NJ: Princeton University Press, 1990.

Zolberg, Aristide R. *A Nation by Design: Immigration Policy in the Fashioning of America*. New York: Russell Sage Foundation, 2006.

Zoltan, Hajnal, and Taeku Lee. *Why Americans Don't Join the Party: Race, Immigration, and the Failure (of Political Parties) to Engage the Electorate*. Princeton, NJ: Princeton University Press, 2010.

Index

affirmative action, 24
  language policy and, 253
  political partisanship over, 243, 250
  racial backlash against, 117–118
  recruitment and training efforts
    compared to, 185
African Americans. *See also* black
    exceptionalism; ethnic group consciousness
  in ANES, 208–209
  assimilation model for, xxii, 10–11
  civil rights movement and, 3, 10–11
  conflicts with other ethnic groups, 95
  as culturally conservative, 252–253
  ethnic identity of, 39, 208–211
  in first U.S. census, xviii
  group consciousness among, xxv, 35–36,
    135, 143, 279–280
  hyphenated identity of, 151, 153
  on immigration policies, 214–216
  issue constraint, 200
  in Los Angeles County, 49
  national attachment, 61–62, 69,
    167, 168
  national identity, 41–42, 160–161
  nativist ideology toward, xix
  one-drop rule for, 98, 280
  opposition to multilingualism, 217
  patriotism, 58, 63–64, 234
  political ideology and national identity,
    235–236
  prejudice and discrimination towards, 35
  racially-targeted policies, 178–186, 193–194
  self-categorization, 149–151
  separatist movements for, 21–23, 126, 167

  soft multiculturalism and, 186–188
  vanguard, 76–79, 139–140
age
  public opinion on multiculturalism by,
    138–140
  vanguard hypothesis and, 144
American dilemma, xix
American flag
  under Flag Protection Act, 230
  legislated protections for, 229–230
  partisan differences, 230
  patriotism and, 64–65, 228–230
  as symbol of national identity, 28
American National Election Studies (ANES),
    46–47
  ethnic identity variables in, 161, 208–209
  feeling thermometer, 164
  issue constraint, 255–256
  multicultural indices, 253–254
  national identity, 46–47
  Patriotism Index, 231
  response rate, 46
  samples, 45
American national identity. *See also* patriotism
  for African Americans, 41–42, 160–161
  for Asian-Americans, 41–42
  assimilation and, 155–161
  boundaries of, 79–86
  as circle of we, 277–278
  civic *vs.* ethnic identity, 79–86, 168–171
  in contemporary U.S., 278–282
  content of, 79–86, 264–265
  cosmopolitan liberalism and, 43, 279
  definition of, 2

American national identity (cont.)
  e pluribus unum and, 26
  ethnic identity and, 267–269
  ethnic self-categorization and, 150,
    171
  hyphenated, 151–155
  in-group identification and, 278
  for Latino-Americans, 41–42
  measures of, 63
  Mexican immigration as challenge to, 4
  multiculturalism and, 43, 279
  national pride index for, 69–70
  Native Americans and, 7
  nativism and, 43
  political models of, 43–44
  self-reliance as part of, 121
  universal character of, 261–262
American racial order, 281
Americanism, xviii–xix
  assimilation and, 173
  civic traits for, 84
  as civil religion, 2
  ethnic traits for, 84
Americanization in the Twenty-First Century
    (Schildkraut), 81–82
Anderson, Benedict, 25
ANES. *See* American National Election Studies
anti-immigration movements, 187
Asian Americans. *See also* ethnic group
    consciousness
  conflicts with other ethnic groups, 95
  ethnic identity for, 158–160
  ethnic self-categorization for, 99–100
  hyphenated identities, 152
  illegal immigration and, public opinion on,
    196–197
  immigration policy and, 13, 195–197
  in Los Angeles County, 49–50
  national attachment for, 71–73, 172
  national identity for, 41–42
  plural identities for, 40
  politicized group consciousness for, 36
  population increases for, 13
assimilation, 34–38
  American national identity and, 155–161
  Americanism and, 173
  black exceptionalism and, 37
  civic identity and, 170–171
  as cleansing process, 8–9
  critiques of, 16
  cultural, 9–10
  definition of, 263–264

  ethnic group consciousness and,
    110, 118
  ethnic identity and, 113–114, 155–161,
    170–171
  group conscious policies, 212
  of immigrants, xxv, 5, 34–38, 71–73
  inter-generational, 111–112, 273–275
  language policy and, 198–199
  language spoken at home and, 158–160
  of Latinos, xxv, 111–112, 273–275
  of Mexicans, 23
  multiculturalism in conflict with, 16, 17
  patriotism and, 57–58, 72–73, 171
  perceived discrimination and, 107
  perceptions of common fate and, 106
  public opinion on, 136–137
  segmented, 42, 112–113
  self-categorization, 156–157
  social multiculturalism and, 125–126
  straight-line path to, 37
  strength of ethnic identity and, 105
  structural, 9
  whites, support for, 171
  during and after World War I, 9
  after World War II, 173
Assimilation in American Life (Gordon),
    9–10, 156
assimilation model, of cultural diversity, xxv
  for African Americans, xxii, 10–11
  contemporary challenges to, 10–13
  of European immigrants, 8–9
attachment. *See* national attachment

Banting, Keith, 17
Barone, Michael, 147
bilingual education, 192–193
  under Federal Bilingual Education Act,
    191, 247
  under Proposition, 227, 193
  public opinion about, 197–201
Billig, Michael, 6
biracialism
  ethnic self-categorization and, 100–101
  intermarriage and, 280–281
  as U.S. census category, 280
birthright citizenship, 188
bisexuality. *See* lesbian, gay, bisexual, and
    transgender community
black exceptionalism, xxii, xxv, 34–38. *See also*
    African Americans
  assimilation and, 37
  changing patterns of, 280

comparison of blacks with US-born
    Latinos, 275
definition of, 34–38, 263, 275–276
ethnic group consciousness and, 94, 98–99,
    118, 143–144
ethnic identity and, 113–114, 160–161
and link between multiculturalism and
    national attachment, 168
model, xxii, xxv
patriotism and, 58, 63–64
perceived discrimination and, 107
perceived ethnic conflict and, 94
perceptions of common fate and, 106
strength of ethnic identity and, 105
Boundaries of Obligation in American Politics
    (Wong), 81–82
Brewer, Marilynn, 41
Brown v. Board of Education, 10
Bush, George H. W., 228
Bush, George W., 226, 228
    immigration reform proposals, 246–247

Canada, multiculturalism in, 16–17
Canadian Multiculturalism Day, 17
census, U.S., xviii
    biracial categories in, 280
chain migration, 12
chauvinism, 60–66
    ethnocentrism and, 211
    International Social Survey Program and, 70
    national pride and, 67
    after 9/11, 69
    patriotism compared to, 66–70
    racial differences in, 67–69
Chavez, Cesar, 245
Cheney, Lynne, 74
Chong, Dennis, 74–75
circle of we, 277–278
citizenship
    birthright, 188
    globalization and, 5–6
    illegal immigration and, 196
    patriotism and, 8
Citrin, Jack, 5, 81–82, 265
City of Richmond v. J. A. Croson and Co., 127
civic creed, xviii–xix. *See also* Americanism
Civic Ideals (Smith, R.), xix
civic nations, 27, 80, 81–82
    ethnic identity in, 147
civic *vs.* ethnic identity, 170–171
    policy preferences and, 220
Civil Rights Act of 1964, xvii, 10

civil rights movement
    African Americans during, 10–11
    multiculturalism and, 3, 18
    women in, 3
cognitive categorization theories, 30–31
coherence of attitudes
    among elites, 225–228
    of multiculturalism, 132–133, 272
    of perceived ethnic conflict, 90–97
    of policy preferences, 133, 199–201, 255–256
Cold War, 228
color-blind racism theory, 32
common fate, perceptions of, 97, 106
    assimilation hypothesis and, 106
    black exceptionalism and, 106
community control, 22–23
Conover, Pamela, 41
constitutional patriotism, 27
constraint issue. *See* coherence of attitudes
constructive patriotism, 59, 70, 264
Converse, Philip, 252
cosmopolitan liberalism
    American national identity and, 43, 279
    Americanism and, xviii–xix
    core principles of, xviii–xix
    cultural diversity and, xx
    discrimination under, xviii
    as inclusive, 278
    liberal consensus and, 1
    multiculturalism and, 24, 128
    nativism and, 2
    soft multiculturalism and, 24
Crevecoeur, Jean de, 6
cultural diversity. *See also* intergroup relations,
        in U.S.; multiculturalism
    academic discussion of, xxi
    cosmopolitan liberalism and, xx
    institutionalization of, 147
    nativism and, xx
    politicized group consciousness paradigm
        and, xxii
    social multiculturalism and, 122
    U.S. national unity and, xviii
cultural pluralism, 9
culture wars, 74, 226, 228

Democracy in America (de Tocqueville), 59, 82
Democratic Party
    affirmative action policy and, 250
    American flag and, legislative protections
        by, 230
    attachment to nation and, 232

Democratic Party (cont.)
  ethnic group consciousness and, 249, 251
  immigration policy and, 244–247
  multiculturalism and, attitudes toward,
    241–242
  polarization of, 223
  realignment of, 223
discrimination. *See also* Jim Crow
  against African Americans, 35
  under cosmopolitan liberalism, xviii
  perceived, 97, 106–107, 115
Dovidio, John, 278
Dubois, W. E. B., 10
Dukakis, Michael, 228

e pluribus unum
  ethnic identity and, 148
  ethnicity and, 26
  multiculturalism and, 3
  nationality and, 26
  as political ideal, 1–6
  racial conflict and, 4
educational institutions
  bilingual policies for, 192–193
  desegregation of, 182
  history standards in, 74
  multiculturalism in curricula, 74
Emerson, Ralph Waldo, xix
Emerson, Rupert, 56
English
  as common language, xviii
  under Federal Bilingual Education Act, 247
  under HR 123, 248
ethnic group consciousness, 97–111
  African Americans, 143, 279–280
  aggrieved, xxiv–xxv, 107–111
  American whites, 94
  assimilation hypothesis and, 110, 111–112,
    118
  black exceptionalism and, 94, 98–99, 118,
    143–144
  contented, 110
  definitions of, 97–99
  ethnic identity and, 211
  by ethnicity, xxiv–xxv, 103–104, 108–109,
    134–136, 266–267
  by immigration status, 112
  Latinos, 112, 194
  in Los Angeles County, 92–93
  multiculturalism and, 94
  national attachment and, 205–219
  partisanship and, 249, 251

  perceived discrimination and, 97, 106–107
  perceptions of common fate as part of,
    97, 106
  perceptions of conflict and, 91, 92, 95
  self-categorization in, 97, 99–102
  sense of group position theory and, 117
  social dominance theory and, 98
  strength of ethnic identification in, 97,
    102–105
  support of public policies and, 179–180, 202
  symbolic, 110
  theories of, 97–99
  typology of, 107–111
  vanguard hypothesis and, 89, 112–113
  for whites, 94, 97–111, 206–208, 249
ethnic identity
  among African Americans, 208–211
  American national identity and, 267–269
  among Asian Americans, 158–160
  assimilation hypothesis and, 113–114,
    155–161, 170–171
  black exceptionalism and, 113–114, 160–161
  civic identity and, 170–171
  in civic nations, 147
  development of, 146–147
  e pluribus unum and, 148
  ethnic group consciousness and, xxii, 211,
    265–267
  hyphenated, xxv, 148–155
  for immigrants, 156, 157–158, 160
  in-group favoritism and, 165
  among Latinos, 159, 166–167,
    208–211, 280
  multiculturalism and, 169, 238–239
  national attachment and, xxv, 148, 161–167,
    172, 173, 220–221
  origins of, 113–116
  perceived discrimination and, 115
  public policy influenced by, 205–219
  recognition of, 263
  religiosity and, 147
  for whites, 167
ethnic nations, 27
  citizen membership in, 80
  classification of, 81–82
ethnicity. *See also* multiculturalism
  e pluribus unum and, 26
  ethnic group consciousness and, xxiv–xxv,
    103–104
  group identification and, 33
  integration with national identity, xx
  issue constraint by, 200

multiculturalism influenced by, 123–124, 130, 193
politicized group consciousness paradigm for, xxii, 265–267
recognition of, xx
self-categorization and, 97, 99–102
socialization and, 42–43
ethnocentrism, 277
national chauvinism and, 211
Europe
multiculturalism policies in, 282
national identity in, 281
European immigration, 8

The Federalist Papers, 6
Flag Protection Act, 230
flags. *See* American flag
Founders, xviii, 6–10
Franklin, Benjamin, xviii, 6

gays. *See* lesbian, gay, bisexual, and transgender community
Gellner, Ernest, 25
General Social Survey (GSS), 134–136, 161
Gitlin, Todd, 3, 238
Glazer, Nathan, 16, 22, 24, 118
globalization
citizenship and, 5–6
national identity influenced by, 5–6
Gordon, Milton, 9–10, 156
group consciousness. *See* ethnic group consciousness
group-centered theories
group competition, 31–32
group conflict, 31
group position, 32
group-serving biases, 31
group-conscious policies. *See also* affirmative action; immigration policy; language policy
anti-out-group hostility and, 212
assimilation hypothesis and, 212
coherence of, 199–201
consensus in opinions on, 177–178, 189
cultural issue index, 254–257
economic issue index, 254–257
in episodic national data, 183–184
ethnic group consciousness as influence on, 179–180, 202, 205–219
ethnic identity and, 205–219
in Europe, 282
factor analysis of, 253
about illegal immigration, 188–190

indices for, 205
in-group pride as influence on, 220
issue constraints, among minorities, 200
issue constraints, among whites, 200
Jim Crow system and, 178–182
in LACSS, 181–182
about legal immigration, 186–188, 195–197
minorities' support for, 208–211
national attachment as influence on, 205–219
in national data, 217–219
national identity as influence on, 207, 210, 212
official English, 191–192
out-group hostility and, 220
partisanship over, 243–252
patriotism of whites and, 217
people of color hypothesis and, 194, 209
post-civil rights, 182–185
psychological origins of, 211–216
race-targeted, 178–186, 193–194, 213–214
racial cleavages over, 193
for soft multiculturalism, 185–186, 188, 189–190, 191–192
vanguard hypothesis and, 212
white support for, 206–208, 218
GSS. *See* General Social Survey

Hacker, Andrew, 3
Hart-Celler Act, 244. *See also* Immigration and Nationality Act
Hartz, Louis, 1
Higham, John, 2
Hollinger, David, 27
honor killing, 20
Horowitz, Donald, 25
Huntington, Samuel, xxiii–xxiv, 4, 11, 76–79, 80–82, 118, 147, 262
on Mexican immigration, 4, 56
hyphenated identity, 148–155
among African Americans, 149–151, 153
American identity as, 151–155
among Asian Americans, 152
dual identities, 278
emotional significance of, 152–153
among Latinos, 151, 152–153
meaning of, 152–155
patriotism and, 154
plural identities, 38–43
among whites, 149

identity. *See* American national identity; ethnic identity; hyphenated identity; national identity
identity politics, 238
illegal immigration
  Asian Americans and, public opinions on, 196–197
  citizenship and, 196
  Latinos and, public opinions on, 196–197
  policies for, 188–190
  political partisanship over, 244–247
  public opinion on, 188–189
Illegal Immigration and Immigrant Responsibility Act, 246
immigrants
  assimilation of, xxv, 5, 34–38, 71–73, 136–137
  birthright citizenship for, 188
  chain migration for, 12
  ethnic identity of, 156, 160
  European, 8
  in LACSS, 72–73
  in U.S., xviii
immigration. *See also* illegal immigration
  of Asians, 13, 195–197
  assimilation model and, xxi–xxii
  birthright citizenship and, 188
  ethnic group consciousness and, 112
  European, 8
  of Mexicans to U.S., 4, 56
  nativism and, xix–xx, 279
  Tea Party response to, 282
Immigration and Nationality Act (1965), xvii, 4, 11, 186, 244
immigration policy, 186–188, 195–197
  African American, public opinion, 214–216
  anti-out-group hostility and, 212
  border hawks and, 244–245
  FAIR and, 248
  Latino public opinion, 189–190, 196, 214–216, 250
  origins of support for, 215
  out-group hostility and, 220
  partisanship over, 244–247
  public opinion on, 186, 187
  Tea Party response to, 282
  whites and, public opinion on, 214–216
immigration reform
  under Bush, G. W., 246–247
  consequences of, xvii
  multiculturalism as result of, 175

Immigration Reform and Control Act (IRCA), 245
immigration status, xxiii–xxiv, 52, 72–73, 137
in-group favoritism, 31, 165
  American national identity and, 278
intergroup relations, in U.S.
  black exceptionalism and, 34–38
  ethnic group identification and, 33
  group competition theories, 31–32
  immigrant assimilation and, 34–38
  politicized group consciousness, 30–33
  psychology of, 30–33
intermarriage, 280–281
International Social Survey Program, 70
IRCA. *See* Immigration Reform and Control Act
Irish Americans, 262
issue indices, 254–257

Jacobson, Gary, 226
Jay, John, xviii, 6
Jefferson, Thomas, xviii
Jim Crow, as public policy, 178–182

Kallen, Horace, 9, 16, 21, 121, 262
Karsten, Peter, 58–59
Kateb, George, 59
Kerry, John, 228
King, Martin Luther, Jr., 10
King, Rodney, 92
Kymlicka, Will, 17, 19–23, 41

LACSS. *See* Los Angeles County Social Surveys
language policy, 191–192
  affirmative action and, 253
  African American opposition to, 217
  anti-out-group hostility and, 212
  assimilation hypothesis and, 198–199
  Bilingual Education Act and, 191
  civic identity and, 220
  coherence with other group-conscious policies, 197–201
  in educational institutions, 192–193
  ethnic cleavages about, 190–193, 198
  in issue space, 253
  Latino opposition to multilingualism, 217
  multiculturalism and, 175–176
  Official English movement, 191–192
  origins of support for, 216
  out-group hostility and, 220
  partisanship about, 247–248
  patriotism as influence on, 221

people of color hypothesis and, 198
public opinion on, 271
as public policy, 190–193, 197–201, 216–217
white opposition to, 216–217
language rights. *See* language policy
language spoken at home
assimilation and, 158–160
for Latinos, 159
LASUI. *See* Los Angeles Study of Urban Equality
Latino National Survey, 126
Latinos. *See also* ethnic group consciousness
in ANES, 208–209
assimilation of, 111–112, 273–275
ethnic conflict perceived by, 95
ethnic group consciousness among, 112, 135, 194
ethnic identity among, 159, 166–167, 208–211, 280
ethnic self-categorization, 99–100, 157
hyphenated identity, 151, 152–153
illegal immigration, public opinions about, 196–197
immigration policy, public opinion about, 189–190, 195–197, 214–216, 250
immigration status, 54
issue constraint among, 200
language spoken at home and, 159
national attachment for, 61–62, 71–73, 167, 168, 172
national identity, 41–42, 159–158
partisanship, 235–236
patriotism of, xxiii–xxiv, xxv, 72, 154, 214, 234
plural identities among, 40
politicized group consciousness, 36
population growth, 12
population transition from immigrant to U.S.-born, 222
public opinion about language policy, 217
public opinion about multiculturalism, 131–132, 137
race-targeted policies and, 214, 222
vanguard, 76–79, 139–140, 222
as voting block, 246–247
legal immigration. *See* immigration
lesbian, gay, bisexual, and transgender (LGBT) community, 3
Levy, Jacob, 20
liberal consensus, 1–6
cosmopolitan liberalism and, 1
liberal nationalism, 276

Lind, Michael, 9
Lipset, Seymour Martin, 2
Los Angeles County, California
African American demographics in, 49
Asian population in, 49–50
demographic description of, 50–55
ethnic conflict in, 92–93
ethnic diversity in, 47–48
immigration status in, 52
languages spoken at home, 53
Latinos in, by immigration status, 54
Los Angeles city compared to, 47
national identity in, 47–55
Los Angeles County Social Surveys (LACSS), 47–50
demography, 49
methodology, 47–55
Los Angeles Study of Urban Equality (LASUI), 106

Mannheim, Karl, xxii
media, multiculturalism in, 74
melting pot, U.S. as, 5, 8–9
The Melting Pot (Zangwill), 8–9
methodology, 46–50
Mexicans
assimilation of, xxv, 23
Huntington critique on immigration of, 4, 56
immigration of, as challenge to traditional American identity, 4
Miller, David, 26, 276
minorities. *See* African Americans; Asian Americans; ethnicity; Latinos; people of color; racial groups
multiculturalism. *See also* group-conscious policies; intergroup relations, in U.S.; political multiculturalism; public opinion about multiculturalism; social multiculturalism; soft multiculturalism
accommodation of groups under, 20–23
African Americans and, 21–23
in America, 16–17
American national identity and, 43
versus assimilation, 16, 17
black exceptionalism and, 168
in Canada, 16–17
civil rights movement and, 3, 18
communal representation and, 269
components of, 15–16
critiques of, 3–5, 168
definition of, xix, 13–16
e pluribus unum and, 3

multiculturalism (cont.)
  in educational curricula, 74
  educational level and, 138–139
  emergence of, 13–16
  equal recognition of cultures under, xx
  ethnic consciousness and, 94
  ethnic identity and, 169, 238–239
  of fear, 20
  group rights under, 4, 15
  hard, xxiv, 18, 23–24, 269, 272–273, 279
  ideological, 15, 168
  for indigenous peoples, 20–21
  individual rights under, 20
  institutional influences on, 18
  issue space in, 252
  justifications for, 19–20
  in media, 74
  multilingualism and, 175–176
  national attachment and, 168–171
  national identity and, 24–14, 168–170
  nativism as influence on, xix–xx
  as normative view, 43
  overriding purposes of, 175
  partisanship over, 238–243, 252–257
  patriotism in conflict with, 257–258
  and perceived ethnic conflict, 94
  policy proposals for, 23–24
  as political movement, 223
  political multiculturalism, 120, 127–132, 142
  politicized group consciousness paradigm
    and, xxii
  as politics of difference, 15
  politics of recognition and, xx, 19
  post-colonial arguments for, 19–20
  as preservation of cultural differences, 125
  promotion of, by white elites, 18
  psychological foundations for, 38–39, 266
  public opinion about multiculturalist norms,
    120, 122–127
  religious, 23, 147, 176, 281
  soft, xxiv, 23–24, 122
  in U.S., 5, 17–18
  vanguard hypothesis for, xxii
  white elites and, 18
multiculturalist policies. *See* affirmative action;
  group-conscious policies; immigration
  policy; language policy
Myrdal, Gunnar, xix

Nash, Gary, 74
National Asian American Survey, 102,
  158–160

national attachment, 60–66, 264–265
  for African Americans, 61–62, 167, 168
  for Asian immigrants, 71–73, 172
  assimilation and, 171
  ethnic group consciousness and,
    205–219
  ethnic identity and, 162–163, 172
  for Latinos, 61–62, 71–73, 167, 168, 172
  multiculturalism and, 168–171
  national identity and, 85–86
  after 9/11, 282–283
  partisanship and, 232, 233–238
  policy preferences influenced by, 205–219
  for whites, 60–63, 171, 209–210, 232
  World War II and, 282
national identity. *See also* American national
    identity; cosmopolitan liberalism; ethnic
    identity
  attachment to nation and, 60–66
  civic *vs.* ethnic identity, 170–171
  civic *vs.* ethnic nations, 27
  common values as factor in, 7
  and culture wars, 228
  ethnic identity in conflict with, 161–167,
    220–221
  ethnicity integrated with, xx
  in Europe, 281
  founders' debates over, 6–10
  globalization as influence on, 5–6
  hard multiculturalism and, 279
  integrating ethnics into nation, xx
  for Latinos, 41–42, 159
  in Los Angeles County, 47–55
  multiculturalism and, 24–14, 168–170, 279
  national attachment and, 85–86
  in nation-building, xvii–xviii
  nativism and, xix–xx, 7, 8, 279
  normative content of, 27
  patriotism and, xxi, 58–60, 233
  plural identities and, 38–43
  political ideology and, 235–236
  political influences on, 38
  public policy on multiculturalism influenced
    by, 207, 210, 212
  socialization of, 42–43
  through symbolism, 28
  value of, 276–278
national unity, cultural diversity and, xviii
nation-building, national identity and, xvii–xviii
Native Americans
  American national identity and, 7
  multiculturalism and, 20–21

nativism, 1–6
  African-Americans and, xix
  American national identity and, 43
  cosmopolitan liberalism and, 2
  cultural diversity and, xx
  immigration and, xix–xx, 279
  multiculturalism and, xix–xx
  national identity and, xix–xx, 279
  public opinion on, 13–14
  racism and, xix–xx
9/11
  national attachment after, 282–283
  national chauvinism after, 69
  national identity after, 81–82
  patriotism after, 65–66
Nixon, Richard, 223

Obama, Barack, 228–229, 263
O'Connor, Sandra Day, 127
Official English movement, 191–192
  ballot propositions for, 193
  political partisanship over, 247–248
one-drop rule, for African Americans, xxvi, 98,
  280
out-group hostility, 220

Parekh, Bhiruck, 20
Parillo, Vincent, 18
partisanship, in U.S. politics, 224–238. *See also*
  Democratic Party; Republican Party
  about affirmative action, 243
  about cultural issues, 227
  among elites, 225–228, 243–248
  group-conscious policies and, 238–257
  history of polarization, 224
  identity politics and, 238
  ideology measures of, 225
  immigration policy and, 243–248
  increases in, 250–252
  language policy and, 247–248
  among Latinos, 235–236
  in mass public, 225–228, 248–252
  national attachment and, 233–238
  Official English movement and, 247–248
  patriotism and, 228–230
  public policy and, 243–252
  sources of, 225–226
patriotism, xxvi
  African Americans and, 58, 63–64, 234
  American flag as symbol of, 64–65, 228–230
  ANES Patriotism Index, 231
  assimilation and, 57–58

associations with Republican Party, 228, 268
black exceptionalism and, 58
blind, 70
chauvinism compared to, 66–70
citizenship and, 8
during Cold War, 228
constitutional, 27
constructive, 59, 70, 264
contemporary level of, 57
dangers of, 59
as emotional construct, 267–268
ethnic differences in, 60–66
ethnic identity and, 162–165, 166, 173
forms of, 59
history of, as political concept, 58–59
hyphenated identity and, 154
ideology and, 233, 237
language policy and, 221
Latinos and, xxiii–xxiv, xxv, 72, 154, 214,
  234
measures of, 162
multiculturalism in conflict with, 257–258
national chauvinism compared to, 66–70
national identity and, xxi, 58–60, 233
after 9/11, 65–66
partisan polarization over, 228–230, 268
pride in specific domains, scale of, 70
public opinion about, 231–238
scale of, 71–73
social identity theory and, 59–60
vanguard and, 73–79
among whites, 60–63, 72, 173, 206, 217,
  257–258
Pearl Harbor, 145, 146
people of color hypothesis, xxiv–xxv, 102
  group-conscious policies and, 194, 209
  language policy and, 198
  as political coalition, 177
perceived discrimination, 97, 106–107
  assimilation hypothesis and, 107
  black exceptionalism and, 107
  ethnic identity and, 115
perceived ethnic conflict
  in Los Angeles County, 92–93
  for minorities, in U.S., 90–97
perceptions of common fate. *See* common fate,
  perceptions of
Pew Hispanic Poll, 195
Pew Immigration Survey, 186, 188–189, 195
Pilot National Asian Political Survey,
  152, 160
Pledge of Allegiance, 229

plural identities
 for African Americans, 39
 for Asian Americans, 40
 intergroup relations and, 38–43
 for Latinos, 40
pluralism. *See* cultural pluralism
policy preferences. *See* affirmative action;
 group-conscious policies; immigration
 policy; language policy
political identity, measures of, 151. *See also*
 national identity
political multiculturalism, 120, 127–132,
 142
 communal representation and, 129
 cosmopolitan liberalism and, 128
 cross-ethnic consensus for, 131
 Latinos, 131–132
 public support for, by ethnicity, 130
 soft multiculturalism and, 131
 Voting Rights Act of 1965 and, 127–128
The Political Tradition (Hartz), 1
politicized group consciousness paradigm, xxii,
 30–33
 for African Americans, xxv, 35–36
 for Asian immigrants, 36
 cultural diversity and, xxii
 definition of, 263
 ethnicity and, xxii, 265–267
 for Latino immigrants, 36
 and perceived ethnic conflict, 94
 in racially-targeted policies, 194
 for whites of European ancestry, 34
politics of recognition, 19
population
 Asian immigration as influence on, 13
 foreign-born, in U.S., 11–12
 of Latinos, in U.S., 12
Portes, Alejandro, 112–113
power theory, 31, 32
Prewitt, Kenneth, 11
Proposition 227, 193
Protestants, as early settlers, xviii
public opinion about multiculturalism, 269–273
 age as factor in, 138–140
 alternative models for, 140–142
 assimilation hypothesis, 136–137
 coherence of multicultural norms for,
 132–133
 educational level as factor in, 138–139
 ethnic and racial cleavages in, 123–124, 193
 group consciousness and, 134–136
 about illegal immigration, 188–189

 about immigration, 186
 about language policy, 191–192, 271
 Latino immigration status and, 137
 maintenance of ethnic culture and, 126
 political multiculturalism, 130
 racial integration and, 126–127
 social multiculturalism, 122–127
 vanguard and, 138–140

race-targeted policy, 178–186, 193–194,
 213–214
 African American support for, 214
 antagonism towards minorities and,
 217–219
 anti-out-group affect and, 212
 in-group pride and, 220
 Latino support for, 214, 222
 origins of support for, 213–214
 out-group hostility and, 212, 220
 white support for, 213–214
racial groups. *See also* African Americans;
 Asian Americans; Latinos; Native
 Americans
 under *e pluribus unum*, 4
 politicized group consciousness paradigm
 for, xxii
 recognition of, xx
racial integration, 126–127
racism
 against African Americans, 35
 nativism and, xix–xx
Reagan, Ronald, 228
Republican Party
 American flag and, legislative protections
 by, 230
 association with patriotism, 228, 268
 attachment to nation and, among
 whites, 232
 ethnic group consciousness and, 249
 immigration policy and, 244–247
 multiculturalist attitudes and, among whites,
 241–242
 polarization of, 223
 support for affirmative action, 250
 Tea Party and, 224, 282
Roosevelt, Theodore, 8

Saguy, Tamar, 278
Salins, Peter, 28
Schildkraut, Deborah, 81–82, 83, 265
Schlesinger, Arthur, Jr., 3, 56–57, 147, 238
segmented assimilation, 42, 112–113

segregation. *See also* Jim Crow, as public policy
  in educational institutions, 182
self-categorization, ethnicity, 97, 99–102,
  150
  vs. American national identity, 148–155, 157,
    159, 169
  by Asian Americans, 99–100
  assimilation and, 156–157
  by biracial people, 100–101
  by Latinos, 99–100, 157
  response categories for, 101
Sen, Amartya, 39
sense of group position theory, 117
separatist movements, for African Americans,
  126, 167
Simpson, Alan, 245
Smith, Rogers, xix, 2, 23
Social Darwinism, 8
social dominance theory, 32
  ethnic group consciousness and, 98
social identity theory, 31
  patriotism and, 59–60
social multiculturalism, 120, 142
  assimilation and, 125–126
  cultural diversity and, 122
  maintenance of cultures and, 126
  public support for, 122–127
  racial integration and, 126–127
  recognition of cultural differences and,
    122–125
  soft multiculturalism and, 125
soft multiculturalism, xxiv, xxvi, 18, 269–270
  African Americans and, 186–188
  cosmopolitan liberalism and, 24
  national identity and, 279
  policies for, 185–186
  political multiculturalism and, 131
  social multiculturalism and, 125
Song, Sarah, 19, 262
Steinbeck, John, 6–7
stereotyping, ethnic, 279
strength of ethnic identity, 97, 102–105
  assimilation hypothesis and, 105
  black exceptionalism and, 105
  white group privilege, 105
structural assimilation, 9
symbolic politics theory, 212
system justification theory, 32

Tamir, Yael, 276
Taylor, Charles, 19, 41
Tea Party, 224, 282

Texas v. Johnson, 229, 230
Theiss-Morse, Elizabeth, 63, 81–82
Tocqueville, Alexis de, 59, 82
transgender community. *See* lesbian, gay,
  bisexual, and transgender community
*Two Nations, Black and White, Separate,
  Hostile Unequal* (Hacker), 3

United States (U.S.). *See also* American national
  identity; Americanism; intergroup
  relations, in U.S.; Los Angeles County,
  California; partisanship, in U.S. politics
  as civic nation, 80
  cultural diversity in, unity and, xviii
  as ethnic cauldron, 90–97
  European immigration to, 8
  foreign-born population increases in, 11–12
  as melting pot, 5, 17–18
  multiculturalism in, 5, 17–18
  as nation of immigrants, xviii
  national identity of, definition of, 2
  national pride index for, 69–70
  patriotism levels in, xxvi
  Protestants as early settlers, xviii
  religious multiculturalism in, 23, 176, 281
  as splintering society, 2–3

Valls, Andrew, 22
vanguard hypothesis, xxii
  among African Americans, 76–79, 139–140
  age as factor in, 75–79, 84–85, 144
  education as factor in, 84–85
  ethnic group consciousness and, 89, 112–113
  group-conscious policies and, 212
  among Latinos, 76–79, 139–140, 222
  multiculturalism norms and, 138–140
  for patriotism, 73–79
  among whites, 75–76, 77, 139
Voting Rights Act of 1965, xvii, 10, 269
  political multiculturalism and, 127–128

Washington, George, xviii, 74
white (group) privilege, 105
whites
  assimilation and, 171
  elite promotion of multiculturalism, 18
  ethnic consciousness, 94, 206–208
  ethnic identity, 167
  group-conscious policies, public opinion
    about, 206–208, 218, 241–242
  immigration policies, public opinion about,
    214–216

whites (cont.)
  in-group pride, 220
  issue constraints, 200, 255–256
  language policy, public opinion about,
    216–217
  national attachment, 60–63, 171, 209–210,
    232
  opposition to multilingualism, 216–217
  partisanship and, attachment to
    nation, 232
  partisanship and, multiculturalist norms,
    241–242
  patriotism among, 60–63, 72, 173, 206,
    217, 257–258
  race-targeted policies, public opinion about,
    213–214

  racial backlash by, 117–118
  racial group consciousness for, 34
  self-categorization of, 148–155
  vanguard hypothesis for, 75–76, 77, 139
Who Counts as an American (Theiss-Morse),
    81–82
women, in civil rights movement, 3
Wong, Cara, 40, 81–82
World War I, assimilation during and after,
    9, 173
World War II
  assimilation after, 173
  national attachment and, 282
Wright, Matthew, 265

Zangwill, Israel, 8–9

Books in the Series

Asher Arian, *Security Threatened: Surveying Israeli Opinion on Peace and War*

Jack Citrin and David O. Sears, *American Identity and the Politics of Multiculturalism*

James DeNardo, *The Amateur Strategist: Intuitive Deterrence Theories and the Politics of the Nuclear Arms Race*

Robert S. Erikson, Michael B. Mackeun, and James A. Stimson, *The Macro Polity*

James L. Gibson, *Overcoming Historical Injustices: Land Reconciliation in South Africa*

James L. Gibson and Amanda Gouws, *Overcoming Intolerance in South Africa: Experiments in Democratic Persuasion*

John R. Hibbing and Elizabeth Theiss-Morse, *Congress As Public Enemy: Public Attitudes toward American Political Institutions*

John R. Hibbing and Elizabeth Theiss-Morse, *Stealth Democracy: Americans' Beliefs about How Government Should Work*

John R. Hibbing and Elizabeth Theiss-Morse, *What Is It about Government That Americans Dislike?*

Robert Huckfeldt, Paul E. Johnson, and John Sprague, *Political Disagreement: The Survival of Diverse Opinions within Communication Networks*

Robert Huckfeldt and John Sprague, *Citizens, Politics, and Social Communication*

James H. Kuklinski, *Citizens and Politics: Perspectives from Political Psychology*

James H. Kuklinski, *Thinking about Political Psychology*

Richard R. Lau and David P. Redlawsk, *How Voters Decide: Information Processing in Election Campaigns*

Milton Lodge and Charles S. Taber, *The Rationalizing Voter*

Arthur Lupia, Mathew McCubbins, and Samuel Popkin, *Elements of Reason: Cognition, Choice, and the Bounds of Rationality*

George E. Marcus, John L. Sullivan, Elizabeth Theiss-Morse, and Sandra L. Wood, *With Malice toward Some: How People Make Civil Liberties Judgments*

Jeffery J. Mondak, *Personality and the Foundations of Political Behavior*

Diana C. Mutz, *Impersonal Influence: How Perceptions of Mass Collectives Affect Political Attitudes*

Hans Noel, *Political Ideologies and Political Parties in America*

Mark Peffley and Jon Hurwitz, *Justice in America: The Separate Realities of Blacks and Whites*

Markus Prior, *Post-Broadcast Democracy: How Media Choice Increases Inequality in Political Involvement and Polarizes Elections*

Paul M. Sniderman, Richard A. Brody, and Philip E. Tetlock, *Reasoning and Choice: Explorations in Political Psychology*

Stuart N. Soroka, *Negativity in Democratic Politics: Causes and Consequences*

Karen Stenner, *The Authoritarian Dynamic*

Susan Welch, Timothy Bledsoe, Lee Sigelman, and Michael Combs, *Race and Place*

Cara J. Wong, *Boundaries of Obligation in American Politics: Geographic, National, and Racial Communities*

John Zaller, *The Nature and Origins of Mass Opinion*

Alan S. Zuckerman, Josip Dasovic, and Jennifer Fitzgerald, *Partisan Families: The Social Logic of Bounded Partisanship in Germany and Britain*